Overcoming My Past

Zaneeya S.

BALBOA.
PRESS

A DIVISION OF HAY HOUSE

Balboa Press books may be ordered through booksellers or by contacting:

Balboa Press
A Division of Hay House
1663 Liberty Drive
Bloomington, IN 47403
www.balboapress.com
1 (877) 407-4847

Because of the dynamic nature of the Internet, any web addresses or links contained in this book may have changed since publication and may no longer be valid. The views expressed in this work are solely those of the author and do not necessarily reflect the views of the publisher, and the publisher hereby disclaims any responsibility for them.

The author of this book does not dispense medical advice or prescribe the use of any technique as a form of treatment for physical, emotional, or medical problems without the advice of a physician, either directly or indirectly. The intent of the author is only to offer information of a general nature to help you in your quest for emotional and spiritual well-being. In the event you use any of the information in this book for yourself, which is your constitutional right, the author and the publisher assume no responsibility for your actions.

Any people depicted in stock imagery provided by Thinkstock are models, and such images are being used for illustrative purposes only. Certain stock imagery © Thinkstock.

Print information available on the last page.

ISBN: 978-1-4525-9230-5 (sc)
ISBN: 978-1-4525-9231-2 (e)

Balboa Press rev. date: 05/25/2018

Chapter One

The Beginning of Life

orn into the world not knowing what to expect, not having a clue about what life would be. I was born March 11, 1989. My mother gave birth to me in an elevator at Highland Hospital. When my mother got out of the hospital, we went to visit my grandma and grandpa. My dad's, mother and father. My grandpa name is Bill.S and my grandma name is Alissa S. Later on that night, we moved in with my auntie Vanessa, my dad's sister. We stay with my auntie for a couple of months. I had two older brothers, Justin Jr. and Qin. After, we moved from my auntie Vanessa house. My mom and her sister Dorthy moved together. We moved to 27th and west. From 27th and West, we moved to High Street. From High Street, we moved to East 16th Street. From East 16th Street, we moved to 32nd and Martin Luther King. There, we moved in with our mother's mom, Stella. When we moved with our granny, my mother was pregnant with my little brother Patrick. I was finally going to be a big sister. A year later, my mom had another baby his name is Ramone. Justin Jr., and Qin taught me a lot. They taught me how to climb trees, jump a fence, and how to put both feet on the walls in the hallway and we would climb up, like we were monkeys. My granny would fuss at us, mostly at my brothers when they were doing something bad. If Qin and Justin Jr., were acting up, she would tell them both to come here, but they wouldn't, because they knew they were going to get a whopping. So my granny would walk towards them and they would run. My granny would say, "Justin Jr., get Qin!" Justin Jr., would get him. My granny whooped Qin. Then she turned around and whooped Justin Jr., and I would laugh.

My brothers went to Chabot Elementary school. My mom enrolled me at Peralta Elementary school. After, my mother took me out of Peralta. My brothers and I went to Hoover Elementary school. After, my mother took me out of Hoover. I finally landed at Golden Gate Elementary school. Life was tough, my brothers and I were not always together and I hated that. My mother was deep into drugs and she needed rehab. Justin Jr., and Qin and I went to live with our dad. While Patrick and Ramone stayed with my granny. My dad was on drugs too. He was in a relationship with our sister Sabreea's mother. Her name is Shay. My brothers and I called Shay mom. Shay had a daughter named, Shonte, and a son, named Travis from a previous relationship. I was three months older than Sabreea. We stayed with our dad for three months. Shay would look after us as if we were her own kids, and I liked that about her. On the weekends, we would go visit our mom in rehab and everytime we would go visit. She would have a gift for us.

I never wanted to leave, and my mom knew it. She would look at me and say, "Cupcake, mommy is coming home soon." I would just look at her and smile. The longer we stayed with our dad, the more I wanted my mom. My dad would play favoritism between my sister and I. Sabreea was his favorite. Nothing she did was wrong in my dad's eyes, but I would get in trouble for anything and so would my brothers. If there was a Barbie doll on the floor, my dad would yell, "Zaneeya, come pick this up." Momma Shay would say, "She didn't have that doll Sabreea did." "I saw Zaneeya playin with this doll." "No you didn't you need to stop picking on her." My mom came to visit us. She told my dad she was taking us to McDonald's, to get us something to eat. My dad said, "Bella, what time are you bringing the kids back home?" My mom replied, "I don't know, and these are my kids and I'm home now!" My dad yelled and said, "Bella, you're not taking my kids nowhere!" "Yes I am." "I'm calling the police Bella." "Call them, I want you too!" When the police arrived to the house, Shay came outside. She said, "What's going on?" The police officer said, "Who kids are they?" My mom said, "These are my kids!" My dad said, "These are my kids." Shay said, "These are my kids." My mom said, "These are my three kids and I let them live with their dad while I was in rehab." The police officer told my mom and dad they would have to go to court to get custody of my brothers, and I. The police officer said, "I'm going to let the kids go back to their mother." So we moved back with our granny. We were happy to feel like our old family again. Soon things got worst. My mom was back on drugs and she needed to go back to rehab. We went back to live with our dad. This time he was with another woman named Tracy. Tracy had a daughter too, her name is Gabbie. My dad, and Justin Jr., Qin and Sabreea, and Tracy, and Gabbie and I went to live with one of my dad's sisters. Her name is Kimberly. We stayed on 79th and Ritchie. It was a house full of kids. Kimberly had two kids of her own. We stayed there for a little while. Then we moved into our own place. My dad and Tracy had a beautiful baby girl named Angelique. We all loved our little sister. Sabreea and I went to the same school and we were in the same grade. We had to wear uniforms at our school. Sabreea would wear the pants three days a week and I would wear the skirt two days a week. We had to use the same asthma pump, and everything else. If I had to use the bathroom, my dad would say, "Zaneeya, slide over a little on the toilet. There's enough room for Sabreea, she has to use the bathroom too." One morning we were getting dressed for school and my dad made us some cereal, but we didn't have any milk. So he gave us water in our cereal and he told us to eat it. I was happy it wasn't just me eating cereal with water. When, we came home from school, we were all playing. Justin Jr., told me to repeat after him, so I did. Not knowing any better. Justin Jr., yelled and said, "Dad, Zaneeya said a bad word!" My dad came in the room and he gave me a whoopin. Then he took me to the bathroom and he washed my mouth out with soap. I cried. I said, "No, dad please don't wash my mouth out with soap!"

He said, "You are going to eat dinner, then you are going straight to bed!" I just wanted my mom, and my dad knew it too. As the days went on Angelique was getting bigger. When she had gotten her first shots, she had an allergic reaction to the medicine. The doctors told my dad that Angelique would be blind. She would only be able to see our shadows. The doctors told my dad, she would never walk or talk and she would not live past 3 years old. Angelique was a happy baby. Everyday she was in pain, but she would always smile. She had long hair just like Sabreea and me. She looked like my dad. She even had his skin tone. Tracy was mean. Not just to me, but to my little sister Angelique. My dad would be at work and she would leave my little sister in her diaper for hours. Then change her right before my dad would come inside the house. When my dad would come home from work, he would shower. Then he would go straight to Angelique before doing anything else. He would have to hold her to feed her. My dad loved Angelique! I could see the love in his eyes for her and it was beautiful. My sister needed all the attention she could get. My dad and Tracy would argue over Angelique. My dad would tell her to take better care of my sister and he was right. Even though I was young, I knew she was, being mistreated by her mother. We moved to the south side of Hayward. We went to live with auntie Kimberly. On the 4th of July everybody was popping fireworks, and one flew down Qin's back. He was yelling and crying. My cousins went to tell my dad that Qin's back had got burned from a firework. My dad looked at his back, and he took care of him. Shortly after the 4th of July, we moved back with our mom. My mom and dad went to court to get custody of us. My dad was late to court. The judge had granted my mother custody of us. The judge told my mom. He liked how she put her own self in rehab and she finished the program, and she was trying to do better for her kids. My mom got a two-bedroom apartment, so that meant we had to go to another elementary school. I was just happy that we all were together again. My brothers and I shared rooms. Justin Jr., and Qin would take the closet doors off and lean them at an angle against the wall. They taught us how to run up the closet doors and slide down them as if they were a slide. We did not have much, and we did not have any furniture, but we had each other. My mother met a new guy named JB, who seemed nice. One night, I woke up and I went inside of my mom's room and as I was wiping my eyes, I seen my mom having sex with JB. I said, "Mommy!" She got up and said, "Cupcake go back to bed baby." "Mommy, what are you doing?" "Mommy is just watching TV." She took me to my room and laid me down, while she had nothing but a sheet over her. We did not always have food. My mom would leave for hours, and Justin Jr., and Qin would be there to look after us. Qin would always find us something eat.

Chapter Two

A New Change

My mom started dating this guy named Dawane. We moved to Modesto, which was a town, and it was country too. My auntie Dorthy moved to Modesto with her kids and her kid's father. We lived up the street from them. Their apartments were blue, and our apartments were brown. I went to Walter White Elementary School for the second grade. Everyday the school bus would come and pick us up, and drop us back off at home. My mom was pregnant again and I told her I wanted to have a little sister. The night, my mom went into labor we went to our auntie Dorthy's house. We stayed there while our mom was in the hospital. When she came home from the hospital, I threw down my backpack and ran to see if I had a little sister. My mom said, "Zaneeya, say hi to your baby brother." I looked at him and said, "I thought he was a girl!" I left my mom's room and went to my room to do my homework. My brother name is Dawane Jr., he was named after his dad. We moved from the brown apartments and we moved in with my auntie Dorthy. We called her house the brick house, because it was a house made of bricks. We lived there for a while. It was a house full of kids. Dorthy had two twin boys, named Jason and Lason. She also had two daughters named Mimi and Christy. When it was time to go to school, my mom would wake up my brothers and I, and my auntie would wake up her kids. My mom would lay out my school clothes at night, so in the morning all she had to do was my hair. She would give me six ponytails. I had long curly black hair. I looked like my mom and my dad. I had my dad's nose, teeth, and mouth. As time went on, everything was going good. My auntie and my mom told my cousins, my brothers and I that we are first cousins and we have to stick together no matter what happens in life. On the weekends, we would play outside. Christy and I would put on Jason and Lason roller skates, that's how we learned how to skate. My brothers and I would visit our dad sometimes *in the Bay Area, and when we did, we would go to our grandpa and grandma house. My grandpa was a great man. He was always nice to me. He would let me lay in his bed with him and we would watch old western movies. My grandpa didn't take no mess from anyone, and he had his shotgun right on the side of his bed, and sometimes he would use it. My grandpa was a handsome man and he loved my grandma and he would never let anyone disrespect her. Their marriage was beautiful! My grandpa served in World War II, and he was highly respected! Not just by his family, but from others.*

One day, my brothers and I were playing and my mom called Justin Jr., and Qin and I to her room. She said, "Sit down I have something to tell y'all." We all stood up, and said, "What is it mom?" My mom looked at us. She said, "Angelique died this morning. Your dad had called and told me to tell y'all." I started crying. My mom said, "Cupcake, are you ok? Come here." I replied, "I'm ok mom." My brothers did not cry at that moment, but I knew they were sad as well. Mom said, "Your dad is coming to get y'all this weekend so y'all can go to Angelique's funeral." Angelique was born 1993 and she died 1997. The weekend came fast. My dad came to pick my brothers and me up. When we made it to the Bay Area, we thought we were going to Angelique's funeral. Instead, my dad dropped us off in Alameda at his house, and he told my brothers and me not to answer the door for anyone. My dad did not come back until later on that night. My brothers and I were hungry. When my dad came back, I was upset. I wondered why my brothers and I could not go to our sister funeral. The next day, I asked my dad why we didn't go to Angelique's funeral. He said, "It wasn't a funeral. Angelique was creammaidit, it's called a wake." Later on that day, my dad took us to Payless Shoe Store. My dad bought me two pairs of sandals. He said, "Zaneeya, I'm buying you some sandals, because I haven't bought you anything in a long time." He told my brothers he would buy them something next time. After, we left Payless we went back to my dad's house. The next day, my dad told us our mom was coming to get us. He told us we can play outside and he told me not to get my sandals dirty. After playing for a while, my dad told us to come back inside the house, so we can get ready to leave. My dad looked at my sandals and he yelled at me. He said, "Zaneeya, I thought I told you not to get your sandals dirty? Damn you can't do anything right!" That really hurt my feelings. I was only 8 years old. What did I know about keeping my sandals clean? Besides, my sandals were light pink. They only had a dirt mark on them, because I was playing jump rope. My mom came to pick us up and yes, I was happy to see her. My dad answered the door. My mom said, "Are y'all ready?" We hurried up and said,

"Yes!" My dad said, "Y'all better give me a hug before y'all leave." We went to give our dad a hug and we said bye to his wife and our stepsister Gabbie. When we got in the car, my mom asked us did we have fun. My mom said, "Did y'all see Sabreea, how was Angelique's funeral?" Qin said, "No, we didn't have fun!" I said, "No, we didn't see Sabreea, and my dad said Angelique was creammaidit." My mom replied, "He still took y'all to her wake right?" Justin Jr., said, "No, we didn't go. My dad dropped us off at his house, and he told us not to open the door for nobody." "What? I'm going to call him later and talk to him about that. Y'all could have stayed home. That wasn't right." One thing about my mom, when it came to her kids and if it was something wrong that my dad did, my mom was definitely going to speak up, and it was not going to be nice either.

When we got back home, my mom called our dad. She asked him why he didn't take us with him to Angelique's wake. My dad said, "Look Bella, I don't have time for all of this. There was no room in the car. Plus, they had on dirty clothes, and I was not going to take them with me looking any kind of way." My mom replied, "Their clothes were not dirty and Zaneeya hair was combed and they all looked nice! So, what are you talking about their clothes was dirty?" "Bella, you cannot be serious right now?" "Yes I am serious! My kids could have stayed home. I bet everybody else went. I know Sabreea went, but that's ok though bye." My mom hung up the phone. My dad called back but my mom did not answer. My uncle Tony was coming home with big candy bars, and jellybeans and just a whole lot of things. Later on, we all found out that he was stealing from his job, but he didn't get fired, because he was a hard worker. Dawane and my mom had an argument one night. Dawane had hit my mom and my mom called the police. We had moved into our own place again. It was on the south side of Modesto. We stayed on Dareta Way. That was the name of the street. Dawane and my mom were still together. My mom had enrolled us at a different school. My mom talked to my brothers and me about the kkk's. She taught us about racism. She told us where we live at their were a lot of kkk's and if we were to ever see any we were to run. We asked, our mom why. She said, "The kkk's do not like black people and they probably will hang you." I know that frighten me a little bit, but my mom wanted her kids to know the truth. I did not know my way to school. Qin, and Patrick and I went to school together. Justin Jr., went to a different school, but his school bus would pick him up at our school. My mom told my brothers to make sure that they walk with me to school and to make sure that I do not get lost. Everyday my brothers and I would walk to school, they would walk in front of me. Qin *and Justin Jr., would look at each other and they would run. So I would have to run too, because I didn't know my way to school. They would do that to make my asthma flare up. Qin and Justin Jr., did that for a week. I finally had enough. So one day, I came home and I told my mom. I said, "Mom, everyday on our way to school, Qin and Justin Jr., would run, and I would have to run too, and that makes my asthma flare up." My mom said, "Justin Jr., and Qin y'all better not do that ever again. I know one thing, if y'all walk to school tomorrow and y'all run. I'm going to whoop y'all butt and I'm not playing. Do it if you want to and see what happen." They said, "Ok mom." My brothers and I would still go visit our dad, and when we did, it was the same old things. When, it was time for us to go to bed at night. My dad would just give Justin Jr., and Qin and I a sheet to sleep with or a thin quilted blanket. While Tracy, Gabbie and Sabreea and him, would sleep with nice warm confronters. My brothers and I would be freezing. When, we lived with him as well, when my mom was in rehab. We would tell our dad we were cold, and he would say, "There is nothing I can do about that, try to stay warm."*

Everyday, my mother would tell us to come straight home from school and do not stop off anywhere. She would say, "If y'all do I'm going to whoop y'all, and if I'm not home wait for me on the porch." We would say ok mom. Sometimes my mom wouldn't be home. Justin Jr., found out their was a woman who sold candy around the corner from where we lived at. She would sell candy for only a five cent. Therefore, if my mom was not home, Justin Jr., would say, "I'm going around the corner to the candy lady house." I said, "You're going to get in trouble." "No, I'm not. I'm going to leave before mommy comes home, and you better not tell either." "I'm not going to tell, you better bring me some strawberry candy back." "Ok I will." If my mom came home before Justin Jr., got home, I would cover for him. We could not go outside on the weekends and play like normal kids. My mom would have us in the house. We would say, "Mom, can we go outside please?" She replied, "No, and if you ask me again, y'all are not going to have any cool laid to drink with y'all dinner, y'all are going to drink some water." We would stop asking for that day. My brothers and I would play baseball in the house. Justin Jr., and Qin would take Lil Dawane stuffed animals and his baby blankets and we would use them for a first base. A second base a third base and so on. We broke many things in the house. Even though we didn't have a lot of furniture. I had a room set, but I did not have any mattress, so I was sleeping on the floor just like my brothers. There was only one TV in the house and the TV was in my mom's room. On Saturday mornings, my brothers and I would wake up early in the morning to watch TV. My mom would make us a bowl of cereal. We would eat our cereal while watching TV. My favorite cereal was Cocoa Puff's. The cartoons we would watch in the morning were the Jungle Book, Pepper Ann, Doug, and Recess. One day, I came home from school and my mom wasn't home. So I waited for her on the front porch, but it was hot that day. I waited for a long time. I thought to myself. I'm going to go to my friend Salena's house. I left my backpack on the front porch and I went to Salena's house. I took a short cut through this park. As I was walking through the park, I saw a group of kkk's. I knew they were kkk's, because I remembered what my mom had told me. She told me some wear all white clothes that look like a robe and their known for wearing their all white hoods. As I seen this group of kkk's they looked at me and I ran for my life. One of the men's saw me. He told one of his kkk friends to get me, so one of the guys ran after me. I kept running and running all the way to Salena's house. When I got to her house, I ranged the doorbell. I ranged it at least five times. Salena's mom came to the door. Her name is Gwen. Gwen said, "Yes, how can I help you?" I said, "Hi is Salena home?" "Yes, come in. What's wrong, what is your name?" "My name is Zaneeya. Salena and I go to the same school.

I seen a group of kkk's and one of the men's ran after me, but I just kept on running." Gwen said, "I'mma get you some water." She brought me a glass of water. She said, "I'm happy you ran. Does your mom know that you are here?" I replied, "No, my mom wasn't home when I left." "I'm going to take you home, because it's a school day and your mother is probably worried about you." "Ok, thank you." "Do you know where you live?" "Yes." I showed Gwen where I lived. As I was getting out of the car, I said bye to Salena. She said, "Bye Zaneeya, I'll see you at school tomorrow." "Ok." I rang the doorbell and I was thinking to myself, I know my mom is going to whoop my butt. My mom answered the door. I said, "Hi mom." She said, "I'm going to get you and you know it." Gwen said, "Hi my name is Gwen, Zaneeya and my daughter Salena goes to school together." My mom replied, "Oh, okay my name is Bella." "Zaneeya came to my house and I asked her does your mom know that you are here. She told me no. So I told her I was going to take her home."

"No I wasn't home, but Zaneeya knows to wait for me on the porch if I'm not home. She is going to get in trouble to for leaving." "I wanted to ask you. Is it ok if Zaneeya goes to church with Salena on Sundays?" "Yes that's fine with me, but I don't have anyway of getting her there." "That's ok, I'll come get her." "Ok thank you for bringing her home." "You're welcome. It was nice meeting you Bella." "It was nice meeting you too Gwen." My mom and I went *inside the house. My mom said, "I'm whooping your butt. You know better for leaving and I told you if I'm not home you are to stay on that porch and wait for me." "I know mom. I'm sorry, I was hot out there while I was waiting for you. So I just went to my friend Salena's house." "Your butt is going to be hot when I'm done with you too." My brothers started laughing. I said, "Mom, I seen a group of kkk's today when I was going to Salena's house." "Where did you see them at?" "At the park, I went through the park to go to Salena's house." "See, that's why I told you to stay home and wait for me if I'm not here." "I know mom, but I ran just like you told me too. I ran all the way to Salena's house." "I'm happy you ran and I'm glad nothing happen to you. Go do your homework then shower and dinner is going to be ready." "Ok mom, are you still going to whoop me?" "Girl just go do what I told you to do." As I showered, I was thinking. I hope my mom do not come whoop me while I'm in the shower. When I got out of the shower, my mom told me to come here so she can do my hair. I walked over to my mom. I sat between her legs. She had a cup of water on the floor. She would dip the brush in the cup of water and she brushed, and greased my hair. She asked me how many ponytails I want. I told her three. I liked how my mom would do my hair.*

Justin Jr., came in the room. He said, "Mom, Zaneeya isn't going to get a whooping?" My mom replied, "No, she's not. Why?" "If that was me you would have whooped me the minute I came in the door." "Boy shut up and go to your room before I whoop your butt right now." Justin Jr., was hoping I got a whooping and he was mad that I didn't. We ate dinner then we went to bed. On Sunday, Gwen came to pick me up for church. I haven't been to church since we moved from our granny house. We went to the 11:00 o'clock service. After, church Gwen took us to McDonald's, to get something to eat. Everybody that went to church that day was Salena, her brother Jamal, and her big sister, and Gwen, and I. Going to church on Sundays with Gwen became an on going thing. Qin and Jamal was in the same grade and they became friends. My brothers started going to church with us. Sometimes, I would spend the night at Salena's house. We would go to her dad's basketball games. We would watch movies and we would have fun. Gwen is a nice person and she is very kindhearted.

As time went on, my mom had met this man through her friend Lisa. His name was Jay. Lisa's husband was Jay's nephew. Jay had four kids. My mom would go to Lisa's house a lot. Sometimes after school, my mom would tell us to meet her over there. Lisa had three kids at the time. She had a daughter and two boys. Christmas was coming up and my mom did not have any money to buy us something for Christmas. So, one of our Neighbours bought us some Christmas toys. My mom was very happy and so was my brothers and I. We moved back in with Dorthy. Qin and I went to Kershan Elementary school. Patrick and Ramon went to Robinson Road Elementary school. Their school was right next door to my school. Justin Jr., went to Mark Twain Middle school. Qin was a bully at school and everybody at school would call him the king of the school. At recess, he would pick on me for no reason at all. If I had a ball in my hand, he would come up to me and take it and that was everyday. One day, I was playing wall ball at school, and Qin came in the middle of the game and he pushed me, and took the ball. I told Qin I was going to tell on him. He said, "Go ahead." Qin pushed me again. So I pushed him back, then we started fighting. The yard duty teacher came over and said, "You guys are both going on the line for fighting each other." That meant we had to stand on the line the whole time we had recess, and we could not play. I was so upset with Qin.

Chapter Three

Momma Picked the Wrong Man

*W*e moved from Dorthy's house and we moved into our own place. It was a nice size house. There were four bedrooms, and two bathrooms. We had a nice size backyard. We had a dinningroom, and a livingroom and a nice size kitchen. I was happy that we had our own place again. I was hoping that we would not have to move from our new house any time soon. We lived five blocks away from my auntie Dorthy. Christy would spend the night at my house with me. My mom would turn on the radio, and when R. Kelly song was playing, "When a woman is fed up, there's nothing you can do about it, it's like falling out of love." My mom would listen to that song while she was cleaning up. My brothers and I were happy my mom kept us all at the same school. I was turning 10 years old. I was sick on my birthday I had the flu. The doorbell ranged. My mom said, "Cupcake, go answer the door." So I did, Salena and Gwen was at the door. I gave them both a hug. My mom told Gwen it was my birthday, and she told her I was sick. Gwen said, "Come on Zaneeya, we are going to leave for a little bit." Gwen took me shopping. After we went shopping, she took me home. I told Gwen thank you and I told Salena to call me. I gave her my phone number. One day, my mom came into the livingroom. She told my brothers and me, she had some good news to tell us. She said, "Mommy has a boyfriend now, y'all met him already. Well, he is going to move in with us." I said, "Are his kids moving in with us too?" "Yes they are, that means y'all have to share your rooms." I did not want to share my room and I just wanted to live with my family, like it has always been!

My mom said, "Jay will be moving in this weekend, and if he ever hit me. All of you are to run to auntie Dorthy's house, and call the police and don't bring this up in front of him. This is just between us!" When the weekend came, Jay and his kids moved in. Jay had two daughters and two sons. Only *one of his daughters lived with us. Jay sons slept in Justin Jr., room we did not have beds, but they came with their beds and really just took over our whole house. Jay's daughter and I shared a room. One night, I went to the garage to wash my clothes. Jay's youngest son had a tool in his hand. He kept swinging it back, and forth, and it slid out of his hand and it hit me right in my mouth. My lip was bleeding and my front tooth was chipped. I ran to my mom's room and started crying. She said, "What's wrong?" I showed her my mouth. My mom yelled, "What happened to you?" Jay said, "I'm about to go find out what happen." When Jay left out of the room, I told my mom what happen. Jay came back and told my mom his son had a tool in his hand and he was swinging it back and forth and it hit me in my mouth on an accident. I was mad! My mom said, "It will be ok Cupcake." Jay said, "Zaneeya, I will buy you a gold tooth to replace the tooth that you had there." I didn't say nothing to Jay. I just wanted my tooth back. Jay's daughter was Justin Jr., age she was three years older than me. She would go to this store called Factory To You, and some times she would take me with her.*

Sometime she would steal. So one day, we went to Factory To You and she showed me how to steal. Therefore, Jay's daughter and I would go and steal bags of candy every weekend. We would sell our candy to the kids in our neighborhood and I would take the candy to school and sell it. One day, Qin said, "Where are y'all getting all this candy from?" Jay's daughter said, "I bought it." "No you didn't stop lying." On weekends, we would have a line of people waiting to buy candy from us. Jay nephew came to live with us, it was a house full of kids. One Saturday, my mom called Jay daughter and I in the house. My mom said, "Where are y'all getting all this candy from?" We said, "We bought it." My mom looked at me and said, "Cupcake don't lie to me. " I replied, "Ok mom, we stole it." "Stole it! How the hell you know how to steal?" Jay's daughter said, "I taught her." My mom said, "Ooh no, I'm telling your dad, and Zaneeya you better not put your hands on nothing you can not buy in the store! Do you hear me?" "Yes mom." "If you steal anything else I'm going to whoop your butt, and I'm not playing, try me if you want too." I knew my mom was not playing. I did not steal anymore from that moment on. One night my mom and Jay had got into an argument and Jay had hit my mom in her head! My mom told us if Jay was to ever hit her, we were to run to our auntie Dorthy's house and to call the police. Qin ran outside to go to auntie Dorthy's house and I ran too. Then Justin Jr., and Patrick, and Ramone ran. As we ran out the house, Jay's nephew and his oldest son ran after us and they brought us back in the house. My mom told us to put some clothes on so we could spend the night at Dorthy's house.

As my mom and my brothers and I were walking to Dorthy's house my mom said, "Stop, we are going back home." I said, "Mom you're not going to call the police?" "No, I don't want to take Jay away from his kids." I did not want to go back home after that. One day, I came home from school and my mom and Jay was gone. I asked Jay oldest son where my mom went. He told me she would be back soon. The doorbell rang so I went to the door and answered it. It was one my friends asking me did I want to come outside and play. I said, "No, because my mom is not home." After I closed the door, Jay's oldest son punched me in my chest. He said, "Don't be answerin no doors around here." I went to my room and waited for my mom to come back. When my mom came home, I told her what happened, but she did not do anything. Jay was very mean and so was his son. When, Lil Dawane would cry. Jay would grab him by his shirt, and put him against the wall and he would shake him. He would say, "Stop crying, stop crying, shut up." Lil Dawane would keep crying, he was only 3 years old. My mom would just smile and say, "Put my baby down." Jay would make my brothers fight each other, something they were not use too. We moved to Ceres into another house. Linn Rena Court was the name of our street. That house was a duplex. We had four bedrooms and two bathrooms, it was a nice house. Jay and my mom would argue a lot, things began to get bad. They would argue everyday. My mom got a job in the Bay Area. She was working at Motel 6. She would drive to work. One evening, she came home and she checked the mailbox. She opened her mail, and her house phone bill was sky high. My mom said, "Jay, why is my phone bill so high?" He did not say anything. She said, "All these Bay Area calls are from your son." Jay still did not say anything. My mom said, "I'm not paying for this either." Jay said, "You better stop all that damn yelling and I don't care about that." My mom was not yelling at all. My mom went outside and she slammed the door. Then she came back inside and she slammed the door again. Jay said, "If you slam the door again, I'mma F you up and I'm not playin." I came inside the livingroom and asked Jay what channel he was watching. I was trying to distract him, so he wouldn't hit my mom and it worked, and that's what I would do all the time. My mom left and went to work and we all were outside playing, and Jay's youngest daughter came to visit. She was outside and she was behind our next-door neighbor car. Our neighbor didn't see her, so as our neighbor was backing up, out of his driveway, he ran her over. One of the kids ran inside the house and told Jay that his daughter had gotten ranned over. Jay came outside *and he started yelling at our neighbor, then he beat him up. So someone called the police. When my mom came home, he started yelling at her. My mom said, "That's not my fault that your daughter had gotten ranned over! Hell, I wasn't even home, I was at work." Jay's daughter was fine she came home from the hospital the same day she got ran over. Jay just wanted to blame my mom, but really he should have been watching his own child!*

I did not like being home, because there was so much yelling, and that made me nervous as a child. I would go to my auntie Dorthy's house on the weekend sometimes. One day Jay's oldest daughter and I rode her brothers bikes all the way to Modesto to my auntie Dorthy's house. Dorthy said, "How did y'all get here?" I said, "We rode the bikes here." "Zaneeya, you rode that bike on the freeway, all the way over here?" "Yes, I did." "Where is your mom at?" "She left with Jay." "Y'all go back home before it gets too late and be careful." "Ok auntie." My mom and Jay were both on drugs, and my mom would leave and I would ask her could I go with her. Most of the time she would say no, but one day I asked her could I go with her and she took me with her. My mom stopped at this house it was night time. She said, "Cupcake, I'mma be right back. Don't open the car door for nobody." "Ok mom." As I waited for my mom to come back to the car, it was getting darker and darker outside, and I was scared. I was cold. I fell asleep in the car. When my mom came back to the car, it was morning. It had to be 5 o'clock AM or 6 o'clock AM, because the color in the sky was changing. My mom said, "If Jay asks you where we went tell him we were at auntie Dorthy's house." "Ok mom. What took you so long to come back?" "I was waiting for my friend to come and I fell asleep." I knew my mom was lying. My birthday was coming up again and I was turning 11 years old. My mom asked me did I want a birthday party, I told her yes. She said, "Ok, what kind of cake do you want?" I said, "I want a fresh strawberry cake" "Ok are you going to call your dad and invite him?" "Yes mom and I want him to bring Sabreea, Gabbie and Agnona." "You better call him. Your birthday is in three weeks." "Mom, I want to call him today." "Ok." We went to the kitchen and called my dad, but he did not answer his phone. So we called again and he answered. I said, "Hi dad, how are you doing?" "Hi Zaneeya. How are you doing?" "I'm doing well. You know my birthday is coming up real soon and I want you to come to my birthday party." "Of course I'm going to come. I wouldn't miss it for the world." "Ok dad, one more thing. Can you bring Sabreea too?" "Yes I can I was just going to ask you did you want your sister to come." "So dad you promise your going to come right?" "Yes I promise." I was happy. I went to school the next day, I would have to leave my class and go to another class, and that class was called resource. The kids that had to go to resource had a learning disability and I was one of those kids. I would have regular classes, but the resource teacher would call my teacher and tell her that I had to go to resource for an hour. That was an everyday routine in school. In resource, we would read and the teacher taught us, how to read fast. They would time us as we were reading. The teachers taught me how to sound out my words and how to understand them! I still had a struggle with learning, and I knew I would have a struggle my whole life. My resource teachers, was extremely sweet and, everyday that I went to my resource class. I was excited to learn how to read better. I admired the fact, that my resource teacher would take her time teaching me, and the rest of the kids.

It was my birthday and I was so happy. I called my dad, but he did not answer. My cousins came over. My mom cooked dinner. She bought me a cake. I kept calling my dad back to back and he finally answered. I said, "Dad, where are you, are you almost here?" He said, "No, I'm not coming. I can't make it today I'm sorry." "Dad, but you promised me that you would come." "I know, but I can't I love you." "I love you too." I hung up the phone, I ran to my room, and I started crying. My mom came to my room. She said, "Cupcake, open the door." I opened the door. My mom said, "Stop crying baby. Your dad is not coming huh?" "No." I started to cry harder. My mom said, "He has to stop doing this to you. It will be ok, come on in play with your cousins." I replied, "I don't want to play and I don't want any party. All I wanted was my dad to be here for my birthday and he lied to me again, it's not fair." "Your dad loves you. I can tell you that, and it's not fair, but, your cousins are here come cut your cake." "I don't want to cut my cake right now. I just want to stay in my room." "Ok do you want mommy to buy you an Easter basket this year?" "Yes mom." "Ok, we will go to the store tomorrow and pick you out one." "Ok mom, thank you." My mom left out of my room and I just laid down crying. I stayed in my room for two hours. Christy knocked on my room door. I said, "Come in." She said, "Are you ok?" "Yes I'm fine. I just wanted my dad and my sisters to be here." "They will come next time. Are you going to cut your cake?" "Yes I am." I went out of my room and went into the kitchen. My mom and everybody were eating. My mom brought my cake out and everyone song happy birthday to me. It got late so everyone left. My mom bought me an Easter basket for Easter. She felt bad that my dad did not come to my birthday party. I liked going to school. At school, I would be happy. Even though I was in resource, I still would get rewards. I was never late to school. I did all of my homework and I would finish all of my classwork. When Qin did not know how to do his math problems, he would ask my mom to help him. My mom would say, "Boy, I do not know how to do that. You better go ask your sister, she is real good in math." Qin would always pick on me, and he was mean to me, and he would cuss at me. So one day, he cussed at me and I called my dad. I said, "Dad, Qin is cussing at me." My dad said, "Put Qin on the phone." I said, "Qin, dad wants to talk to you." Qin got on the phone. My dad said, "Qin, I know you're not cussing at your sister!" Qin replied, "No, I'm not dad." "Boy you better not ever cuss at your sister again or I'm going to come down there and whoop your butt. Do you understand me?" "Man, I didn't even cuss at her." "Do you hear me?" "Yes dad." Qin whispered in my ear, "Watch when you get off the phone, I'mma beat you up." I said, "Dad, Qin said he's going to beat me up when I get off the phone with you." My dad replied, "Let me talk to Qin." I gave Qin the phone. My dad said, "Look, Qin I'm not playing no games with you. You better not beat up your sister. If you hit her, I'm coming down there, and I'm going to whoop your butt, and I'm not playin. I'm not your momma, I'm your daddy and I will whoop you." "Ok dad." My dad said, "Zaneeya, where is your mom at?" "I don't know she isn't here." "Ok, I love you. Call me back if anything happens." "Ok dad I love you too."

Chapter Four

The Woman Beater

It was time for us to move again. We moved to DonPedro that was the name of the street. We still lived in Ceres, but further out in Ceres. The house on DonPedro was bigger. It had four bedrooms, three bathrooms. It had a dinningroom and livingroom they were in separate areas in the house. We had a swimming pool in the backyard. It the first house we had that was upstairs and downstairs. I went to DonPedro Elementary school. The school bus would pick me up on the corner by my house. All the school kids would be waiting in line for the school bus. My first day of school was nice, people came up to me, and they were asking me what my name was. I made friends quickly. When I would come home from school, I would do my homework, and my mom would make me a fried bologna sandwich and she would give me a big cup of coollaid. After I was finish eating and doing my homework I would get in the pool. That was my routine everyday. Justin Jr., would come home, and take off his entire clothes and go skinny-dipping, and I would get out of the pool. Nobody wanted to go swimming with him while he was naked. My mom asked me. Why, would I get out of the pool when Justin Jr., would get in. I told her, because Justin Jr., would go skinny-dipping. My mom said, "Justin Jr., come here right now." Justin Jr., said, "Yes mom." "Boy you better stop, going skinny-dipping. Put your shorts on when you go swimming." "Ok mom."My mom asked me did I want a bike. I said, "Yes that will be nice. I've wanted a bike for a long time." "I know you have, and this weekend I'm going to buy you a bike." I was so excited, I could not wait to go tell Jay's daughter. I told her my mom said she is going to buy me a bike. Jay daughter said, "I know, my dad is going to buy me a bike too. We should get the same bike." I said, "Ok, but it have to be purple, because purple is my favorite color." "Ok that's fine." My mom and Jay took us to the store to buy us a bike. We picked out a purple bike it was nice too. We went home and rode our bikes that day. We would keep our bikes in the garage. One day my mom and Jay left. My mom told us not to go anywhere. I said, "Mom, I'm hungry." "You will eat when I get back." My little brothers were hungry too. Jay's daughter and I rode our bikes to McDonald's, I took Lil Dawane with us. We ordered our food then we sat down and ate.

My mom came inside McDonald's, as we were eating our food. She said, "I thought I told y'all to stay at home?" We said, "We were hungry and we brought Lil Dawane with us." "Jay got something for y'all when y'all come home." I said, "What is it?" "You will see." My mom went back home, so Jay daughter and Lil Dawane and I rode our bikes back home. When we came inside the house, my brothers said, "You guys are in trouble." I said, "Did mommy bring y'all something to eat?" "No, she brought Jay something to eat." Jay daughter and I went inside the livingroom. Jay was sitting on the couch. He said, "Didn't Bella tell y'all not to leave?" We said, "Yeah, but we were hungry so we went to get something to eat." Jay put on a pair of boxing gloves and he told his daughter to get on the floor, and block herself. Then he started hitting her. He hit her in her ribs, her chest, her head and everywhere else. After he was finish, beating his daughter up, he told me to get on the floor and block myself so I did. Jay, hit me in my ribs and my chest and my head. After, he was finish beating me up. I went upstairs and slammed my room door, I was mad. Jay ran upstairs and pulled his belt out. He said, "Who slammed the door?" His daughter said, "It wasn't me!" As Jay went downstairs, he yelled to my mom, "Bella, you better tell your daughter to stop slamming doors before I put those gloves back on and hit her again." Jay's daughter was mad and so was I. She told me she was going to move back with her mom. She told me she was mad at my mom for not protecting her. I was mad at my mom for watching and allowing a man to beat up her daughter. Jay did put his hands on me. My own dad never hit me in my ribs, or my head or my chest. Jay did beat us up and I felt every hit. The drugs were taking over my mom and Jay. Our lights were off, and we did not have food to last us. Not even until the middle of the month! Qin would hit a lick to get money and he would buy my brothers and me food with the money he got. We ate oatmeal for breakfast and for dinner for two weeks straight. We were poor. Things got worst. One day I came home from school, and Jay nephew had came down to visit. Jay's youngest son had a football game. Jay told my mom she could go with him to the game. I went outside to empty my room garbage and I heard a loud banging sound on the wall from my brothers room. So, I ran inside the house. Ramone and Patrick were at the bottom of the stairs. I said, "What's wrong?" I heard my mom yelling and screaming! Ramone said, "Jay is beating up mommy." I ran up the stairs. Jay threw my mom in a corner between my brothers bunk beds, and he was beating her up. He broke the wood from my brothers bunk beds and he tried to hit my mom in her head with it, but my mom moved her head. I stood in the doorway yelling and crying, "Stop, stop hitting my mom. Mommy." I yelled as I was crying! Jay threw the wood down, then he started stomping my mom with his boots on. He was beating my mom in her head and he was stomping her so badly, that she peed on herself. Then Jay ran out of the room and he ran downstairs. He got his son and his nephew and they left. I ran over to my mom as I was crying. My mom said bravely, "Cupcake, everything is going to be ok. Stop crying ok."

My mom was in more pain than me, and even then she would act like everything would be ok, but I was 11 years old, so I knew it wasn't ok. My mom said, "Give me a hug. Do you want to come with me to Lisa's house?" "Yes." "I'm going next door to our neighbor's house, so I can ask her for a ride." The neighbor told my mom she would take her to Lisa's house. My mom took Lil Dawane with us. My brothers wanted to come too, but my mom told them there wasn't any room in the car. My brothers said, "We don't want to stay here." My mom said, "I'll be back later. I'm going to Lisa's house." On our way to Lisa's house, our neighbor told my mom she should go to the hospital. My mom told our neighbor she would be fine. Our neighbor's husband would beat her too. Our neighbor told my mom. She have to hurry up and go home before her husband comes home, because if she was not there by the time he got off work. He would beat her. My mom told our neighbor thank you for giving us a ride. Lisa's husband opened the door. He said, "What happened to you Bella? Hi Zaneeya." My mom said, "Jay beat me up." I said, "Hi Kenny." Lisa said, "Where is Justin Jr., Qin, Patrick and Ramone?" "I had to leave them at home, because there wasn't any room in the car." Lisa said, "Zaneeya are you ok? I know that scared you." I replied, "I don't know why he likes to be mean, and to beat up my mom!" My mom told Lisa that I seen everything. Lisa told me I could go upstairs and play in Veronica's room, which is her daughter. I went upstairs, Veronica was younger then me. We played with her Barbie dolls, but I could not stop thinking about what just happened. So I went downstairs to go sit with my mom. My mom said, "Cupcake, we are going to spend the night at Lisa's house." I said, "Ok, what about my bothers, are they coming to?" "No, they are going to stay at home. Then we will go home tomorrow." "I don't never want to go back there!" My mom called my brothers to see what they were doing. My brothers asked my mom was she coming home tonight. My mom said, "No, I'm coming home tomorrow." They said, "Mom please come home, were hungry." "Ok, I'll be home soon." Lisa said, "So you're going home?" "Yes I have to." "I will take you home, to go get the boys if you want me to, and all of y'all can spend the night." "No, that's ok I'mma just stay at home." I said, "Mom, please can we spend the night?" Lisa said, "Zaneeya, you can spend the night if your mom say it's ok." My mom said, "You can spend the night. Then just get on the school bus when you get out of school tomorrow." "Ok mom." Lisa took my mom home. I called to check on my mom when Lisa got back. My mom told me she was laying down, and she had a headache. I told my mom I loved her and I asked could I speak to Ramone. She said, "I love you too Cupcake." I talked to Ramone. I said, "Is mommy really laying down?" Ramone replied, "Yes she is." "Have Jay tried to hit her again since she's been home?" "No." "If Jay hits mommy again, run outside to our neighbor's house and call the police." "Ok, Zaneeya I will." The next morning, Lisa took me to school. After, she dropped her kids off. She gave me a hug and she told me I could spend a night anytime. I told her thank you, when I got out of school, I went straight home. I went upstairs to see my mom. I gave her a hug and I didn't say nothing to Jay. Qin and I had got into an argument. My mom had left, so he started picking on me once again. He came up to me and pushed me. I said, "Leave me alone Qin, I'm not playin with you." Therefore, I went inside my mom's room to watch TV, so I could get away from Qin. He came up to me and said, "Mommy isn't here now. There is no one to save you." "Leave me alone, your always picking on me!" Qin slapped me in my face. Then I got up and punched him in his face. Then he punched me back and I fell back and hit my head on Jay's rocking chair.

I got up and I ran over to Qin, and I punched him in his face. Qin and I fought all the way into the hallway upstairs. I could not stop fighting him. I knew, if I gave up, he was just going to continue beating me up, and I had enough. So, I finally fought back. Even though, my brother had beaten me, up. That didn't matter. By me fighting him back, I had let him know, that I wasn't going to allow him to keep beating me up and I let him know that everytime. He would hit me, I was going to strike him back and I did! Qin got tired. He said, "Ok, no more. I'm not going to hit you no more." He went downstairs and a few minutes later, my mom came home. I said, "Mom, Qin beat me up." Qin said, "She was fighting me back mom." I said, "I had to fight back to defend myself." My mom said, "Do not put your hands on your sister again, do it again and I'm going to whoop your butt and I'm not playin with you." "Ok mom, I'm not." "Go tell your sister you're sorry." "I'm sorry, Zaneeya. Wait *until she leaves again."I replied, "I'm not worried about you. I'll be waiting for you." Morning came and it was time to go to school. Qin could not find his shoes. He said, "Mom, I can't find any of my shoes. Zaneeya problem hid them from me." My mom called me to her room. She said, "Cupcake, did you hide your brothers shoes?" "No mom, I'm going to be late for school." I said with a smile on my face. My mom said, "Qin, wear my shoes to school today." "Mom, I don't want to wear your shoes!" "Boy you don't have a choice, and you're going to school." I looked at Qin and I laughed. I said, "You have to wear girl shoes. That's cute." "Shut up Zaneeya. I know you know where my shoes are. Just give them to me please. I don't want to go to school in mommy shoes." "Oh okay, you better hurry up, your going to be late." Qin, and Justin Jr., and Jay's daughter left out the door for school. They all went to the same school. I went upstairs to my room to see how far down the street Qin was. I saw that he wasn't far at all. So, I went outside. I picked up some rocks from our front yard, and I threw them at Qin. He looked back to see were the rocks were coming from. I just kept throwing them at him. Then I ran inside house to finish getting ready for school. My mom yelled my name, "Zaneeya come here, I know you had something to do with your brother shoes being missing." I replied, "Mom, when he was sleeping last night. I went inside of his room, and I took every left shoe that he had." "What did you do with it?" "I put his shoes in my room closet." "Go put your brother shoes back and don't do that again girl." "Ok mom." When, Qin came home his shoes was back in his room. I even lined them up for him. My brother Justin Jr., wanted to watch TV and everybody knew Justin Jr., was the bully of the house. Justin Jr., said, "Where, is the remote control?" Nobody did not say nothing, because we wanted to watch, what was on TV. Justin Jr., said, "I'm going to turn the TV off." I said, "I have the remote control. I knew you were going to turn the channel." "Yes I am." He tried to take the remote control out of my hand, but I didn't let it go. He finally grabbed it. I just walked away and started going upstairs to my room.*

Justin Jr., ran after me. He pushed me against the wall, and he slapped me in my face. I went upstairs to tell Jay, that Justin Jr., had slapped me! Jay said, "Don't tell me, that's good for you!" I was mad, so I told my mom when she got home. She told Justin Jr., the same thing she would always say. I'm going to whoop you if you hit your sister again. I was getting tired of her telling my brothers that. I wanted her to whoop them, or put them on punishment! Jay and my mom were on drugs even worst, and this time they could not hide it! One morning I woke up, and I made my mom breakfast. I burned everything. The pancakes, bacon and eggs. She said, "Ooh, Cupcake you made mommy breakfast?" "Yes, but I ruined it." "That's ok mommy is going to have to teach you how to cook." Jay had brought his bb gun out of the closet and he aimed it at my mom. She said, "Don't point that at me." He aimed the bb gun at me. I said, "Do not shoot me with that gun." Jay shot me in my thigh. I said, "Why did you do that?" It might have been a bb gun, but when he shot me, it hurted very bad. My mom said, "Jay was just playing Cupcake." I said, "That's no way to play, and he was not playing." I left out of my mom's room and I went inside of my room. As time went on, my mom and Jay were arguing a lot more. One evening, I went into the livingroom and Jay and my mom was arguing. Jay said, "Bella, if you do not come up with my money that you spent, I'mma kill you and your mother!" My mom replied, "Ok, ok!" My mom sounded like she was scared for her life at that moment, but she could not leave Jay, not right then, and there. After, I heard what Jay told my mom. I called my auntie Dorthy and I asked her could I come spend the night on the weekend? When the weekend came, uncle Tony came to pick me up. That Saturday night, I called to check on my mom. She told me she was laying down, and she did not feel good. I said, "Ok mom I love you." She replied, "I love you too." "Mom let me talk to Ramone." "Ok." When Ramone got on the phone, I asked him did Jay hit my mom. Ramone said, "Yes, he did." I said, "What happened? Go some where, so you can talk, so no one can hear you." "Ok, mommy and Jay were arguing, and Jay tried to hit mommy with a bat, but she moved out of the way. So he slapped mommy." "Where did this happen at?" "Downstairs in the livingroom." "Ok brother, I love you. I'll see you tomorrow, if Jay hits mommy again call the police." "Ok sister, I love you too." We moved in with Jay and his kids. He moved to a two bedroom. It was little, like a little shack! Everything was close together! The house we moved out of went into foreclosure, but my mom could have kept her section 8. She should have looked for a house for us, but instead she lost her section 8 by not moving into her own place. As we were moving, Jay said to my mom, "Do not bring all of your kids belongings to my house either!" After, my mom let Jay and, his kids stay with us, and he brought all of his kid's belongings with him when they moved with us. I did not blame Jay. I blamed my mom, because she allowed it! My mom told me to bring one suitcase with me when we moved. I said, "Mom, what about the rest of my clothes?" She replied, "We will come back for them." I knew she was lying, because I heard what Jay told her. My mom sold my bike. I came home from school one day, and I was looking for my bike and it was not there! I said, "Ramone have you seen my bike?" Ramone said, "No." Qin said, "Mommy sold it." I was upset. My mom left everything.

Chapter Five

Saying Good Bye Is Hard To Do

*W*e all lived at the little shack. We slept in Jay kid's room, on the floor. My mom would sleep in Jay's room or on the livingroom floor. My brothers and I did not want to live there. Jay told my mom that my brothers need to live with my dad because his house was not big enough. One night Justin Jr., got in trouble for cussing. My mom whooped him, and as she was whooping him. I started laughing. My mom looked at me. She said, "Oh, it's funny? Ok, well I'm going to whoop your butt too." My mom whooped me, and as she was whooping me. She was talking to me! She said, "You better not laugh at your brother again, when I'm whooping him. Do you hear me?" I was yelling, "Mom ok." My mom told my brothers that they were going to live with our dad. Qin said, "Why mom, what did we do? Why do we have to go live with him?" My mom replied, "It's time for y' all to go live with him. All of you need to be around y'all dad's more." "That's messed up. You know I don't even get along with my dad." "Well, your dad is coming to get y'all this week." Qin was mad. When my dad came to pick them up Qin said, "Mom, please don't make me go!" My mom said, "Boy, come on." She gave my brothers a hug, and my mom looked like she wanted to cry. My dad said, "It's going to be ok Bella they are going to be fine. I know you love your boys." I told my brothers bye. When we went inside the house after they left my mom cried. Deep down, I think my mom knew she made the wrong decsion. I really didn't want my brothers to leave, but at the time, I couldn't tell them that. I really didn't know how much I would miss my brothers, and I really didn't know how much I needed my brothers, but soon I found out. I finally turned 12 years old. I was a preteen. Jay daughter and I walked to my auntie Dorthy's house. It was a far walk, but I wanted to ask my auntie could I live with her. When we got to Dorthy's house, we rang the doorbell. Jason answered the door. He told me happy birthday. I told him thank you, and I went inside *of Dorthy's room. She said, "Happy birthday Zaneeya." I said, "Thank you auntie. I need to ask you something. Can I live with you?" Uncle Tony came in the room. He said, "Happy birthday niece." I said, "Thank you uncle Tony. Can I auntie, can I live with you?" Dorthy said, "No, because your mom is not going to give me any money or food stamps for letting you live here!"*

Uncle Tony said, "So what if she doesn't give us any money. Zaneeya can live here. She is not a problem. She is the only girl!" I said, "Thank you uncle Tony. I am tired of listening to them argue and stuff!" Dorthy said, "No, I already have four kids." Tony said, "That's messed up! That's your only niece out here." I said, "Ok." I left. I was upset, and I was thinking to myself, how can you tell your niece no. She cannot live with you jus,t because her mom will not give you any money or food stamps. After, the conversation Dorthy and I had. I knew I would not look at her the same. When I went home, my mom asked me what was wrong. I told her what Dorthy and I talked about. My mom said, "She could of let you live with her, but it's ok Cupcake. Things will get better." Jay daughter had moved with her mom. It was only Ramone, Patrick, Lil Dawane, Jay son and I that lived at the shack. Things got extremely worst. One night, I was getting ready for bed, and my mom was sleeping in the livingroom on the floor with Lil Dawane. Jay came out of his room. He said, "Bella where is my money?" My mom replied, "What money? What are you talking about? I don't have your money!" He yelled, "Stop lying!" Jay grabbed the phone from the wall, he picked it up, and he was going to throw it at my mom. I came out of the room. I said, "Stop, don't throw that at my mom, please stop." My mom put her hands up to block her head. My mom said, "Please don't throw that at me, please." Jay threw the phone at the wall and he went to his room. My mom said, "Cupcake, do you want to sleep in here with me?" I said, "Yes." I got my covers and I made me a pallet on the floor next to my mom and Lil Dawane. The next morning I woke up and got dressed for school. Before I left, my mom asked Jay did he find his money. He told her, he found his money in his wallet. I said, "Bye mom, I'll see you later when I get home from school." My mom said, "Wait, it's too early for you to be going to school." "Mom, no it's not. I'll see you later." I left and went to school. My brothers did not have school. They were off track. At our schools, we had blue track, yellow track, green track and red track. I was on blue track, so I was not out of school yet. At school, I had alot of friends. Some were older then me. I wasn't in my right grade. My mom held me back a grade. I had a nice teacher. My best friend's names were Malinda and Ty. Everyday that I went home, I was more nervous as a kid. The arguing got so bad. I would shower at night, and I would put my school clothes on after I would get out of the shower. So when morning came, I would wash up, brush my teeth, and wash my face, and do my hair and I would leave. I hated living with Jay. One Saturday morning, Jay son had a football game in Stockton. My mom and my brothers were going to the game. When they were leaving, Jay said, "Zaneeya, your not coming?" I replied, "No, I'm going to walk to my auntie Dorthy's house." "I wanted to show off my stepdaughter." My mom said, "Come on Cupcake, come with us." I said, "No, I'm going to Dorthy's house, and there's no room in the car and plus, I don't want to go!"

Jay said, "I will make room for you. Ramone get out the car!" Jay made my little brother Ramone get out of the car. Jay said, "Ramone can walk to Dorthy's house and you can come with us." I said, "No, Ramone can go." "Alright, well Ramone can go with you. Come on Bella before we be late." Ramone did not get back in the car. My mom told Ramone and me she would see us later, as Ramone and I were walking to Dorthy's house. I was thinking to myself. How could my mom allow a man, to make one of her youngest sons walk all the way to my auntie Dorthy's house, at his age. If I would of went with my mom. Which I never would of, but if I did. Ramone would have had to walk by himself to Dorthy's house. My mom didn't care about us to me at all any more. When, Ramone and I made it to Dorthy's house. She asked us how we got there. I said, "We walked here." "Where is your mom?" "She went with Jay to his son football game." "I know you didn't want to go. Why, Ramone didn't go?" "He was going to go, but Jay wanted me to go, and I told him no! I was not going, and there wasn't any room in the car. Jay told me he would make room. He told Ramone to get out of the car, and he said Ramone could walk to Dorhty's house, but I told Jay no. I did not want to go." "That's messed up, how can your mom let Ramone walk all the way over here by himself?" "I wasn't going to let that happen. That's why I came with him and I was not going to that game." Uncle Tony said, "Zaneeya are y'all hungry?" I said, "Yes." "Go make y'all an egg and cheese sandwich." "Ok, thank you uncle Tony." "You're welcome." I made Ramone and I an egg and cheese sandwich. We ate, and then we went outside to play. Christy and I played Chinese jump rope. Later on, uncle Tony took Ramone and me home. I told him thank you. Ramone and Patrick had to go back to school. We all would walk to school together. My mom told my brothers and me to walk to Dorthy's house after school, and she will meet us over there. After school, Christy and I walked to her house together. My mom was there waiting for us. When Patrick came in from school, my mom told us let's go. Tony gave my mom five sodas for us.

When we made it to the little shack, Jay had a real bad attitude. He had a crack attitude! Jay said, "Who sodas are these?" My mom said, "Those are my sodas." "Why do you only have five sodas?" "Tony gave me those sodas for my kids." "Why didn't you bring my son a soda?" "I didn't buy those sodas! Tony gave them to me and your son can have my soda." Jay got mad and started calling my mom out of her name and he told my mom to leave. He opened the front door and started throwing my mom stuff out. He threw her purse outside. He threw her sodas outside. He threw out everything. My mom said to my brothers and me, "Come on, we are leaving." I said, "Yes mom, are we going to live with Dorthy?" My mom replied, "Yes we are." "Mom, are you on drugs?" My mom looked at me and said, "Yes I am, but I'm not going to be anymore." I looked at my mom. I said, "Let's just go mom. Everything will be ok." We walked all the way to Dorthy's house. When we arrived to Dorthy's house, she asked my mom what happen that quick. My mom told my auntie and uncle what happened. Uncle Tony told my mom we could stay at their house. My mom told Tony thank you.

My auntie told my mom. She had to give up all of her food stamps, and she had to pay her for living there. My mom should have given Dorthy some money, for letting, us live there, but that was not right. My mom should not have given up, all of her food stamps! Yes, my mom had more kids, but they should have put their food stamps together, and my mom should have spent most of her food stamp, but saved at least $50 dollars in food stamps to herself. See, my mom wasn't the only one on drugs. My auntie Dorthy was on drugs, and so was my uncle Tony. One day, I was using my auntie shower in her room. When, I got out of the shower, my mom told me to ask Dorthy for her hairbrush. I said, "Auntie Dorthy, can I use your hairbrush?" "Go look in my bathroom drawer." "Ok." When I went to look in her bathroom drawer, I saw a crack pipe. I picked it up, and that was not my first time seeing a crack pipe in my aunties bathroom drawer. Dorthy said, "Zaneeya, do you see the brush?" I replied, "Yes, I see it." I put the crack pipe down and I left out of the bathroom. On weekends, everybody would have to clean up. My auntie kids were lazy! Everybody accept for Jason. My auntie would make my brothers and I clean, but her kids would be sitting down. Uncle Tony use to tell my cousins to help. They would only help clean, when Tony made them! Dorthy would tell me to vacuum the hallway floor. Then she would say, "Come vacuum my room too." My uncle Tony wasn't lazy. He would clean and cook before he went to work. On weekends, he would clean the bathrooms. He also would dust, and he would make his kids clean their rooms. Dorthy would even have

Lil Dawane cleaning. We still went to the same school. Patrick and I were in the 6th grade. It was time to go to 6th grade camp and I was excited. At first, Patrick did not want to go. I told him, he should go or he was going to miss out on a whole bunch of fun. He changed his mind, and he told my mom he wanted to go to 6th grade camp. We had to be at school by 7:20 AM, because the school bus was picking all of us up to go to camp. The campsite was called Foot Hill. I was happy to get away.We stayed in cabins. They were nice. We camped for seven days. We would compete with other cabins. They served us breakfast, lunch and dinner. I saw Patrick at lunch. He came and gave me a hug. I said, "You know my cabin is going to come in first place right!" Patrick replied, "Yeah right, we will see. You're going to be mad when my cabin wins." I laughed as my brother walked away. It was only one bathroom, that had showers, and there were only eight showers in the bathroom. Everybody, had 5- minutes to shower, and we could not get dress in the bathrooms. So we had to get dress in our cabins. Everybody had to keep their cabins clean. That's how you got stars and points. The cabin that had the most points and stars was the cabin that won.

We went hiking at night, so we can see the stars. That was my first time seeing the big dipper, and also looking at the planets. When we went hiking, the teachers told us not to touch the plants or trees, because they had poison ivy on them. We had an activity everyday to do. A day before camp ended. They announced the cabin that came in first place, and it was my cabin. I knew we would win! The next morning it was time to leave, to go back home. When we made it to school, I told my friends bye and I walked home. My mom was happy to see me. She said, "Cupcake how was camp?" I said, "It was nice. I had a lot of fun." "Did you see Patrick?" "Yes I did." Patrick came in the livingroom. I said, "I told you my cabin was going to win." Patrick replied, "We just let you win." "Right, that's what they all said." My mom said, "Now you have to get ready for your 6th grade graduation." "I know mom, I can't wait." Christmas came back around, and Justin Jr. and Qin were coming to visit for Christmas break. I was excited to see my brothers. I haven't seen them in a long time. My mom told my brothers to call her, when they get to the Greyhound station, because uncle Tony was going to pick them up. My mom was braiding my hair into a ponytail braid. My brothers called and told my mom that their bus has arrived in Modesto. Tony went to pick them up. When they came inside the house, I told them hi. They gave my mom a hug and they hit me. That time they both hit me, and I knew it was out of love. After, my mom was finished doing my hair. She told Qin and Justin Jr., to come in the livingroom.

My mom said, "How do y'all like living with your dad?" They said, "We don't like living there, and our dad don't even live there." Qin said, "I was late to school one day. So the school called my dad, and he came over. He asked me why I wasn't in class. I told him I was late to school, and I only had ten more minutes left in class. So I didn't go. When the bell ranged, I went to my next class. My dad slapped me in my face that night. I told him, he is not going to be putting his hands on me just, because he is my dad. Then he said he wished he never had me, and he wish his blood wasn't running threw my veins." I never seen my dad, slap my brothers before, but I knew they was not lying on him! My mom said, "What?" Justin Jr., said, "He put his hands on me too." My mom said, "Ain't that about nothin! Don't worry; you guys are not going back." My brothers were happy. My dad and my grandma sent me $20 dollars each. I said, "Justin Jr., and Qin where is my money?" They said, "Mommy took it." "Why did you give my money to her?" They did not say anything. I said, "Mom, why did you take my money?" "Girl your dad didn't give you any money this time." "Yes he did. I talked to him, and my grandma sent me some money too." "I'll give it back to you." "That's messed up, your always taking my money." "Shut up! You better tell your dad that your brothers gave you, your money too." "I'm telling him the truth. My brothers gave you my money, and you took it, just like you always have." Qin and Justin Jr., Lason and Jason were cutting class a lot. One morning they went to school and they came back home two hours later. My mom said, "What are y'all doing back home?" They said, "We didn't want to go to school." The boys would get a free pass no matter what it was.

My brothers told my mom they were smoking weed. My cousins told my auntie and uncle that they were smoking weed as well. My mom knew, she couldn't stop my brothers and my auntie, and uncle knew, they couldn't stop my cousins from smoking weed. My mom and Dorthy told my brothers and cousins to make sure that they do not smoke weed with anyone. They also told them to not buy weed, that's already rolled up. They would go outside in the front yard and smoke. Sometimes my mom would go outside and tell my brothers and cousins to let her hit the weed. They did not have a choice. They would fuss, but she would smoke their weed anyway. Qin was going back to his bullying ways. This time he was not picking on me, he would pick on Christy, when she made him mad. My brothers would want to go inside of Mimi and Christy's room to play their game. Mimi would say yes but when Christy would walk in her and Mimi's room, she would say, "Why are y'all in my room?" Qin said, "Chill out Christy, dang. Mimi told us we can play the game." "This is not just Mimi's room." Mimi said, "I told them they can play the game." Christy said, "I don't care. Y'all can't play the game and get out my room." Qin said, "Come on Christy, just let us finish. Were not even bothering you." "I don't care. Get out my room, I'm telling my mom." "You're always kicking somebody out of your room, with your bald headed self." Dorthy said, "My daughter got hair. She's not bald headed." Christy said, "That's why you don't have your own room, and you have to live with us." Christy laughed. Dorthy said, "That's why my kids have their own room, and their own house and their own beds." What Dorthy said was mean, and how Dorthy would tell Christy to tell my brothers that she had her own room, and they did not, was also mean. Dorthy should have taught Christy. These are your cousins, and they have to live here. You are not going to talk about what you have, and what they don't have, because that's not right. You are supposed to teach your kids! Not, encourage them to treat other people bad. Qin stopped going inside of Christy's room. Qin had got real disrespectful with my mom and she hit him in his chest. Qin was real, out spoken and I think he had a lot of deep feelings. That he never dealt with inside and he was tired of living house from house. My mom would leave at night and I would look after Lil Dawane. Sometimes, I would give him a bath at night. When I knew, my mom did not give him one earlier that day. I washed him up and put Vaseline on him, as my mom would do. I also would put his pajamas on him. I would use my mom lion blanket to sleep with. I would lay Lil Dawane down with me, and we would sleep on the floor, on the side of, Dorthy's bed. When, my uncle Tony came home from work. My auntie would wake me up and tell me to go lay on Christy's room floor, or go lay in the livingroom. My birthday was coming up and I was turning 13 years old. I asked my mom could I go to the Bay Area, because I was off track. She told me I could, but she told me I have to come back a week before school starts. So I could go to my 6th grade graduation. My uncle dropped Justin Jr., and I off at our grandma house.

Chapter Six

I am Not Moving Back To Modesto

*W*hen Justin Jr., and I went inside of our grandma's house. Nobody was there accept our grandma, and our auntie Timberly, which was one of my dad's sisters. We told uncle Tony thank you for dropping us off, and we told him we would see him later. We gave our grandma and auntie a hug. The phone ranged, it was my dad. He told us he would be by later to pick us up, so he could take me somewhere for my birthday. Sabreea was coming up the stairs. I began to hide, because I wanted to surprise her. I went inside of the upper livingroom. When I saw that her back was turned, I tapped her on her shoulder. She turned around. She said, "Hi sister, how did you get here? Are you spending the night?" I replied, "Yes, my uncle Tony just dropped us off." "I'm happy you here. Now I won't be bored." My dad came to pick us up. He brought our little sister Agonna with him. She was 3 years old. My dad had another baby with Tracy. My dad gave me a hug. He asked Justin Jr., was he coming with us. Justin Jr., told him no. So Sabreea, and Agonna, and I went with our dad. My dad went to pick up his girlfriend from work. Her name is Toniya. She was a RN at Highland Hospital. She said, "Hi, you must be Zaneeya? I heard a lot about you." I replied, "Yes, I am hi. How are you doing?" "I'm fine, tired. I've been at work all day, happy birthday." "Thank you." My dad said, "Toniya are you coming with us?" "No, I'm too tired. Plus, I have to get up for work early in the morning." My dad dropped Toniya off at home. Then, he asked me where I wanted to go for my birthday. I told my dad, I wanted to go to the movies or out to eat. Agonna said, "Dad, I want to go to Chucky Cheese." I said, "Agonna, we are not going to Chucky Cheese." "Yes we are. Dad, I want to go to Chucky Cheese." My sister was 3 years old, but she had a conversation with you as if she was 5 years old. My dad said, "Ok, we are going to Chucky Cheese. Your sister wants to go. Plus that's something for her to do." I said, "It's not her birthday. Why, we can't go *to Chucky Cheese for her birthday?" "Zaneeya stop, being selfish." We went to Chucky Cheese and no, I did not play. I sat down the whole time. I really could have just stayed at my grandma's house. After my sister was finished playing, my dad bought us some pizza.*

I did not eat, because I did not eat pepperonis on my pizza. After, they were finished eating, he dropped us off at my grandma's house. My grandma asked me did I have fun. I told her no. I should have just stayed here. I went to bed, the next morning, we called all our cousins that we would hang out with, and we asked them did they want to spend the night at our grandma's house. We called Lil Lamonte, Tommy, and Brain, Janelle, and Deedee. Everybody spent the night over the weekend, accept for Deedee. She already had plans that weekend. Momma Shay came over to spend the night. We would stay up late and the boys would mess with us, while we were sleep. I fell asleep with my glasses on. When I woke up to use the bathroom, I screamed, because I couldn't see anything. Momma Shay woke up. She said, "What's wrong Zaneeya?" "Mom, look I can't see." "Those boys were messing with you while you were sleep. They put shaving cream on your glasses." Sabreea woke up. They put shaving cream on her, as if she had a beard. Momma Shay wiped the shaving cream off my glasses, and she wiped the shaving cream off Sabreea's chin. I told momma Shay I had to use the bathroom, and I asked Sabreea to come with me. She said, "Ok." "Momma Shay said, "Y'all better not mess with the boys either." We said, "Ok mom, and were not." When we went to the bathroom, we came up with a plan to get the boys back. I put Vaseline in Tommy's nose. Then, I got some tissue, and I stuck my hand in the toilet, then I squeezed the water out of the tissue, and I threw it at Justin Jr. Sabreea's job was to mess with Brain. I put hot sauce in Lil Lamont's mouth and I put my grandma's itching cream on Lil Lamont. When they woke up, they were mad. Tommy was yelling, "I can't breathe, I can't breathe." Lil Lamont was mad. He said, "Why do I keep itching? What did y'all put on me?" Justin Jr., and Brain were mad too, we just laughed. They said, "Y'all got us good." My grandma would take us to the Goodwill store to go shopping. We would think we were at Macy or Sears. Grandma would tell us to get four things and that's it. We would be so happy and we would tell grandma thank you. Sabreea and I would get two outfits and if it was something that we really wanted we would go up to grandma and say, "Grandma look can we have this please?" She would fuss and say, "Go ahead and get it, you're not getting anything else." We would smile and say, "Ok grandma, thank you!" Everytime we got on the bus with grandma. We would sit down, but if an older person was getting on the bus.

Grandma would say get up, and she would tell that person they can sit down, and they would. Grandma said, "Anytime their is an older person getting on the bus. You have to get up, to give them your seat. No matter how tired you are, and even if you don't want to, you better always get up." We would have to clean constantly at grandma's house. She would go into the kitchen and make a mess. I mean dishes all over the sink and we would have to clean them repeatedly! We would have to clean the kitchen at least three times a day. We would say, "Grandma, we are tired of cleaning." She would say, "Clean up that kitchen, then y'all can have some fun. Just do it! Don't give me no lip, after y'all clean. I'll let y'all watch a little TV."

We would say ok grandma. Everybody would go over grandma's house. We use to sneak out of the house and go play doorbell ditch. We had a good time when all of us spent a night together. Grandma did not like it when we bought Chinese food, or burritos. She would fuss and say, "I'm not giving y'all any more money, because y'all waste money. Y'all could have made that yourself's." We would say, "Grandma we just wanted to buy something to eat. It's nothing wrong with eating a little fast food." "I'm still not giving y'all any more money, and that's that!" She would go into the livingroom. We knew grandma did not mean what she said, about not giving us any more money. Sabreea and I would say, "Now watch, grandma did all that fussing. Now watch her come in here and ask us for some food." 10- minutes later, grandma would come into the room. She said, "What did y'all order to eat? Do y'all have some chicken and what is that called?" We would laugh and say, "Grandma, do you want some?" "Yes, put little on my plate for me. Thank you." The next day, I called my granny little sisters. They are my great aunties. My auntie Angel answered the phone. I said, "Hi auntie Angel." She said, "Is this Zaneeya?" "Yes, how are you doing?" "Your granny told me you were out here. I'm doing fine." "I'm at my grandma's house. Can I come over and spend the night?" "You know, you can stay as long as you want to. Do you want me to come get you?" "Yes, thank you auntie." "No problem, I will be there soon." "Ok." I told my grandma I was going over to my auntie Angel's house. Sabreea said, "Now I'm going to be here all bored, by myself." "No, you're not. I'm going to come back silly." My auntie Angel came over and her boyfriend Fred. We all called him uncle Fred. Justin Jr., said, "Zaneeya, are you going over to auntie Angel's house?" "Yeah, I'm going to spend the night." Justin Jr., said, "Auntie, can I come too?" Auntie Angel said, "Yeah, you know you can." I gave Sabreea a hug and I gave my grandma a hug and kiss. I told my grandma I would see her later. Angel lived with her other two sisters Letha and Rene and their kids.

Angel has two kids. Rene has four kids and Letha has one child. When we got to Angel's house, we went inside and we said hi to Rene and Letha. They said, "Zaneeya, how are you doing?" "I'm doing well." Rene said, "Tonight you're going to sleep in Alisha and Rebbeca's room." "Ok auntie." Rebbeca and I were close. We all were around the same age. Alisha is Letha's daughter and Rebbeca is Rene's daughter. We all would have fun together. We all stayed up late that night, watching TV. The next day, everybody had to go to school. I woke up and went to the livingroom. Angel said, "Zaneeya, do you want some coffee?" "Yes auntie." Rene and Angel said, "What have you been up to?" I replied, "Nothing, just going to school. I graduate from 6th grades next month." "That's good. What middle school are you going to go to?" "I don't know yet." Later on that day, everybody came home from school. Rebbeca was telling me how she liked the 6th grade. She told me in the Bay Area the 6th grade is part of middle school. I told her in Modesto the 6th grade is part of elementary school.

The next day, everybody went to school. I woke up and went into the livingroom. Angel fixed me a cup of coffee. Angel said, "Zaneeya, I have to take you and Justin Jr., back to your grandma's house today." I replied, "Ok auntie." "I'm going to take y'all, when uncle Fred come home from work. Are you excited to go back to school, to see your friends and to graduate?" "To be honest auntie, I do want to graduate, but I don't want to move back to Modesto." "We will talk about that later." "Ok." When, Fred got off work, they took us to my grandma's house. We all went inside the house and said hi to my grandma. Angel said, "Zaneeya, I'll see y'all later." I said, "No, auntie I want to go back to your house. I want to live with you." "You have to ask Letha can you live there." "Ok, I will ask her." My grandma said, "Zaneeya, your dad told me to tell you, that you cannot leave anymore." I said, "I'm going to call my mom and ask her can I go back over to Angel's house." I called my mom. I said, "Mom, can I go back over auntie Angel's house? My dad told my grandma to tell me that I cannot leave her house?" My mom replied, "Yes, you can! I don't know who he thinks he is, and you always visit Angel, Letha and Rene when you go out there." "Ok mom, thank you." Angel said, "Zaneeya, what did your mom say?" "She said I can go over your house." "Let me talk to her. Bella, is it ok if Zaneeya comes back over my house?" "Of course she can. She can stay over there until she has to come back to Modesto." "Ok, I'll talk to you later my niece." My grandma said, "Well, that's your mom and you live with her. If she says you can go, you can." "Ok grandma. I love you, I'll see you later." "Ok, I love you too." Angel, and Fred and I left. Justin Jr., told me he would be back over Angel's house in a few days. I said, "Ok brother, I'll see you later." When we were in the car, Angel asked me why didn't I want to go back to Modesto. I said, "I'm just tired of the same old things. I just want a better living environment." "Ok, well you can live with us as long as Letha and Rene say it's ok." "Ok auntie, thank you." "You're welcome. You can go to school with Rebbeca and Alisha." "Ok auntie." When, we made it back to Angel's house. Letha said, "What happen, why you didn't stay at your grandma's house?" I said, "Letha I just want to be over here." "Ok." Letha went inside the bathroom she was doing her hair. I went inside the bathroom to go talk to her. I said, "Auntie Letha, can I live here with y'all? Angel said yes and so did auntie Rene, they said now I have to ask you." "Do you think your mom would let you live here?" "Yes, I think she would. All I have to do is ask her." "We will see. What about your 6th grade graduation?" "They will just pass me on to the 7th grade and it's not like I don't have another graduation coming up. I will have an 8th grade graduation." "That's true let me talk to those sisters of mine." "Ok auntie." As the days went on, I got use to being there. Rebbeca, Angel, and Justin Jr., and AD, and Alisha and I would play a couple of cards game. We would play kings corner, speed, and solitaire. We would play for 25cent a game. Sometime I would win. Alisha would win. Rebbeca would win and Justin Jr., and AD and Angel would win. When Alisha did not win, she would say, "You guys are cheating, I'm done with this game." We would laugh and say, "Don't get mad and quit. We need your money." We had a good time.

Sometimes on weekends, Letha, Rene and Angel's dad would come over. Letha, would tell Justin Jr., and I to go hide in Alisha's room. We had to hide, as long as their dad was visiting. We had to hide everytime their dad would come over. It became a pattern. Sometime we would hide for two or three hours or more. One day, Rene had all of us in the backyard, in the garden and we were cleaning up. Her dad came over. Letha said, "Zaneeya and Justin Jr., go inside of Alisha's room, and stay in there until I come get you guys." I did not understand why we had to hide from their dad. I did not understand why they couldn't tell their dad. These are Stella's grand kids. This is our great niece and nephew. These are Bella kids. After, their dad left. Rene came and told us, we could come out of the room. Later on that day, I called my mom and I asked her could I live with auntie Angel, Letha and Rene. My mom said, "No, you have to come back home, so you can get ready for your 6th grade graduation. I only have one daughter." I said, "Mom please, can I live here?" Letha said, "Let me talk to her." I said, "Mom, auntie Letha wants to talk to you." "Ok, let me talk to her." Letha said, "Hey Bella, how are you doing?" "Hi auntie Letha. I'm doing well." "Now Zaneeya ask me could she live here. Rene, and

Angel and I said yes. I will enroll her in school, and she can go to Claremont Middle School with Rebbeca. She will not be a problem at all." My mom replied, "Letha, I don't have any money to pay you for keeping Zaneeya." "Well that's ok. I talked to Angel and Rene and we are all going to buy her what she needs. You know we are not going to let nothing happen to her. Anytime you want to see her, you can. I will never keep her from you. Anytime you want to talk to her, you can. Just call, you have the number. If you want to see her on the holidays, you can. She is in good hands, and when you want to come back and get her you can." "Ok, well that's fine with me auntie. Let me talk back to Cupcake, thank you. After she graduates from the 8th grade, I will come get her." "Ok, that's fine." Letha gave me the phone. I said, "Hello, mom." My mom replied, "Zaneeya, you can live there until you graduate from the 8th grade. Then I will have my own place, and you have to move back to Modesto." "Ok mom, I love you. Thank you." "You're welcome Cupcake. I love you too, and I will be calling you." "Ok mom." After I got off the phone, I was so happy. I went to tell Rebbeca and Alisha about the good news. They were happy too. Rebbeca said, "Zaneeya, I hope we have the same classes." I said, "Me too." Alisha and AD were graduating from the 8th grade. Therefore, the summer was in. Rene called Rebbeca and me to the livingroom one night. She said, "Pack two weeks worth of clothes. Y'all are going to Great America with Glen and Vanessa." I said, "What is Great America?" Rene said, "Great America is an amusement park." Glen is Rebbeca's dad and Vanessa is Glen's wife. Vanessa is my dad sister. The next morning Krystal came to pick Rebbeca and me up. Krystal and Rebbeca are sisters. Krystal is my cousin on my dad side of the family. Glen and Vanessa are Krystal parents. We said hi to Krystal and we gave her a hug. She said, "Hi, you guys are going to spend the night at Sabrina's house tonight." Sabrina is Rebbeca, and Krystal big sister, they all have the same dad. I have not seen Sabrina since I was a little girl. When we arrived to Sabrina's house, we went inside. Sabrina said, "Hi Zaneeya, how are you doing? I haven't seen you since you were a little girl." Rebbeca and I gave Sabrina a hug. Krystal did not stay long. She told us she would see us later. Sabrina said, "Y'all can put your stuff in Emarie's room." We told her ok. Sabrina had three kids and she was married. She had twins, their nick names are Little Man and Big Man and her oldest son name is Emaire. Sabrina told her kids to come here. She said, "This is y'all cousin Zaneeya, come say hi to her." I said, "Hi, can I have a hug?" They came over to me and they gave me a hug. Sabrina said, "Y'all can sleep in the livingroom. I'm going to give y'all some blankets and you guys can eat anything you want. You don't have to ask for nothing." I said, "*Thank you for letting me spend the night at your house Sabrina.*" "*You're welcome Zaneeya. You can stay the whole summer if you want too.*" "*Ok.*" "*We are going to leave early in the morning so we can go to Great America.*" Sabrina's husband came inside the livingroom and he said hi to Rebbeca. Rebbeca said, "*Hi Jonathan.*" Sabrina said, "*Jonathan, this is my cousin Zaneeya, she lives with Rebbeca now. This is my uncle Justin Sr., daughter.*" He said, "*Hi Zaneeya. I just wanted to tell y'all, that y'all could eat whatever y'all want. You do not have to ask for nothing.*" Sabrina said, "*I already told them that.*" "*Did she show y'all where the food and snacks are?*" We said, "*No.*" "*Come on, I'll show you. Remember y'all can eat anything y'all want. Just remember y'all cannot eat my cereal. This is my favorite cereal!*" We laughed and said, "*Ok Jonathan, thank you.*" We stayed up late that night, watching movies and talking to each other. About how many rides we were going to get on at Great America. The next morning, I woke up and showered. Then I ate some cereal. Everybody was getting dress. Some of Jonathan's family members went to Great America with us and uncle Glen went too. Glen gave me $20 dollars and he told me the money was from my auntie Vanessa. I told him thank you. Rebbeca and I went on many rides. We all had fun together. Great America was big at least it was to me. Later on that day, we all took a group picture. It was getting late so we left. We went to Sabrina's house to get our clothes. Rebbeca and I went to Glen and Vanessa's house to spend the night. When we got there, I said hi to auntie Vanessa and I told her thank you for giving me $20 dollars. She said, "*You're welcome Zaneeya. Did y'all have fun?*" I replied, "*Yes, we did. I cannot wait to go back.*" "*Y'all can sleep on the couch bed. I'm going to bring you some covers and some pillows.*" We said, "*Ok, thank you.*" When we woke up the next morning, Vanessa said, "*Y'all can fix y'all something to eat. I'm going to work. I'll be in the office.*" Vanessa was the manager of the apartments where they were living at and Glen worked as the maintenance man. We got dressed. We ate then we went downstairs to Vanessa's office. She said, "*Y'all can go to the playground and play. Your cousin Paris lives here, she's home. Y'all can go say hi to her.*" Vanessa told us what apartment Paris stayed in. We stayed at the playground for a little bit. Then we went to Paris house. We said, "*Hi Paris, how are you doing?*" Paris replied, "*I'm doing well. How are y'all doing?*" "*Were doing good.*" "*I have not seen you guys in a long time. Zaneeya, you still live in Modesto right?*" I said, "*No, I live out here in the Bay Area now. I live with Rebbeca.*"

"*Oh ok, your mom and Rebbeca's mom, are related right?*" "*Yes Rebbeca's mom, is my mom's auntie. My granny and Rebbeca 's mom, are sisters.*"

"Oh, that makes y'all second cousins on your mom side of the family and step cousins on our side of the family." We said, "Yes, we are double cousins." Paris dad and my dad are brothers. Paris showed us around her house, it was nice. Paris said, "Do y'all want something to drink?" We said, "No were fine, thank you." I said, "We are going to 7-elleven. Do you want us to bring you something back?" "No, I'm fine." We said, "Ok, Paris we will see you later. Thank you for letting us come over." "You're welcome. Y'all can come over anytime." We went to 7-elleven we got us some junk food. Then we went inside the house. We spent four nights at Vanessa and Glen's house. Then we went to grandma's house. We stayed at grandma's house for a few days. Then we went back to Sabrina's house. I called Lil Lamont and I asked him did he want to spend the night with us. We would watch the twins for Sabrina. Rebbeca and I would give Little Man and Big Man their baths. A lot of the time, Sabrina would be in pain, because of her arms. I did not mind helping Sabrina at all. Sabrina was a great mother and she also was kindhearted. Sabrina would pay Rebbeca and me for watching the twins. We told her, she do not have to pay us, but she wouldn't listen. She would say, "You guys are teenagers and y'all need to save your money so y'all can have it for when school starts back." Lil Lamont and I were close. That was my best boy cousin my age, and we were thick as thieves. We all would stay up and hang out and watch movies.

Sabrina asked Rebbeca and I did we want to go to her friend house with her. We told her yes. Lil Lamont said, "Where are y'all going?" We said, "With Sabrina to her friend house." "Wait for me, I'm coming too." We all went to Sabrina's friend house. Her friend name is Kayla. Kayla had a daughter and two boys. Kayla' s daughter was Lil Lamont's age, and her oldest son was older than us. Sabrina introduced us to Kayla and her kids. While we spent the summer with Sabrina, Rebbeca and I would hang out with Kayla's daughter. Her name is Tudda. We would listen to music and we would make up dances. One day we went to the store. Tudda had introduced Rebbeca to one of her male friends. Rebbeca and the boy became boyfriend and girlfriend. They only knew each other for a week. One afternoon, Rebbeca said, "Zaneeya, I'm going to Tudda's house." I said, "Ok." Sabrina came downstairs. She said, "Zaneeya, where is Rebbeca?" "She went to Tudda house." "It's getting late! Why are you always doing the dishes?" "Because no one is going to do them, and I know your arms hurt." "Rebbeca needs to do the dishes too. I don't never see her cleaning up behind herself. I'm going to have a talk with her, when she gets back. I'm going to call Kayla, so I can tell Rebbeca to come home." "Ok." Sabrina called Kayla. Sabrina said, "Hey Kayla, what are you doing?

Can you tell Rebbeca it's time for her to come home, it's getting late." Kayla
replied, *"Rebbeca didn't come over here today." "What? Rebbeca told Zaneeya
she was going to your house." "I been home all day and Rebbeca haven't been
over here!" "Is Tudda there?" "Yes, do you want to speak with her?" "Yes, let
me talk to her."* Tudda said, *"Hi Sabrina." "Hey Tudda. Where is Rebbeca?"
"She is with her boyfriend." "What boyfriend? Tudda come meet me at my
house right now. You are going to show me where her boyfriend lives at." "Ok,
I'm leaving my house right now."* Sabrina said, *"Zaneeya, did you know that
Rebbeca has a boyfriend."* I said, *"Yes." "How old is this guy?" "I don't know
how old he is." "Come on Zaneeya. You're coming with me."* When Tudda
came over, we left. Sabrina said, *"Tudda how old is Rebbeca's boyfriend?"
"He is 17 years old." "What? Hell no, that's too old for her! She haven't even
started going to the 7th grade yet!"* Tudda said, *"Rebbeca isn't 16?" "No."*
Tudda showed us where the boy lived. Sabrina knocked on the door and Tudda
and I was on the side of her. Rebbeca's boyfriend answered the door. Sabrina
said, *"Is Rebbeca here?"* He replied, *"Yes, who are you?" "I am her sister. Tell
Rebbeca to come out here right now, so she can go home. My sister is too young
to be your girlfriend! You will not be seeing her again." "I thought Rebbeca was
my age! She's not 17?" "No, she's not. Just go get her!"* He went to get Rebbeca.

Rebbeca came to the door with this blank look on her face. She knew she
was in trouble and she could not blame anyone, but herself! Sabrina said,
"Let's go now Rebbeca!" Tudda said, *"I'm sorry Rebbeca, but I had to tell
Sabrina where you were at. She was looking for you."* Sabrina said, *"Thank
you Tudda go home, because it's already dark outside and it's late." "Ok."*
When we got to Sabrina's house, we went inside of the livingroom. Sabrina
said, *"Rebbeca, why did you lie to Zaneeya, and tell her you were going to
Tudda's house, and you knew you weren't?"* Rebbeca replied, *"I did go to
Tudda's house. Then I went to my boyfriend's house." "Stop lying Rebbeca,
because Kayla has been home all day and she told me you wasn't over there!
Look, you had me worried about you, and you had no business at that boy
house. You didn't even ask me could you go over there, and you're laid up
with some boy. So what were you doing at his house?" "We were just in his
room, watching TV." "I hope you weren't having sex with him Rebbeca!" "No,
I wasn't. I'm still a virgin." "I hope so! You don't need to have sex right now.
You're not even in the 7th grade yet, you have plenty of time to have sex, and
to have a boyfriend. You're to young, and if your mom knew about this. She
would be whooping your butt right now! You know your mom does not play
at all. I let you do whatever you want, when you are over here. In addition,*

you are going to lie to my face! Don't let it happen again, and he is not your boyfriend anymore. Every since you been hanging with Tudda you have changed. You think I do not notice you just been hanging around Tudda and not Zaneeya! What if Zaneeya, did that to you? You just met Tudda you really don't even know her that well! Oh yeah, you have to clean up too. Zaneeya is not doing the dishes anymore while she's here. You're going to, because you never do them and that's not fair." "Ok." Sabrina went to her room. Rebbeca said, "I'm sorry Zaneeya if I've been hanging around Tudda more then you." "It's ok. I'm not worried about that. Lil Lamont is coming back over. So I'm going to be with him anyways." "So now you're just going to hang out with Lil Lamont and not me?" "No, I'm going to hang out with you too, but if you want to act funny like that again. Then, I'm just going to hang out with Lil Lamont." "I'm not going to do that any more." "Ok." Lil Lamont came back over. Sabrina called our cousin Mercy. Mercy is Angel's daughter. She asked Mercy could she come and help Rebbeca, and I out with the boys. She told her she would pay her. So the next day, Sabrina went to get Mercy. We had a week left to spend at Sabrina's house. We stayed with her the whole summer. Mercy would help Rebbeca and me out with the boys. That week went by quick, it was time to go back home. I did not want the summer to end, but I was excited to go to the 7th grade and to have new friends. The next day Sabrina took Mercy, and Rebbeca and I home. Rene said, "Did y'all have fun?" We said, "Yes, we had a good time." Letha said, "Zaneeya, I have to go enroll you in school and Miyesha is going to give you some clothes. That her daughter cannot fit any more, and I'm going to buy you a couple of shirts." "Ok, thank you Letha! Who is Miyesha?" "Your cousin, Wendell's mother, your uncle Alvin baby mother." "Oh ok, I know who you're talking about. I haven't seen her in a long time.

I have to tell her thank you." "Miyesha is coming tomorrow to bring you the clothes." I unpacked my clothes that night, and I went to sleep in Alisha's room. The next day Miyesha came over. She said, "Hi Zaneeya, I haven't seen you in a long time. How are you doing?" I replied, "I'm doing well. How are you doing?" "That's good, I'm fine. These are the bag of clothes. That I have for you. See if you can fit them." "Ok thank you Miyesha." "You're welcome." I tried on the clothes and most of them I could fit. My dad called me, he told me he wanted to see me. He told me he was going to come over to drop me off somethings. Letha said, "Go put your clothes that Miyesha gave you in Alisha's room." I said, "Ok auntie." The next day, my dad came over. He asked me to walk with him to the store. He asked everybody did they want something from the store, they told him no. As my dad and I were walking to the store, he said, "Sindy gave you some clothes, see if you can wear them when you go back home." I said, "Ok dad, tell her thank you for me." "I will, I want to share something with you." "What's that?" "You know I don't have to let you live with Letha right?" "What are you talking about?" "I just want to let you know. I'm the reason why you live with Letha. Your mom is in Modesto and that means I am in control of you. You didn't even ask me can you come over here." "I called and asked my mom. That's who I go to, to ask what I can and cannot do, just like it has always been." "Well, I have custody over you, and I can take you from Letha and there's nothing your mom or Letha can do about it." "My mom has custody over me, and my brothers and my mom said I can live with Letha, and by law, I have the right to say who I want to live with." "I forgot you still think like a kid, and your mind is not mature at all, and your thought process isn't there, but that's ok. Like I said, I can stop you from living with Letha if I want to. So be thankful that I'm allowing you to live with her." "I'm going home! You're always trying to put me down, and I will never live with you." I left and I went back home. Letha asked me what's wrong and I told her what my dad said to me. Letha told me to call my mom. I told my mom what my dad said and my mom told me not to worry about him, because he cannot do anything. After, I got off the phone with my mom. Letha said, "Zaneeya, don't worry. I'm going to fix him!" School had started and it was my first day of school. Letha took me to enroll in school. She told the principal that my dad is not allowed to come pick me up, and his name will not be on my emergency card. The principal told us no one could take me out of school, unless their names are on my emergency card. When Letha was enrolling me in school, they asked her did she want to put me in my right grade. Letha said, "Zaneeya, do you want to be in the 8th grade?" I replied, "No, because I would be behind on what I didn't learn from 7th grade." "Ok, I'll just put you in the 7th grade."

The next day, I went to school. I walked to school with Rebbeca. I told her I was nervous. I never had so many classes in one day. I hope I don't get lost. Rebbeca said, "Zaneeya, you will not get lost. You will get use to it, and we will meet in the front of the school, when school is out." I replied, "Ok." I walked to my 1st period class. There weren't many students in my class. My teacher was friendly. Each class was an hour long. I had lunch 4th period. I had lunch with all the 8th graders and some 7th graders. I was standing in the snack bar line at lunch. I bought me something to drink and I bought me some chips. Then I went to sit down in the cafeteria. This girl came up to me, and she told me I could sit with her. Her name is Desseire. I sat with Desseire and her *best friend Jessica. They said, "Are you new here?" I said, "Yeah, today is my first day." "Where are you from?" "I'm from the East, but I just moved from Modesto." "Where is Modesto?" "It's by Tracy and before Turlock." "Oh ok." When the bell rang to go to class, we all said bye to each other. I had a nice teacher. Her name is Miss. Harrison she was my resource teacher. Rebbeca and I had Miss. Harrison class together. When we got home, Letha, Rene and Angel said, "Zaneeya how was your first day of school? Did you meet anybody?" I replied, "It was ok auntie. I met these girls named Jessica and Desseire." "Oh ok." "I'm going to do my homework. Then I'm going to put my clothes out for school tomorrow." The next day Rebbeca and I walked to school together. At lunch, Jessica asked me did I want to eat lunch with her and Desseire. I told her yeah. Desseire said, "Zaneeya, you're not eating?" "I don't want anything to eat." "I'm going to buy you something to eat and drink anyways." "No, I'm fine. I don't want anything, but thank you." Desseire bought me some chips and some juice anyways and I told her thank you. After lunch, we all went to class. I was always happy to go to Miss. Harrison class. She made me feel like I didn't have a learning disability, even though I knew I did. We had helpers in Miss. Harrison's class. They would help us if we needed help with our classwork. One of the helper's name was Mrs. Jackson. I had a teacher named Miss. Jackson too. After school, Rebbeca and I walked home. When, I went home. I did my homework, and auntie Rene told us to change clothes and come help her in the garden, so we did. We helped pull weeds, and we planted some new flowers. After we were done, we went inside the house. I showered. Then I ate, and went to bed. Every morning Rebbeca and I would walk to school together. At lunch, Jessica said, "Zaneeya, can you or Desseire give me a dollar so I can catch the bus home after school? I will pay you back tomorrow." Desseire did not say anything. I said, "Here Jessica you can have a dollars! Is that all you need?" "Yes, thank you Zaneeya. I'll give it back to you." "No, that's ok. You don't have to pay me back." When the bell rang, we went to class. I saw Rebbeca. She said, "After school, there is suppose to be a fight." I said, "Who is fighting?" "This girl named Ria and Desha." "Oh ok." "I don't know where the fight is going to be at, but we can go. If it's not too far, but you know we would have to hurry up. So we won't get in trouble by Rene and Letha." "Yeah, your right, we don't want to be on punishment for seeing a fight."*

After school, Rebbeca and I saw a crowed of people. She said, "I think their going to the fight." I replied, "Let's go see where everybody is going." We went to see if the crowed of people were going to watch Ria and Desha fight, and they was. The fight was in the ally. Everybody was standing around watching the fight. Desha friends were yelling, "You better beat her up Desha." Ria's friends were yelling at her and telling her the same thing. Ria hit Desha first. Desha was fighting back, but Ria won the fight. Rebbeca and I left. We hurried up and went home. Rene said, "Go change y'all clothes, and come help me in the garden!" We stayed in the garden late that day. I didn't mind helping my auntie Rene. She taught me how to pull weeds. How to plant flowers. She told me what to do when a flower is dying, and she told me, how often you need, to water your flowers. The next day at school, everybody was talking about the fight. Soon, Desha's mom removed her from Claremont Middle school. Everyday it was the same routine. Go to school. Go home, and help with the garden and anything else in the house. I started meeting more people at school and Jessica, and Desseire and I became best friends. This boy name DD would beat on the hall lockers, with his pen and his fist. One of the songs he would do the beat to was. *"Closer to my dreams, I'm getting higher, and higher closer to my dreams."* Those were the lyrics to the song. DD and I had Miss. Harrison class together. He would call me his sister, and I looked at him, as he was my brother. My friends did not know I was in resource. I hid that from them. Before, the bell would ring, for Rebbeca, and DD and I to get out of school. We would line up by the classroom door, 5- minutes before class ended, and we would hurry up and walk in the hallway. So, nobody would see us leaving from our class and we would do that everyday. Miss. Harrison would say, "You guys shouldn't have to hide the fact that you're in resource from your friends. They should accept you for the way you are! It's not your fault that y'all have a learning disability. You were born with it." Rebbeca and I said, "We just don't want people in our business." "Ok, I'm here for the both of you. I just wanted to let you know, how I felt." Miss. Harrison was definitely there for me and I really appreciated it! Auntie Angel had found her own place. She moved out, and Rebbeca, Mercy, and AD and uncle Fred and I helped her moved. Angel told us, we could spend the night at her house anytime. After, Angel moved out. Rebbeca had Mercy's old room. Which was originally the nook, AD had his on room, and Angel's old room was going to be Ilesha's room. Rene's youngest daughter and the room they gave me was a wash area. It was like a hallway. It was big enough for a little bed and a dresser. Everybody, would have to go threw my room to get to the backyard. Alisha and AD would have to go through my room to get to their room. Rene and I painted my room yellow. Miyesha bought me a new blanket for my bed and she bought me an iron. Rene made me a little shelf in my room so I could *put my lotion and other things on. Even though, the room was small. I was happy to have a bed to sleep in!*

One weekend, I asked auntie Rene could I use her phone, so I can call Sabreea. Rene told me I had 5- minutes to talk. I laughed and said, "Ok auntie." I called Sabreea to see what she was doing. Sabreea asked me if I wanted to come over her house on the weekends. I told her I have to ask Letha. My mom had called one evening. Rene said, "Zaneeya, your mom is on the phone." "Ok, here I come." My mom said, "Hi Cupcake, what are you doing?" I said, "Hi mom, I just got done doing my homework." "How do you like going to school out there?" "I like it. I wasn't use to a lot of classes, but now I am and my teachers are nice to me and I have two best friends now." "I'm happy you're doing good Cupcake! When, do you get your report card?" "Next week." "Ok, I will call you next week to see how you're doing, and to see what your grades are looking like." "Ok mom." "I know you're not worried about your grades. You have always gotten good grades." "No, I'm not worried. I get good grades on my homework and all of my teachers said that I'm doing well, in all of my classes." "Ok, I know you are your smart Cupcake!" "Thank you mom." "You're welcome." "Tell my brothers I said hi, and tell them I love them." "Ok, I will and I'll talk to you later." "Ok." One day I was in my room getting dressed, and Angel came over. It was Memorial Day weekend, and Rene, Letha and Angel was cooking. My room and the kitchen was only one inch away from each other, if that. I heard Letha talking about my mom. Letha said, "That's a shame, Bella is on drugs and she don't even pay me for keeping Zaneeya. I know I said she don't have to give me any money, but damn. She don't send nothing at all." Rene did not say anything! Angel said, "Where are the boys?" "I don't know. I guess with Dorthy." I walked out of my room! Angel said, "Hey Zaneeya, what's wrong?" I repled, "Nothing." I went outside and wrote in my diary. I wrote a poem as cried. I was not use to hearing people talk about my mom or about her being on drugs. Even though, I knew, she was on them. I stayed on the front porch for a long time. Alisha came outside. She said, "Zaneeya, what's wrong with you?" "Nothing Alisha, I just miss my mom and my brothers right now." "Oh, you should call her?" "Maybe I will later." Angel came outside and said, "Zaneeya come eat." "Ok auntie I will." I waited for another hour then I went inside the house. I ate. Then I went to bed. Rene would help me with my school projects. Mostly my science projects, my report card came in the mail, and so did Rebbecca's. Letha said, "Zaneeya your report card came, come here!" I went to the livingroom. Letha said, "If you have any bad grades, you are going to be on punishment." I replied, "I'm

*sure, I don't have any bad grades!" "You better not have any C's, D's or F's."
"I don't auntie." Letha opened my report card. She said, "You did good, better
then what I thought you would do." I was proud of myself. I had a 3.17 grade
point average. Rebbeca opened her report card and she did good as well. She
had a 3.00 gpa. I said, "See Rebbeca were not doing bad in school, and we are
in resource!" Rebbeca said, "I know, I'm proud of us."*

*As the school year went on, Rene got sick. We did not know what was
wrong with her. Letha told Rene, if she does not feel better, she is going to take
her to the hospital. Rene said, "I'm fine. I don't need to go to the hospital."
Mercy came over to spend the night. I slept in the livingroom. I was helping
Mercy watch Rene. Rene got up to use the bathroom in the middle of the night
and she was stumbling. Mercy and I helped Rene walk, as she was going to the
bathroom. We knocked on Letha's room door and we told her what happened.
Letha said, "Rene you are going to the hospital tomorrow." The next morning
I woke up for school, Letha said, "Zaneeya, braid Rene hair in a of couple
French braids. I'm taking her to the hospital." "Ok, I will auntie." After, I got
dress. I braided Rene's hair. Letha said, "If I'm not here when you get home
from school, somebody will be here." As Rebbeca and I were walking to school,
I told her I hope auntie Rene is ok, and I hope nothing happens to her. Rebbeca
said, "I hope nothing happens too my mom either. I do not want to be stuck at
the house with Letha!" I was worried about Rene. After school, Rebbeca and
I rushed home, but Rene was not there. Angel said, "Rene is going to be in the
hospital for a long time. She had a stroke and a heart attack." Toya was at the
house too. That was Rene's oldest daughter. Rebbeca and I asked Angel how
long was, Rene going to be in the hospital. She told us she did not know. Letha
was at the hospital with Rene. Angel said, "Rebbeca when you come home from
school tomorrow. I'm going to take you to go see Rene." I knew Rebbeca, AD,
Toya and Ilesha missed their mom! We all missed Rene, but to me her kids
missed her more. Toya was a great cousin and she was always sweet. The next
day we went to school, I couldn't get my mind off of Rene. I started crying at
lunch. I went into the bathroom, so I could get control over myself. I was use to
seeing Rene everyday. I was use to talking to her, and watching movies with her
like, **Lord of the Rings** and other movies. When the bell rang, I went to class.
Rebbeca said, "Zaneeya were you crying?" "Yeah, I couldn't stop thinking
about Rene." "I cried today too, I miss my mom!" When the bell rang to get
out of school, we went straight home. Angel and Fred took Rebbeca, Ilesha and
AD.To the hospital go see Rene. Letha called Alisha and me to the livingroom.
She said, "We are all going to visit Rene on the weekends, We are going to take*

turns visiting her, and I'm going to tell Rebbeca and AD that when they get back. While Rene is in the hospital, we are going to clean up this house, and get rid of the thing that she doesn't need." Alisha said, "When are we going to do that?" "This weekend, everybody is going to help out even Ilesha! She don't never like to clean, but she is going to start cleaning up now!" When AD, Rebbeca and Ilesha got back from the hospital, Letha told them the same thing she told us. Letha said, "Ilesha, you're going to take out the recycling everyday, when you come home from school, and you're going to have one day out of the week to clean the bathroom. Rebbeca you guys are not going to the hospital every weekend to see Rene either." Rebbeca just looked at Letha. After Letha was finish talking, we went to our rooms. Rebbeca knocked on her bedroom wall, we would do that when we wanted one another to come here. That was our signal for each other. I went to Rebbeca's room. She said, "That's messed up Letha said we can't go to the hospital every weekend to see my mom!

That's my mom, not hers. I'm going to the hospital. I don't care what she says!" "Your right, you and your siblings are going through it much harder then anybody else is, because that's your mom. I know Ilesha is missing her like crazy, and AD, he's a momma's boy, so I know it's not the same for him either." "Watch, Letha is going to start taking over the house and doing what she wants to do. She's probably going to try to get rid of all of my mom stuff. If it gets too bad, I'm going to go stay with Angel until my mom gets out of the hospital." "No, you better not leave me here." "I'm not, but Letha gets on my nerves!" We looked at each other and laughed. One weekend Letha woke us all up. She said, "Get up, come on. We have a lot of work to do. The faster y'all hurry up, the faster y'all can have the day to yourself's. After we clean up, I'm going to make some grits, eggs and some bacon." We cleaned the inside of the house first. Then we went outside and cleaned the garage. We cleaned the basement, and we cleaned Letha's storage room. It was very hot outside and the more we cleaned, the hungrier we were. After, we were finish cleaning Letha said, "All of you did a good job." We all ran inside the house. Soon as I went inside the house, I showered and so did Rebbeca. Letha yelled and said, "Y'all have 5-minutes to use my water. Y'all butts aren't that big. Hurry up, water ain't free." Letha cooked breakfast and we all ate. Later on that day, Letha's auntie Jade came over, and she brought some food she had made for us. She made some stuffed bell peppers, fried chicken, and many other different types of food. As time went on, we would go to the hospital to visit Rene. I was happy she made it through the stroke and heart attack that she had. She looked good and I was happy that she was living! Rene stayed in the hospital for a while.

Rebbeca and I would go pick Ilesha up, from school on Wednesdays, because we got out of school early on that day. One day, we came home from school, and Letha told us Rene would be coming home tomorrow, we were all happy. I think Ilesha was the happiest. She was use to her mom spoiling her and seeing her go to school everyday, and picking her up from school. I think she missed being under her mom. Rene loved all of her kids. All four of them, and they loved her too! The next day, we went to school. Rebbeca said, "I can't wait to go home to see my mom." I replied, "I can't wait to see her too." After school, Rebbeca and I ran home. When we made it home, we saw Rene sitting in the livingroom on the couch. Rebbeca gave Rene a hug and so did I, Rene wasn't in a good mood, because everybody was telling her what she could eat and what she could not eat. Letha said, "If y'all see Rene, with some sunflower seeds. Take them from her or come get me, because she is not supposed to eat sunflower seeds and she cannot drink Coke Cola's either." We said, "Ok auntie." Everything was back to normal. We all helped by keeping an eye on auntie Rene, none of us wanted her to go back to the hospital again.

My dad would call me sometimes, and when I did call him, he did not always answer. I called my dad to see if I could spend the night at his house. Even though, my dad and I did not get along. I really did love my dad! I called my dad. I said, "Hi dad. How are you doing?" He replied, "I'm fine Zaneeya. How are you doing?" "I'm doing well. I called you to ask you can I spend the night at your house." "That's nice of you to want to spend sometime with your dad. I would love for you to spend the night." "Ok, I'm going to ask Letha and see what she says." "Let me talk to Letha." I gave Letha the phone. Letha and my dad did not talk long. After, she got off the phone. She looked at me with this mean look on her face. Letha said, "Zaneeya, did you ask your dad, can you spend the night at his house?" "Yes I did!" "Don't do that again! If your dad wanted to see you, he would have asked you to spend the night at his house. I'm going to let you go this time, but do not do that again!" "Ok." My dad came to pick me up. Then we went to pick up Sabreea. We looked at houses with our dad and Toniya over the weekend. The houses were big and beautiful. They all were five and six bedroom homes. The house Sabreea and I told them to get, was a five-bedroom home. It had four–bathrooms and it had two kitchens. The main kitchen was downstairs and there was a second kitchen, on the second floor of the house. The house was nice. My dad and Toniya said they liked that house as well. We had fun that weekend. My dad and I did not even argue. When it was time for me to go home, he dropped me off first. I told Sabreea and Toniya bye. My dad walked with me up the stairs, *he gave me $20 dollars and a hug. He said, "Thank you Letha, for letting my daughter spend sometime with me." Letha replied, "No problem." My dad said, "Zaneeya, how are your grades in school?" "There fine. I'm doing well in school." Letha said, "Her grades are good. When her first report card came, she got a 3.17gpa. Then her second report card, she got a 3.57gpa." My dad smiled, I think he was shocked! He said, "What, you have to be kidding me? Look at my daughter. You're smart girl, go head on. Look at you." Letha showed my dad my report card, so he could see for himself. I truly can say my dad was very proud of me. He gave me a hug. Then he left. I went to my room and got ready for bed. The next morning, I woke up for school, Letha and Rene's dad was there. I spoke to him. Then I went to school. I was always happy to go to school, and I didn't miss a day. At lunch, Jessica asked me what I did over the weekend. I said, "I went to my dad's house, and we looked at houses, and we bonded for the first time ever!" "Did you have fun? Was it just you and your dad?" "I had fun. I was with my sister Sabreea and my dad's girlfriend." "I didn't know you had a sister." "I have three sisters, but Sabreea's older sister I call her my sister too. So, I usually say I have four sisters and five brothers." "Wow, that's a lot of siblings!" When I got out of school that day, I was tired. Letha, Rene and Angel's dad was still there. I always spoke and said hi to everyone when I came in the house. Letha said, "My dad is moving in with us. Alisha he is going to take your room for now. Then you will get your room back after, we fix his room up." Alisha was mad. She did not want to give her room up. She said, "Why he can't sleep in Angel's old room? He can't come here and take my room." Rene said, "Yes he can. This is really his house." Alisha was mad and she just went to her room. Letha fixed up Angel's old room for Alisha. She painted the walls and she bought Alisha a new bed and dresser.*

Letha would give me $2 or $3 dollars for lunch. I would save my money and eat, when I came home. Whatever Rene would cook I would eat. When, Letha would go to Wendy's, which is a fast food restrurant. She only would buy me a dollar cheeseburger and I would still be hungry after eating that! One day, Angel was over and Letha came from Wendy's, and she brought me a dollar cheeseburger. Angel said, "Zaneeya, do you want to go to Wendy's with uncle Fred and Rebbeca? I will buy you something to eat. You need more then just a cheeseburger! That is not going to fill you up." I replied, "Yes, auntie thank you." When we got back from Wendy's, Letha said, "Zaneeya, where did you get that from?" Angel said, "I bought that for her. She can eat more then just a chessburger." Letha said, "Well you can buy her food then." "Anytime that I am over here Zaneeya, if I eat, so will you! We are family. I'm *not going to buy my kids something to eat and only bring you back one thing, knowing you are still going to be hungry." Letha just went to her room. I said, "Thank you auntie Angel." See everytime I would go to the corner store. I would ask Rene, Angel and Letha did they want me to bring them something back. Sometimes they would say no, and sometimes they would say yes. Auntie Rene would say, "Bring me a RC soda" and I would. As time went on, things started to change. Christmas came up. Letha, Angel and Rene bought me some gifts for Christmas. I got a VCR a cd player, and a cd. I was happy. I got dress and I went outside to listen to some music on my cd player. That was my first Christmas with out my mom and brothers, so I was a little sad. I went inside the house and asked Rene could I call my mom and tell her Merry Christmas? Rene said, "Yes." I called my mom and after I talked to her, I felt much better. My dad called me. He said, "Zaneeya, you're out of school for another week huh?" "Yes I am." "Ok do you want to come to my house tomorrow?" "Yes, can you pick Sabrina up too?" "Yes I will go get her, you really love your sister and that's a good thing. Let me talk to Letha." I gave the phone to Letha. My dad told Letha, he wanted to pick me up tomorrow. Letha said, "I think we are doing something tomorrow." My dad replied, "Well, what are y'all doing?"*

"I'm not sure yet, but I will let you know." "Well, I just want my daughter to spend the night with me tomorrow, and I will bring her back." "Well, that's up to her." "Zaneeya don't have a problem spending the night, I asked her. I will pick her up tomorrow around 4 or 5 o'clock PM." "Ok, I'm going to let her go this time." Letha said, "Zaneeya, did you ask your dad to spend a night over his house?" "No, he asked me did I want to spend the night and I said yes." "Why did you do that? You should of came and asked me first." "I just want to spend sometime with my dad and I do want to spend the night at his house." "You don't know what we were going to do tomorrow." "What are we doing tomorrow?" "Nothing, but you're not going to be at your dad's house just, because he's your dad! You can go tomorrow." "Ok, thank you." The next day Rebbeca said, "Zaneeya I want to go with you to your dad's house." "You know my dad would not mind. I'mma call and ask him." I called my dad and I asked him. Could Rebbeca spend the night? He told me yes. I said, "Dad, can you pick us up from Angel's house?" He said, "Yes just be ready when I get there." Uncle Fred took Rebbeca and me to Emeryville to go shopping. I bought Letha a cd that she had been wanting. When we got to Angel's house, I called my dad to see where he was. He told me he was picking Sabreea up. Then he would be on his way to come pick me up. Rebbeca and I waited for my dad to come. It was only 5:35 PM. My dad did not get to Angel's house until 6:15 PM.

When my dad picked us up, he gave me a hug and he gave Rebbeca a hug. He said, "Zaneeya, are y'all ready?" I said, "Yes we are." "Come on." The phone ranged. Rebbeca and I told Angel bye. Angel said, "Hold on, that was Letha on the phone. Zaneeya, Letha said you cannot go with your dad, because it's too late to be leaving." I replied, "What?" My dad said, "That's crazy! You have to be kidding me?" Angel replied, "No, that's what Letha said." My dad said, "Call Letha!" Angel called Letha back. My dad said, "Letha, why can't Zaneeya come with me? I told you yesterday I was coming to get her." Letha said, "It's too late for her to be leaving." "I am her dad, and nothing is going to happen to her while she is with me, and I'm not about to play these games with you Letha." "She can't go, and I'm not playing games." Letha hung up the phone, and she called right back. Angel said, "Zaneeya, Letha said if you leave, you're going to be on punishment for a month." My dad said, "That's messed up. I'm not about to play these games with Letha mean self." Sabreea said, "That's crazy." Rebbeca said, "Letha is always messing up something." My dad said, "Give me a hug. I'm going to talk to your mom about this." My dad gave me $20 dollars and he gave Rebbeca $20 dollars too. I was mad. Letha called back and told Angel to have Fred bring me home. Fred took me home and I was the only kid at home. Rene said, "What are you doing back?" I replied, "Letha said I couldn't go with my dad, because it's too late." Rene just shook her head. I went straight to my room. Letha came to my room and said, "It's too late for you to go with your dad." I gave her the cd that I bought her. She said, "How much did this cost?" I shrugged my shoulders up and down. Letha gave me $10 dollars for buying her the cd. I just went to bed.

The next day, Letha said, "Zaneeya, you're going to start going to your granny house on weekends." I replied, "Ok, that's fine with me." Every two weeks I would go to my granny house, to wash my clothes. My granny was taking care of my brother Ramone at the time. He lived with her for a couple of years. My granny would wash my clothes, and she would cook breakfast and dinner. My granny was a great cook. She would cook greens, banana pudding and stake. Whatever we wanted to eat, my granny would cook. Two weeks went by. Then three weeks went by. Then a month went by. After a while, Letha stopped letting me go to my granny house! I said, "Letha why can't I go to my granny house any more?" Letha replied, "Your just not going to your granny house any more, and you can wash your clothes at home and dry them on the line, outside." Rene had a clothesline hanging up outside in the backyard. My grandma called me on Rene's phone. She asked me, did I want to go to her house once a week to spend time with her. I said, "Yes grandma, but I would have to ask Letha." My grandma said, "I will ask her." "That's ok grandma, I will ask her." "Just let me talk to her." I said, "Letha my grandma wants to talk to you." I gave Letha the phone. Letha said, "Hi Miss. Alissa." My grandma replied, "Hi Letha, I want Zaneeya to spend some weekends at my house! Is that ok?" "I don't have a problem with Zaneeya going to see you, every once in a while, but not every weekend and Zaneeya will not be spending the night, at no ones house for a long time." Letha gave me back the phone. When I got on the phone, my grandma was telling me what she asked Letha. My grandma said, "Zaneeya, you need to leave from over there. She won't even let you see your people. She's probably not gonna let you see your mother too." "If it gets that bad grandma, I'm leavening." "I love you and you should leave." "I love you too grandma, things are going to get better." A couple of months went by and it was my birthday. I turned 14 years old. I went to school that day, everybody told me happy birthday. When I got home from school, Letha gave me a shirt and a pair of pants that she had bought me. She said, "Zaneeya, your dad is coming to pick you up, and take you out for your birthday." "Ok." My dad picked me up and he brought Sabreea with him. He said, "Zaneeya where do you want to go for your birthday?" I replied, "Let's go to the movies." "Ok." We went to the movies. Then we went to get some pizza. My dad said, "Zaneeya, I think I'm going to make you come live with me!" I replied, "I don't want to live with you." "It doesn't matter. It's not what you want. You are going to live with me or you're moving back to Modesto, to go live with your mom." "I'm not moving back to Modesto and I'm not living with you, I will visit you." "You might have too. You never go see your grandma, and my mother is getting up in age." "It's not my fault and you know that! Letha won't let me go anywhere." "I'm tired of Letha." "I'm not hungry anymore." I was thinking to myself. I am not living with him and I am not moving back to Modesto. When my dad dropped me off, I gave him a hug and I said bye and I went straight to my room.

Letha came in my room. She said, "What's wrong with you?" "Nothing, I'm just thinking." "Did your dad make you mad?" "Yes." "That's why you need to stay away from him." The school year was ending, and my mom was calling and telling me that I was going to be in the 8th grade this year and after I graduate, I have to go live with her. I would tell my mom, that I did not want to move back to Modesto. She would say, "Well, when are you going to come back home?" I said, "We do not have a home, and I just want to go to school out here at OT High." "I will think about it Cupcake." My auntie Dorthy came down to visit. She spent a night. She was telling Letha in front *of me, that my mom should be getting out of jail soon. I said, "Dorthy, my mom is in jail? I just talked to her last week." She said, "Yes your mom is in jail. You didn't know that?" "No, I didn't know that!" Dorthy said, "Letha you didn't tell Zaneeya, that her mom is in jail?" Letha replied, "No, she don't need to know about that." I said, "That's my mom, and I do need to know. Everybody else knows about my mom being in jail, but me." I just went to my room. Dorthy came in my room and got me. She said, "Zaneeya walk with me to the store." "Ok auntie." As we were leaving, Letha said, "Zaneeya, where are you going?" Dorthy said, "She is going to the store with me." "Ok, next time tell me that you're going to the store." I did not say nothing, I just kept walking. Dorthy said, "Do you like living here?" I said, "No, not really." "You can always come home." "What home? I don't have a home! Where are my brothers at?" "They are at my house, and you can come live with me." "I asked you could I live with you before I moved out here and you told me no! Thank you auntie, but I'm going to stay out here for now and finish school." "Ok." Dorthy gave me $20 dollars. I said, "Thank you auntie." "Put it in your pocket. How much money, does Letha give you for lunch everyday?" "$2 or $3 dollars!" "That's not enough money. You could only buy a soda and some chips with that." "That's what I eat for lunch!" "That's a shame." The next day I went to school, auntie Dorthy gave me $20 more dollars. I told her thank you. She said, "You're welcome. Give me a hug. I'm not going to be here when you come home from school. I'm going back to Modesto today." "Tell my brothers I love them, and tell my cousin I said hi, and I love them too." "Ok, I love you. Have a good day at school." "Ok, I love you too auntie." As I was walking to school, I could not stop, thinking about my mom and my brothers. That was my mom first time going to jail, and I was thinking, I hope my mom is ok. I wondered who was taking care of Lil Dawane. I was a nervous wreck. When I got out of school, my granny called me, as I was walking in the door. Rene said, "Hold on, Zaneeya your granny wants to talk to you." As Rene gave me the phone Letha said, "Sit right here in talk. Don't leave out the livingroom, and go to your room with the phone." Letha wanted to see what I was telling my granny. My granny said, "Hi Zaneeya. You know your mom is out of jail now." I replied, "HI granny, she is?" "Yes she is." "I'm so happy. I was worried sick about her and my brothers." "Well, now you don't have to worry. You don't know when you can come over here huh?" "No, Letha won't let me go to your house anymore. You have to ask her." "That's a shame, but that's ok.*

I love you. I will talk to you later." "Ok granny, I love you too." When, I got off the phone with my granny. Letha said, "Zaneeya, why did you tell your *granny, that I won't let you spend the night at her house anymore?" "It's the truth! You said I can't go over there, so I told her the truth." Letha just looked at me, with that mean look on her face. The school year had ended. My mom and Dorthy got $15,000 dollars. From their grandma that died on their father side of their family. Letha said, "Zaneeya call your mom, she got some money, and she needs to give you some." "Ok." I called my mom. I said, "Hi mom. How are you doing?" "Hi Cupcake I'm doing well, I have some money for you." "You do?" I asked all excitedly! "Yes! Do you need anything right now?" "I need some lotion, some body wash, some hair grease, some clothes, and some shoes." "Ok, I'm going to come out there and take you shopping." "For real mom?" "Yes for real Cupcake!" "Ok, don't lie mom." "I'm not lying. Let me talk to Letha." I gave Letha the phone. My mom told Letha, she was going to give her some money, for taking care of me. Letha said, "You don't have to give me nothing, just buy your daughter some clothes." My mom replied, "Ok, I am auntie." I did not hear from my mom for a while. I called her three weeks later. I said, "Mom, I thought you were going to take me shopping!" She said, "I am, I promise." "No, you're not. Can you just send me some money? Can you just give me $100 dollars please?" "I can do that. Is that all you want?" "Yes." "Ok, I'm going to mail it to you tomorrow." "Ok mom, thank you." Everyday I would ask Rene did I get any mail. Rene would say no. I called my mom two weeks later. I said, "Mom, I thought you said you were going to send me some money." "I'm going to, I haven't forgotten." "You know you're not going to send me any money, just stop lying!" "Who the hell do you think your talking to little girl?" "You need to just stop lying. That is a shame. You only have one daughter and I don't even live with you, and you came into $15,000 dollars and you can't send me a $1 dollar." "I have other kids besides you. Who I take care of! I had to give your brothers some money, and I didn't get $15,000 dollars." "Yes you did. Stop lying! It's ok, I am not moving back to Modesto. I don't care what you say take care of your other kids, bye." I hung up the phone. I would write in my diary. I was sad and I didn't feel loved by parents or anyone else. I cried every night for a whole year. I knew, I was not happy in life, and I wanted to commit suicide, and this was not my first time wanting to do it. The first time that I wanted to commit suicide, I was 12 years old. That's when Jay kicked my mom and us out, and we had to go live with my auntie Dorthy. One day, I was sitting on the couch in the livingroom, and I was thinking about everything that my mom and my brothers and I went through. I stood up and I went to the kitchen and I grabbed the biggest knife out of Dorthy's kitchen drawer, and I stuck the knife on the side of my pants,* *by my waist, so nobody would see me. I went to the bathroom, and I locked the door. I got on the floor and I pointed the knife at my chest. As I was crying and rocking back and forth, I felt the point of the knife hit my chest, and a voice spoke to me. The voice said, "Put the knife down Zaneeya, you are not going to kill yourself." I didn't know where the voice came from. There was no one in the bathroom, but me. I put the knife down, and I walked out of the bathroom, and I went to the kitchen and I put the knife back in the drawer. Even though, I was young. I knew I was going threw something, and I was going threw it by myself. I would think about my mom. I would pray to God every night and I would ask God to please help my mom get off drugs, and to please keep Jay away from her. I also would ask God to please take care of my brothers. I truly loved my mom. No matter how much she was on drugs and I loved my brothers. I would say, "Letha, I wish I had some money, so I can take care of my brothers." Letha would look at me and say, "That's not your job to take care of your brothers. That's your mom's job. Even, when you make it in life and you become successful. If they ask you, can they come live with you, you tell them they can stay for two nights. Then after that, I will give you some hotel money for three days, and that's it." I said, "I couldn't do my brothers like that." "You need to do your mom like that. Your dad and whoever else, that wants to live with you. You are too kindhearted. You will find out when you get older." I thought to myself, maybe Letha was right, but I had to find out for myself!*

Chapter Seven

Seventh Grade Summer

*S*chool was out summer was in. My dad called and spoke to Letha and he asked her could he come get me for the weekend. Letha told him yes. My brother Justin Jr., would come by and spend the night with me. We were close. Justin Jr., would tell me everything and I would tell him everything, but I did not tell him what I was going threw deep down inside. When my dad came to pick me up, Justin Jr., came with me. My dad said, "Y'all are going to spend the night at Sabreea's house tonight." When, we went to Sabreea's house. Shonte was leaving. She gave Justin Jr., and I a hug. I said, "Shonte where are you going?" She said, "I'm having a beach party for my birthday." "You look cute." "Thank you, I will see y'all when I get back." "Ok." We went upstairs, momma Shay was happy to see us. Sabreea said, "Zaneeya, y'all should spend the night or spend the whole summer with me." "I know that would be nice." My dad said, "Shay is it ok if Justin Jr., and Zaneeya spend the night?" Shay replied, "Do not ask me a silly question like that. You know they can spend the night. Let them stay for a week or two." "Ok, thank you Shay." My dad gave Justin Jr., and Sabreea, and I some money. He also gave momma Shay some money, for letting us stay there. We stayed up late that night talking. Sabreea, and Justin Jr., and I would go swimming, and we would walk to the dollar store with momma Shay, and we would hang out at the mall. Sabreea liked this boy. He came over one night and she washed his hair, and she braided it for him. She went to her room and she told me she wanted to kiss him. I said, "Go kiss him. Just, don't do anything else." Therefore, while she was in the kitchen doing his hair, no one was looking at her. So, she kissed him. She looked at me and smiled. I smiled back at her. My dad came to pick Justin Jr., and I up, but we were not ready to leave yet. We said, "Dad can you come back and pick us up next week?" He said, "Ok I will." It was the 4th of July. Momma Shay took Sabreea and me to Jack London

Square. We looked at the fireworks. Then she took us to the movie and she took us to Fridays the restaurant. Then after we ate, we went home. Sabreea told me that she let her friend, use some of her clothes, and she let borrow her necklace, and her friend will not bring her stuff back to her. I said, "Sabreea we are going to your friend house, and she is going to give you all of your things back to you!" She said, "Ok." Momma Shay and I was walking back from the dollar store. Sabreea didn't want to come with us to the store that day. So she stayed home with Shonte. As momma Shay and I were walking. This girl said, "Hi mom my momma Shay." Momma Shay replied, "Hi Moe. How are you doing?" "I'm doing well." I kept walking, to see if the girl was going to think that I was Sabreea, and she did.

Moe yelled, "Tweedy, where are you going?" I turned around and walked back towards her. Moe said, "Where are you going? Wait you're not Sabreea." Momma Shay said, "This is Sabreea's sister, Zaneeya." I said, "Your name is Moe right?" She replied, "Yes." "You have my sister clothes, and her necklace that she let you borrow, that you won't give her back right?" "Yeah, I haven't had time to bring them to her yet." "Ok, well I'm just letting you know, you don't have any more time! I am not Sabreea. I am Zaneeya, and my sister wants her clothes, and you have until the end of today, to bring them to her, or I'm going to have a problem with you! I do not play when it comes to my sister, and you do not want a problem with me! Do not forget my sister necklace either." "I will bring them today!" "Ok, I will see you later. It was nice talking to you." Moe did not say nothing else. Momma Shay and I walked back to her house. Momma Shay said, "Sabreea you don't have to worry about Moe not giving you, your necklace or your clothes back to you. She's going to bring them to you today." Sabreea said, "She is?" "Yes she is. Your sister told her she has until the end of the day to bring you, your clothes or it's going to be a problem." Sabreea said, "Thanks Zaneeya." There was a knock on the door. Momma Shay opened the door it was Moe. Moe said, "Here Tweedy, thank you for letting me use your clothes, here's your necklace too." I said, "Thank you." Moe smiled and left. Momma Shay told Justin Jr., he had to leave, because she did not have enough food at her house, and the money my dad gave her was gone. Shay said, "If I had more food I wouldn't mind, but I don't." Justin Jr., did not want to leave, and I did not want him to neither. My dad came in got Justin Jr.I told him I would see him when I get back home. I stayed at Sabreea house for a few more weeks. Shonte heard on the radio, that there was going to be a dance competition in Alameda and whoever wins will get some money. Therefore, Shonte asked Sabreea and I did we want to be in the *dance competition. We told her yes. Shonte said, "Ok, Bernice is going to dance with us." Bernice is Shonte best friend. Shonte said, "We are going to practice, and practice for hours." We told her ok, not knowing what we was getting are self's into. Everyday we would practice for hours. When we would leave out the room, Shonte would say, "Where are y'all going?" We said, "We are tired, we need something to drink." "Hurry up, y'all need to come on. We have to practice!" We would go into the livingroom, and sit down on the couch next to momma Shay. Sabreea would say, "Mom, Shonte is working us too hard!" I said, "I know mom, can you talk to her?" Shonte would yell, "Sabreea and Zaneeya come on, so we can practice." Momma Shay said, "Shonte hold on their tired!"*

"No their not, come on y'all we are almost done, I promise." We would just get up so we could finish practicing. When it was time to go to the dance competition, we all wore fishnet shirts and blue jeans. When we arrived to the dance competition, it was around the corner from my house, where I lived at with Rene and Letha. We went inside, we seen a lot of people standing around and some were dancing. We found out that it was not a dance competition at all. It was a dance studio, and whoever wanted to join could, but you had to pay an amount of money. We all were upset. We said, "All that practicing for nothing." Shonte said, "I know, I'll buy y'all something to eat." After we ate, we went back to Sabreea's house. Mamma Shay said, "What are y'all doing back so quick?" We said, "It wasn't a dance competition." Momma Shay laughed! She said, "All that practicing y'all did was for nothing!" We said, "Mom, that's not funny!" "Yes it is!" Momma Shay could not stop laughing. Then we all started laughing. Momma Shay and her husband took Sabreea, and Bubba and I to Boomers. At Boomers, you can ride on the go-carts, play laser tag, golf, and other games. We had fun. I was with Momma Shay and her husband, while Sabreea was with Bubba. The next day, my dad picked Sabreea and me up. He told us we were going to spend a few nights with him. Before, school started back. My dad said, "Zaneeya, grandma is going to buy you some more glasses." I said, "Ok, I have to call her." I needed some new eye glasses. I had some big goofy glasses, and I told Rebbeca I was not going to the 8th grade with those glasses on my face. So I broke my glasses in half. Sabreea and I stayed at my dad's house. We stayed up watching this movie called The Hannibal*. It was a scary movie. We fell asleep, while watching the movie and my dad woke us up and told us to get in bed. The next morning, we woke up and my dad took us home. My dad dropped me off first. My dad and I went inside the house. Letha said, "Zaneeya, what makes you think you can stay gone for the entire*

summer?" I replied, "I was with my dad, and you knew where I was." My dad said, "Letha, I'm not going to be trippin with you about, how long my daughter can leave, and when she has to come back! It is the summer. School is out, and I have the right to spend time with her for the whole summer if I want too, and Zaneeya should not be on punishment, because of that! I have a big family, and yes, she spent some time with her sister. That shouldn't be a problem." Letha said, "I bought her tickets to go to the B2K concert and I had to give them away! She cannot be gone for that long. Zaneeya lives with me and she will not be going any where for a while." "I will give you, your money back for those tickets, that's not a problem! How much did the tickets cost?" "No, that's ok." "My mother is going to buy Zaneeya, a new pair of glasses. So, she has to spend a night over my mom's house so she can go to her appointment." "Her uncle Ike was going to buy her some glasses, but she wasn't here." "Listen, that's ok. My mom is going to buy her some glasses. Everything is going to work out. Zaneeya I love you. I have to go, call your grandma." "Ok dad, I love you too."

Chapter Eight

The Beginning of 8th Grade

I was excited to start 8th grade. I did not have any new clothes, but I was just happy to be going to school. I had all new teachers, accept for Miss. Harrison. She also taught eighth graders, and I was happy to have her as my teacher again. The first day of school, everybody was happy to see each other. I had PE first period. My PE teacher name was Mrs. Dumbly. She was nice. This girl in my PE class was sitting all by herself. After class, I went up to her. I said, "Hi, you're new here huh?" She said, "Yes. Is this your first day here too?" "No, this will be my second year here." "Oh ok, my name is Jasmine." "My name is Zaneeya." "I don't know where all of my classes are. I know I'm going to get lost." "No you're not you'll get use to it. What class do you have next?" She showed me her schedule, and I told her where her classes were. So she would not get lost. I said, "I have one class with you." She replied, "Which class do you have with me?" "Miss. Avera class 4th period." "Ok, we can sit by each other in class." "We can, well I'll see you in 4th period." "Ok." I went to my next class and time went by fast. When 4th period came, Jasmine was in class already sitting down. She waved her hand at me, and I sat next to her. I said, "How do you like your classes? Are your teachers nice?" She said, "My teachers are nice, but the people at this school are not friendly at all." I laughed! I said, "Why you say that?" "People just don't like to speak, but they can stair at me, and roll their eyes." "Everybody is not going to be nice, but just be yourself, and don't worry about them." "Your right, I am. Where are you going for lunch?" "I'm going to the snack bar line to go meet up with my friends, you can come with me." "Ok." Miss. Avera class was full. She had many students. She taught US History. When the bell ranged to go to lunch, everybody rushed out the classroom to leave. Jasmine and I went to the snack bar. I saw Jessica, we gave each other a hug, and I introduced Jessica *and Jasmine to each other. We all sat down and ate. We could not believe we were in the 8ᵗʰ grade, we all was excited.*

Before, the bell ranged to go to class. I told Jasmine that she could eat lunch with me everyday, if she wants to. Jasmine said, "Ok, thank you Zaneeya. You are so nice." "You're welcome." The bell ranged to go to class. I told Jessica and Jasmine that I'll see them after school. When I got to class, Rebbeca was sitting down in her seat. I said, "I didn't know we had a class together." She said, "Neither did I." We had Miss. Harrison class together. Miss. Harrison said, "Hi Zaneeya. How was your summer?" I replied, "Hi, Miss. Harrison my summer was nice. How was your summer?" "I had a nice summer as well. I couldn't wait to get back to work. Rebbeca and you are cousins and you both have my class again." "That's right."

"Did you and Rebbeca do anything together over the summer?" Rebbeca said, "No, she left me by myself for the whole summer." I smiled and shook my head. I said, "No, I did not leave her, but I was gone for the summer. I was with my sister. Rebbeca could have come too, but she didn't want too. Plus Rebbeca was having fun with her cousins." "What cousins and what fun? Now you know, I did not enjoy my summer with out you." Miss. Harrison said, "Aww, she missed you Zaneeya." I said, "I missed her too, and she knows that! She went to a concert with out me." Rebbeca replied, "No, Zaneeya had a ticket to go to the concert, but she didn't know about it. She was supposed to come too." Miss. Harrison said, "You guys are close, and you should always stay close." Rebbeca said, "We are." I replied, "Rebbeca's is right about that." Miss. Harrison said, "Zaneeya are you close with any of your other cousins?" "Yes, my cousins that live in Modesto, we all use to live together, and my cousin Christy and I are like sisters. I think about her everyday. I really miss her, and my brothers, and my other cousins." "Well, the holidays are coming up. Maybe, you will see them over the holidays." "I hope so. I would like that." Rebbeca and I would sit by each other in class. Everybody knew we were cousins and we for sure had each other's backs. When the bell would ring to get out of school, we would leave, and I would tell Rebbeca to come with me. To go meet up with Jessica and Jasmine and she would sometimes. Sometimes, after school, Rebbeca and I would go buy us some smoothies. When I would get home from school, I would do my homework, shower and eat, talk to Rebbeca and watch some TV. Then go to bed.

Rebbeca and I would walk to school together everyday. I knew who she did not like at school, and I knew why, she did not like that person. Rebbeca told me about this girl named Sandy. She told me, she did not like Sandy, because she acted as if she was better then everybody and she was stuck up. I was soon going to find out for myself. One day, Rebbeca and I were in the snack bar line, and Sandy was staring at Rebbeca and me. So, Rebbeca rolled her eyes at her! I said hi to Sandy, with an attitude, but she did not speak back. Rebbeca said, "Zaneeya, don't speak to her." I replied, "She was staring, so I just wanted to say hi." Later on that day, when we went home, Angel came over. Rebbeca had told Angel what happen. Angel said, "That's ok, don't worried about her." I said, "I'm not..." The next day we went to school. Rebbeca and I went back to the snack bar line. Sandy said, "Hi. Your name is Zaneeya right?" I replied, "Yeah. Why?" "I didn't say hi to you yesterday, because I didn't know who you were." "Even, if you didn't know who I was, if someone says hi to you. You are supposed to speak back to them, but I only said hi, because you were staring at us. I wasn't being nice to you." "Ok, hi Rebbeca." Rebbeca did not say anything, so I nudged her. Rebbeca said, "What?" I said, "It's ok to say hi." Rebbeca said, "Sandy, all this time you and I have been going to school together and you have never spoken to me. So you don't have to now." Sandy replied, "Well, I just wanted to say hi, and I have spoken to you before and you didn't say anything." Rebbeca and I bought are food and we left. I knew one thing. Rebbeca was right about Sandy. See I had a class with Sandy. She had Miss. Avera class with Jasmine and I 4th period, and she would never speak. Even, if you spoke to her. Matter of fact, Sandy and her friends would roll their eyes at Jasmine in class constantly. After Sandy and I spoke, she started speaking to me in class. She would say, "Zaneeya sit right here by me." I did not like her friends and I really didn't know her. I said, "No, I'm going to sit by my friend Jasmine!" "Ok." Jasmine said, "I don't like her or her friends." "I don't like her friends either." Jasmine and I became close, and it was a lot of new people enrolling into Claremont Middle School. This girl named Javon and I became friends. Rebbeca had her on friends too.

As time went on, it was getting closer to Thanksgiving. My mom called and asked me did I want to go to Modesto for Thanksgiving. I told her yes. I have not seen my mom or my brothers over a year. My mom said, "Ok, let me talk to Letha." I gave Letha the phone. My mom said, "Letha I want Zaneeya to come to Modesto for Thanksgiving." Letha replied, "I don't know what were doing out here yet." "What does that have to do with her coming out here? I haven't seen my daughter over a year. You don't let her go over my mom's house, any more and you don't let her see her grandma Alissa. That's not right!" "None of the kids get to leave every weekend, and I'm not keeping your daughter from you. You can come see her anytime you want to. I'm not letting her go to Modesto for Thanksgiving." "I didn't know it was going to be like this. After, Zaneeya finish the 8th grade, she is coming to move back with me." "That's fine with me." Letha got off the phone. She said, "Zaneeya, if your mom comes to get you, you're leaving with the clothes on your back. You're not taking anything with you!" "Why I can't take my clothes with me?" "Your mom is going to sell them or wear them herself." "You didn't even buy me most of my clothes. They were giving to me from Sindy and Miyesha." "I don't care, your still not taking them with you." I just went to my room. I knew Letha was just being mean, and if she really cared about me. She would want me to take my belongings with me. I knocked on Rebbeca's, room door and I told her what Letha said. Rebbeca said, "You know Letha is very mean. Letha don't care about nobody but herself and her daughter. She acts like she care about other people, but she don't." "I see, I'm going to bed. See you in the morning." "You're going to bed this early? Stay up with me." "I'm going to bed. I'm tired and I'm upset. Good night." "Good night Zaneeya, don't worry about what Letha said." The next day at school, everybody was talking about what they were going to do for Thanksgiving break. Jessica said, "Zaneeya what are you doing for Thanksgiving?" "I don't know, but I do want to see my mom and my brothers and my cousins. I miss them! This is the longest I have ever been away from my family." "Just tell Letha you want to go see your family for Thanksgiving." "I did tell her that, and she told me no." "That's messed up." "I know." After school, I went home. Letha told me that my granny called, and asked could I go to Modesto with her for Thanksgiving, and she said that my mom really wants to see me. Letha told my granny. I could not go to Modesto for Thanksgiving. On Thanksgiving, my brother Justin Jr., came over. I was happy to see him. He said, "Zaneeya are going to Modesto today, to go see mommy?" "No, Letha will not let me." Justin Jr., said, "Auntie Letha, can Zaneeya come with me to Modesto for Thanksgiving? Nothing is going to happen to her, she will be ok." Letha replied, "When are you leaving?" "I was going to ask you for a ride to the Greyhound station." "I'll take you." Rene said, "Letha come here for a minute." Letha went to see what Rene wanted. Rene said, "Letha, you should let Zaneeya go see her mother for Thanksgiving. She haven't seen her mother over a year, and she should spend the holiday with her mother. That's the right thing to do!" Letha said, "Now I have to buy her a ticket." "I'll buy it."

"No, that's ok I will buy it." Letha called me to the livingroom, I went to see what she wanted. She said, "I'm going to let you go to Modesto for Thanksgiving, but you better come back with Justin Jr., and I'm not playin." I

said, "Ok, thank you." "If I have to go down there, and get you, you are going to be on punishment for a long time. Hurry up and go pack your bags. Your bus will be leaving shortly." I could not believe that Letha was letting me go to Modesto. Rebbeca said, "You're leaving me again." I replied, "Come with me let's ask Rene can you go." We went to the livingroom, to ask Rene could Rebbeca come with me to Modesto. Letha said, "No Rebbeca, you don't need to go, and y'all are always trying to leave together." Rebbeca said, "I'm asking my mom." "Don't get smart Rebbeca." Rene said, "Rebbeca you are going to stay here, but next time you can go with Zaneeya." "Ok mom." Before I left, I said bye to everybody. Mercy said, "Zaneeya, are you happy that you are going to Modesto?" "Yes I am. I cannot wait to see my mom, my brothers, and my cousins." Letha said, "Come on let's go before you stay here. Tell your mom I was going to let you go to Modesto the whole time. I just wanted to surprise her." "Ok, I will." Letha bought my ticket and she waited until my bus came to leave. I told her bye. She told me to call her when I make it to Modesto.

That was my first time on Greyhound. Justin Jr., sat on the side of me. The bus held more passengers then what I thought. The bus driver had to stop at a couple of places before we got to Modesto. When, we made it to Modesto. I said, "Justin Jr., are we going to call uncle Tony so he can pick us up?" "No, we are going to walk. It's not that far sis, let's surprise mommy. Give me your bags, I will carry them." "Ok brother, thank you." We walked from the Greyhound station which is downtown Modesto, to the west side of Modesto. Justin Jr., said, "See, it's not a far walk at all." I replied, "Yes it is, I'm tired." As we were walking, I told Justin Jr., we have to stop, because my asthma kept flaring up. He said, "Ok, take your time little sis." I took two puffs of my asthma medicine. Then we started walking. When we arrived to Dorthy's house, her front window was open. I heard my mom say, "Who are those people?" Justin Jr., said, "Open the door." My mom said, "Hi son, hi Cupcake." She smiled and gave me a hug and a kiss. She kept kissing me. I said, "That's enough now, stop kissing me mom. You no I don't like that!" "I'm just so happy to see you." "I'm happy to see you too." I walked over to my granny, and I gave her a hug and kiss and I gave my bothers a hug. I said to my brothers, "Do not kiss me!" They laughed and they told me ok. I gave my cousins a hug and auntie Dorthy and Tony a hug. I was happy to see Lil Dawane.

Christy said, "Zaneeya, you finally came back!" I replied, "You know you missed me!" "I did, you know we did everything together." "Who do you hang with out here?" "Erica." "Oh, Ok." "That's my best friend now." "Look at y'all." We laughed. Christy said, "You left me out here, now you're all *close with Rebbeca." "You and I will always be close! Now I have two favorite cousins, you and Rebbeca. You are like a sister to me, and that is how it's always going to be. We were close, and we still are. The only difference is, I do not live out here anymore. So we don't see each other everyday,and we don't talk everyday, but if I could talk to you everyday, I would." Christy and I been threw a lot together. When she would fight someone, I was right on the side of her! I said, "I don't even talk to my mom or brothers everyday. I haven't talked to my brothers on the phone since I lived with Letha." Christy replied, "I know they don't let you use the phone a lot." "I will ask auntie Rene can I use her phone, and she will tell me, but Letha will not let me use her phone." "That's messed up." "Let's just have fun while I'm out here." My brother Ramone came inside of Christy's room, and he told me that my mom wanted me. I went to the livingroom to see what she wanted. My mom said, "Come here. Sit down, how are you doing in school?" "I'm doing good in school, I get good grades. I'm happy I'm in the 8ᵗʰ grade now!" "I know you are. You know that's messed up Letha wasn't going to let you come down here for Thanksgiving!" "I know." "What made her change her mind?" "She told me to tell you, that she was going to let me come to Modesto this whole time. She wanted to surprise you." "She was not trying to surprise me. I don't believe that for one minute." "Rene talked to her this morning and she told her to let me come out here." "That's why she did it. Rene knew Letha was wrong for saying you could not come out here and I have not seen you over a year. Do you like living with Letha? Be honest Cupcake!" "Yes, I like living there." "Ok, as long as you're happy!" The truth was. I was not happy at all, and I didn't want to live there any more, but I knew I couldn't tell my mom, because if I did. She wouldn't allowed me to go back to the Bay Area. I knew I wanted to graduate with my friends, and I wanted to go to OT High School. So I just kept how I really felt to myself. Christy and I went to Erica's house. We knocked on the door, and Erica opened the door. She said, "Hi Zaneeya. How long are you going to stay out here?" I said, "Hi Erica, just for Thanksgiving break." "Ok, I have to go back in the house, because my mom isn't home." "You better go back inside the house before you get in trouble. You know you can't leave the front porch." Christy said, "Right, ain't nothing changed at all." Erica said, "Shut up." We said bye to Erica and we left. I introduced Erica and Christy to each other, when we were younger. When my mom and I lived on Rose court, we were walking to Dorthy's house one day. Erica was in her driveway playing with her little sister and her mom Cassy was watching them play. Cassy said, "Hi. What's your name?" My mom said, "Hi. Do I know you?"*

"No, I just moved out here, and I haven't met anyone out here yet." "Oh ok, my name is Bella, and this is my daughter Zaneeya." I said, "Hi." Cassy said, "Hi you are so pretty, these are my daughters Erica and Faith, and I have an older daughter too." My mom said, "Do you live here?" "Yes I do." "Ok, we only stay two blocks away from you."My mom showed Cassy where we lived at. Cassy said, "Is it ok if your daughter and my daughters play together?" "Yes, that's fine with me." I said, "I have some cousins too, we can all play together." My mom said, "Yeah, I have two nieces." After talking to Cassy, my mom and I walked to Dorthy's house. One day, I knocked on Erica's door, and asked her mom could she play outside, and I brought Christy with me. I introduced Erica and Christy to each other and every since then they have been best friends. After, Christy and I left Erica's house. We went to my friend Ty house, but she was not home. Then we went to my friend Joanna house, and she was not home either, so we went back to Christy's house. My mom told me that my brother Qin wanted to see me. I asked her where he lived. She said, "He stay with his girlfriend, and their family around the corner." I said, "Ok." Mimi said, "Zaneeya do you want me to go over there with you?" I replied, "Let's go over there tomorrow." The next day, my mom, and Mimi, and I walked around the corner to Qin's house. Qin said, "Mom don't ask me for no money, because I don't have any." My mom said, "Shut up Qin! I don't be asking you for money, you're always showing out." I said, "Hi brother." He said, "What's up sis?" He gave me a kiss and a hug. He said, "What have you been up to?" "Nothing just going to school, that's it." "I know you have a boyfriend. Tell him I said don't play no game with you. Tell him your brother, don't mind shooting at all." I smiled. I said, "Qin, I don't have a boyfriend and I'm not worried about having one right now!" "Good, keep your head in the books. What do you want to go to college for?" "I want to be a lawyer then a judge and an actress." "That's good. I'm going to need a lawyer. I can use you as one." "You shouldn't be thinking like that." "It's the truth. I'm just letting you know. Zaneeya do you like gold?" "Yes I do." "I got something for you." Qin went to his room and he told me to come here. He said, "This is from Ranesha and me, I hope you like it." I said, "Thank you Ranesha, thanks brother." "You're welcome." They gave me a gold bracelet. Qin said, "It's real gold too. Make sure you always wear it." "Ok, I will. It's cute I like it." My mom said, "I'm ready to go, let's go Cupcake." I said, "Ok mom." Qin said, "Just, because your ready to go, that doesn't mean Zaneeya have to leave yet." "Shut up Qin, I'm tired of your mouth. You have one more thing to say smart to me and see what happens." Qin said, "Sis you can stay longer if you want too." I

replied, "I'll come back tomorrow." "Ok, come back. We will be here and you can come chill with us." "Ok, I will see y'all tomorrow."

As we were walking back to Dorthy's house, my mom said, "Qin is always showing out with his disrespectful self. He makes me sick." I said, "He was probably just playing with you." "No he wasn't, but that's ok." Later on that night, Qin came over. He told my granny he just stopped by to see her. Qin said, "Sis, don't forget to stop by tomorrow." I replied, "Ok, I'm going to come over tomorrow with Christy or Mimi." "You can bring Mimi, but not Christy bald headed self." Christy said, "Qin, Shut up, you always got something to say. Go home, bye." Qin replied, "Shut up, make me get out." I said, "Y'all need to stop, y'all still argue back and forth!" Christy said, "Girl, your brother is not going to change. He's always talking mess!" Qin left, the next day we woke up and got dressed and we walked to Qin's house. Qin said, "Zaneeya you can come in, but Christy you're going to have to wait outside." Christy said, "Qin, stop playing with me!" "I'm not playing with you, watch." Christy said, "Ranesha, can you tell Qin to let me in the house?" Ranesha said, "He's just playing you, you know you can come in. Qin leave her alone." We stayed at Qin's house for a little while, then I told him bye. He said, "Zaneeya you have to leave tomorrow huh?" "Yes." "Ok little sis. I love you." "I love you too brother." "Wait, Zaneeya when are you coming back out here?" "I don't know!" "That's crazy how Letha won't let you see granny or grandma, and she won't even let you come out here. Don't let them brain wash you!"

"I'm not brother. Everything will get better soon." "Ok, we will see." Christy and I left, we went back to her house. We stayed inside the rest of the day, we played the PlayStation, and we talked, and ate. The next morning, everybody was getting ready for school. I woke up and I told my brothers bye, and I told them I love them. I told Mimi and Christy bye, and I told them I love them as well. Christy said, "I probably won't see you until another 3 years." I replied, "That's not true, I'm not gonna let that happen!" "Yeah ok, we will see." "You sound just like Qin." When, everybody left. I went back to sleep for an hour. Then I woke up and showered, then I got dress and I made me a bowl of cereal. Then I played **Mario Brothers on the Nintendo** in Christy and Mimi's room. Jason came in the room. He said, "Do you like living in the Bay Area cousin?" I replied, "Yes I do." "Are you ever going to move back out here?" "I don't think so. I don't see myself living in Modesto any more." "It's crazy, because we all grew up together." "That's true! I miss all of you. We were close. I use to do your hair for you, you use to get mad and kick Christy and me out your room, because we didn't ask to play your PlayStation. You *taught me how to play football. When my brothers didn't want Christy and I to follow y'all, you use tell us to go back home. Christy would go back home and I would say cousin can I come please? Justin Jr., and Qin would say no and you would say yes, you can come.*

I miss those days!" Jason said, "I miss those days too. We all used to have fun together. At least you're doing well in school. Remember to keep your grades up." "I am cousin." Jason left out the room. Then my mom came in the room. She looked at me with a sad look on her face! She said, "You're really going to leave your mom Cupcake?" I replied, "I will see you again. Don't say it like I'm never going to see you. Maybe Letha will let me come out here for Christmas Vacation." "She better!" "My uncle Tony said, "Are you ready niece? Let's go, I have to go to work." I said, "I'm ready uncle Tony." My mom walked me outside. I said bye to Dorthy and Lason. Jason came outside and said bye to me. He said, "I love you cousin." I said, "I love you too." "Don't forget about what we talked about, keep your grades up!" "I'm not going to forget. I'll see you later." I gave my mom a hug and kiss. She wanted to cry. I said, "Don't cry mom. I'll see you soon." She replied, "I just miss my daughter, that's all!" "Mom, things will get better soon. I love you. I will call you this week." "Ok Cupcake." I got in the car and we left. Uncle Tony dropped me off, after he took my granny home. We went inside the house. Tony told Letha and Rene hi then he left.

Letha said, "Zaneeya, I told you about leaving my house, and not calling to check in." "I was with my family, trying to enjoy myself, and I did call. I spoke with Angel." "I'm not Angel." I went to my room to unpack my clothes. Rene came in my room. She said, "Zaneeya, did you have fun?" "Yes, I had a good time auntie. That's just what I needed. I needed to see my family." "I'm happy you enjoyed yourself." Letha was in the kitchen. She heard me talking to Rene. Letha said, "You can move back to Modesto after you graduate." I replied, "I know I can." "Don't get smart!" When, I went to school the next day. Jessica and Jasmine asked me did I go to Modesto for Thanksgiving. I told them yeah. They asked me did I have fun. I said, "Yes, I couldn't wait to be around my family." Jessica said, "I'm happy you went, because I know you've been waiting to see your family, and I know you miss them." "I'm happy I went too. How was y'all Thanksgiving?" Jasmine said, "My mom cooked and I spent Thanksgiving with my family." Jessica said, "I was with my family too." When the bell ranged, we went to class. Miss. Harrison said, "Zaneeya how was your Thanksgiving?" "It was nice. I went to Modesto to go see my mom, my brothers and my cousins." Rebbeca said, "Yeah, she left me again."

I replied, "I wanted you to come with me, but auntie Rene wouldn't let you. I think Rene will let you come with me next time." When we got out of school, we went home. Rebbeca came in my room so we could talk. She asked me did I miss living in Modesto. I said, "I miss living with my brothers, and my mom and I miss seeing my cousins everyday." She said, "Are you going to move back to Modesto?" "No." "Good, stay out here with me and let's go to OT High School together." "I am."

Every weekend, I stayed inside the house. I could not go anywhere and I was getting tired of that. Sabrina would call Rene and ask her, can Rebbeca and I go over her house to watch the twins for her. Rene would say yeah, but she would tell Sabrina, she has to ask Letha because she takes care of me. Rene would give Letha the phone and Sabrina would ask Letha could I go to her house with Rebbeca to help watch the twins. Letha would say, "No because it is not fair to the other kids. Zaneeya and Rebbeca leave together all the time." Sabrina would say, "I'm sure the other kids leave on the weekends too." "Sometimes they do, but Zaneeya will not be going to help watch the twins anymore." I said, "See Rebbeca, she don't never want me to go anywhere. I am leaving after the 8th grade!" Rebbeca said, "Don't leave, where are you going?" "I'm not moving back to Modesto, but I'm going to figure out something." "Ok, I'm going to leave too." "I'll see you when you get back home, have fun without me. Tell Sabrina I said hi and I love her!" "Ok, I will." When Letha would go shopping or out of the house for a few hours. Rebbeca and I would take her food. We would take Letha's box of pasta, and we would cook it. Rebbeca and I did that all the time. We were hungry. Letha would fuss about her pasta being missing, and auntie Rene would ask Rebbeca and I did we eat it and we would say no. Rene would say, "Y'all better leave Letha's food alone." Rebbeca and I would just smile and say ok. I was so bored at home. Alisha was at her sister house. Ilesha and AD were at their sister's house. I was the only kid at home once again. Rene said, "Zaneeya, come in the livingroom with me and watch a movie." Rene I stayed up watching movies. I went to sleep in the livingroom. The next day, I just did my homework. I stayed in my room and I wrote in my diary. I was always sad. Even though I would put on a smile, behind my smile I had a lot of pain. The next day, everybody came home. I stayed in my room to myself. Rebbeca knocked on her wall and I knocked back. She opened her room door. She said, "Zaneeya come here." I replied, "No, you come here." "Zaneeya no you come here." "I'm not getting up." "No, I can't talk about what I need to tell you in your room." "Here I come. Did you have fun and did you tell Sabrina I said hi? What do you have to tell me?" "Nothing, I just wanted

*you to come here and yeah I told Sabrina what you said." "I'm going to bed."
"No, it's too early to go to bed." "I know, but I just want to get some sleep." I
was really going through a deep depression, for over a year and to me it was
getting worst. Christmas vacation was coming up. We had two weeks out of
school. My mom called. She said, "Letha I want Zaneeya to come out here for
Christmas. She spent last Christmas with you guys." Letha replied, "Zaneeya
is staying out here for Christmas. She was just in Modesto for Thanksgiving."
"After she finishes the 8th grade she's moving back to Modesto." "That's fine
with me, like I told you before." When, Letha and my mom got off the phone.
Letha said, "Zaneeya, you're staying out here for Christmas." I said, "I can't
go to Modesto for Christmas?" "No, you just saw your mom last month." I
stayed in my room more, and more, and when I was not in my room, I would
sit on the front porch. I would write in my diary, about how much I missed
my mom and brothers and my cousins. I started writing poems and I would
make up raps to different beats.*

*One day I was in my room and Letha called me to the livingroom. She
said, "Why are you always in your room? You're starting to be an antisocial."
I said, "Oh." I just went back to my room. Letha asked me what I wanted for
Christmas. I told her I just wanted a movie. The movie I wanted was called,*
Friday After Next. *On Christmas, I asked Rene could I call my mom, so I
could tell her Merry Christmas. I called my mom and she was happy to hear
my voice. I told her I loved her and to tell my brothers I love them and to tell
my cousins the same. After I got off the phone with my mom, I called my
grandma and I told her happy birthday. It was Angel's birthday too and she
was coming over.*

*Angel came over. She cooked, we ate and I just stayed in my room
and watched the movie that Letha had bought me. Angel called me to the
livingroom. She said, Zaneeya, do you want to spend the night at my house
tonight?" "Yeah, that would be nice, but I have to ask Letha." "Don't worry
about Letha. Rene is going to ask her can you come over my house." Rene asked
Letha could I spend the night at Angel's house. Letha said, "No, she needs to
stay home." Rene said, "Zaneeya is always home. She's home more then my
kids and your child. She needs to get out of the house." Angel said, "Letha,
it's not going to hurt you if she spends a night at my house. Rebbeca is coming
too." Letha said, "Rebecca and Zaneeya are always trying to leave together."
Angel said, "What is wrong with that? They are close, that's a good thing."
"No, Zaneeya is staying home." Rene said, "She's going to Angle's house."
Rene came into the livingroom she said, "Zaneeya come here. Pack your bags,*

you're going to stay a few nights with Angel." "Ok, thank you Rene, thank you Angel." Letha said, "You're not going anywhere." Rene said, "What is the damn problem?" Letha said, "You know what, I'mma let you go this time, but you are not going nowhere else for a while." Angel said, "Come on Zaneeya." When we got to Angel's house, she told us we could sleep in the livingroom. Angel had a couch bed. Rebbeca and I stayed up listening to music with Mercy. Mercy had all the CD's, anything you wanted to listen to she had. I asked Mercy. Did she have this rapper named Eve CD. She told me she did. So I asked her could I listen to it. I played this song called, *"Love is blind and it will take over your mind, what you think is love, it's truly not, you need to elevate and find love is blind"* those was the lyrics to the song. I played that song repeatedly. I liked that song. I thought about my mom when I would listen to that song. I knew the next time that Jay was going to hit my mom. It would be the worst beating that she ever got from him.

We stayed at Angel's house for three nights. We cooked. Watched TV, we ate whatever we wanted and listened to music and we just had fun. We had to go back home so we could get ready for school. Christmas break was over. Rebbeca and I went to school like we normally would and we would go home. February 1st 2004 my cousin Jason died. My granny had called Rene and told her that he was dead. I went to my room and started crying. He died from alcohol poison. I couldn't believe, that Jason was not going to be with us anymore. I knew Mimi, and Christy, and Lason, and Dorthy, and Tony were going through it. I knew my brothers were going threw it too, because they were close. Toya and her boyfriend Joey came over. I was doing my hair in the livingroom. Joey said, "Zaneeya are you ok? I heard what happen." I replied, "Yeah, I'm ok. Thanks for checking on me." Letha said, "Is she ok. Are we ok, were the aunties." I knew Joey asked me was I ok, because I use to live with my cousin and we were close. Jason was like a brother to me. Not just a cousin, but Letha always had something to say. We went to Modesto. Letha said I could stay out there for Jason's funeral. Rebecca stayed too. When the funeral took place, I was a mess and so was Christy. Jason had a lot of people at his funeral. He was truly missed and he was truly loved. After the funeral Angel said, "Rebbeca, and Zaneeya let's go." My mom said, "She has to leave already?" Dorthy said, "Are you ready to go Zaneeya?" I replied, "No!" Angel said, "You have to come back with me." My mom said, "I'm going to call Letha and see if you can come back later. Rashon is going back to the Bay Area later on tonight. You can ride back with her." I said, "Ok mom." Angel said, "If Letha says you can stay, that's fine with me."

Dorthy called Letha. She said, "Letha is it ok if Zaneeya goes home later on tonight? Tony's auntie Rashon will bring her home, when she leaves. She lives in the Bay Area as well." Letha said, "I don't know her and Zaneeya don't neither." "Zaneeya does know her. She has been knowing Rashon every since she was a little girl. I am not ready for her to go back yet, and Zaneeya and her cousins are close. I just lost my son, so I want to spend a little more time with my niece and Bella wants to spend some more time with her daughter." "Ok, but make sure she comes home." Dorthy gave me the phone. I said, "Hello." Letha said, "You better make sure you get in that car or you're not going anywhere for a long time." "Ok." Angel said, "I'll see y'all later. Zaneeya, I'll see you when you get home." Rebbeca and I told each other bye. Then I went outside to talk to Sabreea, and Christy and Mimi. We left Modesto at 9:00 PM. When Rashon dropped me off at home, it was 10:45 PM. I went inside and I spoke to Rene. Letha came to my room. She said, "Zaneeya, do not ask to go anywhere for a long time." I could not even look at her and I did not say anything to her.

I went to school the next day. Jessica asked me was I okay. I said, "I don't think I can live with Letha much longer!" Jessica said, "Who are you going to live with?" "I don't know, but I will figure it out just like I told Rebbeca." At lunch, I ate a sandwich and some chips. I choked on my sandwich. So Jessica went to get me some water. After, the bell rang. I went to class. My asthma started to flare up real bad. I had an asthma attack. My teacher called 911. My principal called Letha and told her that the Paramedics' are giving me an asthma treatment. He asked Letha did she want them to take me to the hospital. Letha said, "No, I want her to stay at school." My principal came and told my teacher what Letha said. Miss. Harrison said, "Zaneeya needs to go to the hospital." My principal said, "Her auntie said no, but I will make sure she gets another asthma treatment." After school, Rebbeca and I walked home slowly, because I did not want my asthma to flare up again. When I got home, Letha said, "Zaneeya, do not call 911 again from school." I replied, "I did not call 911. My teacher did." "I don't get any money for you or any insurance. Anytime you call 911 and the paramedic's comes out and treat you. That's a bill, and that bill will be on my credit, not yours." I just went to my room and did my homework. Rene came to my room to check on me later on that night. The next day, I asked Letha, could she take me to buy Jessica a cake for her birthday. Letha said, "No, I'm not spending my money on getting a cake for your friend." I said, "I will buy it." "Where did you get money from?" "I always save my money." Rene said, "Call Toya and asked her can she take you to the store to buy Jessica a cake." I called Toya and asked her, could she take me to the store to buy Jessica a cake for her birthday. Toya said, "Yeah, I will pick you up tomorrow." The next day, Joey and Toya picked me up. They took me to the store to buy Jessica a cake. When I went to school, I put Jessica's cake and ice cream in her teacher classroom. When it was lunchtime, I told Desseire that I bought Jessica a cake and I needed her to go get Jessica for me. So she did. When Jessica came in the classroom, she was shocked. She was smiling from ear to ear. She almost cried. We all sung happy birthday to Jessica. She said, "Zaneeya, thank you so much. No one has ever done anything like this for me, before." I replied, "You thought I forgot about your birthday huh?" "Yes, I did, because everytime I would bring my birthday up. You would never comment on the conversation." We ate some cake and ice cream and we talked. Everybody told me how much of a great friend that I am to Jessica. Jessica was a good friend to me as well. When I got home, Rene said, "Zaneeya did Jessica like her cake?" "Yeah she almost cried, she was happy, she thought I forgot about her birthday."

I could not believe that it was my birthday and I was turning 15 years old. When I went to school, none of my friends told me happy birthday and I was a little upset. When it was time to go to lunch I saw, Jessica, and Dessiere and they looked at me and they kept on walking. I yelled at them, "Hello today is my birthday." They just kept on walking. Jasmine came up to me. She said, "Zaneeya, Miss. Christonchro wants to see you. She said she needs to talk to you about your grades." I replied, "There is nothing wrong with my grades. Science is one of my favorite subjects. I have an A+ in her class. I'm extremely smart in science." "I'm just telling you what she said. I will walk with you to her classroom." "Ok." When Jasmine and I was walking to Miss. Christonchro class, all of the lights were off. Jasmine said, "I'm going to cover your eyes." I said, "Jasmine, what's going on?" She covered my eyes up with her hands. When we got inside the classroom, I saw Jessica, Desseire, Moe Mae, Rebbeca, Rudy, Yvette, and Miss. Christonchro, they all song happy birthday to me. I was definitely surprised and shocked. Jessica bought me a cake some balloons and a gift, I was happy. Jessica said, "You, thought I forgot about your birthday huh?" I smiled and said, "Yes I did, y'all was ignoring me all day. I didn't know what was going on. Thanks Jessica, I appreciate this a lot." "You're welcome sis." Mrs. Franklin bought me some Chinese food. She was a security guard at my school. Mrs. Franklin was always nice. She was a sweet person. I shared my Chinese food with Rebbeca and Jessica.

After the bell ranged, we all went to class. After school, I met up with Jessica and Jasmine. When I got home, Rene said, "Zaneeya did you have fun today?" I replied, "Yes, Jessica bought me a cake some balloons and a gift for my birthday." "That was nice of her." Letha said, "Zaneeya do not walk down the street like that again." I said, "Like what?" "With balloons in your hand." "I had to bring them home. What was I supposed to do with them?" "Just don't do it again." I went to my room. I did my homework, ate, and went to bed. I got sick I did not feel good. The next day Letha said, "Zaneeya, if you don't feel good stay home." "I don't want to miss school." "I think you should stay home. You don't need to go to school sick." "It feels like I have the flu." "Go to your room." I went to my room and I stayed in bed all day. The next day, I didn't go to school. Rene came in my room. She she said, "Zaneeya your friends are here for you." I went to the door and it was, Jessica, Lala, and Sunny." I said, "What are y'all doing here?" They said, "We came to check on you. You weren't at school for two days and that's not like you."

"I'm sick I have the flu, but I will be at school tomorrow if I feel better." "Ok." "Thanks for checking on me, I love y'all." "You're welcome, we love you too." I went to school the next day. I was happy to see my friends, and the school year was ending. 8th grade graduation was coming up. I was excited and all of my friends were too. As I was walking to the bathroom this girl named Trudy came up to me. She said, "Zaneeya, I have to tell you something." I said, "What?" "If I was you, I would not speak to Sandy, because she is so fake. All she do is talk about you and your mom." "What are you talking about? She doesn't know anything about me!" "Sandy told everybody that you had to move out here, because your mom is on drugs. That's why you live with Rebbeca, and your mom doesn't buy any of your clothes and everything that you have someone gave you." "Ok, thanks for telling me what she said." I seen Rebbeca and I told her what Trudy told me. I told Rebbeca I want to fight Sandy. Rebbeca said, "If you do. I'm going to make sure, no one jumps in." After school, Rebbeca and I went to look for Sandy, but she was gone. When we went home, Rene asked us what was wrong with us. I told Rene what happened. I said, "I'm going to beat the mess out of Sandy tomorrow." Rebbeca said, "I'm going to fight her sidekick, Yay." Rene said, "Wait just a damn minute. Y'all are not fighting anyone." I said, "Yes I am auntie. I do not bother anyone, but she talked about my mom and that's not coo. How does Sandy know that my mom is on drugs anyway?" "I don't know." Rene called Letha to the livingroom. She told Letha what happened and she told her what Rebbeca and I said. Letha said, "Zaneeya, you better not fight her.

You never put you hands on anyone first. If someone hits you first then you better beat them up." I said, "Auntie, she was talking about my mom." When Angel came over, they told Angel what happened. I said, "How does Sandy know that my mom is on drugs? How does she know that I'm wearing clothes that other people gave me?" Rene looked at Angel and it clicked in my head. Angel had told Sandy's auntie Debra that my mom is on drugs and everything else. See Debra and Angel are friends. I said, "Angel, did you tell Debra that my mom is on drugs?" "No, I didn't. Did you tell Sandy that your mom is on drugs?" "No I did not! Why would I? That's nothing to be proud of." Angel said, "Well, I'm going to call Debra and let her know what happened." Letha said, "Yeah, get Debra on the phone. They need to tell Sandy to keep her mouth shut." Angel called Debra and told her what had happened. I just went to my room. I was so mad. Letha called me back to the livingroom. She said, "We talked to Debra. She is going to call Sandy's mom and let her know what happen at school today. When you go to school tomorrow, do not touch her or your going to get in trouble." "Ok, but I am definitely going to confront her about what she said!"

The next day, I went to school I seen Sandy and I went up to her. I said, "So, what makes you think. It's your place to go around school, talking about my mom and me? You think it's ok that you told everyone that my mom is on drugs, and I wear clothes that other people give me? Let me tell you something. You are no better than anyone else. Your friends do not even like you! The next time you speak on me or my mother. I'm going to beat the mess out of you and that's my word. The only person that is saving you right now is Letha. So maybe you should thank her." Sandy said, "I'm sorry about what I said. I wish that never happened." "You're hella fake, do not speak to me at all. We are not friends." I went home after school and I told Rene what I said to Sandy. Rene said, "I'm glad, that you did not put your hands on her, and you never bother anyone. You get good grades in school. You mind your own business. You didn't deserve that, but I am happy you put her in her place." "I wanted to beat the mess out of her, but I knew I was going to get in trouble by Letha and you and it wasn't worth it." Letha came inside the livingroom. I told her what happen. Letha said, "I bet Sandy will not be talking about anyone else. She got lucky this time." I asked Rene could I use her phone, so I can call my mom. When I called my mom, my auntie Dorthy answered the phone. I said, "Hi auntie. Can I talk to my mom?" "Hi Zaneeya, your mom doesn't live here anymore." "Where does she live at?" "She lives with Lisa." "Oh ok. What's Lisa number?" "I don't have Lisa number." "When you talk to my mom can you tell her to call me?" "Yes I will tell her." The next day Letha got a call. I heard her say, "He jumped on Bella. She did something to him to make him jump on her." When she got off the phone, she told Rene what happen and I was in the livingroom too. Letha could not even look at me and tell me what happen to my mom. Instead, she talked about it in front of me and she blamed my mom for the reason why Jay had jumped on her. I said, "My mom and Jay is not even together Rene." Letha said, "How do you know? You live out here." "I know for a fact that my mom is not with him." I went to Alisha's room. I asked her could I use her phone so I could call and check on my mom. I called my auntie Dorthy. She answered the phone. I said, "Hi auntie. Is my mom there?" "Hi Zaneeya, yes she is here. Hold on." Dorthy gave the phone to my mom. I said, "Hi mom. How are you feeling?" My mom replied, "My whole body is sore Cupcake." "What happened mom? Why did he beat you up?" "He's just mean, all the kids went to school he waited until everybody left. He kicked the front door down. I was laying on the couch. He ran over to me and started beating me. He hit me in my head. He hit me in my ribs and one of my eyes felt like it was going to come out of my socket." "Mom, don't go back to him." "I'm not with him now! I don't have anything to do with him. He jumped on me for no reason! My eye is black and purple. My ribs hurt so bad, it hurts to hug people." "What did Qin say about this?" "Qin came to Dorthy's house, with all his thug friends. I did not know Qin knew that many people. They had cars and trucks filled with guns. Qin took me outside and said mom what gun do you want me to kill Jay with? I said please Qin, please do not kill him."

"Jay needs to be dead. Think about what he just did to you. I wish I was out there with Qin so I can help him shoot him." "Don't say that Cupcake. That's not nice." "I'm not trying to be nice. He wasn't being nice when he was beating you! What did Qin say after you asked him not to kill Jay?" "Qin said mom your crazy. Jay is going to pay for what he just did to you. I'm not a kid any more. I bet he will not put his hands on you again. You can believe that. I just kept telling Qin and his friends that it is not worth it and to let God deal with him. The police came to Dorthy's house, but I didn't want to press changes against Jay." "You should have pressed charges, after what he just did." "Well, I'm going to bed Cupcake. I don't feel good." "Ok mom, stay away from him. I'm going to ask Alisha can I use her phone, so I can call and check on you. I love you." "I love you too." After, I got off the phone with my mom. I asked Alisha could I use her phone tomorrow. So I could call and check on my mom. She told me I could use her phone anytime. I went to my room and I sat on my bed. I had my legs propped up, as I wrote in my diary. As I

was writing, Eve song popped up in my head. "£ove Is Bfind." I just started crying. I couldn't stop thinking about my mom. I knew my mom wasn't lying when she said Jay had beat her up for no reason. He was a mean cold hearted man, and that is just who he is. As I was writing, I went into a deep thought. I thought about what my mom said. How my brother Qin showed her all those guns that his friends and him had. I was thinking to myself. I wish I could just get my hand on one of those guns so can shoot Jay myself. My mom did not deserve to get beat up, and no woman did. The next day I went to school, I was sad. Jessica asked me what was wrong. I said, "Nothing." She replied, "Something is bothering you. I can tell." "I can trust you right?" "Yes, I'm not gonna tell nobody. I am not like that, and your best friend I wouldn't do that to you." I told Jessica what happened to my mom. She said, "Sis, I am so sorry that happened to your mom. I really am. No woman deserves to be treated like that." "I know, especially not my mom." "I am here for you remember that." "Ok thank you." "You're welcome." When I was in class, I did not want to talk to nobody. My teacher said, "Zaneeya what's wrong?" "Nothing, I just don't feel good today." "Maybe you will feel better tomorrow." Rebbeca said, "Do not worry about your mom Zaneeya, she is ok now." "I know now! I still hate that happened to her." I walked over to Miss. Harrison and I asked her could I put my head down on my desk .She told me I could. After, I did my classwork. I put my head down and I closed my eyes. I just played Eve song "£ove Is Bfind." Over, and over in my head. After school, I went straight home. When I got home, I said hi to everybody. Then I went to my room. I did my homework. Then I asked Alisha could I use her phone so I can call my mom. I said, "Hi mom, how are you feeling today?" She replied, "I'm still sore." "Ok, get some rest. I'll call you later. "Ok, I love you Cupcake."

"I love you too mom." I gave Alisha her phone back. She said, "Zaneeya, anytime you need to call your mom just let me know and I will let you use my phone." "Ok, thanks Alisha." Angel called me. She said, "Zaneeya do you want to spend the night at my house this weekend." I said, "Yeah auntie. My mom birthday is coming up." "When is it?" "May 10th. "I think that's Mother's Day." "I wish I can see my mom on Mother's Day." "I know you do. Fred is going to pick you up on Saturday." "Ok auntie." "Tell Rene I will call her back later. I love you my niece." "I love you too auntie." Fred and Angel picked me up over the weekend. Angel said, "Zaneeya, somebody is waiting for you upstairs." I said, "Who?" "Somebody you been waiting to see." I went inside of Angel's house, I saw my mom. She was sitting down as she was smiling. I said, "Mom, why you didn't tell me you were coming out here?" She replied, "I wanted

to surprise you." "You surprised me alright." We gave each other a hug. My mom said, "Don't hug me so tight my ribs are still sore." "Are they? I'm happy your eye doesn't look so bad." "It was worse then this." "Mom, how long are you staying out here?" "I'm leaving tomorrow." "How did you get out here?" "My boyfriend Charles brought me out here." "Boyfriend, when did you get a boyfriend? Where is this boyfriend Charles at?" "He's outside. He went to his car right before you came in." "Oh ok. Uncle Fred I need to talk to you for a minute." Fred said, "Ok Zaneeya." "Fred, can you take me to Longs Drugs or Safeway? I want to buy my mom something for Mother's Day and I want to get Angel something too. I want to get up early in the morning. Like around 6:00 AM so I can cook them a big Mother's Day breakfast." "Yeah, I'll take you Zaneeya. That's nice of you. What if Angel ask where were going?" "I'm going to tell her don't worry. It's a surprise for y'all." "Ok." When I went back into the livingroom, I said, "You must be Charles!" My mom said, "Charles, this is my Cupcake." He said, "Hi, how are you doing?" "I'm doing fine. How are you doing?" "I'm fine." "You better take good care of my mom because the next man that put their hands on her I'm going to shoot them myself. They don't have to worry about Qin." "I am a good man. I am not a woman beater." "Ok." I said, "Uncle Fred are your ready?" "Yeah, here I come Zaneeya." Angel said, "Where are y'all going?" I said, "Don't worry. We will be right back, it's a surprise." "Y'all hurry up and come back, where ever y'all going." "Ok."

When we got to Long Drugs, I bought my mom a Teddy bear and it came with a box of Chocolate. I bought Angel a box of Chocolate too and I got them both a Mother's Day card. Fred and I went to Safeway grocery store to get some food. I bought some fresh strawberries. Some pancake mix and some bacon. Angel had everything else at her house. When we got back to the house, Angel and my mom were sitting in the livingroom. They said, "What do y'all have in those bags?" I said, "Nothing." I put the food up and I hid my mom and Angel gifts that I had bought for them. I stayed up talking to my mom for a few hours. Then I went to bed. The next morning I woke up, it was 5:30 AM. I showered. Then I cooked breakfast. I made some strawberry pancakes, some grits, eggs, bacon, and some waffles. After, I was finished cooking. Angel came out of her room, she smiled. She said, "Zaneeya, I knew you were up to something. I have to make me some coffee." I said, "Ok, after you make your coffee get out the kitchen and go into the livingroom. I'm going to bring my mom and you, you're plates." "Ok, I have to wake your mom up." Angel woke my mom up. They both went into the livingroom. I brought both of them their plates. They told me thank you. My mom said, "I have a sweet daughter."

Angel said, "You sure do. That's my niece." After I ate, I gave my mom and Angel their Mother's Day gifts. My mom said, "Thank you Cupcake. I love you." She gave me a hug. I said, "I love you too mom." Angel said, "Thank you Zaneeya." "You're welcome auntie." My mom stayed for an hour then Charles and her left. She said they had to leave before it got dark. She had to go home to my little brothers, because they had school the next day. Fred took me home after my mom left. Rene said, "Zaneeya, did you enjoy seeing your mom?" I replied, "Yes I did auntie. I cooked her and Angel a Mother's Day breakfast." "That was nice of you." "I miss her already." I went to my room and watched a movie. The same movie I watched over, and over Friday After Next. I went to school the next day. My teacher said there would be an 8*th* grade field trip to Great America. The only people that were going were the people who were graduating from the 8*th* grade. I was happy because I knew I was going. I came home, and I told Letha about the field trip. I asked her could Jessica spend a night, so we can leave together the morning of the field trip.

Letha said, "I don't know, I'm going to think about it." I said, "Ok." The next day, Letha told me Jessica can spend the night, but she have to ask her parents. I went to school and I told Jessica what Letha said. When Jessica spent the night, Rene said, "Jessica can sleep in Rebbeca's room. So she can have her own privacy, and Rebbeca can sleep in your room with you." "Ok auntie." We stayed up that night watching TV and talking. Letha asked Jessica did she want some ice cream. After Jessica was finished eating her ice cream, we went to bed. The next morning I woke up first and I got dressed. Then Rebbeca and I woke up Jessica. After, she got dressed we went to school. We all rode on the bus together, I wish my cousin Dudy would have came. We would have been cracking jokes and laughing the whole ride there. On the bus ride to Great America, everybody was just talking. When we got there, everybody had split up into groups and everybody had a chaperone. Jessica, and Desseire and I were together in a group, and Rebbeca was in a group with her friends. We stayed at Great America for a while we all were having fun. I got a chance to get on some rides. That I did not get on when Rebbeca and I went the last time. We had a real good time. Jessica, Desseire, and Trudy and I went on this ride called the drop zone. As we were being lifted into the air Trudy yelled, "I want to get down, I want to get down." Cearly she couldn't, because we was so high up in the air. After, we got off the ride Trudy starting crying as she ran to her mom. Everybody started laughing at her. Trudy mom said, "If you knew you were scared, you should not have gone on that ride." It was getting late, so we all had to go back to school. That's where the bus dropped us off at.

Jessica's dad picked her up from my house. Jessica said, "Zaneeya I'mma call you later." "Ok." I said hi to Jessica's dad. His name is Henry, but I called him uncle Henry. He said, "Hi Zaneeya, did you and Jessica have fun?" I replied, "Yes, we had a good time." "Ok, I'll see you later. Maybe you can spend the night with Jessica on the weekend." "Ok, that will be nice." I could not believe it was time for us to graduate and our 8th grade dinner dance was coming up. Letha said, "Zaneeya and Rebbeca come here. Y'all have to take pictures at the dinner dance and we have to go shopping for y'all dress." The next day we went shopping. I did not find anything. Rene bought Rebbeca's dinner dance dress and it was cute. A couple of days later, Letha went shopping by herself and she bought me a dress. It was baby blue, it had roses on the dress and it was sleeveless, I really liked it.

Chapter Nine

My 8ᵗʰ Grade Graduation

*T*he night before our dinner dance, Letha pressed Rebbeca and my hair. She gave us different hairstyles, which was fine with us, because we didn't want the same hair style going to the dinner dance. My hair was long. It was all the way in the middle of my back. Letha got a chair and she told me to sit down in it, so I did. She had some scissors in her hand. I said, "Letha, what are you doing?" She replied, "Just be still. I'm cutting the ends of your hair. Your hair is uneven." "My hair does not need to be cut and I do not want my haircut." "Well, you're going to get it cut anyways." I was mad and Letha knew it. When Letha was finish cutting my hair, it was way more then just my ends she cut. I said, "My hair is short now. You cut most of my hair." Letha said, "It will grow back." Rene said, "Zaneeya, you needed your ends cut." "Auntie Rene, she cut way more then my ends." Rene looked at my hair and said, "Yeah, but it will grow back." "That's messed up, I always had long hair. Letha just did that for meanness." My hair was pasted my shoulders, but I still was mad. Rebbeca said, "Why did Letha cut so much of your hair off?" "I don't know." I went to my room. The next morning, I woke up all excited. I couldn't wait to go to the dinner dance. Rebbeca and I got dressed around 3:00 PM. We went outside and took pictures. Then Letha and Rene dropped us off at the dinner dance. Letha said, "I'mma pick y'all up, where I'm dropping y'all off at. Do not forget to take pictures." Rene said, "Have fun." We replied, "Ok." We took pictures with are friends when we got there. The dinner dance was at the boathouse around the lake. We ate, we danced and we talked. Jessica and Desseire looked nice. I think everybody looked nice that night. Jessica had a crush on this boy named Frank. She was staring and smiling at him most of the night. I said, "Jessica, go dance with Frank." She replied, "No, he has a date." "So what, we all know their not together, their just friends." "No, you know I'm shy." Jessica wasn't *lying about that, shy she was. It was time for Rebbeca and I to take pictures and we did. They played a lot of rap music. We all danced until it was over.*

After, the dinner dance was over, we all waited for our rides to come. Letha got there quick, she asked us did we have fun. We said, "Yeah, we had a great time." I said, "I will never forget about this night." The next day, Jessica called me and asked me did I want to spend the night at her house? I said, "Yeah, but I have to ask Letha." I asked Letha could I spend the night at Jessica's house. She said, "Yeah, but you're not going over there every weekend." I said, "Ok." I called Jessica. I said, "Jessica, Letha said I can spend the night at your house." She said, "Ok." When Jessica picked me up, I got in the car. I said, "Hi auntie Betty, hi uncle Henry." They said, "Hi Zaneeya, how are you doing?" "I'm doing fine. How are you? Thank you for picking me up." "You're welcome. No problem, anytime.Were doing fine." When I went to Jessica house, we watched TV. Then her dad took us to get something to eat. Later on that night, her parents took us to the movies. We had fun. We stayed up late that night talking about the dinner dance and how much fun we had. We couldn't believe we were going to graduate. The next morning we woke up, Jessica's parents took us to Denny's. After we ate, they dropped me off at home. When I got home, I washed my clothes. Cleaned up my room and I did my chores around the house. Letha bought me an outfit for my 8th grade graduation. I wore a long sleeve white shirt and a black skirt and she bought me a pair of black high heels shoes to wear with my outfit. The day of my graduation, the 8th graders did not have to go to school, but I went anyways. When I got out of school, I went home and I painted my fingernails then Letha did my hair then I got dressed. My mom and Charles came to my graduation. My dad called me. He said, "Zaneeya, do you have a ticket for me and Toniya?" "No, I only have a ticket for you." "Toniya and I are one, so that means you should have a ticket for her too." "Well, I don't have a ticket for her and Letha is giving my tickets out. She bought my tickets." "Ok, I'll see you later." "Ok." I hung up the phone. Letha said, "Zaneeya you did the right thing. I told you to tell your dad that we do not have a ticket for his girlfriend. So what if he does not like it." Letha couldn't find my graduation tickets, so I helped her look for them. Letha found the tickets in her room. When we arrived at our graduation, Rebbeca and I went to join the rest of the graduates. As we were walking to our seats, I could hear everybody family yelling their names. It was a very proud moment. As we were sitting down, the principal gave a speech and Desseire gave a speech too. Desseire's speech was nice. She spoke highly and well of her grandmother and how happy, she was to graduate. After, Desseire's speech was over, it was time for us to walk across the stage.

When, it was time for the row, that I was in to walk across the stage. I was nervous. I stood in line smiling. When, they called my name. I walked and I shook my principal hand, I posed then I finished walking across the stage. As I was walking down the stairs, my cousins was taking pictures of me, and my dad was throwing rose petals at my feet. After, they called everyone's name we got up and hugged each other. Some of us were crying. We took pictures. Then I went to find my family. When I found them, Letha was yelling at me. She said, "Zaneeya, what took you so long to get over here?" I replied, "I was taking pictures with my friends and it has not even been 10-minutes since the graduation has been over." "Boonie bought you a graduation card and she gave it to your mom and your mom ran off with your money." My dad came up to me and gave me a hug. He said, "Zaneeya, where are you going after this?" "I'm going home, then I'm going to my friend graduation party." "Ok, do you want to ride with me home? I will take you home." I said, "Letha can my dad take me home?" She said, "Yeah, but come straight home." As my dad and I were walking to his car, I saw Jessica's parents. They said, "Hi Zaneeya congratulations." I said, "Thank you, uncle Henry, thank you auntie Betty. This is my dad Justin Sr. Dad this is my best friend Jessica's parents." My dad said, "Hi, how are you doing?" They said, "Hi, were doing well. We are proud of Jessica and Zaneeya for graduating." "I am proud of them too." Auntie Betty said, "Zaneeya, are you going to the graduation party?" "Yes, I'm going." "Ok have fun."

When my dad and I were in the car, he said, "I am so proud of you. Now you are going to be in the 9th grade this year." I replied. "I know dad, I am so excited." "Do you want to come with me, instead of going to that party?" "No, I really want to go to this party. It's a celebration for everyone who graduated, and I want to be with my friends at this party." "You know what Zaneeya. You are so damn selfish. You never go over your grandma's house, and you never call her. You never see my side of the family. So you can just stay away for good this time and if my mother dies, don't come to her funeral." I just sat there the whole time as my dad was yelling at me. I did not say anything. I was thinking to myself, my dad is never going to change. When we got to my house, I hurried up and opened the car door. My dad said, "You're not going to give me a hug?" I replied, "No!" I got out of the car and slammed the door shut. I ran up the stairs, and I went straight to the bathroom and cried. Rebbeca knocked on the door. She said, "Zaneeya what's wrong?" "Nothing, I'll be out in a minute." "Let me in." "I'll be out in a minute." Rebbeca left then she came back. She said, "Your granny wants you." I said, "Ok." I left out the bathroom and went into the livingroom.

My granny said, "Come here Zaneeya, sit down by me. What's wrong, what did your dad say to you?" I told my granny what my dad said. My granny said, "He was wrong for telling you that! Don't let him mess up your day." My mom came in the door and she heard my granny and me talking. My mom said, "You're dad got a lot of nerves talking to you like that! Hell, it's not your fault why you don't see your grandma. Letha won't let you. You are doing what you are told to do. I'm going to call him and tell him about hisself." Letha said, "Zaneeya, do you still want to go to that graduation party?" "Yeah I do." "Ok go get ready." Rene's dad came in the livingroom. He gave me $20 dollars and he told me congratulations for graduating.Then I went to get dressed. After I got dressed, I went back into the livingroom. I said, "Mom, where is my graduation money that Boonie gave you to give to me?" She said, "What money? Boonie gave that money to me." "No she did not. Why would she give you graduation money and it's not your graduation?" "That wasn't your graduation money. She just gave it to me." "I can't believe you stole my graduation money." "Girl, that wasn't your money. I'm about to leave." After my mom left, Fred took Rebbeca and me to the graduation party. When we got there, it was a lot of people there. Shanti had the party in her backyard. We danced and listened to music. Before the party was over, Shanti's mom came outside with her graduation cake, and some apple cider. Shanti's mom said, "I want to congratulate all the graduates of class 2004." We all toasted to that. Fred came to pick Rebbeca and me up. As we were leaving, we said bye to everyone. When we got home, it was late. Rene asked us did we have fun. We said, "Yeah, we had a good time."

We went to our rooms and went to bed. The next day, we woke up and got dressed. Rebbeca and I went to Wendy's to get something to eat. Summer was in, but I knew I was not going anywhere over the summer. I knew I was staying in the house. Over the summer, Rebbeca and I just stayed in the house and we walked to Wendy's a lot to have lunch. I couldn't wait until school started. Jessica called me and she asked me did I want to go to this Usher Concert with her. I said, "Yeah, but I have to ask Letha." She replied, "Ok, let me know." "How much do the tickets cost?" "Don't worry about the tickets my dad is going to buy them." "Ok, I'mma ask Letha. Then I'mma call you back to let you know what she say." I went inside of Letha's room and I asked her could I go to the Usher Concert with Jessica. Letha said, "When is it?" I said, "A week before school starts." "I'm not paying for you to go see Usher." "Jessica's dad is buying my ticket." "Ok, you can go, but you're not going anywhere else for a while." I asked Rene could I use her phone so I could call Jessica. I called Jessica. I said, "Jessica, Letha said I can go with you to the Usher concert." "Ok, I'mma let you know what day it is." "Ok."

Two months went by, and it was time for us to go to our 9th grade orientation at OT High School. Letha and Rene took Rebbeca and I to OT High, so they can enroll us in school. I saw Jessica in line. We gave each other a hug. She said, "Zaneeya, come get in line with us." I said, "Letha, Jessica is going to let us get in line with her." Letha said, "Ok." We took are 9th grade id pictures and we got are class schedule for school. Letha said, "Zaneeya I'm leaving. You can stay up here so you can find your classes." "Ok, thank you." Rene and Letha left. Jessica, and Rebbeca and I went to find our classes. After, we were finished finding them we walked back home. Jessica came with me. She asked her parents could she come over my house for a little while. When we got home, we went to the store. I asked Rene could I have some of her cheese so I can make me some nachos. I made Jessica and I some nachos. We sat in the kitchen and we talked. An hour went by so Jessica called her parents, so they could pick her up. When her dad came to get her she said, "I'm going to call you later sis." I replied, "Ok." Letha bought me four pairs of pants and five shirts and two pairs of shoes for school. It was time for Jessica and me to get ready for the Usher Concert. Letha told me I could wear one of my new outfits that she had bought me for school. I never had been to a concert before. This was the first one. Jessica and her dad picked me up. She said, "You look cute sis." I said, "Thank you, so do you. Thank you, uncle Henry for buying my ticket and picking me up." He replied, "You're welcome Zaneeya, no problem." Uncle Henry dropped us off at the Coliseum, when we went inside and it was a long line. We went to the bathroom first. Then we went to find our seats. When we found our seats, somebody was sitting in them. We said, "Excuse us, but you're sitting in our seats." They got up and moved. Jessica and I sat down, the concert was starting. I will never forget what Usher was wearing. He wore a white suit and man he looked good. As Usher was singing, everybody got up and started singing too. Usher said he was going to choose a woman from the audience to get on stage with him. So I raised Jessica's hand. She was trying to put her hand down, but I didn't let her. The girl that Usher picked to go on stage, she was beyond excited. As Usher was singing to her, she nearly fainted and it was a great concert. After the concert was over, we went outside to go wait for uncle Henry. When he picked us up, he said, "Did y'all have fun?" We said, "Yes, we had a good time." I said, "Jessica, that's just what I needed before school starts back." She laughed and said, "Me too." They dropped me off at home. I thanked uncle Henry again for buying my ticket. I told Jessica I would call her tomorrow. She said, "Ok, I had fun with you sis." I replied, "I had fun with you too."

Chapter Ten

Finally In High School My 9ᵗʰ Grade Year

When I went inside the house, I went straight to bed, but I could not stop thinking about how good Usher looked in that white suit. When I woke up the next day, Rebbeca said, "So, Zaneeya did you have fun at the concert?" "Yes, I did. I had a wonderful time. I always have fun with Jessica." "I wish I could have gone. I know Usher was looking good." "Yes he was girl, he is fine." I said as I smiled. Rebbeca said, "Oh yeah, you must have been dreaming about him last night." I replied, "No I wasn't dreaming about him, but I did think about him before I went to sleep last night." "I cannot believe that we are going to be 9ᵗʰ graders tomorrow." "This school year is going to go by fast." Later on that night, I called Jessica. We said we were going to meet in the back of the school tomorrow. I laid my school clothes out at night for school. I went to bed early, because I knew I had to get up early in the morning. Rene woke us up in the morning. She was cooking her dad breakfast, and she made him some coffee. I went in the bathroom first to get dress, then Rebbeca, then AD. Rebbeca and I said we were going to meet each other in the back of the school, so we could walk home together. We told AD, he didn't have to wait for us after school. When I got to school, I did not see Jessica. I thought she was running late. When the bell ranged I went to my 1ˢᵗ period class, it was science Biology. My teacher name was Mr. Kiem. I didn't know anyone in my class. My teacher just went over the class rules, and he told us what we would be learning in class for the rest of the year. After 1ˢᵗ period, we had 2ⁿᵈ period. After 2ⁿᵈ period, we had 3ʳᵈ period. Before 3ʳᵈ period, started we a 15- minute break. I went to the back of the school to find Jessica. Jessica seen me, she ran up to me. She yelled, "Sis." All excitely! I replied, "Hi sis." We gave each other a hug. I said, "Where were you at this morning?" "I was running late. You know I'm not a morning person." "I thought so." We talked until the break was over. When the bell rang, we went to class. After 3ʳᵈ period was over, we had 4ᵗʰ period. After 4ᵗʰ period, we had lunch.

Lunch started at 12:45 PM until 1:30 PM. We all went to Wendy's, for lunch. Wendy's was packed with kids. We waited in line to order our food. Then we sat down and ate. After we were finished eating, we went back to school. After lunch, we had 5th period. I had math 5th period. My teacher name was Mr. Hutter. He was a nice teacher. He went over the class rules and he had us do a few math problems on the board. After 5th period, it was time to go to 6th period. My teacher name was Miss. Regeiro. She was my Spanish teacher. I liked all of my teachers so far. When school was out, I went to go meet Rebbeca in the back of the school. I told Jessica I would see her at school tomorrow. Rebbeca and I walked home when we got home Rene said, "How was school?" We said, "It was nice." "Did y'all get lost looking for y'all classes?" I said, "No, because I remembered where they were, when we looked for them the day of orientation." I went to my room to go do my homework. After I did my homework, I took a shower. Then I ate. Then Rebbeca came to my room so we could talk. She said, "Zaneeya, there, are so many cute boys at school." I replied, "Oh really!" "Don't act like you haven't seen any." "I'm not thinking about any boys right now." "You don't have to think about them, but I know you seen a cute boy in one of your classes" "Yeah, I did. I saw two handsome boys today at school." "What are their names?" "I'm not telling you, so you can tell them." "What are their names, tell me?" "I'm not tellin you." "I'm going to ask Jessica." "She is not going to tell you, that's my best friend." "I'm going to find out." "Ok, I'm going to bed good night." "Good night Zaneeya see you in the morning." The next morning, Rebbeca and I walked to school together. AD was still sleeping. I went to all of my classes. When it was time to go to the 15- minute break, I went to go meet Jessica in the back of the school. We seen Rebbeca and Susan, they came up to us. Rebbeca said, "Jessica, who does Zaneeya like up here?" Jessica smiled. She said, "I don't know." "Yes you do." I said, "No she don't, and plus like I told you. That's my best friend she is not going to tell you." Susan said, "I wonder who he is." I said, "Y'all need to give it up. I'm going to class." Rebbeca was yelling, "Zaneeya, I'm going to find out." I shook my head and kept walking. I went to class and I could not wait until lunch, because I was so hungry. When the bell ranged to go to lunch, I went to the back of the school to go meet Jessica and Desseire. We went to Burger King. I seen this boy who I thought was cute. He looked at me and smiled. I smiled back. Jessica said, "Zaneeya, who are you smiling at?" "Nobody!" "Zaneeya I just seen you smiling at someone. Who are you smiling at?" "Let's order our food so we can eat." We sat down and ate our food. After we were finished eating, we went back to school. After school, I met up with Rebbeca and Jessica.

Jessica said, "Zaneeya, who were you smiling at in Burger King?" "I'm not telling you, it's no big deal. I'm happy I go to school here though." I laughed as I smiled! Jessica said, "I'mma call you tonight so we can talk." I said, "Ok." Rebbeca and I walked home. I did my homework. Then Rene told us to come help her in the garden, so we did. I changed my clothes and I put on some sweat pants, because I did not want to get my school clothes dirty. We stayed in the garden for 45- minute that day. After we were done, I went inside to shower then I went to bed. As I went to school everyday, it was the same routine. Go to school meet up at the 15-minute break. Go to class. Then go to lunch. Then back to class. Then go home after school. Everything was going good at school, but at home. Things were not good and I wasn't happy any more. Letha would give me $2 or $3 dollars for lunch money. I would say, "Auntie, can I have another dollar so I can get me a full meal for lunch, because I still be hungry after I eat?" Letha said, "No, that's all you need, and if you're still hungry. You can eat when you come home." "You barely cook." "Don't you eat every night?" "No, not every night. I have gone to bed hungry." "If there's nothing cooked, don't I buy you something to eat?" "A little cheeseburger and nothing else." "I'm going to buy you some snacks, so you can take with you to school." "Ok." I asked Rene could I use her phone so I can call my grandma. I called my grandma. She said, "Hello." I said, "Hi grandma, how are you doing?" "I am fine. Who is this?" "This is Zaneeya your son Justin Sr., daughter." "Oh hi, I didn't recognize your voice. How do you like the 9th grade?" "I like it, grandma I need a job. I need to work. Do you have auntie Jannette's number? So I can call her and see if she's hiring." "Yeah, hold on let me get it out of my phone book." "Ok, take your time." My grandma got back on the phone. She said, "Hello Zaneeya, are you still there?" I replied, "Yes, I'm still here grandma." She gave me Jannette's number. She said, "Make sure you go to Jannette's job tomorrow." "Ok, I'm going to call her first." "Ok, you know you can come live with me." "Thank you grandma, I'm going to call you and let you know what happens. I love you." "Ok, I love you too. Check you later." That was my grandma's way of saying bye.

After I got off the phone with my grandma, I went to give Rene her phone back. The next day, I went to school. I asked Jessica could I use her cell phone so I could call my auntie. I called Jannette's job the receptionist answered the phone. I said, "Can I speak with Jannette." She said, "Hold on, let me transfer you over to her department." The phone ranged someone answered. I said, "Hi, can I speak with Jannette?" They said, "Who's speaking?" "Her niece Zaneeya." "Hold on let me go get her." Jannette got on the phone. She said, "Hello." I said, "Hi auntie!" "Who is this?" "Zaneeya, your brother Justin

Sr., daughter." "Hi my niece, how are you doing? Grandma said you go to OT High, that's right by my job." "Yes, I do. Auntie, I need a job. I need to make my own money." "Ok, come to my job tomorrow on your lunch break." "Ok, thank you auntie." When I got off the phone, I gave Jessica back her phone. Jessica said, "Why are you so happy?" I replied, "No reason. I'm not going to lunch with you tomorrow, because I have to go to my aunties job." "Ok for what?" "I'll tell you tomorrow." After school, I went straight home. I was excited to go see my auntie and even more excited to get a job. The next morning, I woke up for school early. When the bell ranged to go to lunch, I walked up the hill to my aunties job. I ranged the doorbell so the receptionist would let me in. I said, "Hi, I'm here to see Jannette." The receptionist told me where to go. I went straight into the diningroom. Jannette was sitting down eating lunch. She gave me a hug. My auntie Kimberly was working there too. Jannette hired her as a cook. Kimberly gave me a hug too. Jannette said, "Zaneeya, do you like going to OT High?" I replied, "Yes, I like my school. I just want to work and I know I need my own money." "I'm hiring right now. How are your grades? I heard that you get good grades." "My grades are good. I get A's and B's. I only have one C." "That's good. I'm going to hire you." "Ok, thank you auntie." "You're welcome." Jannette introduced me to her employees. She said, "Zaneeya, come see me two days from today. So I can have you fill out your job application, so you can start working." "Ok auntie, thank you." "You're welcome, now go back to school." When I left Jannette's job, I was happy. I feeling so good about having my first job. I went back to school. After school, I told Jessica about the job. She said, "That's good sis. I'm happy for you. You're going to be the first one working, getting a real pay check." I replied, "I know, I can't wait." I told Jessica I would see her at school tomorrow. I didn't see Rebbeca after school so I walked home. When I got home I said, "Rebbeca come here, I have something to tell you." She said, "What is it?" "I'm going to start working for my auntie Jannette. One of my dad's oldest sisters." "When?" "Real soon!"

"I want to work too. What are you going to be doing?" "I'm going to be a waitress. I have to bring the residents their food and beverages and I have to bust the tables. I have to set the tables with placemats and soupspoons. Stuff like that." "Can you get me a job too Zaneeya?" "I'm sure I can, after my auntie hires me. I need to make my own money so I can buy my own things." "That's good you are going to be working. What if Letha doesn't let you work?" "What do you mean if she doesn't let me?" "What if you asked Letha can you work and she say no." "I'mma still work! I need lunch money. I need clothes. I need a jacket, and I need a whole bunch of stuff." "When are you going to ask Letha?"

"Tomorrow." "Ok." *The next day I got ready for school. I said, "Letha, can I have some lunch money?" She said, "Here's $3 dollars." "Thank you." When I was leaving, Rene said, "Zaneeya do you have enough lunch money?" "Can I have a dollar auntie?" "Yeah, is that all you need?" "Yes, thank you auntie Rene." Rebbeca said, "Mom, where is my lunch money?" Rene gave Rebbeca some lunch money then we went to school. I used Jessica's phone again, to call Jannette. To ask her do she still want me to go to her job tomorrow so I can fill out the application. Jannette said, "Can you come up here today on your lunch break?" I replied, "Yes I can." "Ok I'll see you later." Rebbeca said, "Zaneeya, can I go with you?" "Yeah." When the bell rang to go to lunch, I met up with Rebbeca. Then we walked up to my aunties job. I gave her and Kimberly a hug. I said, "Jannette you remember Rebbeca?" She replied, "Yeah I remember her. She came with you when I took you shopping when you were younger and I bought her an outfit too. That's Glen's daughter." Rebbeca said, "Hi auntie." She gave Jannette and Kimberly a hug. I filled out my job application. Rebbeca said, "Zaneeya, don't forget to ask Jannette can she give me a job." "I'm not. Auntie Jannettte can you hire Rebbeca after you hire me." She said, "Yeah, after I hire you. Rebbeca you are going to have to wait a week or two then I will hire you." Rebbeca said, "Ok thanks auntie, that's fine with me. I want to work too." Jannette said, "What does your grades look like? Do you have good grade?" "I get A's and B's and some C's." "Ok, I'mma let Zaneeya know, when I want you to come up here to fill out your job application." "Ok auntie." Jannette said, "Zaneeya go back to school. I'mma call you. So I can tell you what day to come to work. After school, you need to be here on time. You need some black pants a white shirt and some all black shoes." "Ok auntie, thank you. I love you." "I love you too." Rebbeca and I left, we went back to school. Rebbeca said, "See your going to start working. I can't wait to work too."*

When I went home, I said, "Letha, I want to work so I can make my own money. You wouldn't have to give me any lunch money or anything. My auntie said she will hire me and I already talked to her. I filled out my job application and she hired me." She replied, "So, you're not working. You don't need to work, just worry about school." "I have always gotten good grades in school, and I would go to work after school. I get out of school at 3:30 PM. I have to be to work at 4:00 PM and it's only two blocks away from my school." "No, you are not working and do not go back up there to your aunties job neither." Rebbeca said, "Mom, can I work?" Rene said, "Maybe Rebbeca." "Please mom, I can make my own money. You would not have to worry about giving me money. You can just give it to AD, and Ilesha." "We will see." "Ok."

I asked Rene could I use her phone. I called my grandma and asked her can I come live with her. She said, "Yeah, when are you coming?" I said, "Two days from today, but don't tell nobody grandma." "Ok, I'm not." I called Jannette and told her what Letha said and I told Jannette that I'm still going to work. When, I got off the phone with Jannette, I went to Rebbeca's room. I said, "Rebbeca I'm moving in two days." "Where are you moving to? You know Letha is not going to let you take your clothes and the rest of your belongings with you." "I know, I'm moving with grandma and I'm still going to work for my auntie." "I'm coming too." "Come on. I'm going to wash my clothes today and tomorrow. Then I'm going to pack slowly. When Alisha leaves for school in the morning, I'mma go to the corner, so I can put my clothes in the bushes. Then I'm going to take them out, on our way to school. Then I'm going to get on the bus and go to grandma's house." "Ok." I washed my clothes for two days, the day before I left. Rebbeca said, "Zaneeya I'm not going. I'm going to stay here so I can look after my mom." "Ok." The next morning I got up for school, and soon as Letha took Alisha to school. Rebbeca and I took my clothes and we put them in the bushes on the corner by the house. Then we ran back home so nobody would see us and we got dressed for school. When Letha came back home, she said, "Zaneeya, it's time to go to school." "I'm leaving auntie." "When you get home from school, I'm going to take Alisha, and Rebbeca and you out for ice cream." "Ok, see you later." I said good morning to Rene's dad, and then Rebbeca and I left. We joked with Rene as we were leaving out the door. I said, "I love you auntie Rene, I'll see you later." Rene replied, "Ok, I'll see you when you get home. I love you too." Rebbeca and I hurried up and got my clothes out of the bushes. We went to the bus stop and we waited for the 51 bus. Rebbeca said, "Now I'm not going to have anyone to talk to." I replied, "You have somebody to talk to, you have Alisha." "Real funny!" The bus came, so we got on the bus. Rebbeca said, "I'm going to cry." I said, "You better not cry. We are still going to see each other. I'm still going to OT High everything is going to be fine." "Ok, I'm going to call you." We hugged each other then Rebbeca got off the bus to go to school.

When, I got off the bus downtown I notice that my bags were heavy. After, I got off the 51 bus. I got on the 40 bus. The 40 bus dropped me off at the store, which was two blocks away from my grandma's house. I carried my bags up the hill. My asthma started flaring up, so I dropped one of my bags of clothes by my grandma's house. Then I went inside her gate to drop the rest of my bags. Then I went to get the bag that I left on the sidewalk. When I came back, I ranged my grandma's doorbell. She opened the door. She said, "Zaneeya you made it."

"Yes, I'm finally here." "Your asthma sounds like it's flared up. I'm going to get you some water." "Ok." Krystal was at grandma's house. She said, "Zaneeya, how did you get here? Aren't you supposed to be at school?" I replied, "Yeah, I caught the bus here. I left Letha's house. I'm going to live with grandma for now, until I find some where else to go." "Does grandma know that you left Letha's house?" "Yeah she knows. She told me I could live with her." Krystal laughed and said, "Y'all are crazy." I said, "Krystal, where are you going?" "To Jake's house." "Can I come?" "Come on." Krystal was a great cousin and she was sweet, and if I wanted to go anywhere with her, she would always take me. I took my clothes inside of grandma's house. I told grandma I would be back later. I told her that I was going with Krystal for a minute. My grandma said, "Ok, bring your clothes inside my room." After, I put my belongings in my grandma's room. I told grandma to come lock the door. I got into the car with Krystal we went to Jake's house. We stayed there for a while. I was always happy to see Vicky. That was Jake's mother name. Vicky was a sweet kindhearted person. I went to school with Jake's niece. Her name is Jamie. We got alone well. She was like a cousin to me. It was getting late, so Krystal took me back to grandma's house. I ranged the doorbell grandma opened the door. She said, "Zaneeya, you can sleep in my room." "Ok, grandma thank you. Can I use your phone?" "You better not make any long distance calls." "I'm not. I want to call my best friend so I can let her know that I made it to your house safe." I called Jessica. I said, "Hi sis." She replied, "Hi sis, you made it to your grandma's house safe." "Yeah." "Are you going to live there?" "For now, until I decide where I want to live." "Are you going to go to school tomorrow?" "No, I'm not. I probably won't be at school for a couple of days." "Ok, call me and let me know what's going on." "Ok, I will. Remember if Letha calls you, you don't know anything." "Letha called and she talked to my parents and she asked me have I seen you at school. I told her no." "Ok, thank you. I'll call you tomorrow good night." "You're welcome, good night."

After, I got off the phone with Jessica. I went to bed. As I laid down I so was comfortable, and my mind was at peace. The phone ranged, so I went to the livingroom to answer it, but my grandma picked up the phone. She said, "Hello." I sat down in the chair at my grandma's diningroom table. Letha asked my grandma have she heard from me. My grandma said, "Yes." Letha said, "Is Zaneeya at your house?" "Yes she is!" "What is she doing over there?" "I don't know, you tell me. She left your house." "Let me speak with Zaneeya." "No, you cannot speak to her." My grandma hung the phone up in Letha's face, but Letha called back. Letha said, "I'm going to send the police over there." My grandma replied, "You better not send the police over here! If you do, you will not be able to do it again." My grandma hung up the phone in Letha's face again. My grandma said, "Zaneeya, dial your dad's number for me." "Ok grandma." I called my dad. My grandma spoke with him first. She said, "Justin Sr., Zaneeya is at my house. You need to get over here right now." He replied, "Ok momma. I will be there in 10-minutes." My dad got to grandma's house fast, he said, "Give me a hug girl. What are you doing here?" I replied, "I have to tell you what happened." My grandma said, "You need to let Zaneeya spend a night with you tonight. Letha is talking about calling the police." My dad said, "For what?" "Zaneeya have to tell you what happened." "Ok, Zaneeya did you bring any clothes with you?" I said, "Yeah I did." "Ok, get your clothes and come on." I got a couple of outfits and I put them in my backpack. As we were leaving, I gave my grandma a kiss and I told her I would see her later. When I got in the car with my dad, he asked me what was going on. I said, "Well, I got tired of living with Letha, so I left." My dad said, "You left?" "I really left." He looked at me with a big smile on his face. He said, "That's the best thing you ever did." He laughed as he was driving. He said, "I am sorry for saying what I said to you on your graduation. That was not right, and I apologize for that." "Ok, thanks for apologizing. So where are we going?" "Do you want to go to Sabreea's house?" "Yeah." "Call, Shay on my cell phone for me." I called momma Shay. She answered the phone. My dad said, "Well hello Miss. Thomson. How are you doing?" Shay replied, "I'm doing well Justin Sr. How are you doing?" "I'm doing fine. Look, I have Zaneeya with me, and I need to stop by your house real quick so I can talk to you about something." "Ok, when are you coming?" "I'm on my way right now. I'll see you when I get there." "Ok bye." When we got to momma Shay's house, my dad knocked on the door. Shonte answered the door. She said, "Hi Zaneeya. How are you doing?" "I'm doing well." I gave her a hug. Sabreea looked surprise to see me. Sabreea and I gave each other a hug. Then I gave momma Shay a hug too.

My dad said, "Shay, I need you to keep Zaneeya for me for a few days." Shay replied, "Ok, that's fine." "Ok, thank you. I have to go." My dad gave Sabreea and me $20 dollars, and he gave momma Shay some money for letting me stay at her house for a couple of nights. Momma Shay said, "Zaneeya what happen? Why are you with your dad?" I told momma Shay that I left Letha's house. She said, "I'm happy you left. Now you can spend some time with your family." Sabreea said, "What school are you going to go to?" I said, "I'm still going to OT High. I really like my school and all of my friends go there." After *we talked for a while, we went to bed. I slept in Sabreea and Shonte's room. The next morning, when I woke up, Sabreea was already in the livingroom. Laying on top of her mom like she was a big baby. It was nice to see how momma Shay showed Sabreea love. Sabreea was truly a momma's girl and I couldn't blame her. I said good morning to everyone then I took a shower. When I got out the shower, I made me some cereal. After Sabreea got dressed, we walked to the store to get some junk food.*

Sabreea asked me did I like any boys at my school. I told her yeah, she asked me who. I said, "I'm not telling you!" She replied, "Why not?" "Anyways, are you and your boyfriend still together?" "Yes, we are still together." "Oh ok. Does mom let him spend the night?" "No, but I'm going to ask her if he can." "Mom is going to tell you no, watch. To be honest, both of you are too young to be spending a night together." "Zaneeya, you and I are the same age." "I know, but I am not trying to spend the night with any boys. Are y'all having sex?" Sabreea smiled and said, "No." "Yes you are! You better use a condom Sabreea for real! You do not want to get pregnant." "I'm not having sex. We only kiss." "Yeah right!" Sabreea had a big smile on her face. She said, "I'm serious Zaneeya, for real. What, you don't believe me?" "No!" Later on that night, we watched a movie and we talked before we went to sleep. When I woke up in the morning, momma Shay was cooking breakfast. Momma Shay said, "Good morning Zaneeya, breakfast will be ready soon ok." "Good morning mom. Ok, I'm going to take a shower first." "Ok Zaneeya." As I was taking a shower, Sabreea came knocking on the bathroom door. She said, "Zaneeya, I have to use the bathroom." "No, you don't. You just want to see me naked." "I do have to use it, for real. You're going to make me pee on myself." I opened the door. Then I got back in the shower. I said, "You better not be, taking a number two neither!" She replied, "It's too late. I'm sorry sis. I couldn't hold it."

"I am never letting you back in the bathroom again, when I am showering. Next time you will booboo on yourself." I got out the shower and I went into Sabreea's room to get dress. Shonte was still sleep, so I made sure that I did not make any noise. After, I finished getting dress. I went into the livingroom. Momma Shay said, "Zaneeya you can eat when you want too. Eat as much as you want." "Ok, mom thank you." I ate some bacon, eggs and some pancakes. Shonte came out the room. She said, "Good morning. Who cooked breakfast?" I said, "Mom." "I can't wait to eat." After, I was finished eating, my dad called momma Shay. He said, "Shay, I'm coming to get Zaneeya in a few hours so tell her to get ready." "Ok, Justin Sr." Momma Shay said, "Zaneeya, your dad is coming to get you. So get your bags together." "Ok." Sabreea said, "Zaneeya

what are you doing for Halloween?" I replied, "Nothing why? What are you trying to do?" "My cousin Courtney is coming over to spend the night and I want you to spend the night too. We are going to Sobrante Park, so we can go trick or treating. Courtney goes with one of Bubba's friend and I want you to talk to one of Bubba's friends as well." "I am not talking to none of Bubba's friends and I mean that." "Please sis, you're going to like him." "No!" "I will call you tomorrow and tell you more about it. You're going to spend the night right?" "I don't know." "Come on sis, please." "Ok, I'll ask dad to drop me off, but I'm not talking to none of Bubba's friends." My dad came to pick me up. I gave Sabreea, and Shonte and momma Shay a hug. I told momma Shay thank you, for letting me spend a couple of nights at her house. Momma Shay said, "You're welcome Zaneeya. You can spend a night anytime you want too you know that. Justin Sr., can you bring Zaneeya to my house on Halloween? So she can spend the night with Sabreea, and Courtney. They are going trick or treating together." My dad replied, "Yes Shay. That's not a problem. I'll see y'all later. Sabreea be good and stay away from those boys. I love you." Sabreea laughed as she told my dad she loved him too. On our way to grandma's house, my dad said, "So, Zaneeya what school do you want to go to?" "I want to continue going to OT High. I can get up early in the morning and catch the bus to school." "Ok, you have to get up around 6:00 AM. Do you think you will be there on time?" "I will be at school bright and early." When we arrived to grandma's house, my cousin Janelle opened the door. Janelle and her mother Sherrie lived with my grandma at the time, and so did Timberly. I gave my grandma a hug and kiss and I spoke to Sherrie and Timberly. My grandma said, "Zaneeya, you can sleep in my room at night."

"Ok grandma, thank you." My dad gave me some lunch money. He said, "Zaneeya, do you have a bus pass?" "No." My dad gave me some money so I could buy me a bus pass. I told him thank you. He said, "You're welcome. I'll call and check on you tomorrow. Listen to your grandma." Grandma said, "Zaneeya always helps me and listen to me out of all the grandkids." My dad gave me a hug. I told him I would see him later. I locked the door then I went to bed. The next morning I had school. I woke up at 6:00 AM. Janelle was getting ready for school and Sherrie was getting ready for work. After, I got dress I said bye to grandma. Then I walked to the bus stop and I waited for the bus to come. When the bus came, it was crowed it. The bus was filled with many school kids and people who had to go to work. When, I got off the bus downtown. I caught the 51 bus to school. When I got off the 51, I stopped at the donut shop. That was the hang out spot in the morning. So everybody would be

there buying food or getting something to drink. When I went inside the donut shop, I saw my friends and my cousin Dudy. Dudy said, "Zaneeya, where have you been?" "I been MIA for minute, but I'm back now. " "Why did you get off the bus? You don't stay with Rebbeca anymore?" "No, I live with grandma now." "Oh ok. I'm happy you're back at school. I'll see you later cousin." "Ok." I seen this boy who I thought was cute. He came inside the donut shop. He said, "Hi. What are you getting some coffee?" I replied, "No, I have enough nervous energy already. I do not need caffeine to exacerbate it." He smiled. He said, "What is your name? I see you around school a lot." "My name is Zaneeya. What is your name?" "My name is Brandon." "Everytime I see you, you're always smiling at me." "I like what I see. Why wouldn't I smile?" I smiled at him then I walked away. When I went to class, I was nervous. I didn't know what to expect, and I knew Letha called the police on two of my older cousins, when they left her house. Their names are Eva and Tina. They are sisters, and when they left Letha's house, she called the police and reported them as a run away. My teacher said, "Hi Zaneeya, you haven't been here in a couple of days. I'm going to give you some of the homework that you missed." I did my homework in class and when the bell ranged, I went to my next class. I was nervous in 2nd period too. When the bell ranged to go to the 15- minute break, I went outside to go meet Jessica. She did not know I was coming to school. When I seen Jessica, I ran up to her and I put my hands over her eyes. She said, "Who is this? Move your hands off my eyes." I started laughing. Jessica said, "Zaneeya." We hugged each other as if we have not seen each other in years. Jessica said, "I did not know you were coming to school today. I'm happy you're here, now we can catch up."

I replied, "I know, we have so much to talk about." "I missed you sis." "I missed you too." "We will talk about everything at lunch." "Ok." Brandon walked passed me. He looked at me and smiled. Jessica said, "Sis, do you like him?" I said, "No! Why you ask me that?" "I saw him smiling at you. So I figured y'all must like each other." "I have to go to class." "We are going to finish this conversation later Zaneeya, don't think were not." I shook my head and yelled, "No were not." I went to class, I was still nervous, because I did not know if the principal was going to come in my classroom and tell me to leave. After, class was over it was time to go to lunch. I went to the back of the school like always and I waited for Jessica. I seen Rebbeca, she ran up to me and gave me a hug. She said, "Zaneeya, I miss you." "I miss you too. We are so use to being with each other everyday." "I know, now I don't have anyone to knock on the wall with me anymore." "Yes you do, you have Alisha." "Real funny

Zaneeya, it's not the same." "Where are you going for lunch?" "I'm going to Burger King with Susan." "Where are you going?" "I'm going to Wendy's with Jessica." "Come with me to Burger King?" I said, "Jessica do you want to go to Burger King?" "Yeah, we could go." When we went to Burger King, we waited in line to order are food. Brandon walked in. He looked at me and said hi. Jessica looked at me and smiled. I said, "Why are you smiling Jessica?" "Oh, you know why I'm smiling Zaneeya?" Rebbeca and Susan said, "We want to know too." Everybody looked at Brandon and I, and I just shook my head. Jessica asked Brandon what his name was. Rebbeca and Susan went to order there food. I was so happy, because I knew Jessica was going to ask Brandon some questions and I did not want them to comment on nothing. It was time for me to order my food. I told Jessica to come on as she was questioning Brandon. After, Jessica ordered her food I asked her what she asked Brandon. Jessica said, "Nothing, I didn't say nothing!"I replied, "Yeah right, just tell me!" "Do you really want to know?" "Tell me." "Ok, but let me ask you something first. Do you think he's cute?" "Yes, I do!" "So do you have a little crush on him?" "Just a little one." "I asked him did he have a girlfriend and he said no." "Oh ok. I'm not talkin to him. Their are too many girls that like him up here." "So, what does that have to do with you?" "No, it's not going to happen, give it up!" After we ate, we went back to school. When I was in 5th period, the phone ranged. My teacher hung up the phone and he walked over to me. He said, "Zaneeya, Mrs. Williams want to see you in her office." "Ok." As I was walking to the principal's office, I was becoming even more nervous. I went inside the office and knocked on Mrs.Williams door. She opened the door. Mrs. Williams said, "Zaneeya come in, have a seat." I sat down in a chair directly across from her.

Mrs. Williams said, "Do you want some water?" I replied, "Yes, thank you." "Your auntie Letha came up here and said that you ran away from home. She told me to call the police on you when you come back to school, because she reported you as a runaway. Tell me what happened. Why did you leave?" "I left, because I was tired of living there. I was tired of being mistreated. I could not see my mom or my grandmothers or no one else. When Letha finally allowed me to visit my mom, a whole year went by. I would spend the night, and wash my clothes at my granny's house every two weeks. My mom's mother, which is Letha's sister. That lasted for a month and I couldn't see her any more. Letha would give me $2 or $3 dollars for lunch, whenever she wanted to give it to me. I talked to Letha before I left. I told her that I wanted to get a job, and my auntie is going to hire me. I want to work so I can provide for myself. I told Letha she would not have to buy my school clothes or give me any money. She told me no! I don't need to work. That was my final straw! So I called my grandma, my dad's mother and she said I can live with her. I packed my bags and I left. I had to ask before I ate out of the refrigerator, and I just got tired of the same things. I didn't feel loved and I would cry myself to sleep every night. I was extremely unhappy and I'm depressed right now." "Wow, that's a lot for a young lady to go threw. I do feel for you. Do you still want to go to OT High?" "Yes, I do. I do not want to go to no other school." "Ok, well I'm not going to call the police. I looked at your grades, you have all A's and B's. You only have one C and you have been getting good grades since you were in middle school. You're not a bad girl at all. You're a good girl. You get excellent grades and you don't have a history of bad behavior! So, I'm going to let you stay here at OT High." I smiled and said, "Yes!" All excitedly. I said, "Thank you Mrs. Williams!" She replied, "Call me auntie." She smiled at me and said, "I'm going to need your grandma, or whoever else is taking care of you, to come up here and sign some papers." "Ok, thank you auntie!" "You're welcome. Now go to class and I will be checking on you." "Ok." It was 6th period. When I went to class, I felt so good inside. I knew I was going to be ok, and I knew I would work and go to school. My teacher said, "Zaneeya, where have you been? You're in trouble. Mrs.Williams said when you come back to school to tell you to go to her office." "Miss. Regeiro, I spoke to Mrs. Williams already. I just left her office." "Ok, you have to catch up on your homework." "Ok, can I do some of the work that I missed, today in class?" "Yes, but when you are done you have to do today's classwork as well." "Ok."

When, the bell ranged to go home. I took Miss. Regeiro my homework that I finished. I said, "I finished all of my homework that I missed and I finished today's lesson as well." She said, "You are extremely smart in Spanish. I knew you would be done with all of your work. How are you doing? I couldn't believe you ran away from home. You're a good student, I was worried about you?" "Thanks Miss. Regeiro. I'm doing well. I didn't run away! I walked away and I'm still going to attend school here. I know things are going to be much better now." "I'm happy you're doing better. I will see you in class tomorrow ok." "Ok, see you tomorrow." I went to the back of the school to go meet Jessica she had a uniform on. I said, "Are you a cheerleader now?" "Yes I am!" "Oh ok congratulations! I'm going home. I'll see you tomorrow." "Ok, I have to go to practice." When I made it home, I ranged the doorbell. Janelle opened the door for me. She said, "Hi Zaneeya." "Hi Janelle, how long have you been home?" "I just got home not too long ago." I spoke to my grandma and Sherrie.Timberly *was sleep. My grandma said, "Zaneeya, I want you to go in the kitchen and do the dishes, and Janelle is going to sweep the floor." "Ok grandma." After, I did the dishes I took a shower. Then I did my homework. Then I went to bed. The next morning I woke up, I got dress and I went to school. When, I came home from school, soon as I stepped one foot in the door. Grandma said, "Zaneeya, do those dishes and Janelle is going to sweep and mop the floor." I said, "Ok grandma." After, I was finished doing the dishes I took a shower. Then I did my homework. Then I went to bed. I lived with my grandma for a week. One day I came home from school. My grandma said, "Zaneeya, get in the kitchen and do those dishes." I replied, "Ok Grandma, let me sit down for 10- minute then I will go do the dishes. I don't feel good." Sherrie came in the livingroom. She said, "Hi Zaneeya." "Hi Sherrie." "You don't look to well. Do you have a fever?" "I don't know, but I'm very cold. It feels like I have the flu or something!" "Do you have any soup or medicine?" "No." "I'm going to take you to the store. I will buy you some soup and medicine." "Ok, thank you Sherrie." "You're welcome." Grandma said, "Ok, get up. You have been sitting down long enough. I want those dishes done before it gets too late." I went to the kitchen and grandma had dishes everywhere. She would always make a mess, but I never seen it like this before. I started doing the dishes before I left. After, I was done doing the dishes. Sherrie took me to the store to get me some soup and to buy me some medicine. When we came back to the house, grandma had made more of a mess in the kitchen. She said, "Zaneeya, I want you to go do those dishes and Janelle is going to sweep and mop the floor." I said, "Grandma, I just did these dishes before I left and I'm not doing any more dishes tonight. I am sick and I am tired." "Girl I said go in the kitchen and do those dishes now." "Grandma, I am tired. I am not doing any more dishes tonight. I haven't eaten, nor did my homework and I still have to get in the shower."*

Grandma said, "Call your dad. You cannot live here since you don't want to do the dishes." "Ok." I called my dad and grandma said, "Let me talk to him. Justin, you have to come get Zaneeya! She don't want to clean up." He replied, "I'm on my way." When, my dad came to grandma's house. He said, "What's going on and why you don't, want to do what grandma told you to do?" I said, "I did do what she told me to do. I did those dishes when I came in from school. I am sick and I'm tired. I went to the store with Sherrie. She bought me some soup and some medicine. When we came back, the kitchen was in a mess. Grandma told me to go in the kitchen and wash the dishes again. I told her that I am not doing any more dishes tonight. I don't feel good. I'm sick and I'm tired. I haven't done any of my homework or showered and I haven't eaten." Sherrie said, "Justin Sr., Zaneeya does everything that grandma tells her to do. When she comes home from school, she does the dishes and whatever else grandma tells her to do." Grandma said, "I said she doesn't and that's that." I couldn't believe grandma lied on me. My dad said, "Well, momma Zaneeya did the dishes when she came home from school. Are you upset, because she's not doing them now?" She replied, "No, I'm not upset. She just needs to live with you, because we clean up over here and she doesn't want to." "Momma stop saying that. That's not true at all, and don't go around in the family telling people that either, because it's not true. It's a lie. That's ok, she can come stay with me. Come on Zaneeya, get your stuff and take it to the car." "Ok dad," I took my stuff to the car. Then I came back inside the house and gave Sherrie and Janelle a hug. I said, "Thank you Sherrie for telling the truth about what happen and standing up for me." "You're welcome Zaneeya, anytime." I said, "Bye grandma, I love you. Thank you for letting me stay with you." "You're welcome. You can come over on the weekends, but you have to clean." My dad said, "Bye momma, come lock the door." Even though, my grandma lied on me. I still loved her, and that will never change. When my dad and I was in the car, he told me that I might have to go to school in Antioch. I told him that I wanted to stay at OT High. He said, "Ok, well you're going to have to get up at 4:00 AM every morning. We are going to leave Antioch at 5:20 AM, because there is going to be traffic." "Ok dad." When we made it to Antioch, my dad told me I could sleep in the guest room. I got all of my belongings out of my dad's car, and I took them upstairs to the guest room. I didn't unpack, I just kept my clothes like they were. I put my pajamas on. Then I turned the light off. Then I laid down to go to bed. My dad came in the room. He said, "Are you going to bed?" I replied, "Yeah, I'm tired." "Don't go to sleep without telling me you're going to bed. Good night we are going to talk in the morning ok and you probably won't go to school tomorrow." "Good night, see you in the morning."

The next morning, I woke up and I did not go to school. I showered then I went downstairs. My dad was already downstairs. He said, "Good morning, do you feel a little better?" "No, I feel worst." "Ok, well we need to talk. Who house can you stay at in the Bay Area when you get out of school? I'm not going to pick you up, when you get out of school to take you home, because that means I have to take you to Antioch. Then drive back to the Bay Area. Then drive back to Antioch when Toniya get off work. That's too much driving and that's too much gas that I'm wasting." "Ok I can stay at my granny's house when I get out of school. She wouldn't mind at all." "I'm not going all the way to your granny's house to pick you up every night. That's going out of the way." "I can stay at my best friend Jessica house after school. I know if I ask her parents they would let me." "I don't know her parents. I'm going to have to talk to them. So, call Jessica when she gets out of school today. So I can talk to her parents and if they want me to pay them for letting you stay over, there for a couple of hours a day then your just going to have to go to school in Antioch." "Dad, Jessica parents don't want nothing from you and they wouldn't take any money from you. Her parents are not like that. They are nice people." "Ok, a lot of people are nice, but they still want money. If they don't want any money that's good. You can use the house phone anytime you want to. You can call long distance, because it's free." "Ok, thanks dad. I'm happy you said that. Can I call my mom? I know she is tremendously worried about me." "Yeah you can. You haven't talked to your mom since you left Letha's house?" "No I haven't, but I want to call her and talk to her." "Ok, that's fine. You can call her now if you want too." "Ok." I picked up the house phone and I called my mom. She said, "Hello?" I said, "Hi mom, how are you doing?" "Hi Cupcake, where are you? I've been worried about you, but I have not worried myself sick, because I know you are not a fast girl. So I knew you didn't run away behind a boy and plus your smart. So, I had a feeling that you went to your dad side of the family. I knew you weren't in the street and I knew nothing bad had happen to you." "I don't want you to worry mom, I'm fine. I went to my grandma's house when I left Letha's house. I stayed with my grandma for a week. I just moved with my dad last night." "Oh ok, so are you going to live with your dad?" "I am right now, but I know my dad and I do not get alone. So I know we are going to but heads at some point" "Well, Cupcake you know you can always come home." "What home mom?" "I have my own place now and you have your own room here, so you don't have to live with your dad if you don't want to." "Thanks mom, but I am going to stay out here, and go to school. I have to do what's best for me and if my dad and I do not get alone. I will ask granny if I can come live with her." "Ok Cupcake. I'm happy you called me. I had a feeling this was you calling, because I didn't recongnize this number."

"This is my dad house phone, so I will be calling you from this number ok." "Ok Cupcake let me talk to your dad." "Ok mom. Dad my mom wants to talk to you." I gave my dad the phone. He said, "Hi Miss. Bella, how are you doing?" My mom said, "I'm fine, how you are?" "I'm good. Did Zaneeya tell you that she lives with me now?" "Yes, she did. Thank you for letting our daughter live with you. I appreciate that." "You don't have to thank me Bella. That's what I suppose to do. Zaneeya is going to be ok now. Don't worry about nothing. How

is Justin Jr., and Qin doing?" "They are doing well. Justin Jr., is still in the Bay Area, and Qin live with his girlfriend. He's doing good too." "Well, is Qin in school yet, what's going on with that?" "No he's not in school yet. I have to enroll him. He will go to school soon." "Well, don't you think you need to hurry up in enroll him in school, so he can get use to going back to school again? I know he is selling drugs. He, thinks he's grown, and he don't know the first thing about being grown." "Look, I'm not about to go there with you. I wanted to talk to you so I can thank you for letting Cupcake live with you, that's all. Qin will go to school and it's never too late to go back to school. Let me talk back to Cupcake." "Ok, there's no need to get mad Bella it's the truth, but here is Zneeya hold on." I got on the phone. I said, "Mom." "Yeah Cupcake, your dad gets on my nerves sometime. He's lucky I didn't cuss him out, but I love you. I'll call you tomorrow. I will let your brothers know that I talked to you. They were worried about you too." "Ok mom, tell them I love them and tell them I said hi." "Ok I will." When I got off the phone with my mom, I went to make me some soup. After I ate, I took a nap. As I was sleeping, my dad woke me up. He said, "Zaneeya, I'm going to leave for a little while. I sat the alarm system on the house. If you need anything just call me." "Ok dad." I went back to sleep. When I woke up, I did my homework. After, I was done I called Jessica. I said, "Hi sis, what are you doing?" She replied, "Hi sis, I just got home from cheerleading practices. What are you doing and who number is this?" "I just got finished doing my homework, and this is my dad's number." "I thought your dad lived in Antioch. You live out there now?" "He does and yeah I live in Antioch now." "So you're not going to OT anymore? Come on, really! Why did you move way out there? I thought you were still going to continue going to OT?" "I am still going to OT. Clam down. I had to move out here. My grandma said I couldn't live at her house any more, because I didn't want to do the dishes. So my dad came in got me. Now I live with him." "Oh ok, as long as you're still going to OT with me!" "Jessica, I need to ask you something." "Ask me, what is it?" "I want to know if I can come to your house with you after school, and my dad will pick me up from your house after he picks up his girlfriend from work." "That's what you wanted to ask me? Yeah, of course you can you know that." "Can you ask your parents to see if it's ok with them?"

"I don't need to ask them, their going to say yes." I heard the front door open and the alarm system went off. I said, "Hold on Jessica." I ran downstairs. My dad said, "It's just me." "Ok dad." He said, "Who are you talking to on the phone?" I replied, "I'm talking to Jessica." "Did you tell her to ask her parents can you stay over there after school until I pick you up?" "That's what I'm

doing right now. Jessica said her parents don't mind." "No, tell her I want to talk to her parents so I can ask them myself, so they can know what's going on." "Ok dad, Jessica can you just ask your parents while were on the phone? Tell them my dad wants to talk to them so he can get a clear understanding." Jessica yelled, "Mommy, can Zaneeya come over here everyday after school, she lives in Antioch? Her dad cannot pick her up right after school so she wants to know if it's ok. Her dad will pick her up after he picks up, his girlfriend from work. See, I told you Zaneeya my mom would say yes." "I know, but let me ask her." Jessica said, "Mom can you tell Zaneeya yourself, because she will not listen to me." Auntie Betty got on the phone. She said, "Hi Zaneeya." "Hi auntie, how are you?" "I'm fine. Yes, you can come over here after school, tell your dad I said yes. You know we don't mind at all, that's not a problem." "Ok auntie, thank you. I'll let my dad know." My dad said, "No let me talk to her. Tell her your dad wants to talk to her." I said, "Auntie, my dad wants to talk to you." "Ok." My dad said, "How are you doing Miss. Betty? I am Zaneeya's dad Justin Sr. I wanted to ask you can Zaneeya go to your house after school and I will pick her up when my wife gets off work, remember I met you the day of their graduation." "Yes, I remember and that's fine with us. We don't have a problem with that. I told Zaneeya to tell you that." "She did tell me, but you know their kids, and I just wanted to hear it from you." "Yes that is fine with us we love Zaneeya." "Ok thank you, she will be at your house tomorrow and I will see you tomorrow." "Ok, you're welcome bye." My dad gave me back the phone. I said, "Jessica, I am so happy that your parents are going to let me stay at your house after school." She replied, "I am too. Are you going to school tomorrow?" "Yes I am." "Ok, are you ready to see Brandon?" "I am not worried about that boy." "You don't have to worry about him, but I'm going to hook y'all up." I laughed. I said, "Good night Jessica, I'm going to bed." "Ok sis, I'll see you at school tomorrow. Good night I love you." "I love you too." After, I got off the phone with Jessica. I went to put the phone on the charger. Then I went upstairs to get ready for bed. My dad came in the room. He said, "Do you feel better, do you want to go to school tomorrow?" "I don't feel better at all, but I do want to go to school tomorrow. I need too." "Ok, are you going to bed now?" "Yes I am. I need all the rest I can get." "Ok, good night. I'll wake you up in the morning." "Ok, dad good night."

I slept through the whole night. When I woke up to see what time it was, it was 4:25 AM. After I got dressed, my dad knocked on the door. He said, "Zaneeya it's time to get dress for school, you have 30-minutes." "I'm already dressed dad." He looked at me and said, "You sure are, look at you. Well, I'll be *finish getting dress in about 20-mintues ok." "Ok dad." I went downstairs and sat on the couch as I waited for my dad. He came downstairs. He said, "Come on Zaneeya let's go." My dad set the alarm on the house then we went to the car. It was freezing cold outside. That is the earliest that I have ever been up for school. On my way to school, my dad stopped by one of his friends houses, he told me to wait in the car. I was cold, as I waited for my dad to come back to the car. He stayed inside of his friends house for about 20-minutes. When, he came back to the car. He said, "Are you cold? I'm going to take you to school right now." "Yes I'm cold, it's freezing." "Next time, I will leave the keys in the car." I went to sleep in the car for a little while, when I woke up, we was in the Bay Area. My dad dropped me off at Burger King, because my school was not open yet, it was too early. He gave me $20 dollars. He said, "I'll pick you from Jessica house later tonight. What's her phone number?" I gave him Jessica's number then I went inside of Burger King. I bought me some breakfast. I waited until 8:00 AM to leave Burger King. I went to school. I had to be in class before 8:30 AM or I was going to be late. I went to all four of my classes. Then when the bell ranged to go to lunch, I went to the back of the school to go look for Jessica. She was standing up talking to Desseire. I said, "Jessica where do you want to go for lunch?" "I want Burger King." "No, let's go to Wendy's. I ate Burger King this morning." "Ok." We walked up the hill to Wendy's. We ordered are food. We sat down and ate. Jessica told me she has to go to cheerleading practice after school. After we ate, we went back to school. We sat down in the back of the school for a little while. Then when the bell rang to go to class, we left. When school was over, I went to meet Jessica in the back of the school. We hung out for a little while. Then I went with her to cheerleading practices. I did my homework while I waited for Jessica. When practice was over, her mom and dad came to pick us up. I said, "Hi uncle Henry. Hi auntie Betty. Thank you for letting me stay at your house after school." They said, "No problem Zaneeya anytime." Uncle Henry took us to get something to eat. Then we went to their house. Jessica and I ate are food. We watched TV, and we talked. She asked me would I go out with Brandon. I told her no. She said, "Why not, just tell me why and I hope it's a good reason too?"*

I said, "I think he has a girlfriend right now. I just don't want to go out with anyone right now. I need to figure out how everything is going to play out with my dad, because I know I'm not going to stay with him for long." "If you don't live with your dad, are you going back to Modesto?" "No, I'm not moving back to Modesto. I'm going to call my granny and ask her if I can come live with her." "Ok, maybe you should just live with your granny and things will get better." "I think that's what I'm going to do." My dad called Jessica's phone. She said, "It's your dad." She gave me the phone. I said, "Hi dad." "Hi Zaneeya, I'm on my way right now. Give me her address. I'm going to call you when I make it outside ok."

"Ok dad." I gave Jessica back her phone. My dad called back less than 5- minutes later. He said, "I'm outside." I told uncle Henry and auntie Betty bye. Auntie Betty said, "I'm going to walk you outside." Jessica and auntie Betty walked with me outside. I introduced my dad to Jessica. He said, "Hi, I'm Zaneeya's, dad. Thank you again for letting her stay over your house after school. It's finally nice to meet you Jessica. I heard so much about you. Boy your best friend sure loves you." Jessica said, "We love each other." "Good, y'all are best friends and y'all have to stick together no matter what happens in life." Auntie Betty said, "That's right, bye Zaneeya I'll see you tomorrow." I replied, "Ok auntie." Jessica said, "Bye sis." I said, "Bye sis, I'll see you tomorrow." My dad said, "Bye, see y'all tomorrow thanks again." I got in the car. I told Toniya hi. She said, "Hi Zsneeya how was school?" "School was good. How was work are you tired?" "Yes I am. I just want to shower and go to bed." My dad said, "Jessica parents are nice. They are really nice people you don't see that everyday." I said, "They are very nice." When we got home, I went upstairs, I showered then I went to bed. Everday I would get up at 4:00 AM. I would shower. Then my dad would drop me off at Burger King and I would go to Jessica's house after Cheerleading practices. Then when Toniya got off work, he would pick me up. My dad and Toniya had another car. They had a Jaguar. So Toniya was driving herself to work and my dad would still pick me at 10:00 PM every night. Everytime I was laying down in bed, my dad would come in the room. He would say, "Zaneeya, we need to talk. You might have to go to school in Antioch. You know I have custody over you now. Not your mom and it's because of me that I let you go to school in the Bay Area." "Dad, I am tired, and I'm going to bed. It's after 12 o'clock at night. I have to get up in a couple of hours. I'm not about to argue with you."

I lived with my dad for a week an a half and I was not happy there. I called my granny one day when I got out of school. I said, "Granny, can I come live with you?" She replied, "Yeah, I guess so." "Ok, I'm coming over this weekend." I went downstairs so I could talk to my dad. I said, "Dad, I want to go live with my granny. It will be better for me." "I don't know about that. You need to stay here." "I want to live with my granny. We don't get alone! I'm not happy here and you wouldn't have to get up in the morning to take me to school everyday. I would catch the city bus to school everyday." "I don't care *about your happiness! You know what? I'm not a bad father at all. I busted my butt to take care of you and your siblings when y'all were younger. Bella moved around and I couldn't find y'all. Now I have custody over you. Not your mom and you're going to do what I say do, and you're not going to live with your granny, now!" "You didn't have to come look for us. I was told that was lie and that does not have anything to do with me living with my granny. I am going to live with my granny." "You know what? Yeah, you can live with your granny. When do you want to go?" "Tomorrow!" "Ok, that's fine with me. We are going to drop you off early so pack your bags tonight." "There already packed." "Good." I went upstairs and went to bed. I woke up early the next morning. I took my bags downstairs and placed them by the front door.*

Toniya came downstairs. She said, "Good morning Zaneeya." "Good morning Toniya. How are you doing?" "I'm a little tired. So you're going to leave me huh?" I smiled. I said, "Yeah, I think this will be best for everybody." "I'm sorry I couldn't spend anytime with you!" "That's ok. I know you have to work I understand that." My dad came downstairs. He said, "What are y'all talking about?" Toniya said, "Nothing." My dad said, "Zaneeya are you ready to go? You don't have to worry about coming over here for a long time." "Ok, that's fine and yeah I'm ready." I took my bags to the car. When, we got in the car. My dad said, "I'm not going to your granny house everyday to bring you lunch money, or to give you bus fare." I said, "You come to the Bay Area everyday, but you can't come bring me some lunch money or bus fare?" "Yeah you're right. I do come to the Bay Area everyday, but I'm not going to your granny house everyday. So you better figure something out." "Ok, that's fine." I already had a plan. See, I knew I was going to get a job. My dad dropped Toniya off at work. We said bye to each other. Then he dropped me off at my granny's house. When we got to my granny's house, my uncle T opened the door. He was living with her and Justin Jr., was over there too. Justin Jr., said, "What's up little sis, what's up dad." I gave Justin Jr., a hug. I said, "Hi brother."

I went inside of my granny's room and I spoke to her. I gave her a hug and a kiss. My dad said, "Thank you Miss. Stella for letting Zaneeya live with you. I'm going to give her some lunch money for school." My granny said, "That's my granddaughter and they all use to live with me. So I can't turn my back on her now." My dad said, "Zaneeya, I'm leaving." "Ok dad. Thank you for letting me live with you and thanks for the $20 dollars. I love you." "You're welcome. Call me later, I love you too." My dad left. My granny told me to put my clothes in her closet. So I did. I told my granny that I was going to get a job.

I didn't go any where over weekend. I just stayed in the house. I watched TV, and ate some good food with my granny. I slept in the bed with my granny. She slept on one side of the bed and I slept on the other side of the bed. When Monday came, it was time for me to go to school. My granny woke me up at 6:30 AM. My granny said, "I'm going to walk with you to the bus stop every morning." I said, "You don't have to granny, just tell me where the bus stop is." "I'm going to walk with you. It's not that safe over here, just get dress then were going to leave." "Ok granny." After I was finished, getting dress we walked to the 19 bus stop, which was a block away from my granny house. When we got to the bus stop, it was a few other kids waiting for the bus as well. The bus didn't take long at all, we waited for 10-minute. When the bus came, my granny gave me a kiss. She said, "I'll see you when you get home." "Ok granny I love you." "I love you too." I got off the bus downtown in front of the Marriot Court Yards. Then I got on the 51. The bus was, packed as usual. Some kids would have their radios in their backpacks, and they would play their music so loud, that the bus driver would tell them to turn their music down. If they wouldn't turn it down the bus driver would say, "I'm not moving the bus until whoever is playing the music turns it down." So, everybody on the bus would tell that person to trun their music down and most likely they would. Then the bus driver would start the bus back up. When I got off the bus, I went to get some coffee from the donut shop. I saw Brandon. He said, "Hi Zaneeya." "Hi." "You're going to be late for class. You better hurry up and get there." "Look who's talking. I see I'm not the only one that's going to be late. You just make sure you don't make any stops on your way to class, Brandon." He smiled and said, "I'm going straight to class, matter of fact, we can walk together." "I don't need you knowing where my classes are." "I already know where your classes are. So we mind as well walk together."

"Maybe, next time I will let you walk with me to class. I don't want you to get in trouble by your girlfriend." "I don't have a girlfriend." "Right! See you around school, bye." Brandon shook his head. He yelled, "What, you don't believe me?" I kept walking. I went to class. I was happy I didn't have to worry about catching up with my homework, because I did it all. When the 15-mintue break came, I went to the back of the school to meet Jessica. Then we went to the cafeteria to get some chocolate chip cookies. Jessica said, "I don't have practices today so were going straight to my house after school." I replied, "Well, I'm not going to your house after school any more." "Why not, is this your last day at school? Don't tell me you're going to another school?" "No silly. I told you I'm going to stay at OT. I moved with my granny over the weekend. So now I live

with her." "Ok. Do you like living with your granny?" "Yeah I like it so far. My granny is laid back. She don't trip off a lot of stuff." "Well that's good. You finally have some where you can live and you don't have to worry about moving or not being wanted." "I know I made the best move by living with my granny. I don't have to worry about no drama, or her talking about my mom or nothing like that. I had to deal with that while I was living with Letha and my dad." "I know, now you want be so stressed out and we can hang out on weekends. We can go to the movies, and to the mall." "Yeah we can." On my way to class, I seen this boy named Nathan. He was very short, but he was fine. He said hi to me and I said hi back to him. At lunch, I did not see Jessica. I figured she went to eat lunch with Desseire. So I left and I walked to the deli, which was right across the street from OT. The deli was packed with students. I ate a sandwich for lunch, and some French Onion Sun chips and I bought a Dole Apple juice to drink. After, I got my food. I walked back to school, and I sat in the back of the school and ate my lunch. As I was eating, I saw Jessica walking towards me. I said, "Where did you go for lunch?" She replied, "I went to Wendy's. I waited for you, but I did not see you so I left." As we were talking, I saw Brandon. He was with his friend Bernard. Bernard said, "What's up Zaneeya." "What's up Bernard?" Brandon said, "Y'all know each other?" We said, "Yeah." The bell ranged to go to class, as I was walking to class. Brandon said, "Zaneeya, you still don't believe me?" "No, I don't. I don't even know you to believe you." I said as I laughed. Bernard said, "What are y'all talking about?" I said, "Nothing, it doesn't matter." I walked away and went to class.

I liked my math teacher Mr. Hutter. He explained math very well. He would ask us if we wanted to do some math problems on the board and I would raise my hand. Mr. Hutter said, "Zaneeya come up here." I would do a few math problems on the board then I would sit back down in my seat. It was a boy in my math class that I liked his name was Sammie. We sat next to each other in class. After the bell ranged to go to class, I went to Mrs. Williams office. I knocked on her door. She opened it. She said, "Zaneeya, I'm having a meeting right now. I'll see you in a little bit, and why aren't you in class? Nevermind, we will talk about that when you come in my office." "Ok auntie." I waited in the office until her meeting was over. 6th period was almost over. When Mrs. Williams came out of her office, she told me to come here. She said, "You better have a good reason for why you're not in class." I replied, "I just wanted to tell you that I don't live with my dad anymore. I live with my granny out here and I wanted to know could I make some changes on my emergency card. I need to do my paper work over too." "You need to keep the same address for *now and your granny needs to come up here and change your emergency card and the rest of your information." "Ok, but my granny can't come up here, she has legs problems." "Ok, I'll let you make the changes." "Ok, thank you auntie." "You're welcome. How is everything else going for you?" "It's going good. I'm caught up with the rest of my homework, everything is going well." "I've been checking on you. Your teachers said that you're doing good. Keep up the good work, here's a pass to go back to class." "Ok, I'll see you tomorrow." Mrs. Williams looked out for me and she always made sure, that I was on top of my work, and I thank God for putting her in my life. I left and I went to class. My teacher said, "Zaneeya you're late. Class is almost over." "I know I was in Mrs.Williams office. I had to talk to her about something. Here's my pass." "Ok, here's the homework, it has to be done in two days. I will go over it with you more tomorrow and where going to watch a movie tomorrow in class. That's part of the homework." "Ok, thank you." The bell ranged to get out of school. I went to the back of the school. Jessica, and Desseire and I hung out for a little while. Then Jessica's dad picked her up. I said bye to Jessica and Desseire then I walked to the bus stop. Jessica yelled, "Sis, do you want a ride home?" I said, "No thank you." "My dad said come on, he'll take you home." "Ok." I got in the car. I said, "Hi uncle Henry. Thank you for taking me home." "Anytime Zaneeya." Uncle Henry dropped me off at home. I told Jessica I would call her later.*

As I lived with my granny, I got use to it. A month went by and I was doing good. My dad called me and asked me did I want to spend the weekend with him. I told him yeah and I asked him could he go pick up Sabreea. So she could spend the night as well. My dad and Sabreea came to pick me up. I gave my granny a kiss and I told her I would see her Sunday. I gave my dad and Sabreea a hug. My dad said, "Sabreea and Zaneeya, do y'all want to get in the Jacuzzi tonight?" We said, "Yeah, but we don't have any bathing suits." "Don't worry about that. I'm going to take y'all to Wal-Mart to get some, but right now, we are going to hang out. I have to get some work done." "Ok." We were happy to hang out with our dad. We went to meet up, with his best friend who we called uncle Muhammad. I always enjoy seeing my uncle Muhammad. He was always nice to me. Muhammad and my dad did some work together. My dad was making a lot of money. We went to the Olive Garden in Hayward. We stayed there until it closed. Then my dad took us to Wal-Mart to get us some bathing suits. When we got to Wal-Mart, we did not find anything. Everything we seen we didn't like. My dad said, "Did y'all find something?" We said, "No, nothing is cute here." "Ok, well let's go." When we were leaving, Sabreea said,

"Wait, look sis." We had seen this cute bikini. It had flowers on it. It was pink, green and white. My dad said, "Do y'all want it?" We replied, "Yes." "Get it then." After we left Wal-Mart, we went to our dad's house. When we got there, we went to go put on our bikini. Then we went downstairs and told our dad that we were ready to get in the Jacuzzi. He said, "Ok come on. Let me show y'all how to work it." My dad took the top off the Jacuzzi and he showed us what the buttons was for. Then he went back in the house. Sabreea and I stayed in the Jacuzzi for a while. We just talked. She asked me who did I like at school again. I said, "Do you really want to know?" She replied, "Yes, who?" "I like this boy name Sammie and this boy name Brandon." "What, you like two boys? You can't like two boys!" "Yes I can. I don't go with neither one of them. I just think their cute." She laughed and said, "Which one are you going to go with?" "Neither one! I need to be working right now and focusing on that." "Sis, we are young. We don't have to work right now, and you should go with one of them." "Maybe you don't have to work, but I do. I need some money, clothes, shoes and everything else." "How are you going to get a job? Nobody is going to hire you, because you're too young?" "No I'm not. I'm going to work for auntie Jannette at the retirement home. I'm going to be a waitress. I have to keep up my grades and have a work permit from my school to give to Jannette. You have to have a work permit in order to work when your in high school, and you have to have a 2.00gpa or higher to work."

"Oh, that's all you need? I didn't know that." "Yeah, let's get out the Jacuzzi. I'm getting sleepy." We put the top on the Jacuzzi and we went upstairs to shower. I used the shower upstairs and Sabreea used the shower downstairs. After we got dressed, my dad came in the room. He said, "Are y'all going to bed?" We replied, "Yeah." "Good night, I hope y'all turned off the Jacuzzi." "Good night dad, we did." Sabreea and I laid down in bed, as we listened to one of Usher songs. I remember the words that Usher was saying in his song, *"So long, I waited for this night to get excited look in your eyes and tell me baby take me I'm yours, and if you feel anything like I feel, by the end of the night I'm certain you'll be screaming for more!"* Sabreea and I took turns singing parts of the song until we fell asleep. The next day when we woke up, it was 11:30 AM. We showered then went downstairs. My dad said, "Look who finally decided to get up. Are y'all hungry?" We said, "We was tired dad and yes were starving." "Ok, I'm going to make y'all a buffalo burger and y'all can eat some chips with it." Sabreea said, "Ok dad." I said, "Dad I don't want a buffalo burger! Can you just make me a regular beef burger?" "No, you are going to eat buffalo just like Sabreea." "You can make it, but I am not going to eat it. I'm not eating anything that I do not like." "Ok, I'll make you a beef burger." Sabreea and I went in the backyard and we sat down. My dad came out and brought us are burgers, I took my tomatoes off mines, because I did not like tomatoes. I took a bite of my burger and it was good, so I ate all of my food. I went back in the house to wash my plate. Then Sabreea and I watched a little TV. My dad came in the livingroom. I said, "Thanks dad for making us lunch, it was good." "You're welcome. You know you were eating buffalo." "What, I was?" I shook my head. I said, "I should have known you were going to make me a buffalo burger anyway." "That's right. That buffalo was good huh?" I laughed and said, "It was." My dad said, "Zaneeya, what are your grades looking like?" "My grades are still good, and I'm happy right now. I think I'm going to get two jobs." "You don't need two jobs, you only need one." "I know, but I really want two jobs. I'll be fine. I can handle it." "Ok, just make sure you pass the 9th grade." "Oh, I am for sure! I know I can do it." "What about you Sabreea? You're not saying nothing. How are your grades?" Sabreea replied, "My grades are good dad." "Yeah, ok. You better make sure you pass the 9th grade too and I'm not playin with you." "I am dad." "So let me ask y'all something. Are y'all having sex? Are y'all going down on boys? Please don't tell me y'all do!" I said, "No, I am a virgin still! Why would you ask us are we going down on boys?" "I want to know that's why! What positions do y'all like? Do y'all like it from the back? Sabreea what about you, your still not saying nothing. Are you a virgin, no huh?"

I said, "If I wasn't a virgin I would not tell you what positions I like. That's nasty! You don't need to know that! You sound like a pervert!" Sabreea said, "Dang dad, how are you just going to say no? Yes, I am a virgin still." "Ok, I just want to know that's all. I'm going to ask y'all four months from now and see what y'all say then, and Zaneeya I do not sound like a pervert." "I'm still going to be a virgin. My answer is still going to be the same. You can ask me six months from now, and when I start having sex, I'm not going to tell you, you don't need to know my business." Later on, that night, Sabreea and I watched a movie on my dad's portable DVD player. My dad left. He went to get us something to eat. Sabreea said, "I can't believe dad asked us something like that." I said, "I can and I know he is going to ask us again." We didn't see Toniya, because she was always in her room sleeping. She was tired, because she worked a lot. When my dad came back he brought our food to us. We ate then we went upstairs to go to bed.

The next morning we woke up, we ate some cereal. Then my dad came downstairs. He said, "I'm going to take y'all home in 45-mintues ok." We said, "Ok dad." After we ate, we went upstairs to get are bags. We took them downstairs and sat them by the front door. My dad said, "Are y'all ready? Go upstairs and tell Toniya bye." We went upstairs and knocked on Toniya's room door. We said, "We just wanted to come upstairs to tell you bye, and thank you for letting us spend the night at your house." She replied, "You're welcome. This is y'all house too, remember that ok." "Ok." "Next time y'all spend the night, we are all going to do something as a family." "Ok." We went to the car. My dad said, "I had fun with y'all. Hopefully y'all can start spending, some nights on the weekends with me." Sabreea said, "Yeah, we can dad. That will be nice." I said, "I will come over on some weekends." My dad said, "Zaneeya you're not going to come watch." "Yes I am." My dad dropped me off at home first. I said bye to Sabreea and I gave her a hug and kiss. Then I gave my dad a hug. My dad gave me $20 dollars for lunch and he told me he would see me later.

My granny asked me did I have fun at my dad house. I said, "Yes, I did granny. Sabreea and I got in the Jacuzzi. We went out to eat to the Olive Garden. We had fun and I think my dad really enjoyed us too." "That's good. I'm happy you enjoyed yourself. The holidays are coming up. I'm going to Modesto for Thanksgiving. Are you coming?" "Yes, I'm coming granny. I can't wait to see my mom and brothers." Thanksgiving break was finally here. My uncle Tony called and told my granny he was coming to pick us up at 3:00 AM. When, he gets off work. So my granny, and T and I packed our clothes. So when Tony come, we can just leave. Justin Jr., had called he said he was going to Modesto with us. I laid down until Tony came, when Tony came, it was 3:00 AM. We put our bags in the car and we got on the freeway to go to Modesto. When we made it to Tony's house, everybody was sleep, but my auntie Dorthy was woke. I went upstairs and said hi to her and I gave her a hug. She said, "Zaneeya, you can put your clothes in Christy and Mimi's room." "Ok auntie." Christy woke up. I said, "Wake up I know you have been sleeping all day." She said, "Shut up Zaneeya, you can put your bags in my closet." "Ok." After I put my clothes in Christy's closet, I went back downstairs. I told granny good night. Then I went upstairs and I went to sleep. I woke up at 10:00 AM. Everybody was downstairs. I showered then I did my hair. Then I went downstairs. I said hi to everybody. Christy said, "Zaneeya do you want to come with me to my friend house? She lives next door." "Yeah, I'll go with you." My granny said, "Zaneeya, can you do my hair before you leave?" "Yes, granny I will do it after I eat." Mimi said, "Zaneeya, can you perm my hair while you're out here?" "Yeah, I'll do your hair later. You're not going anywhere today. I know you still be right under yo momma." "Your right and I'm not going any where today." I ate some cereal then I straightened my granny's hair. Then Christy and I went to her friend house next door. She introduced me to her friend. We stayed over her friend house for a little while. Then we went back to Christy's house. When we got back in the house, my mom and my brothers were there. I gave my mom a hug and I told my brothers hi. My mom said, "Cupcake, I'm so happy to see you. Now I don't have to worry about not seeing you. You can come out here for the holidays. Now you can see your family with no problem." "I know mom. I'm happy too and I don't have to worry about nothing living with granny."

"Cupcake, can you do your mom a favor?" "It depends on what it is there is no tellin what you want." She smiled. My mom said, "I don't want much. Can you do my hair for me?" "Yes, I'll do it right now. Everybody wants their hair done. I'm going to start charging y'all!" "You can't charge yo momma!" "Yes I can. I need some money." "You better go to work." "I am, soon as I go home." My mom sat in a chair while I straighten her hair. As I was doing my mom's hair, she was constantly complaining about the way that I was combing her hair, because she's tender headed. She would say, "Ouch Cupcake that hurts." "Mom, I'm holding your hair as I comb it, and your hair isn't even that tangled, woman up." "Look, I'm tender headed. Let me see that comb I'll do it myself." "I don't have time for this mom. I'm not gonna do yo hair if you don't hurry up." "Ok, go ahead Cupcake." After, I was finished doing my mom's hair. I said, "That's the last time I'm doing your hair. You're too tender headed!" "Thank you Cupcake, it looks nice, and it feels good. I don't have to worry about my hair not being done at least for two weeks." "You're welcome mom." Mimi was sitting on the couch. I said, "Come on Mimi so I can do your hair." She replied, "Ok Zaneeya let me go get my perm." "I can do you hair upstairs that will be better." "You can do my hair in my mom's room." "Ok." I walked upstairs so I can do Mimi's hair. Before I did her hair, I put some plastic gloves on my hands. So I wouldn't get the perm on my hands. Then I applied the perm on Mimi's head by doing sections at a time. I told Mimi that we were going to let the perm sit in her head for at least 25-mintues to 30-minutes. After, I was finish putting Mimi's perm in her hair I washed my hands then I went downstairs to make me a sandwich. As I was eating my sandwich, Mimi was yelling my name. She said, "Zaneeya, my hair is burning. My hair is burning." "It hasn't even been 20-minutes yet. Clam down. I'm coming, but *first I'm going to finish my sandwich." "Come on, you can eat when you're done." "Girl please, I'mma bout to finish this sandwich. I'm almost done you can wait 5- minutes." "Hurry up Zaneeya please." "I told you I'm coming. I am not going to let your hair fall out." After, I was finished eating. I went upstairs, and I washed Mimi's perm out of her hair. Then I blow-dried her hair. After blow-drying her hair, I straighten it out with my flat irons. When I was done I said, "Next time I'm going to charge you." "Thank you cousin." She said with a smile on her face." I replied, "Yeah, now you want to smile huh?" "What are you talking about? I'm always smiling and don't charge me, we are first cousins. I like my hair. This is what I needed." "I'm happy you like it."*

Later on that night, I ate and went to bed. When I woke up the next day, it was Thanksgiving. My granny was baking homemade sweet potato pies, and she made a pineapple cake for my cousin Lason. I showered then I went downstairs and said happy Thanksgiving to everyone. Christy woke up, and asked me. Did I want to go to her friend house with her? I said yeah. We went to her friend house. I stayed there for about 15-minutes. Then I told Christy I was going back to her house, because I wanted to eat Thanksgiving dinner with my own family. So I left. Christy said, "Ok, I'll be over there in a little while." When I got in the house, everybody was eating. I washed my hands and I made me something to eat. My granny made some greens, potato salad, candy yams, turkey, Ham, dressing, sweet potato pies, and a lemon pie. After, I was finish eating my food Lason came in the kitchen. He said, "I do not want anyone eating my cake that granny made me." I said, "Can I have some cousin?" He replied, "No, because if I give you some I have to give everybody some." "Wow, really? I can't have a piece of your cake?" "Maybe, I'll think about it." My granny made Lason a cake that was big enough to feed 40 people. Lason cut him a piece of cake then he went upstairs. I sat down in the chair and I thought about what he said. So, I went in the refrigerator and got his cake and I cut me a piece. Lason came downstairs. He put his plate in the kitchen sink. Then he turned around and looked at me. "Zaneeya, why did you cut a piece of my cake?" He said as he stuttered

He said, "I told you, that I do not want anyone eating my cake!" "You did tell me that, but you have enough cake to share. It's not like your going to miss a piece." "Don't eat no more of my cake. You can eat that piece, but that's it." "I know I'm going to eat this piece. That's why I cut it. I wanted some." "Ok cousins, don't eat no more please." "Ok, I won't." After Lason went back upstairs, everybody came and cut them a piece of his cake. When, Lason came back downstairs. He had a half of cake left, and yes, he was fussing. We all stayed in the house, and ate, and we talked about what we use to do. When, we were kids. I always had a good time with my brothers and my cousins. The next day Christy asked me, did I want to go to the fun house? I said, "What's the fun house?" She replied, "It's a club for 15 years olds and 18 years olds." "Oh yeah, let's go. How are we going to get there?" "My dad is going to drop us off." "Ok, let's ask Mimi if she wants to come." "Mimi is not coming, but we can ask her." I went upstairs and asked Mimi did she want to go with us to the fun house. She said, "No, I'm staying at home."

The next day, Christy and I caught the bus to the mall. We went shopping for a little while. Then we got a bite to eat. Then we went back to her house. Christy and I picked out our outfits that we were going to wear to the club. After, we got dressed uncle Tony and my mom dropped us off. Uncle Tony said he would be back around 12:30 AM to pick us up. We said ok, we told them bye and we went inside the club. The fun house packed. Christy and I was dancing, we had a real good time. I saw my stepsister Gabbie. She looked at me and said, "Hi Zaneeya." I replied, "Hi Gabbie." She came up to me and gave me a hug. She said, "I haven't seen you in a long time. How are you doing? What are you doing here?" "I'm doing well, and I came to dance and to have a good time." We laughed. Gabbie introduced me to her friend Precious. He said, "You're so pretty let's dance." We started dancing. I gave Gabbie a hug, and I told her, and Precious bye. I had to go find Christy. After, I found Christy. We danced to Usher, Lil John and Ludacris, song they had made together, called Lovers and Friends. *As we were dancing, Tony called and told us that he was outside. On our way back to Christy's house, my mom and Tony asked us did we have fun. We said, "Yes, we did." I said, "I can't wait to go back. Next time we have to stay a little longer." My mom said, "Y'all stayed long enough. I'm happy y'all had fun."*

When we got in the house, we put are pajamas' on and we went to bed. The next day, uncle Tony took us back to the Bay Area. I said bye to my mom, my brothers and my cousins. When I got back home, I unpacked my clothes and I did some homework. Then I ate, and went to bed. The next day, I had school. Sammie had written down his phone number on a piece of paper and he told me to call him. I saw Nathan at school we spoke to each other again. After school, I went home. I did my homework then I took a shower. I ate and went to bed. I was thinking about calling Sammie, but I said to myself no. I'll wait a few days. As the school year went on, Nathan and I became closer. I started to look at him as my brother. We became best friends. We would hug when we seen each other, and we talked on the phone. I knew who he liked at school, and he knew who I liked at school. We were just close. One day, I called Sammie. I said, "Hi, is Sammie their?" He said, "This is he." "Do you know who this is?" "Keep talking." "What are you doing? You probably thought I was never going to call you huh?" He giggled in the phone. He said, "Oh, Zaneeya I didn't think you were going to call me." "I had to wait a few days." "Why is that?" "I just had too." I smiled, as I was on the phone. Not that he could see me smiling. I said, "What are you doing?" He replied, "I'm vacuuming my granny's room floor and I'm cleaning up right now." "Oh, do you want to call me back?" "No, it's ok. I can talk and clean at the same time. What are you doing?"

"I'm just doing my homework." Sammie and I talked on the phone for a while before we got off. The next day, I watched some old western movies with my granny. We ate, and we watched Tombstone. *That was one of my granny's favorite movies and she would laugh and talk to the TV as she watched it. Before I went to bed, I put my school clothes out for the next day. At school, Jessica and I discussed what we did over, Thanksgiving break. I saw Brandon. He came up to me, and asked me where was I going to eat lunch at?" I said, "I don't know." He said, "You're probably going to eat lunch with your boyfriend." "Who is my boyfriend?" "That boy you always be with, and y'all always be hugging." "Nathan? That's my best friend that's my brother, you're crazy." "Yeah, ok that's your best friend." "I'll see you later. I'm going to class." I went to lunch with Susan. I said, "Susan, why are you always smiling when Bernard comes around?" She replied, "No reason." "Yeah right. You like him huh you want to be with him huh?" "Yes, I do like him, and I do want to be with him, but I don't think he's into me." "He probably don't know that you like him. I'm going to tell him you like him." "Ok, when are you going to tell him today or tomorrow?" "I'm going to tell him today after school." "Now I'm nervous." "Good, you should be." "Since you're going to talk to Bernard for me, I'm going to talk to Brandon for you." "I don't need you to talk to Brandon for me. I am fine. I don't want to date Brandon right now." "Why not? I'm going to tell him that you have a crush on him." "You just won't stop will you?" "No."*

After, Susan and I ate lunch, we went back to school, we seen Bernard and Brandon sitting down. I went up to Bernard and I told him that I needed to talk to him. I said, "Bernard, do you have a girlfriend?" "No why, what's up?" "Well, I wanted to tell you that Susan like you. A lot and she want to talk to you." "Doesn't she go with somebody up here?" "No, not any more. She's y'all yours if you want her." He smiled. He said, "I don't know, we can be friends for now. I don't want a girlfriend right now, but she is pretty though." "Ok, well

friends y'all will be. You can give her your number and she can give you her's."
"Ok. I'll get it from you." "No, you need to get it from her." "Ok Zaneeya."
As we were walking back towards Susan and Brandon, they were talking and
I heard Susan tell Brandon that I had a crush on him. I said, "Oh really? I
do Susan?" She replied, "Yes, you do Zaneeya." "He is ok lookin, he's not all
that." Susan said, "Please." "It's time for me to go to class. I'll see y'all later."
"No, I'll see you after school." "No you won't, because I'm going straight home
after school." "You have to tell me what you and Bernard talked about." "I
will, but it want be today. Bye, see you tomorrow."

"I'm not gonna see you tomorrow, because you're going on a field trip
tomorrow remember. So, I'll call you tonight so you can tell me." "No, I will
tell you when I come back from the field trip." "No, because I'm going to want
to know while I'm at school, that's torture." "Pay back is something isn't it?"
I laughed as I walked off and went to class. I completed all of my classwork,
and homework in class. When the bell rang to get out of school, I went straight
home. Susan called my name as I was walking to the bus stop. I yelled, "I'll
see you tomorrow." When I got home, I showered. My granny said, "Zaneeya,
you can eat dinner when you want to the food is ready." "Ok granny, thank
you." After I ate, I called Nathan to see if he was still going on the field trip
tomorrow. He said he was. So I told him I would see him at school and I got
off the phone and went to bed. I went to school the next day. Everybody that
was going on the field trip with Mr. BoveraMacho class had to line up, on the
side of the school, by the boys gym.

Mr. BoveraMacho took roll to see how many students that was going on
the field trip. The students that Mr. BoveraMacho picked, to go on the field
trip were the students who was the most athletic, and who passed their PE
test. It was another PE teacher going on the field trip with us. I was talking
to Nathan and Rebbeca then Brandon stood next to me. He said, "Zaneeya,
you're going on the field trip too?" "Yeah, I'm going. What are you doing over
here? Are you going too?" "Yeah I'm going." Rebbeca spoke to Brandon, and
as we were walking to West MacAuthur Bart station, I was talking to Nathan
and Rebbeca. Brandon was talking to someone else, but he was right behind
me. When we made it to the Bart station, we all got on this bus called the
Emery go round. After we got off the bus, we walked a block to our destination.
We were going in door rock climbing. When we got there are teachers gave us
instructions on what to do, and what not to do. After they gave us instructions,
we waited outside for a little while until we could go in. Nathan and I was
talking, we said we were going to rock climb together. Brandon stood on the

side of me. He said, "See, I told you that's your boyfriend." I said, "That's not my boyfriend, that's my best friend. Ask him yourself." "No, I'm not going to ask him. Matter of fact, I will." Brandon said, "Nathan, do you and Zaneeya go together?" Nathan giggled. He said, "No, that's just my best friend. That's my sister. Why do you think we go together?" "You guys are always together, and y'all are always talking and hugging." I said, "Yeah, we are close, and if I had a boyfriend or he had a girlfriend we still would interact like that. Were just best friends, you need to understand that. You heard that from me and you heard that from him." "Ok, I believe y'all."

We went inside to go rock climbing. The employees told us what to do, and they helped us put are gear on. Rebbeca went with her boyfriend. His name was Ferryman. Nathan asked me was I going to rock climbing right now. I said, "No." He said, "Can you hold my hat for me best friend?" "Yeah, give it to me. I'll just keep it while were here, then when you're done rock climbing just come get it." "Ok, thanks best friend." "You're welcome." Nathan went rock climbing. Brandon and I were talking. He said, "See, if y'all not together why are you holding his hat?" I replied, "He is going rock climbing, and he asked me to hold it, and I am ok with that. You need to let that go." I walked away as Brandon was shaking his head. I went rock climbing with Nathan and Brandon went to go do his own thing. I was having a good time while I was rock climbing. We ate lunch there. When it was time to go, Nathan came to get his hat. We all walked backed to the bus stop. We got on the bus. After, we got off the bus we walked back to school. Nathan, Rebbeca, and Brandon and I walked together. Brandon had asked Rebbeca did she think, Nathan and I were together on the low. Rebbeca said, "No, they are best friends. If they were together, they would tell you. Zaneeya, Nathan stop, wait for a minute." We said, "Stop for what?" "I have to say something. Brandon, do you want to be with Zaneeya?" "I do, but I think she really talks to Nathan." Nathan said, "Man, we not gonna keep tellin you that were not together. We are just best friends."

Brandon said, "Zaneeya, I do want to be with you though, and if y'all aren't really together then I do want to be your boyfriend." Rebbeca said, "Zaneeya, stop acting like you don't like him, because you do and you know it." I said, "Your right, I do like him, but Brandon I do not want to hear nothing else about Nathan and I again." "Ok, you do not have to worry about that." Nathan said, "So, y'all are together now." Brandon said, "Yeah Zanneya, now you're my girlfriend." I smiled and said, "Ok." Nathan said, "Brandon you liked my best friend all this time. Why you just didn't tell her? Y'all could have been together?" "She knew I liked her, she was playin hard to get, but that's

ok." "Well, you got her now just treat her right, that's my best friend." "I am."
As we walked back to school, Brandon and I was walking and talking. He asked
me where I was going when we got back to school. I said, "I'm going straight
home." "You're not going to find Susan to tell her that we are together?" "No,
I'll tell her tomorrow." "Where are you going when we get back to school?"
"I'm going to wait for my mom to come pick me up, she'll be here soon. Then,
I'm going to call you tonight." "Ok, I'll see you tomorrow." I got on the bus and
went straight home. When I got home, I showered then ate. My granny said,
"Zaneeya, did you have fun at school? How was your field trip?" "I had fun
granny. We went rock climbing. I had a good time." "That's good. I'm glad you
did." "Granny, do you know a boy name Brandon that goes to your church?"

"Yeah, that's my pastor's grandson. If were talking about the same boy. I
have known him every since he was a little a boy. Your Godmother TT Neadda
use to babysit him. When, you use to go to church with me, you would fall
asleep at church. You would sleep on Neadda's lap, and Brandon would come
running to her and she would give him a piece of candy. Why, does he go to
your school?" "Yeah he goes to my school, he is going to call me tonight?" "Ok,
I can't wait to talk to him. I see him every Sunday." Later on when I was in bed
Brandon called me, I answered the phone. I said, "Hello." He said, "What are
you doing?" "I'm laying down, on my way to sleep." "What are you doing?"
"I'm in bed too. What time are you going to school tomorrow?" "I'll be there
around 8:00 AM. Why?" "I'm going to be in the side hallway, right before
you get to Mr. Nickolas classroom. So come meet me over there. Then I might
walk you to class." "Ok, I'll meet you over there, and you know you want to
walk me to class, and you are. There's no mite." He laughed. He said, "Your
right, I am." "I'm going to bed, good night. I'll see you tomorrow." "Good night
Zaneeya. See you tomorrow and be on time." "Demanding, how cute boy bye."
After, we got off the phone. My granny said, "Zaneeya was that Brandon?"
"Yes granny that was him." "When you go to school tomorrow tell him that
your granny goes to his church and tell him I said hi." "Ok granny, I will."

The next day, I went to school I got there at 8:15 AM. I went to go meet
Brandon in the hallway. He was sitting down in a chair, talking to his friends.
I walked up to him. He got up and gave me a hug. He said, "You're late." I
replied, "No, I am on time. How long have you been sitting here?" "I have been
here for 15-miuntes now, waiting for you." "You have not been waiting for me
for 15- minutes, because I'm on time." "Where are you going for lunch?" "I
want Burger King, but I don't want to eat there." "Let's eat lunch in Susan's
teacher classroom. The teacher she got 5th period." "Mr. Wing's class? Ok, are

you going to get something to eat first? If so, can you go to Burger King for me and I'll wait for you in Mr. Wing class?" "Yes, I'll just go soon as the bell rang to go to lunch." "Ok, thank you." "Can I have a kiss?" "No, I am not kissing you just, because were together. I don't know where your lips been." "My lips ain't been nowhere, but ok." When the bell ranged to go to class, Brandon gave me another hug. Then he walked me to class. He said, "What do you want from Burger King?" I said, "I want a chicken tender bacon ranch sandwich and I want the meal and I want a strawberry soda." "You're greedy, you're lucky we go together or I wouldn't be buying you this." "Yeah right, you have been waiting to get with me, so you can buy me lunch, and stuff. Stop frontin." I smiled.

"Yeah, ok. I have never bought lunch for any girl." "I know you haven't, and I know why." "Why?" "Cuz she ain't Zaneeya." I laughed. He smiled and said, "I'll see you in Mr. Wing's class." As I sat in class, I couldn't wait for lunch to hurry up and come. When class was over, I went to my next class, and on my way there, I seen Nathan. We talked for a minute then we went to class. At the 15-minute break, I saw Susan and Jessica. Susan said, "So Zaneeya, what did you and Bernard talk about?" "I told him, that you like him. I also told him that y'all could exchange numbers." "What did he say?" He said, "Ok." "Does he want a girlfriend right now though?" "Um, not right now, but he did say you were pretty and y'all can be friends." "Ok, well give him my number." "Ok, I will. You can't wait to call him huh?" Susan laughed. She said, "I really can't. How was the field trip yesterday?" I smiled. I said, "It was nice. I had a good time." Rebbeca walked over to us. She said, "What are y'all talking about?" Susan said, "I just asked Zaneeya how was the field trip yesterday." Rebbeca said, "We had fun. Zaneeya their goes your man." Brandon came over to me. He just looked at me and smiled. I smiled back. He had some chips in his hand. He asked me did I want some! I said, "Yeah, thanks." He said, "You can have them. I'll see you at lunch." Jessica and Susan said, "What's going on with y'all now? What are y'all doing at lunch and Rebbeca why did you say that's her man?" I said, "Nothing and Rebbeca don't say nothin."Jessica said, "Zaneeya, we want to know what's going on." "I'm going to class. I'll see y'all after school." "Why after school you're not eating lunch with us?" Rebbeca said, "No, she's not! Didn't you hear what her man said, he will see her at lunch, y'all better catch on." Jessica and Susan said, "Wait, y'all go together? When did this happen?" They both smiled as they were talking. Rebbeca said, "Yesterday while we were on the field trip." I said, "Thank you Rebbeca for telling everything." "You're welcome Zaneeya." Susan

said, "So are y'all really together?" I replied, "Yes we are, and I am going to class." They said, "Wait, where are y'all going for lunch?" "We are going to Mr. Wing's class for lunch." Susan said, "Oh, you are going to my class for lunch? I definitely will be there." Jessica said, "Y'all have to show me where Mr. Wing class is at, because I have to see them too together." When I went to class, I was trying to remember some of my homework for 6ᵗʰ period, because I had to take a test on it. When the bell ranged to go to lunch, I went to Mr. Wing class. I asked Mr. Wing could I eat lunch in his classroom, and I can I use his computer. He said, "Yeah, go ahead. None of the students that come in my classroom for lunch is my students, but everybody loves to come in Mr. Wing class. Just make sure you throw away your garbage after your done eating." "Ok, thank you Mr. Wing."

It only took Brandon 15-mintues to bring me my food. He came in the classroom. He said, "The line wasn't long at all. I'm happy I left soon as the bell ranged to go to lunch." He gave me my food and I told him thank you. As we were eating, Bernard came in the classroom. He said, "Oh, so this is where you are." Brandon said, "I told you I was going to be in Mr. Wing's class with Zaneeya." "You guys are eating lunch together now, do y'all go together?" Brandon said, "Yes, we go together." "When did this happen?" I said, "Yesterday." "Ok, look at y'all." I said, "Brandon do you want some fires?" "Yeah, I'll take some." After, I was finished eating. I threw my trash away. Then Susan came in the classroom. She said, "So what are y'all doing?" I said, "We just got done eating lunch." Susan said, "Hi Bernard." He replied, "Hi Susan, what's up? You know are friends go together now." "I know they didn't need our help." I said, "Susan, while you're in my business you need to tell Bernard how much you like him and stop playin." Brandon said, "Bernard, you need to tell Susan how much you like her." Susan said, "I think your cute Bernard." "I think you're pretty." I said, "Bernard, don't you think you need to take down Susan's number." "Ok, what is it?" Susan said, "Zaneeya, how do you know that I want to give him my number?" I replied, "Look, you need to stop playin. You were just tellin me today that you want me to give Bernard your number, so stop it." Bernard said, "Do you want me to have your number or not?" Susan replied, "Yeah I do." "Ok, I'm going to text you, so you can save my number in your phone." Brandon and I were talking, and Bernard and Susan were talking. When the bell ranged to go to class, I told Brandon bye and I left. While I was in class, I did a few math problems on the board. When the bell ranged to go to my next class, I was thinking about the test that I had to take. When I arrived to class, my teacher took roll then she gave us our test. When, Miss. Regeiro handed me my test. She said, "Take your time Zaneeya. You get good grades on all of your homework, and your classwork. You can do this." "Thank you, Miss. Regeiro." As I was taking my test, I was trying to remember the time in Spanish, and the days of the week, the numbers and the months. I looked at the clock in class, and that's how I remembered how to say the time in Spanish and everything else just came to me. When I turned in my test, I was very confident that I passed my test. When, the bell ranged to go home. Miss. Regeiro said, "Zaneeya, how do you think you did on your test?" "I think I did well. I know I got at least an, A+ or a B+.

Miss. Regeiro looked at my paper. She said, "You did a great job. I'm going to grade your paper right now. You got an, A+ congratulations! See, it's not to many people with a learning disability that try's and works hard like you. Your very determine in many ways, and you show it in your classwork, homework, and now your test. If you just need 10- minutes before taking your test to remember it, just tell me. I'll let you go outside to clear your head." I replied, "Thank you so much Miss .Regeiro. You are a wonderful teacher! I like the way you teach and you are so hands on with your students and some teachers are not like that." After, I left Miss. Regeiro class I seen Brandon, he walked over to me and we talked for a little while. Then I told him I was going home. He gave me a hug and he told me he would call me later on tonight. When, I made it home. My granny said, "Zaneeya, did you tell Brandon what I told you to tell him?" "Oh, I forgot granny, but I'll tell him when he calls tonight." "Ok, make sure you do. Dinner is ready, so you can eat when you want to." I did my homework first. Then I showered. When I got out the shower, I ate dinner. My granny made some turkey wings, white rice, cabbage with some smoke neck bones in it and some corn bread. When I was eating, Susan called me. I told her I was eating and I was going to call her back. As I was eating, I told my granny that the food was good. She said, "I'm glad you like it." I called Susan back. She said, "Zaneeya, I can't believe you didn't tell me that you and Brandon are a couple." "I was going to tell you and Jessica at the same time. Have you talked to Bernard?" "No not yet. I wanted to text him. Do you think I should?" "If you want too, but I would wait a couple of days first, but you can still talk to him at school." "Ok, that's what I'm going to do." Brandon was calling me on my other line. I said, "Susan, I have to go I'll see you at school tomorrow." "Why are you getting off the phone?" "Brandon is on my other line and I'm going to click over for him." "Ok, talk to your boo bye." I answered the other line. I said, "Hello." He replied, "It took you long enough to answer." "I was talking to Susan. What are you doing?" "I'm playin the video game and talking to you." "You cannot multitask, so stop trying." "Yes I can, watch. What are you bout to do?" "I was going to read my Spanish book, so I can study my vocabulary. I thought you were going to call me later." "I was, but I want to talk to you right now. Do you want to go back to Mr. Wing's class for lunch?" "Yeah we can go. I don't know what I want to eat for lunch tomorrow. I think I just want a sandwich, or some nachos and some juice." "That sounds good. I think I want some nachos too, everybody be talkin about how good the donut shop nachos are. I'm going to try them tomorrow."

"Brandon, do you know an older lady at your church by the name of Miss. Stella? She use to sit with Sister Davis when she was living, they were best friends." "I think I do know a lady at my church name Miss. Stella. Why?" "That's my granny, and Sister Davis is my Godmother. I use to go to your church when I was between the ages three and five years old." "No you didn't. I would have remembered you." "I did, I use to go to Sunday school early in the morning. I would always wear a dress to church and I would have a hat on my head. When it was time for Sunday school, my TT Neadda would take me upstairs. When Sunday school was over, they would line us up on the side of the church, and we all would walk into church together to attend 11:00 o'clock service. Your grandpa is Pastor Cobs, and every Sunday after church, he would give me $2 dollars. One day, I left my hat at church and my TT Neadda took me back to church, to get my hat and Pastor Cobs had it, and I went to get it from him. He gave me $2 dollars." "Dang, all this time we were around each other when we were kids and we didn't even know it. We went to the same Elementary School Peralta, Church and we have the same Godmother." "That's my Godmother not yours." "She was my Godmother too. She use to watch my sister and me at her house." "I miss her. I would be with her all the time. I would go with her to her doctor appointments. She would take my brothers and me to the movies. One day she dropped my brothers and I off at home, after leaving the movies and I did not want to go home. I was only five. I told my brothers bye. My TT Neadda said, "Zaneeya you have to go too." I said, "I'm going to your house." She said, "I'll pick you up tomorrow." Brandon said, "That is your Godmother! I remember her dog named Pebbles." I replied, "Yeah, I told you. My granny told me to tell you hi, I forgot to tell you when I was at school." "I know you did forget. You were so happy to see me that you couldn't think straight." "You're so funny, ha-ha, don't flatter yourself. I'm going to sleep, I am tired." "Ok good night, dream about me." "Good night." The next day I went to school, I went to go meet Brandon in the hallway. He walked me to class. At lunch, we went to the donut shop, and we

bought some nachos. Then we went to Mr. Wing's class. I showed Brandon a picture of my Godmother, and me when I was a little girl. She was hugging me in the picture. I had on a dress and she was dropping me off at home. Brandon looked at the picture. He said, "Aw look at you, you was a pretty little girl and my Godmother is gorgeous." We ate our lunch and we talked. Then when the bell ranged we went to class.

On my way to class, I saw Jessica. She asked me did I want to take driver's ed with her. I told her yeah. Driver's ed was a class that was early in the morning. To enroll in the class, you had to be in line at school by 6:50 AM or no later than 7:00 AM. It was first come, first serve. The driver's ed teacher was going to teach us about driving, and how to prepare us for our written permit test, that you would have to take in order to pass the class. If you study and passed your driver's ed class, you would be able to pass your written test at the DMV. When school was over that day, I went home and I told my granny about the driver's ed class. She asked me what time did I have to be at school. I told her around 7:00 AM at the latest. My granny said, "Ok, I'll walk with you to the bus stop, and you're going to have to catch the 13." "Ok granny, thank you." Brandon called me later on that night. My granny answered the phone. She was talking to him. She said, "I told Zaneeya I've known you ever since you were a little boy. Hold on, I'mma let you talk to Zaneeya, and I'll see you at church Sunday." I got on the phone. Brandon said, "Zaneeya, granny is so funny." "Don't be calling my granny, granny. She is not your granny!" "Yes she is my granny, and I'm going to tell her what you said too." "Go ahead. Who side you think she's going to take?" "My side once I see her, that's my granny like I said." "Yeah ok, are you going to sign up for driver's ed?" "I want too. I was thinking about it. Are you?" "Yes, I am going to be there early, because I know the line is going to be long. I just hope I can wake up every morning on time." "You will, but that's too early for me to be in school." After, Brandon and I got off the phone I went to bed. Everything was going good between Brandon and me, so I thought. I talked to Brandon and Jessica the night before driver's ed and they both said they would meet me at school. My granny waited with me at the bus stop. It was dark outside. The post office, was only a block away from are house. I was still sleepy it was 6:20 AM. The bus did not take long at all to come. My granny gave me a hug and she said, "I'll see you when you come home from school." I replied, "Ok granny." My granny walked back home. When I made it to school, I got in line. I did not see Jessica or Brandon.

I stood in line for 20-minutes then Jessica came in got in line. I said, "I thought you were going to meet me up here, and you were going to be on time." She replied, "I was, I had a hard time getting up. You know I'm not a morning person." "That is besides the point." She laughed. She said, "Where is Brandon, I thought he was coming?" "I don't know, he said he would be here." The driver's ed teacher opened up the door, to let us in the class. He said, "I will let all of you know when the class is too full. I am not able to take anymore students today, but when we have another opening for driver's ed. You all may come and sign up. Remember, it's first come, first serve. Thank you all for coming." The driver's ed teacher went back in the classroom. Jessica and I sat in the third row in the classroom. Are teacher told us the rules in class, and he told us that we would be taking our permit test today, just to see where everybody was. He said we were going to watch videos in class, about driving, and wearing your seat belts. He also was going to cover everything else that had to do with driving. He passed out the permit test and he went over the test before he let us take it. When I was taking the test, I was thinking to myself. I don't know any of this. I know I am going to fail this test right now. After, I was finished taking my test I looked at it. We had to pass are test up, to the person that was sitting right in front of us, so the teacher could collected it. The teacher graded our test before class was over. I didn't pass my test, which I knew I wasn't. I got 19 problems wrong. I was just happy, that I wasn't the only one in class that didn't know what they were doing, because most of the class got 17 problems and more wrong. When class was over, Brandon was standing outside waiting for me. I gave him a hug. He said, "I seen you when you were going inside of the classroom, but I didn't want to cut everybody else in line. So I just waited for you to come out, and I walked around the school." "Oh, ok. Jessica, where are you going?" "I'm going to find Desseire." "Ok, I'll see you at the break." Brandon and I went downstairs to sit down. When the bell ranged, I went to class. At the 15-minute break, I went outside to talk to Jessica, and Susan. I asked Susan has she talked to Bernard on the phone yet. She said, "Yeah, I just started talking to him on the phone." I said, "Oh, look at you and you're boo, I know your excited." "I am, and he sounds so sexy on the phone." "I don't need to know that, but I'm glad to see you happy."

When lunch came, Brandon and I went to Mr. Wing's class and Susan, and Bernard came in there as well. We all were talking. Brandon and I were making fun of Susan and Bernard. When the bell ranged to go to class, I saw Nathan, we started taking. He said, "Dang best friend we don't talk every night no more ever since you and Brandon got together." I replied, "Yes we do, stop it. You are my best friend, cut it out." "I'm just playin, I'll see you later best friend." "Ok." I went to class. When, I was in class. Sammie said, "Zaneeya *do you go with Brandon?" "Yes I do. Why you ask me that?" "I just wanted to know. Somebody said you did, and I just wanted to ask you myself, man I don't like him!" "You don't like Brandon?" "No, and I don't know why you like him. He is so cocky and he thinks he can have any girl he wants. I don't know what you see in him, he use to go with MJ." "Oh, I didn't know that and he's nice to me."*

"Would you break up with him if he cheated on you?" "Yes I would and he knows that too." "Just be careful with him, I do not like him." "Ok Sammie, I will. Don't worry about him though." When class was over, I went to my next class. I did my classwork and my teacher put on a video. 30-minutes before the bell ranged to get out of school. As I watched the video, I kept thinking about what Sammie said. When the bell ranged, I left. I went to say bye to Brandon. When I got home from school, I did my homework. Then I showered, ate and went to bed. Brandon called me. So my granny woke me up and gave me the phone. She said, "Zaneeya this is Brandon on the phone." I said, "Hello." He said, "Wake up, why are you sleeping so early?" "I'm tired. I've been up since 5:00 AM this morning." We talked for a little while, Brandon told me that he would be waiting for me outside of my driver's ed class, when it over. I said, "Ok." The next morning I went to my driver's ed class, we watched a video. Then when class was over Jessica and I left. I didn't see Brandon. So as Jessica and I was walking down the stairs. I looked down the hallway, and I seen Brandon hugging another girl, as she was resting her head on him. Jessica said, "Zaneeya what are you looking at?" "Brandon and Celie is hugged up girl, hold on a minute. I'm going to walk over there." "No, don't do that. Don't even let him know you see him." "Just wait, I want to make eye contact with him, to let him know that I see him." "Ok." Brandon turned around and I looked at him, and smiled. He looked at me like he just seen a ghost. He pushed Celie off him. I shook my head at him and went down the stairs. I said, "Come on Jessica let's go." She replied, "Did he see you?" "Yeah he did. I'm done with him." "You're going to break up with him?" "Yes I am. He supposed to be my boyfriend, and he's going to disrespect me like that. By being hugged up with the next chick, and he no, I don't even like her and she ain't seven cute, he can have her."

"She's really not though, and maybe you should talk to him about it first, before you just break up with him." "I'm not talking to him about nothing. So he can lie about it. I know what I saw and it ain't nothing he can say or do that's going to make me stay with him. I'm done and I'm not going to speak to him today." I went to class. I was mad at Brandon, and I was thinking

about the look that he had on his face, when he seen me. When it was time to go to the 15- minute break, I went to buy me a cookie. Then I went to talk to Jessica and Susan. Susan said, "Zaneeya, Brandon is over there sitting by Bernard." "I don't care." "What's wrong with you now?" Brandon walked by us and Susan spoke to him. She said, "Brandon, what did you do to Zaneeya?" Brandon just stared at me and he walked toward me as if he wanted to give me a hug. I said, "I'll see y'all later. I'm going to class." Susan said, "Barndon what's wrong with Zaneeya?" He replied, "I don't know." At lunch, I ate by myself. I did not want to be bothered. I seen Brandon and I did not say nothing to him. Bernard said hi to me and I said hi back to him. Bernard said, "Why y'all not eatin lunch together?" Brandon said, "I don't know what's wrong with her." I said, "You know why, but I'm not mad, and you know what you did! Think about it." Bernard said, "What happen?" The bell ranged to go to class. I said, "Brandon, I'm happy you enjoyed your time with Celie, while y'all were hugged up. Y'all can be hugged up everyday. You don't have to worry about me. I'll see you later Bernard." Bernard said, "Ok Zaneeya." Brandon said, "We were not even hugged up, I do not want her I want you. She was crying and I gave her my shoulder to cry on, that's all." I replied, "That's good, and you can continue to give her your shoulder too. I'm not mad at you anymore, trust me." I went to class and just did my classwork. When the bell ranged to go home, I went to say bye to Jessica and Susan. Jessica said, "I'll call you later." I said, "Ok." Brandon just looked at me. I looked backed at him and shook my head and I walked to the bus stop. When, I got home from school. My granny said, "How was your day, and did you see Brandon at school?" I replied, "My day was ok granny and yeah I seen him." I did my homework, and I talked to Nathan for a little while. I told him what happened. He couldn't believe it, he asked me was I going to break up with Brandon. I said, "I'm not with him, far as I'm concern and I will let him know that tonight. I know he's going to call me later." After, I got off the phone with Nathan. I got my school clothes out for the next day. Then Brandon called me, so I answered. I said, "Hello." He said, "What are you doing?" "What's up?" "I just wanted to talk to you."

"Call Celie, and talk to her. You didn't want to talk to me earlier this morning. When you was supposed to meet me, after my driver's ed class was over. You think what you did was ok, and it makes me not want to be with you even more. You would not like it if my head was on Sammie's shoulder or his head was on my shoulder, and you know it." "Your right. I wouldn't like it, but it's not even like that. I was on my way to your class, but she said hi and I said hi and she started crying. She came up to me and she put her head on

my shoulder." "I was looking at you for 5-minutes, and when you seen me you pushed her off of you." "I don't want her, I want you!" "Well, I can't be with you. It's over, I'm not going to let that slide at all. I told you if you cheated on me, I'm not going to be with you." "I didn't cheat on you though." "You didn't far as I know, but hey you could have kissed her. How I know? If I didn't see you hugged up with her, I know you wouldn't have told me."

"Yes I would have, you're taking this too far." "No, you did when you decided to be hugged up with her." "So you're really breaking up with me?" "Yes I am. You can talk to whoever you want too! I have to go." I hung up the phone and I got in the shower. After, I got out the shower. I went to bed. The next day at school, I did not say anything to Brandon. He looked at me and he would walk over to me, but I would just walk away. I did not speak to Brandon for three weeks. He finally walked up to me at lunch. He said, "Hi Zaneeya, so are you really going to keep ignoring me?" I replied, "Hi Brandon." He smiled. He said, "Can I talk to you for a minute." "You have 5- minutes." "Are you still mad at me?" "No I'm not." "I don't want her. I told you it wasn't like that. Can we be friends at least?" "I don't know." "Stop acting like that, we use to be close." "I thought we were too, but clearly you did not feel the same way." "Yes I did. That's why I was trying to talk to you. I didn't want us to break up, and you know that. So can we be friends and start from here?" "Yeah we can be friends and that's it." He smiled and said, "Ok, that's all I want. Now I can tell Susan were friends." He yelled, "Susan we are back together!" She said, "Y'all are back together?" "Yeah we are." I said, "No were not! We are just friends, and that's it. We are not getting back together." He said, "Can I have a hug?" "No you cannot, I am going to class." "I'm going to call you later." I kept walking.

I went to my auntie Jannette's job after school. So I could talk to her. She said, "You're going to work every weekend, and every holiday. I'm going to give you five days a week to work. You need black pants, a white shirt and all black shoes. You need to come to work already dressed in your uniform and ready to work. You have to clock into work everyday at 4:30 PM. So be on time. I will see you tomorrow." I replied, "Thank you auntie." I gave Jannette a hug. I went home and I told my granny that I have a job. My granny said, "That's good you're going to be working. What time do you start work, and what time do you get off work?" "I start work at 4:30 PM and I get off work, at 8 o'clock every night. I am going to work five days a week." "How are you going to get home after work?" "I'm going to catch the bus. Jannette said all of her employees catch the bus home too." "Make sure you be careful on your

*way home." "I'll be fine granny. Soon as I get off work, I'm going to walk to
the 51 bus stop. Then, I'm going to get off downtown and get on the 19 bus
to come home." "Ok, when do you start working?" "I start work tomorrow.
I already have some all black shoes and pants, and I have an all white shirt.
I am so excited granny. I cannot wait to work, and I can still work for my
school. Now I have two jobs!" "I know, now you will have more money."
After talking to my granny, I showered, ate then I got ready for bed. The next
morning I went to school. I did not tell anyone that I had a job. I couldn't
wait to get out of school, so I could go to work. The day went by fast. Before
school ended, I asked Miss. Regeiro could I go to the rest room everyday, before
the bell ranged. So I could change into my work clothes. She said, "Zaneeya,
you have another job?" "Yes." "Congratulations, I am so happy for you and I
am so proud of you." "Thank you, Miss. Regeiro." "You're welcome and yes.
You can leave 20-minutes before the bell rang, to go change your clothes. Just
come back." "Ok, I will." Before the bell ranged, I went to get dress for work,
and I put my clothes that I had on in my backpack. When I went back to
class, everybody was looking at me. When, the bell ranged to go home. Miss.
Regeiro said, "Have a good day at work Zaneeya." "Thank you." I walked
up to Nathan. He said, "Best friend, where are you going dressed like that?"
"I'm going to work." "You have another job?" "Yes, I do and I am so happy."
"Congratulation best friend, I'm proud of you! Call me tonight." "Thank you
best friend and ok, I will."*

*Rebbeca came up to me. She said, "Zaneeya where are you going? Wait,
you started working with auntie Jannette huh?" "Yeah, today is my first day at
work." Rebbeca smiled. She said, "I am so happy for you." "Thanks Rebbeca."
"Can you still get me a job there?" "Yeah, I haven't forgotten. I'm going to talk
to Jannette tomorrow for you." "Ok Zaneeya, I know you're going to hook me
up. You're my best cousin." "I got you just let me handle it." Brandon came
up to me. He said, "Zaneeya, why are you dressed like that?" Rebbeca said,
"She's going to work, that's why." "Oh, you have another job?" I replied, "Yes
I do and I'm on my way to it. I'll see y'all later." Brandon said, "You look
good in your uniform too." Rebbeca said, "You're just nasty." Brandon said,
"What, I can't give her a compliment? She do look good, it's the truth." When
I arrived to work, I went straight to the breakroom. It was only 4:00 PM. I
was 30-minutes early. Some of the employees came in the breakroom and
spoke to me. Some didn't speak at all, and I didn't either. Vida came in the
breakroom. I've been knowing Vida for a while, because Vida and Jannette
are best friends. Vida said, "Zaneeya, Jannette wants to see you in her office."*

I went to Jannette's office. I said, "Hi auntie?" She replied, "Hi niece. Are you ready to work?" "Yes I am." "Put your stuff behind my door and turn off your phone. You cannot have your phone out on the floor." Jannette told Vida to come here. Jannette said, "Vida I need you to train Zaneeya today. Show her how to do everything in the diningroom. Show her how to put out the butters, and creamers, and the cracker baskets. Show her how to make the coffee, and show her how to do the salad bar. I want her to set up the diningroom tonight. Give her the back diningroom. Show her where everything is and show her how to make a busting cart. Then next week, we will put her on pots and pans." Vida replied, "Ok Jannette." Vida showed me how to do everything. I clocked in early, because Jannette told me too. I filled up the cracker basket. I put the butters creamers out. I washed out the chairs, and I put the juice and the salad bar out. Then I made some coffee. When, the 4:30 crew came to work. They said, "Jannette, everything is out already. What do you want us to do?" She replied, "Clean out the chairs, it's something to do. Vida make them clean. Keep them busy." Vida was my supervisor. She was lead supervisor. Vida gave me a section, but she showed me what to do. I had to ask the residents what they wanted to drink and what they wanted to eat for dinner.

At each table, there were five residents, accept for the long tables and we only had two of those. The long tables sat six people. Everybody had a full section and everybody had five tables, unless you were a floater. A floater had to go and help each person in his or her section. Rather it was pouring the residents juice or taking the food out to the residents, or bringing them their desert. Vida said, "Zaneeya you can only take five plates at a time. Make sure you always get the residents orders right and never argue with the residents." After, the residents ate their food I brought the residents their desert. Dinner started at 5:00 PM and it ended at 6:00 PM. After dinner was over, we had to bring the residents there walkers and wheel chairs to them. After the residents left, we had to bust the tables that were in our section. I had to put the plates in buckets. The glasses in one bucket, the coffee cups in one bucket, and the silverware was all together in a bucket with soap in water. I had to throw the placemats away and wash off the tables with soap and water. When I was done, I had to take my busting cart to the kitchen. Then I went to set up the diningroom, by putting placemats on the tables and napkins. I had to set 22 tables. I had to go to the kitchen to get my glasses, coffee cups and coffee plates and my silverware. After, I was finished setting the dinningroom up, I had to vacuum the floors. Then I filled up the cracker basket and sugars. I was tired, by the end of the night. Vida said, "Zaneeya you can sit down. Are you tired?"

"Yes Vida. I have never worked like this before." "You will get use to it trust me. I'll give you two more days. You're a quick learner and your fast on your feet too." "Thanks Vida." Vida said, "It's 8:00 PM. It's time to clock out let's go." "Ok, Vida I'll see you tomorrow." "Ok Zaneeya, be careful." "Ok, I am." I walked to the bus stop and my co-workers did too. I got on the bus and I went straight home. When I got home, I was tired. I hurried up and took off my shoes. My granny said, "How was, work?" I replied, "Work was fine. I learned a lot, I'm tired now." "I know you are tired." After talking to my granny, I got in the shower. Then I ate and went to bed.

The next day, I went to work after school. Vida was still training me. I learned quickly on what to do. After work, I went home. My granny was waiting for me on the front pouch. When I walked up, the OG's said, "Here she comes momma." They were looking out for me. My granny said, "I just walked back out here to see where you were." I said, "Granny, you better stay inside the house. It's too dangerous for you to be comin outside at night." "I'm not going any further then the porch and everybody be looking out for me. When I come outside they say momma, were looking out for you. She hasn't made it yet." Living in the Bay Area was ruff. People were getting killed everyday. People would fight constantly. It was crack heads outside. Soon as I step foot outside, people was selling drugs. The Bay Area was full of violence. When I came in the house, I only was there for about 15- minutes and there was a knock on the front door. My uncle T said, "Who is it?" It was my dad and Toniya. They both walked into my granny room. My dad said, "How was your first day at work?" I gave Toniya and my dad a hug. I said, "Today wasn't my first day at work, but work was good." My dad said, "Today wasn't your first day at work?" "No, it was not." "Well, how is school going?" "School is going good." "Well, I went up to your school today and I talked to your principal Miss. Petter." "Why are you going up to my school?" "I went up to your school so I can get a copy of your report card. I went to the attendance office and they told me that I was not on your emergency card. So, they couldn't give me any information. I asked them could I speak with someone, like a principal, and they told where the principal's office was. So I waited and I went to talk to Miss. Petter. She said what can I do for you? I told her I was your dad and I wanted a copy of your report card. She said I am not on your emergency card, but she gave me a copy anyways. You're not doing too well in school and you have one B+, three C+ and two D." "I know what my grades are." "Look, I thought you said you were doing good. Evidently, you're not and I can go get a copy of your grades anytime. I want too and there is nothing you can do *about that." "Actually, there is something I can do. I'm not worried about you. You will never get another copy of my grades. That's why I took you off my emergency card. You're not the type of parent to help me bring up my grades. You just wanted to get a copy of my grades, so you can be nosy and make fun of me." "I'm not being nosy. I can have you removed from OT High and it is funny. You said you're doing good and you're not."*

"I am doing well, and you can never have me removed from OT trust me." "I can make you come live with me right now it's, because of me you live with your granny." "You cannot make me do anything and I will never live with you again." "Ok Zaneeya, that's why you're failing in school and you're not going to make it to the 10th grade." "You wish, but that's not going to happen and I am done talking to you." My granny said, "Justin, by law you are not supposed to get a copy of her report card. She lives with me and I am going to make sure I talk to her principal. By law, she is at the age where she can say where she wants to live and you do not have custody over her! Bella does and I am not going to have this in my house period." He replied, "I have custody over her too. Bella and I share custody." "You do not share custody! Bella and you went to court when those kids were younger. When I was living on 32nd and Martin Luther King and you were late coming to court. When you got there, the Judge already granted Bella soul custody over Justin Jr., Qin and Zaneeya, and it's been that way ever since." I said, "That's right granny." Toniya said, "Let's go." My dad said, "I'm still going up to your school now." "I know you are, but you are not going to be able to get any more copies of my report cards. While you are putting all this energy into what I am doing, you need to go find your daughter." "I'll call Jannette and tell her to fire you right now. The only reason why she hired you is because, I told her too." "Their you go lying again! You did not know anything about me wanting a job with Jannette because I didn't tell you and Jannette didn't either. This been took place before I left Letha house. So stop trying to make yourself look good in front of Toniya. You did not have anything to do with Jannette hiring me, and you cannot have me fired. Sorry you do not have those rights." "That's what you think. You are not on my level of thinking anyways. I forgot I was talking to a 15 year old, who does not have a brain at all. You cannot even think on an adult level. I am so much smarter then you, and even when you get older, I will always be. Keep failing in school, all of your friends are going to go to the 10th grade and you are still going to be in the 9th grade. You already got held back once you'll think you learned your lesson!" "Say whatever you want too. That's why none of your kids do not have a relationship with you. What type

of dad, makes fun of his daughter and say the things you say? None and I am done talking to you bye leave."

"*Oh I'm leaving, but you can't shut me up and nothing you said is true. Toniya knows about everything.*" "*I can shut you up, bye Toniya.*"*I shut the front door in my dad's face as he was still talking. My granny said, "Your dad just wanted to go up to your school to make fun of you and to have something to talk about. He is not the type of dad that will help his kids if they were failing in school. He just wanted to throw it in your face that's all. I'm happy you spoke up, you needed too. Your dad has said mean things to hurt you and your brothers over, and over, and that's not right. When you go to school tomorrow, tell Miss. Petter to call me. I'm going to call your mom and tell her what happened.*" I replied, "*Your right granny, I will.*" "*Do not worry about what your dad said.*" "*I am not worried about him. We are always going to have a relationship like this! He is not a father at all! He has always said mean things to my brothers and me. He told Justin Jr., and Qin he wish his blood wasn't running through their veins. He told us that we weren't supposed to be here and we are mistakes.*" "*That's so discussing! If he was a real father, he would not say those things to his kids, but he never was a father to y'all anyway. Yes your brothers and you lived with him a couple of times when y'all were younger, but it wasn't for a year or anything like that.*" "*I know granny. I am not worried about my dad, and I am not going to let him say mean things to me and get away with it any more forget that*" "*I do not blame you. That's why Qin does not have anything to do with him.*" After, my granny and I finished are conversation. I went to take a shower. After I got out of the shower, I did my homework and went to bed. The next day, I went to school, I went straight to Miss. Petter's office. I said, "Hi Miss. Petter I need to talk to you. " "Ok, what's going on Zaneeya?" "My dad told me that he came to see you yesterday, and he is not on my emergency card. I took him off. So why did you give him a copy of my report card?" "Well, your dad is a charmer. He was saying he's the one who takes care of you even though you live with your granny. He was really concern about how you were doing in school." "He lied! My dad does not take care of me! I do live with my granny. I lived with my dad for a week an a half and that was it. He does not give me any money and he has never bought me any clothes. If I don't have any money, my granny will give it to me. She is very upset right now, because you gave him a copy of my report card and I am too. My dad came to my house last night and we got into it over this.*"

"*I am so sorry Zaneeya. I did not know you and your dad did not get along. He is not on your emergency card! So, I will not give him any more copies of your report cards or anything else, but he is a charmer and your dad is fine. He was telling me about how he works, and how he always took care of you and your siblings." "Well, he lied to you and he does not take care of none of us! Did my dad tell you that he has six kids?" "No he didn't." "He has five kids living and my two older brothers and I have the same mom and dad. I have a sister who I am three months older than. Yes, he was with my mom and he cheated. He don't even know where my younger sister is. He lied to you, just so he can get a copy of my report card. Let me guess, he was flirting with you as well, and he was telling you how beautiful you are and maybe y'all should go to lunch." Miss. Petter shook her head. She said, "Yes he did! Damn your dad is a charmer. He has a lot of kids, let's call your granny." Miss. Petter called my granny. She said, "Hi, this is Miss. Petter. Zaneeya's principal. How are you doing?" My granny replied, "Hi Miss. Petter. I'm doing fine. I wanted to talk to you, because Justin Sr., doesn't have a right to get a copy of her report card. She does not live with her dad. She lives with me. She took her dad off her emergency card. So I don't know why he has a copy." "Well, Miss. Stella that was my fault. I knew he wasn't on her emergency card, but he was saying he took care of her and a whole lot of other things, but you don't have to worry about that again. I will not give him any more copies of nothing else." "Justin Sr., lied. He doesn't take care of none of his kids. He owes child support for all his kids, but thank you so much for calling me." "Wow, he acts like he has been a great dad to all of his kids, but you're welcome. Zaneeya is my girl. She is really a good student, her grades dropped a little, but she has enough time to pick them back up. It's not like she's failing. She just don't have the grades that she normally would have right now, but she is very determined and she will be fine." "Thank you and yes she will. It was nice talking to you. Tell Zaneeya I will see her when she gets off work." "Ok, it was nice talking to you too bye." Miss.Petter hung up the phone. She said, "Zaneeya you have another job?" "Yes I do. I go to work after school." "Look at you, go ahead girl. Just keep going to school and working, everything will work out, and don't worry about your dad, go to class ok." "Thank you Miss. Petter, I need a pass to go to class." "Ok, I'll right you one, here you go. I'll see you later." "Ok bye." I walked to class. When I got to class, I gave the pass to my teacher. Then I did my classwork, when the bell ranged I didn't go to the 15- minute break I went straight to my next class.*

When I went to class, I asked my teacher could I start my classwork. Then could I start my homework, after I was finished with my classwork. She said, "Yeah." My teacher explained my classwork to me. Then she explained my homework to me then I started to work on it. When the rest of my classmates came inside the classroom, I was already doing my classwork. I told myself I was going to do my homework in class everyday. So I wouldn't have to do my homework when I got off of work. When lunch came, I seen Rebbeca and we went to lunch. I seen Nathan and I started talking to him. Nathan asked me did I like changing old people diapers. I said, "I do not change the residents diapers, they have a nurse to do that. I work in food services. I bring the residents there food and drinks." "Oh ok best friend, I thought you changed their diapers." I laughed. I said, "I cannot wait until the school year goes by." He replied, "Why?" "So I can work more hours at work, so I can buy my school clothes and get the things that I need." "I feel you. Your birthday is coming up. What are you doing for your birthday?" "I don't know yet. Whatever I do I want you to come with me."

"Ok, I will best friend just let me know ahead of time." "Ok I will." When the bell ranged I went to class. I asked my teacher could I start on my classwork soon as I got in class, and after I was done with my classwork can I do my homework. He said, "Yes, and if you need help just raise your hand and I will help you." I did all of my classwork and my homework in class. When I went to 6ᵗʰ period, I knew Miss. Regeiro would let me do my homework in class. I went to class and asked Miss. Regeiro can I do my classwork and homework in class, she told me yes. Before the bell ranged to go home, I went to the bathroom to get dress for work. When, I went back to class. I turned in my homework and my classwork. When the bell ranged I left. I went to go talk to Nathan, Jessica, and Rebbeca and Brandon for a little while. Then I walked to work. When I got to work, I told Jannette what happened between my dad and me. I told her that my dad said he could get me fired. Jannette said, "That's a damn shame my brother acts like that with his kids. Do not worry about him. He does not have a say in what goes on here, and I did not hire you because of him. I hired you because you wanted to work. He never talked to me about getting you a job! You called me on your own. Do not worry about your dad. I'm telling you, my brother know not to come up here with all that foolishness. Trust me he knows better. Your auntie does not play when it comes to that.

Go clock in and get ready for work. Put everything out for me. Tonight you're going to have your own section. I know you can handle it. You're a fast worker and a quick learner." "Ok auntie." I put the juice out, the butters and creamers, the cracker baskets and I filled up the sugars. Then Vida showed me how to set the trays for room service. Each tray had an order written out on it, stating what type of food they wanted and what room they were in. When,

I would deliver the food to the residents room. I would ring the doorbell and the residents would say come in, or they would come to the door and get their tray. Some of the residents rooms smelled like pee, booboo and cigarettes. After, delivering their food, I would go back to the kitchen to take the cart back that I had. Then I would go to the diningroom and start working in my section. I would take the residents walkers and line them up against the wall. Then I would get a pitcher of cranberry juice or tomato juice and I would pour them a glass. I would take their order, and then I would go to the kitchen and tell the cooks what I wanted. Vida said we only could take five plates at a time, but I took ten plates at a time and so was everybody else. Some of my co-workers asked me did I need help. I told them no, but thank you and I finished working. When dinner was over, I did the front diningroom. Jannette was leaving. She said by to everybody. After my co-workers and I was finished working. Vida would let us sit down. My cousin wife worked in the same department as I did. Her name was Gena. She would say hi to me and we would talk a little. When it was time to go home, we all clocked out and left. I said bye to Vida, and I walked to the bus stop. When I would get off work, it would be so dark outside. I was kind of nervous, because so much was going on in the Bay Area. People were getting shot from left to right. Some of the people that went to my school, they would sell drugs on the corner by my house. When, I went in the house. My granny said, "Zaneeya, your birthday is coming up. What do you want for your birthday?"

"I don't know yet granny, surprise me." "Ok, I'll think of something. You know what I was thinking. You should tell your auntie Jannette about what your dad said to you, about how he can get you fired." "I did granny. She told me not to worry about that." "Ok, I'm glad you told her." I did my daily routine then I went to bed. The next day at work, I talked to auntie Jannette. I asked her could she hire Rebbeca. Jannette said, "Is she responsible, and what if her mom doesn't let her work and I hire her? That means, I wasted my time and I would have to find someone else to hire!" I replied, "Her mom would let her work, and she would show up to work everyday. She is responsible and she needs a job too. Auntie, if things don't work out while Rebbeca is here, you do not have to hire anyone else that I recommend." "Ok, tell her to come up here in two weeks with you after school. Tell her to be ready to work. Tell her I do not play and she has to come on time, and take this application to her, have her fill it out and bring it back to me. Tell her to wear all black shoes, all black pants and a white shirt."

"Ok auntie I will, thank you." "I'm taking your word on this Zaneeya, she better be ready to work." "She will be auntie." After work, I couldn't wait to go home. I did not want to call Rebbeca and tell her over the phone that I got her a job. I wanted to tell her in person. So, I went home and I told my granny that Jannette is going to hire Rebbeca. My granny said, "That's good that y'all will be working together. Are you going to call her and tell her?" "No, I'm going to tell her at school tomorrow." I showered, ate, then did my homework and I went to bed. I couldn't wait to tell Rebbeca the good news. It felt like I was getting a new job and I already had two jobs. At the 15-minute break. I told Rebbeca to meet me in the back of the school, so we could go to lunch, because I had to give her something that was extremely important. She said, "What is it Zaneeya, tell me now?" "No, I don't have time. We have to go back to class, but I will give it to you at lunch." "Now, I'm going to be wondering what it is that you're going to give me." "Well keep wondering. I have to go class, bye see you at lunch." When it was time to go to lunch, I told Rebbeca to let's go get something to eat. She said, "What's the surprise." I replied, "We have to sit down first. Then I'll give it to you." "Ok, where do you want to eat at?" "Let's go to Burger King. I want two double cheeseburgers with fires and an apple juice." "Ok." So Rebbeca and I walked to Burger King. After we got our food, we sat down and ate it. Rebbeca said, "Now can I have my surprise please?"

"Oh yeah." I said as if I forgot. I said, "Here, read this." I handed her the application. As she was reading it, she started smiling. She said, "I thought you forgot all about me. I knew you were going to get me hired, but I just didn't know how soon." "I didn't forget about you. I talked to auntie Jannette yesterday. You need to wear all black pants and shoes. You need an all-White shirt. Oh yeah, you also need a tie to wear. We all have to wear ties now, but they are ordering us some bow ties, but I'm still going to wear a tie or switch them up. You also have to be to work on time everyday. Fill this application out, because I have to take it back to her today. Then, in two weeks you are going to start work." "Ok, thank you Zaneeya. I cannot wait to work. Is the work hard to do?" "No, it's not hard. You are going to be very tired when you get off work, but you'll get use to it. It's kind of fun to be honest. I like my job. I learn something new everyday." "Ok, I'm going to fill this out in class and I'm going to give it to you after school." After we ate, we walked back to school. Then we went to class. After school, I meet up with Rebbeca and she gave me her application then I went to work. When I got to work, I went in Jannette's office and I gave her Rebbeca's application. Jannette said, "Zaneeya, I might need Rebbeca before two weeks, because I think I'm going to fire someone. So *tell her to come here tomorrow. Matter of fact, call her for me. Do you think she can get her work clothes and everything else today?" "Yes she can. I'm going to call her right now, she should be home." I called Rebbeca she answered the phone. She said, "Hello, Zaneeya." "Rebbeca I'm calling you for auntie Jannette. She wants to talk to you." Auntie Jannette got on the phone. She said, "Hey Rebbeca, I'mma need you to start work tomorrow. Do you think you can buy your work clothes today?" "Yes I can auntie that's not a problem." "Ok good, I'll see you tomorrow. Come to work with Zaneeya." "Ok auntie thank you." When, Jannette got off the phone. She said, "Zaneeya I need you to clock in for me and get to work." I said, "Ok auntie." I had another supervisor besides Vida. His name was Thomas. He was nice too and he was very helpful. When Jannette needed something done, she would call Vida and Thomas and they would come. Jannette had a beautiful relationship with Vida and Thomas. Even though Vida and Jannette were best friends and Jannette was Vida's boss, they got along great. They knew how to separate the two and Jannette looked out for Vida and Vida looked out for Jannette. They respected each other, and they truly loved each other and I liked their friendship, they were like sisters.*

When an employee got mad and they did not want to do what Vida told them to do. They would go get Jannette, and Jannette would say, "Do what Vida told you to do or you can go home." Jannette did not take no, mess from nobody and you were not going to disrespect Vida and not listen to her, because Jannette was not having it and Vida was not either. The girls at work started speaking to me. I got along with everybody accept for this girl named Kathy. She was always rolling her eyes at me. She would play a lot at work and Vida would always have to talk to her. When she didn't listen to Vida, that's when Jannette stepped in. Jannette would say, "Look Kathy, I'm going to send you home for good if you don't listen to Vida. I'm not playin with you at all and either is Vida. When Vida ask you to do something you do it, and if you don't you're going to be fired." Kathy would say, "Jannette I'm going to listen. I love you Jannette." "You heard what I said." After dinner, we would make our busting carts, and Kathy was in the back of me and she was huffing and puffing. She said, "Dang Zaneeya can you hurry up and walk?" I didn't say nothing, I just took my time. When I came back in kitchen from busting my tables, I saw Kathy roll her eyes again. I got some glasses that I needed for the diningroom, so I can set my tables. Kathy said, "You can't take those glasses until the rest of them are done. So leave those here then come back." "I'm taking these glasses right now. Then I'm going to come back for some more."

"You have to come back for some more, so why not wait and just go put your placemats out ok." "You need to mind your business and worry about what you are supposed to be doing, like doing the dishes. Jannette did not leave you in charge. I will not be taking orders from nobody, but my boss and that's Jannette, Vida and Thomas and you do not look like any of those people." "Ok, whatever you're new. I'll take my time on these dishes." "That's what you're not going to do! I'm not gonna play no games with you at all. Trust me you will be setting the diningroom up yourself after you're done with the dishes, so hurry up." Vida came in the kitchen and she heard Kathy and me arguing. She said, "I'm going to get Jannette." Jannette came in the kitchen. She said, "What's the problem now?" Kathy said, "I was telling your niece, that she does not need to take, those glasses that's in the rack already. She needs to go put her placemats on the tables first. Then come back for some glasses, but she won't listen." I said, "And I told Kathy, she needs to mind her business. I am not taking order from nobody, but Jannette, Vida and Thomas. If she takes her time doing the dishes, she will be setting up the diningroom herself." Jannette said, "Kathy you don't tell nobody what to do and I'm not going to have any more mess from you. You need to worry about yourself. You don't give orders, I do. She can have those glasses there ready and Zaneeya has to set the diningroom not you. So why are you in her business? The next time you start mess with somebody you're going to get fired, I'm tired of you.

Zaneeya don't argue with anyone. Next time just come get me, Vida or Thomas ok." "Ok auntie, I'm sorry for arguing, but I don't like her." "Let me handle Kathy." "Ok auntie." When Jannette was leaving, she said bye to everyone. After, everybody was done with their job duties, they all came and sat in the diningroom. When it was time to get off work, we all clocked out and left. I walked to the bus stop with a few co-workers. When I got off the bus downtown, I went inside of Burger King to get me something to eat. After, I got my food. I got on the 19 bus to go home. When I got home, my granny said, "How was work?" I told her what happen. My granny said, "That's good Jannette checked her, next time you should just go tell Jannette and that way you don't have to worry about arguing." I said, "Granny, I am not going to run and tell Jannette about an argument. In less I get mad enough where I am going to hit somebody and you know I am hot headed." "I know you are." I took a shower. Then I talked to Nathan on the phone for a little while. Then I went to bed. The next day after school, Brandon asked me to hang out with him for a while. I told him I had to go to work. He said, "Call in, don't go." I said, "Boy please, I'm not about to call into work for you. That's my job and I need my job. That's my income and I need my money, but I'll see you later." "You can call off work today." "I can, but I'm not going too." *Rebbeca and I went to work. As we were walking to work, Rebbeca told me she was nervous. I said, "You'll be fine." When we arrived to work, we went to Jannette's office. Jannette said, "Zaneeya, I need you to clock in. I know it's early, but I'm going to have you clock in everyday at 4:00 PM instead of 4:30. Plus, that's a little extra money in your pocket. After you clock in, come back to my office." I went to clock in, and I said hi to my other boss. His name is Ryan. Ryan's dad was the owner of the Claremont house and they were good friends with Jannette and my grandma. Ryan called my grandma, mom and they were like family. Ryan would joke with us at work. He was very nice and so was his dad. After I clocked in, I walked back to Jannette's office. She said, "Niece, I want you to train Rebbeca. Your good enough, you will be showing her everything that she needs to know. I want you to train her in your section tonight." I replied, "Ok auntie." "Thank you niece." "You're welcome auntie." I showed Rebbeca where everything was and how to set up everything.*

At dinner, Vida gave Rebbeca and me a section to work in. I showed *Rebbeca how to greet the residents and how to serve as a server. I said, "Rebbeca, we are only supposed to take five plates at a time. That means one table at a time, but I take two tables at a time and everybody else does too. It's faster that way. You just have to remember what your residents asked for." Rebbeca and I worked good as a team and I was happy that I got her hired. After serving dinner, we bought the residents their desert. After they ate their desert, we gave the residents their walkers back. We went to the kitchen and I showed Rebbeca how to make a busting cart. After we made our butting carts, we went back into the diningroom to bust are tables. I showed Rebbeca how to set the tables for the next day. I showed her where the napkin goes on the placemats. Where the water glasses goes and where the coffee cups went and where the forks, knifes, spoons and soup spoons went. After we were finished, we vacuumed the floors. Jannette came inside the diningroom. She said, "Good job my nieces. It looks good in here and Zaneeya you did a good job training Rebbeca. I need you to train her for two more days. Then she's going to be on her on, in her on section. I'll see y'all later." I said, "Ok auntie, thank you." Rebbeca said, "Thank you auntie for hiring me." "You're welcome. Your cousin really spoke up for you. She has your back." "I know I got hers too." After Jannette left, we sat down and I felt so tired like it was my first day at work. Rebbeca said, "I'm so tired. I don't know what to do. I can't wait to go home and rest." I said, "I know what you mean, me too." When we got off* work, we left. I walked up the hill towards Wendy's and I waited for the bus to come, and Rebbeca went home. When I got off the bus, it was extremely quite outside. I knocked on the door and my granny opened it. As I was going inside the house, I looked behind me and I saw this boy crossing the street. I came in and shut the door. When I shut the door, I heard a loud sound from a car, as if somebody had gotten ran over. My granny said, "Zaneeya did you hear that?" "Yeah, I heard it granny. I wonder what happened that quick." I looked out of my granny's bedroom blinds and the same boy that I seen crossing the street. He was laid out in the middle of it. He got ran over. I said, "Granny look, a man just got out of his car, and now he is going through the boy pockets. A van just pulled up on the side of him and their trying to put him in there, but they can't. It looks like the body is too heavy, so they just left."

A woman and two men's came running and the woman was yelling, "What happen to my son, what happen?" She looked at her son and started screaming no, as she was crying. She dropped to the ground and started hugging him as she was yelling, "My baby, my baby." As she cried, the police came in the ambulance and the fire truck. Then everybody came outside and stood on the corner and in the front of their house, to see what was going on. That was the first time I ever heard a mother cry and yell for her child. My heart went out to the mother and her family. I did not sleep well that night. The next day, people went to the corner and they brought flowers, roses, teddy bears and even candles. Everybody would do that in the Bay Area when somebody got killed. As time went on, my dad called me and he apologized for what he said to me. I told him that I accepted his apology and I apologized as well. I knew my dad, and I were always going to argue, and I knew my dad was going to say more, hurtful things to me! My dad called me before my birthday. He said, "Zaneeya what are you doing for your birthday this year?" "I don't know. I'll probably go hang out with my friends." "I would like it if you would come out here. You can invite three of your friends and you can hang out and y'all can get in the Jacuzzi and I'll take y'all bowling." "I don't know dad, because I don't want us to get into an argument." "Were not going to argue we are going to have a good time for your birthday." "Ok dad, thank you. I'll call in invite some friends, but how are we going to get out there, are you going to pick us up?" "Toniya is going to come get you when you get out of school. So, tell your friends to have their bags packed and tell them to bring their bags to school with them." "Dad, where are we going to put our bags at when we get to school? Everybody doesn't have lockers?" "I don't know. I'm sure y'all will come up with something." "Can I invite Lil Lamont and Brain *and Justin Jr.?" "You can, but I don't know how they are going to get here, I'm not going to get them." "What if they catch the Bart? Would you pick them up from the Bart station?" "Yeah, I'll do that." "Ok, I'll see you Friday. Thank you for letting my friends and me spend the night at your house." "You're welcome, I'll see you Friday."*

After, I got off the phone with my dad. I told my granny I was going to my dad's house for my birthday. My granny said, "Well, I hope you have fun and you enjoy your birthday." "Hopefully my dad and I won't argue." "I know." I called Jessica, Susan, Rebbeca and Desseire to see if they wanted to come spend the night with me in Antioch for my birthday. Desseire said she couldn't go and Rebbeca said she had to work and Jessica and Susan said they were coming. I told them to bring their clothes to school with them Friday. Susan and I would hang out sometimes. I would spend the night at her house, I would do her hair and we were just close. Jessica and I were best friends, so we were extremely close too. Desseire had spent a night in Antioch with me before. We would just chill and stay in the house like Sabreea, and I would. Susan's mom had brought me an outfit for my birthday. Susan and I had the same outfit. Hers was green and mines were light pink. I called my cousin Meech to see if he could take me to buy some shoes. He picked me up and took me to Bay Fair mall. He took me to a shoe store called Georgio's. Meech asked me what shoes did I want. Susan and I said we was going to wear some Chuck Taylors with are outfits. So I told Meech, I wanted a pair of chucks. He said, "Ok, I'm going to buy them for you." I replied, "Thank you cousin." "No problem baby. If you need something, just call and ask me and I'll get it for you ok." "Ok Meech." Meech dropped me back off at home. I said bye to him and I gave him a hug. My cousin Meech is a great man. He is sweet, and he is kindhearted and I look up to him. When I went inside the house, I showed my granny my shoes that Meech bought me. She said, "Those are nice. That was really nice of him." "I know granny. I can always call Meech and he will always be here for me! I love my cousin." The next morning, I left for school. I told my granny, I would see her when I got home Sunday and I told her I would call her when I made it to Antioch. She told me ok and she gave me a hug. She said, "Zaneeya be careful." "I am granny, I love you." "I love you too don't forget to call me now." "Ok." I went to school happy. When, I made it to school. I went inside of the girl's locker room and I put my clothes inside of my gym locker, because I did not have a hall locker. Then I went to class. When the bell ranged for the 15- minute break, I went to go meet Jessica, and Susan. I asked them did they bring their clothes to school with them. Susan said, "Mines are in my locker." Jessica said, "My bags are at home, I don't have anywhere to put them. Will Toniya be mad at me?" "I don't know." "I don't live far from the school though." "I know, I never seen her mad before, but I'm not saying she don't get mad, because she do. We are all human, but I don't think she's going to be mad, she is a sweet person." After are break was over, we went to class. When it was time to go to lunch, I seen my old friend Jasmine. We hugged and we were happy to see each other. I asked Jasmine did she want to come spend the night with me at my dad's house in Antioch. She said, "Yes.

How are we going to get out there?" "My stepmom is going to come pick me up after school. So I can ask her to take you home, so you can get your clothes." "Ok, I just have to ask my mom she be trippin, but let me see what she say and I'll meet you at your school. When, I get out of school." "Ok, just meet me at the side gate of OT. That's where I'll be." "Ok Zaneeya, I'll see you later." After school, I went to get my bag out of my locker. Then I went to meet Jasmine. We all were waiting for Toniya. When Toniya called, she said she was in the front of the school. So we went to the front of the school to go meet her. When we got in the car, I introduced Toniya to Jasmine and Susan. I asked Toniya could she take Jessica home, to go get her bags and could she take Jasmine home, so she can pack her bags. When we got to Jasmine's house, her mom wanted to talk to my dad. I called my dad and Jasmine's mom and him talked…. After, we left Jasmine's house. We went to Jessica's house. Then we got on the freeway to go to Antioch. When, we made it to the house. Toniya parked in the garage, she called my dad. She said, "Were here." As we walked in the house, I noticed the lights were off. My dad and Justin Jr., were standing in the kitchen singing Happy Birthday to me. As they were holding my birthday cake and some balloons in their hand that, my dad had bought for me. I was definitely surprised, I said, "Thank you dad. I had no idea you was going to get me a cake and some balloons. That was nice of you." He gave me a hug. He said, "You're welcome Zaneeya. What do you want to eat?" "I want some pizza." "Ok, you know we don't eat pork in my house, but I'll order some pizza with some chicken on it." "Ok dad that's fine." I introduced Jasmine and Susan to my dad and Justin Jr. Then, we went upstairs to go put our bags in the guest room. Toniya niece was living with her. She was taking care of her for a while. Her niece name is Alexia. She was a pretty little girl. My dad went to pick Brain up from the Bart station. We all ate some pizza and we watched a movie downstairs. Susan was flirting with Justin Jr., she was throwing herself at him. Brain and Jasmine was flirting as well, but Jasmine was not throwing herself at him! The movie was boring and it was getting late, *so I went upstairs. I gave Jasmine and Susan a blanket to sleep with. Then I went to the guess room, so I could go to sleep. Then Jessica came upstairs right after me. Jessica said, "I wonder if they are going to sleep downstairs." I said, "I don't know. They better sleep upstairs, because if my dad wakes up and their sleeping downstairs with the boys, he is going to be mad." So I went downstairs. I said, "Susan, and Jasmine when y'all get sleepy come upstairs, because y'all can't sleep downstairs with the boys."*

They said, "Ok." I went back upstairs to go to sleep. The next morning, when I woke up, I stayed in bed for a little while. Then Jessica woke up. She said, "Zaneeya where is Jasmine and Susan?" "It looks like they slept downstairs. I wonder what happened." "Do you think Susan and Justin Jr., messed around last night?" "It wouldn't surprise me. You know how Susan is and she was throwing herself at my brother! To be honest they probably did mess around, but Justin Jr., just wants some sex." "He really do." Jessica and I laughed. Jasmine came upstairs. I said, "What happened to you last night?" She smiled. She said, "Nothing, what are you talking about? I simply watched a movie and I fell asleep. I didn't even see the whole movie, but your cousin is cute." Jessica said, "So that's all that happened, really Jasmine?" "Yeah that's what happened. Girl, I'm still a virgin and he is cute and everything, but I was not about to have sex. We wasn't even talking like that." I said, "I believe you, because I know when you're lying." Susan walked in the room. Jessica said, "Susan what did you and Justin Jr., do last night?" She smiled. She said, "We didn't do anything. We just talked and watched a movie." I said, "Stop lying. You do not know how to just watch a movie. What were y'all doing?" "We wasn't doing anything, but your brother is very handsome and I did want to have sex with him, but I didn't." "Stop lying, I saw y'all under his covers together. What was going on?" "I asked him did he want some of my cover, and when we went to sleep, he slept under his own cover." "Yeah, y'all messed around. You're nasty, you don't even know him!" "He's your brother." "I know, but you do not know him." "We didn't have sex at all. I wanted too though." My dad knocked on the bedroom door. I said, "Come in." He said, "Good morning. If you want to go bowling it's going to be later on." I said, "Ok dad that is fine with me." "Tonight y'all cannot sleep downstairs with the boys. Nobody is going to get pregnant while you're spending the night at my house, it's not going to happen. So tonight when you get sleepy just come in the room and make a pallet thank you." We got dressed and we hung around the house. Later on that night, my dad took us bowling. Susan and I had are outfits on that her mom bought us. Jessica said, "Where is my outfit? We could have all dressed alike?" I said, "Susan's mom bought this for me for my birthday." Jasmine said, "You guys look cute." "Thank you Jasmine." When, we got to the bowling alley. My dad said, "I'm going to pick y'all up in two hours. That's when the bowling alley would be closed, so be ready ok." We all said, "Ok." When my dad left, we all bowled and we had a good time.

We all were talking mess about who was going to win the game and I'm very competitive. So of course, I knew I was going to win and I had my game face on. I won one game and Justin Jr., won one game. When my dad came, we left. When, we got to the house. My dad said, "Y'all can get in the Jacuzzi if y'all want too." I told the girls if they wanted to get in the Jacuzzi they could. I was tired and I wanted to go to bed. So Jessica, and Jasmine and I went upstairs and we went to sleep. Susan stayed downstairs with Justin Jr., and Brain. I heard my dad say, "Susan when you get sleepy come upstairs and sleep." Later on that morning, Susan came upstairs and laid down. When we all woke up, we went downstairs to eat breakfast. My dad made us pancakes for breakfast. I told him thank you. He said, "I'm going to take y'all home, in two hours. So after y'all eat get dress." After I ate, I showered. Then I got dressed. I put my bags downstairs in the livingroom by the front door and I told the girls to bring their bags down, after they were finish getting dressed. My dad said, "I'm going to take Brain to the Bart station. Then I'm going to take y'all home." I told Brain bye. When my dad came, back to pick us up. I said bye to Justin Jr., and I thanked Toniya, for letting my friends and me spend the night at her house. She said, "You're welcome. Did you have fun?" I replied, "Yes I did." I gave her a hug. When we got to the Bay Area, my dad dropped Jessica off first. Then Susan and Jasmine, then he dropped me off. I said, "Thank you for surprising me for my birthday and thank you for letting my friends and me spend the night." He replied, "You're welcome. I'm happy you enjoyed yourself. See, I told you we were not going to argue." "Yeah, you were right dad." My dad gave me a hug. Then I went inside the house. My granny said, "Zaneeya did you have fun?" "Yes I did granny, I enjoyed myself." "That's good you did." I unpacked my clothes. Then I talked to Nathan on the phone for a little while. After I got off the phone with Nathan, Brandon called me. He said, "Zaneeya how was your weekend?" "It was nice. I had a good time with my family and my friends. How was your weekend?" "It was good I thought you were going to call me." "I never said I was going to call you. So I don't know how you figured that." He giggled. He said, "I know you didn't tell me that. I just thought you would call." "Oh, well that's what you get for thinking, but I'm going to bed. I'll see you at school tomorrow, good night." "Good night Zaneeya." I went to bed. The next morning, I woke up. I got dressed and I went to school. I could not believe, the school year was going to be over and the summer was coming. I knew I was going to be working a lot over the summer. I seen Susan at lunch and she asked me to go to Jack in the box with her, so I did. We sat down and talked. She asked me is it ok if she talks to my brother!

I said, "Go ahead, but don't get mad at me when it doesn't work out." She replied, "I don't know if he even likes me?" "I don't know. We don't talk about you." We stayed at Jack in the box for a while. When I looked to see what time it was it 2 o'clock. We cut 5th period and that was the first time I ever cut class. I said, "Come on Susan let's go back to school." "Let's just wait until school is over!" "Girl please, I'm not about to wait until school is over. That means we would cut two classes and I'm not doing that. I'm going back to school, I'll see you later." "Come on Zaneeya let's just stay." "No, you can, but I'm not." "Ok, here I come." We walked back to school. We went to one of the side doors of the school, so somebody would let us in. I went to my class and Susan went to her's. When I walked in my class, I went straight to my seat. Miss. Regeiro said, "Zaneeya, where have you been?" "I'm sorry I'm late. It will not happen again. I lost track of time while I was sitting down eating lunch." "Ok, I believe you. You're a good student, here is the homework and don't worry about the classwork." "Thank you, Miss. Regeiro." When, the bell ranged to get out of school. Susan, and Nathan, and I went to the job that we had after school together. I had two jobs, and Brandon came too. We would have to meet up in a classroom, with our boss Dianna. Dianna would write poems on the board in class. Then we would have to write the poem that she wrote down, and we had to finish it off. When, we were finish writing. We would read are poems out loud and all of us would say how we felt, about that person's poem. We would come together as a group in class, and talk about, what we were going to put in are magazine that we was making. We went to Claremont Middle School, to talk about the violence in schools and the gangs and we gave are magazine out. We spoke in one of my old classrooms, my science teacher Miss. Christonchro class. After we were finished speaking, we left and we went home. When I got home from school Justin Jr., was there. He said, "What's up little sis." I said, "Hi brother." My granny said, "Zaneeya come here and dial this number for me." "Granny who am I calling?" "Just dail the number and go into the livingroom girl." I heard a phone ring. I saw this box, so I picked it up. I yelled, "Granny, you bought me a cell phone?" "Yeah girl and when your minutes run out that's it. You have to wait until the next month to talk." "Aw, thank you granny." I gave her a hug. I said, "I'm going to talk on the house phone until my minutes are free." "No you're not you better use your cell phone, that's what it's for." "Granny you just want my minutes to run out." "That's what there for, so go and use them." My granny was giggling as she was talking.

I was so happy that I had a cell phone of my own, but my granny would let me take her cell phone to school. The next day I went to school, I gave Susan and Jessica my number. Susan said, "Granny bought you a phone? Let me see it." It was a Cingular flip phone, it was black and gray. Susan said, "That's cute, I know you're happy." I replied, "I am and I appreciate my granny buying me a phone." Later on that day, I saw Brandon. My phone was ringing so I answered it. It was my granny calling me. She said, "You don't suppose to be answering your phone in class." "I'm at lunch granny." "Oh ok, I was just calling to make sure that this was your number that I wrote down. I'll see you when you get home." "Ok granny, I'll see you later." I hung up the phone. Brandon said, "Who phone is that?" I said, "This is my phone, why?" "Oh, let me see it. Granny bought you, your own phone, finally?" He said as he laughed. "Ha-ha, real funny. Give me back my phone, thank you." "Dang, you're not going to give me your number!" "I was waiting for you to ask me for it!" "It's like that? If I was somebody else you would have given me your number, without me even asking!" "Who are you talking about?" "Nobody, what's your number?" I gave Brandon my number. I said, "See you later, I'm going to class." "I'm going to text you." "I am not going to be texting you while I'm in class, so I can get my phone took." "Just, text back please." "Bye Brandon." I went to class and while I was doing my classwork, my phone was vibrating. I looked at my phone it was a text from Brandon. I did not reply to him. When class ended, I texted him back. After school, I went home. When, I got home from school. My granny said, "Did you use your minutes up yet?" I replied, "No granny, I see all of my friends at school. So I don't need to call them until the weekend. On the weekend, my minutes are free, and if I come home from school, I'll just use the house phone. I'm going to save my minutes." "You need to use your minutes. Dinner is ready. I made some homemade chili beans and some rice and corn bread. You can eat when you want to." "Ok granny, thank you." As the school year went on, I was still working both jobs. I also was spending time with Brandon after school. When I did not have to work and we would talk until I had to go to work. We became close friends. Nathan and I still were best friends and so was Jessica and I. Desseire and I wasn't as close, but we all still hung out and I still had her back. Everybody was getting sad, because the school year was ending. Susan's mom was removing her from OT, because she was failing and she had to go to summer school to pick her grades up. She also said she did not want Susan and me going to the same school, because we would cut class together.

Susan and I wasnt cutting class together all the time, but her mom did not know that. Susan would go to whatever boy she was dating at time house and she would cut class. I cut class with Susan three times total. Brandon was going to another school too. He got kicked out of OT High. On the last day of school, it wasn't mandatory that we had to go to school. Susan, Jessica, and Brandon, and Bernard and I stayed in the same classroom that day. It was a substitute teacher in every class. Brandon went inside of Mr. Hews classroom and he threw a water balloon at him and ran. I stayed outside. Mr. Hews poked his head out the window. He said, "Brandon I'm calling security." Brandon said, "I'm already kicked out of OT High." I said, "Why did you do that? That was mean?" "He deserved it. He was mean for giving me a D for a grade on my report card." "You gave yourself that D by cutting class and not doing what you are supposed to be doing. Do not blame anyone, but yourself!" "Ok, when you get a D. I'm going to tell you the same thing." "I have had a D and I cannot blame my grades on nobody, but myself." After school, we all said bye to each other and I went home. Over the summer, Jessica and Susan, and I would still hang out. Susan birthday was coming up and I told Jessica we should take Susan to Boomers for her birthday. So, we went to Susan's house the day of her birthday. Jessica, Susan and her two cousins and I caught the Bart and we went to Boomers. We rode on the go-carts and we took pictures. We ate, we played laser tag, and we just had a good time. When it was time to go, Susan called her mom to come pick us up. When her mom picked us up, she was fussing. She said, "Y'all could have taken the bus and Bart back." Susan said, "The bus isn't running." As we pulled out the parking lot, Sally saw a bus driving by. She said, "Susan why did you lie? I see the bus right there and you had me come way out here." When we got back to Susan house, we all changed clothes then we went to the movies. After the movies, we went home. Over the summer, I worked a lot and my mom called me. She said, "Cupcake, Justin Jr., birthday is coming up and your auntie Dorthy is giving him a surprise party. Are you coming?" "If I don't have to work, I'll go." "Ok, let me know." Sabreea called me and she gave me her new number. She said she was going to spend the night at my grandma's house and she wanted me to go over there to spend a night with her. I told her I would. When the weekend came, I went to my grandma's house. My mom was going to pick me up and take me to Modesto. So I could go to Justin Jr., party. When Sabreea arrived to grandma's house, she came in with her auntie. Her uncle's wife on her mother side of her family, we said hi to each other and we hugged.

I said, "Sabreea, I cannot spend the night with you, because I have to go to Modesto tonight for Justin Jr., birthday party." "How are you going to get out there?" "My mom is on her way to come get me right now." "I want to go too. How long are you staying out there?" "You can come. You know my mom wouldn't mind and I'm staying out there for the weekend. I have to come back, because I have to work." Sabreea asked her auntie is it ok if she comes with me to Modesto. Her auntie said, "No, you can't go. You came over here to spend time with your grandma and I don't know those people, or where they live at." Sabreea said, "That's my sisters mom and I want to see my brothers." "I don't know about that." I said, "Sabreea my mom is on her way. I'm going to the nail shop to get my nails done before she gets here." Sabreea kept asking her auntie could she go to Modesto. Her auntie said, "I have to speak with her mom and she's not here." I said, "I can call my mom for you if you want to talk to her." I called my mom. Sabreea's auntie said, "Hi, my name is Brandy. I'm Sabreea's auntie. Sabreea said she wants to go to Modesto with her sister, but I told her I do not know where she would be staying." My mom replied, "She would be staying at my house. I can give you my address, that's not a problem. If you're at Miss. Alissa house, I'll meet you in a little while. I'm on my way right now." "No, I have to leave, but I guess I'll let Sabreea go. I don't want nothing to happen to her. Shay left her with me and she's my baby." "Nothing is going to happen to her. She's safe with me and Shay knows me." "Ok well, I'll let her go with you. I'll call you tomorrow and get your address and everything." "You can get it right now if you want too." "Can I have your phone number too?" My mom gave Brandy her phone number. Brandy said, "Ok, I'll call you tomorrow and check in with you to see how Sabreea is doing. I'll call her phone too." Before Brandy left, she gave Sabreea some money. Then Sabreea and I went to get our nails done. As we were talking in the nail shop, we both looked out the window, and it was a man holding a gun in our cousin Lil Kevin's face. I ran outside the nail shop and I stood in front of Lil Kevin. I said, "Please don't shoot him! He's only 13 years old. He's only a kid." The gunman said, "Well, tell him to stop runnin his mouth and to stop banging his set on my block." Lil Kevin said, "Man shoot me. I'm not scared and I'm going to keep throwin up my set." I said, "Shut up Lil Kevin. Shut up right now stop runnin yo mouth! He does not mean that. Please don't shoot him please!" The gunman said, "I'm not gonna shoot you and I'll let him live this time, but if he come back down here on my block, he won't be livin!"

The gunman left. I watched him while he walked away. I wanted to see where he was saying his block was. It was a block away from my grandma's house. After, the gunman left. I said, "Lil Kevin go to grandma house and don't come back down here. That man is not playin with you! You need to stop talkin mess to people.That's not coo and he could have shot you and me." He replied, "I'm going to get Lil Lamont." "Now you're just being stupid. Don't none of you have guns on you and you're going right back down there to start drama. You're going to get shot." "Whatever, he is not gettin away with this." "You're hard headed. You'll learn one day." I went back in the nail salon. Sabreea said, "Sis, I thought he was going to shoot y'all. Lil Kevin is always into something. He needs to sit down somewhere. He thinks he is so bad." As Sabreea and I were walking back to grandma's house, we saw Lil Kevin showing Lil Lamont where the gunman was. I said, "Lil Lamont it's not worth it. Lil Kevin was runnin his mouth and banging his set to them. So that's why that man pulled out his gun, but that don't make it right, but Lil Kevin needs to mind his business. If you go down there Lil Lamont you're crazy too, and y'all are going to end up gettin shot." Lil Lamont replied, "I'm not going down there and Lil Kevin you need to stop runnin yo mouth and banging yo set! Your lucky Zaneeya was there, because he probably would have shot you." Sabreea and I waited for my mom to come. When she came, we said bye to grandma and to Lil Lamont. I told Lil Kevin to be careful. When, we were on our way to Modesto. My mom said, "I'm so happy that y'all are coming. We are going to have a good time." When we got to Modesto, we went to Dorthy house, Justin Jr., was shocked to see us. We spent the night at Dorthy house. We stayed outside with Justin Jr., for a little while. Gabbie was there too and we all was together again like the old days. When, it got late. Uncle Tony let Justin Jr., use his car to take Gabbie home. Justin Jr., was tipsy. He really didn't need to be driving. So Sabreea and I went with him to take Gabbie home. Then we went back to Dorthy's house. Sabreea and I slept in Christy's room. The next day, Nicky came over with her best friend Tammie. Tammie was going with Lil Brad. Which is uncle Tony's nephew, and Nicky was Tony's niece. Christy asked us did we want to go with her. She was going with Nicky and Tammie to the park, because there friend was having a bbq. I said, "Yeah." When we arrived to the park, Tammie introduced us to her friend. His name is Xavier. Xavier said hi to all of us. Then Xavier introduced us to his two cousins.

Xavier asked us are age. Tammie hurried up and said, "They are 18 years old, all of them." He said, "Ok." Justin Jr., girlfriend was with us too. Xavier and his family were leaving. We stayed at the park for a little while. Sabreea's auntie was calling her and telling her that she needed to come home. Sabreea said, "You said I can spend the weekend out here with my sister. I only spent one night, and my sister mom is not going to drive us back to the Bay Area today." Brandy said, "Well, I'm going to call her and tell her that you have to come back home." My mom called Sabreea. She said, "Sabreea your auntie is calling me and she said you have to come back home, because your mom is trippin. What is your mom's number? I'm going to call her myself. I'm not taking you home today and I told that lady I wasn't. I don't know what she don't understand." My mom called Shay and she told her what was going on. My mom called Sabreea back. She said, "Sabreea, I just talked to Shay, and she said she doesn't mind that you're out here. She said you could stay the whole summer if you want too. I'm going to call your auntie and tell her, before I have to cuss her out." When, we left the park. We went to Dorthy's house and as we were getting out of the car. Tammie said, "Which one of Xavier's cousin do y'all think is cute?" I said, "The one who had the shirt on his head was cute." Christy said, "David." Tamie said, "That's David Zaneeya." Sabreea said, "I have a boyfriend, so I do not know." As we were walking in Christy's house, Tammie yelled my name. She said, "Zaneeya come here, someone wants to talk to you." I replied, "Who is calling me on your phone?" "It's David. Xavier's cousin." I got on the phone. I said, "Hello." He said, "Hi, how are you doing? I'm David. I was the one who had the shirt on his head." "Oh ok, I'm doing well. How are you?" "I'm doing well. I wanted to ask you do you have a boyfriend." "No not at this moment. Why?" "I wanted to ask you for your number. Is that ok? So we can talk and get to know each other!" "That's fine, but I don't have a phone right now, but you can call me on my cousin phone. We are together all the time." "Ok Miss. Zaneeya. Where do you live at?" "I live in the Bay Area. Where do you live at?" "I live in Stockton. So does your family lives in Modesto?" "Yes, I have family out here." "Ok well, I'm going to talk to you later. Oh, yeah when you are going back to the Bay Area? I'm just asking you, so I can know when to call you!" "I'm leaving in two days." "Ok Miss. Zaneeya, I will be calling you. Enjoy the rest of your evening." "You do the same bye." After I got off the phone, I gave Tammie her phone back. She said, "David said he wanted to speak with the girl with the turquoise shirt on. He wants you Zaneeya." I said, "We would probably just be friends. I don't see it being nothing serious." I went inside the house. That night Christy and her uncle got into it. They were going back and forth. Sabreea and I were just laughing. Even though Christy was young, she was not about to let him talk crazy to her. After they finished arguing, we went upstairs.

It was a lot going on that night. Justin Jr., was trying to beat up his girlfriend and Sabreea and I came between them. I told Justin Jr., he should be a shame of his self for putting his hands on a woman. We took his girlfriend in Christy's room with us and I told her she was crazy for being with a guy who puts his hands on her. I said, "I do not care if he is my brother. You don't take that from no one. I'm younger then you and I know that." An hour late, she went back in the room with Justin Jr. Sabreea and I said, "Let's go check on her." When, we went inside of Lason's room. We walked in on Justin Jr., and his girlfriend having sex. We hurried up and shut the door. Then we went back in Christy's room. I said, "I see they made up." Then we went to bed. The next day, my mom, Patrick, and Ramone and Lil Dawane came to pick Sabreea and me up. We went to Lisa's house. Lisa said, "Hi Zaneeya, I haven't seen you in a long time." I gave Lisa a hug. Then I introduced Lisa and her kids to Sabreea. We all hung out that day. We spend a night at Lisa's house. The next morning my mom woke us up. She said, "Wake up come on, we have to go. I have to stop by Qin's house." We went to Qin's house. He had his thug friends over. When we seen Qin we gave him a hug. He said, "Zaneeya and Sabreea do y'all want to stay here for a little while? I'll order us some pizza." We said, "No, we can't. We have to go back home today." "You guys can't stay out here and kick it with your big brother?" I said, "No we can't, I have to go to work, but we will come back." "Ok, I'll see y'all later with y'all black self's." I said, "Shut up Qin, you're always talkin mess." My mom took us to Dorthy's house to get are clothes. We said bye to everybody. Then we went to my mom's house. My mom was fussing a little bit, because Sabreea and I did not spend a night at her house. I knew it was out of love. So I did not mind. I said, "Next time, we will spend a night with you at your house." We stayed at mom's house until it cooled off, because Modesto was scorching hot. My mom wanted to wait so her car, wouldn't over heat while she was driving. When it was time to leave, my mom dropped Ramone and Lil Dawane off at Dorthy's house, but Patrick came with us. On our way to the Bay Area, my mom called her brother Ike to ask him for some money. When we arrived to the Bay Area, we got lost. Ike gave my mom the wrong directions to his house. So we parked at this Chinese food restaurant. My mom called Ike, so he could come meet us. When Ike came, my mom followed him to his house.

We didn't stay long. I asked my mom to take me to my cousin Tameka's house. Who I was spending the summer with. My mom said, "I don't know my way around Hayward and you don't neither and I'm not going to get lost again." I said, "Mom, I'mma call her and ask her for directions." "No, she can pick you up from yo grandma's house." My mom drove us to my grandma's house. Patrick, and Sabreea and my mom went to the back room to go to bed. My mom said, "Cupcake, you mind as well come lay down with us. Tameka is not coming to get you and I don't blame her. It's late at night, go to sleep." I replied, "I'm not spending the night. I'm going to Tameka's house. I'll see you when I go back to Modesto." I called Tameka. I said, "Hi Tameka, can you come get me? I'm at grandma's house." She replied, "Girl it's too late to be getting up. I'll come get you tomorrow." "No Tameka, come get me tonight. I have to work tomorrow and my work clothes are at your house." "Zaneeya it's late." "It sounds like you're up already. Come on Tameka. You know you love me and plus I miss my baby." "Your right about one thing, I do love you. I'm on my way. Be ready to come outside when I get there." "Ok thank you. I'll buy you something to eat when you pick me up." I went in the room and I sat down on the bed. My mom said, "You still think your cousin is coming to get you huh?" "She is coming to get me. Now how you like that!" "No she's not. You're going to fall asleep sitting up." "Ok you'll see." Tameka called me 20- minutes later. She told me she was out outside. I told my mom, Sabreea, and Patrick and my grandma bye. My mom said, "Cupcake you're really leaving?" "Yes I told you I was. I was not playin." "Tameka is really outside? Let me go see." My mom and I walked outside. My mom said, "Hi Tameka look, at you, you are so pretty. You're all grown up now." Tameka said, "Hi Bella, thank you." She gave my mom a hug. Tameka said, "How are you doing?" My mom replied, "I'm doing well. You came for your girl huh!" "Yeah, she's lucky I love her." My mom said, "Cupcake you could have spent the night with me." "Mom, I'm not trying to hear that. I'll see you later and there's nowhere for me to sleep at anyway." "You could sleep in the bed with us." "I am not about to be squished. It's not enough room. I'll go to Modesto soon, I love you mom. I'll call you tomorrow." "Ok Cupcake, I love you too." Tameka and I left. On our way to her house, we stopped at Jack in the box to get something to eat. Tameka said, "I have not for got about what you said. I want everything that's on the menu." When we made it to Tameka's house Kelly was sleep. Kelly is Tameka daughter.

Kelly and I took pictures together, that was my baby. Tameka shared a house with her sister Paris. Paris is older than Tameka. Tameka and I ate are food. I told Tameka, that David would be calling her phone. She said, "Who is David, and where did you meet him at?" I replied, "I met him in Modesto." "Oh ok, when he calls, I will let you know." We went to bed. When I woke up the next morning, I got in the shower then I got dressed for work. Tameka was getting dress for work too. She would drop me off at work and at night. I *would catch the bus to her job, and wait for her to get off work. She worked at the Hilton hotel in the Bay Area. Tameka introduced me to her boss and all of her coworkers. They were nice and friendly.*

Before we went to work Tameka's phone ranged. She told me to answer it. It was David calling me. I said, "Hello." He said, "Hi, may I speak to Zaneeya." "This is she." "Hi, how are you doing? I told you I was going to call you." "Yes you did. I'm doing well, I'm on my way to work. How are you doing?" "I'm good, I was just thinking about you." "How are you thinking about me and you don't even know me?" "I like what I seen and I'm highly interested in you and I want to get to know you better, if that's alright with you." "We can be friends and get to know each other." "Ok, Miss. Lady, have a good day. Is it ok if I call you when you get off work?" "You can call me, but I won't be with my cousin until 10 o'clock tonight. So you can call after 10 o'clock." "Ok, I'll talk to you later." "Ok, bye." After, I got off the phone with David.Tameka said, "Zaneeya was that David?" "Yeah, he is going to call me later on when I get off work." "You guys are going to be together." "I do not know about that Tameka." "Yes you are watch. " I said bye to Paris and my little cousins then Tameka and I went to work. She dropped me off at work. Soon as I went inside the breakroom, Jannette asked Vida who was in there. Vida came inside the breakroom. She yelled, "Jannette, Zaneeya is here." Jannette said, "Niece, come here." I went to see what she wanted. I said, "Yes auntie." She said, "I want you to go to the store for me across the street. I need some icy hot patches ok. Your auntie is in a lot of pain. My arthritis is killing me right now." "Ok auntie." "When you come back from the store just clock in, and start working ok. So we can get everything done today." "Ok." I went to the store to get some icy hot patches for Jannette. Then I stopped at Jamba Juice and I bought Jannette, and Vida and I a smoothie.

When, I went back to work. I went to Jannette's office and I handed her, her icy hot patches, and her smoothie that I had bought for her, and I gave Vida her smoothie as well. I made sure I put everything out that we needed to serve with for dinner. That consisted of the juice, coffee, cracker baskets, butters creamers and everything else. I was finished with my duties extra early that day at work. So I just helped Rebbeca in the diningroom. Rebbeca asked me did I have a good time in Modesto. I said, "Yeah I did. Justin Jr., got drunk on his birthday." "Did you miss me?" "Girl you know I did." "You left me at work by myself and went to Modesto." "I had to go, it was Justin Jr., birthday party and you had to work, but the next time I go out there. I want you to come with me." "Ok, for sure." After we were finished working, we clocked out and left. Rebbeca and I said bye to each other and I caught the bus to Tameka's job. When I arrived to Tameka's job, her co-workers and I would speak to each other. Then I would go to the gift shop and look around. Then I would go back to the lobby and wait for Tameka to get off work. Tameka worked at the front desk. We would talk while she was working. When a customer would come, we would stop talking and she would assist the customer. After she was finish helping all the customers, she gave me her phone. David was calling me. He said, "Hi Zaneeya I hope you had a good day at work today." "Thank you. I had a nice day." David and I talked until Tameka got off work. When we left, we went to get something to eat. We ate are food at the kitchen table. Tameka said, "Zaneeya, so how old is David and where do he live at?" "He is 18 years old and he lives in Stockton Ca." "Do he have any brothers or sisters and who do he live with in Stockton?" "He lives with his mom and his stepdad and he have three brothers. He has a few sisters on his dad side." "Is he a momma's boy?" "Yes he is." "So do you like him?" "He seems like a good guy, but we have to get to know each other first." As Tameka and I was talking David called me. He said, "Zaneeya, I know I told you good night, but I just wanted to call you so I could hear your voice." I said, "Aw how sweet." "Good night Zaneeya." "Good night David." Tameka said, "He seems like a nice guy." "Yeah he does, but we will see." Tameka and I went to bed. As the summer went on David and I would talk every morning. We would talk on my lunch breaks and every night. We stay up on the phone until we fell asleep. Lil Lamont and Brain would spend the night at Tameka and Paris house with me. Brain liked Paris best friend daughter and they started dating.

Brain and Lil Lamont and I spent most of the summer together. Tameka and Paris took all of us to the beach. We had a great time. Of course, Lil Lamont went and he was looking for him a woman, even though he already had a girlfriend at the time. He was truly a player and he was smooth with it too. We stayed at the beach and we relaxed. When it was time to go home, we all left. I would always be in Tameka's room or in the livingroom. One day, I was on the phone talking to David, and I told him to hold on, because somebody was calling Tameka on her other line. I said, "Hello." This guy said, "You finally answered for me." "This is not Tameka hold on. Let me go get her for you." "Oh, I'm sorry thank you." I clicked over and I told David I was going to call him back. I gave the phone to Tameka. She said, "Hello, who is this?" She started smiling. I grabbed Kelly and I started playing with her. For some reason, Tameka was giggling the whole time she was on the phone. So I gave her a smile and I pointed my finger to the phone. I said, "Whoever that is, he got you overly excited."

When, Tameka got off the phone. I said, "Who was that?" She replied, "Oh, this guy name Dan. He's a football player. He just got signed to the OR football team. It's nothing serious, we are just friends. I just met him." "It seems like you like him already." "He is a nice guy. I'm going to Napa. Do you want to come with me? I'm going to see Dan?" "Yes I'll go with you." So the next day we went to Napa. We went to the hotel that Dan was staying in. Dan came to the car. He was tall and buff. He looked like a football player. Tameka introduced us to each other. She said, "Zaneeya, I'll be back. I'm going to his hotel room. You can wait in the car or you can walk around." I said, "Tameka, I'mma take one for the team this time." Dan said, "I'll give you one of my key cards, so you can get inside the hotel, and you can order what you want. I'll have them put it on my card." I replied, "Thank you so much for your offer, but I'm going to sit in the car until Tameka gets back. Take your time. Don't worry, have fun and play nice." Tameka and Dan laughed. She said, "Ok, I won't be long at all." "Yeah right, just take your time." I talked to David while I was waiting in the car for Tameka. David said, "When are you going to come see me?" "I do not know, maybe before the summer is over." After, we got off the phone. I dozed off and went to sleep. When I woke up, Tameka was getting in the car.

When, Tameka got in the car. She said, "See I didn't take long at all." I said, "Yes you did, but that's ok I'm hungry. So did you have fun?" "Yeah we just talked you know." "No, I don't know and y'all were not talking. I have not been around you my whole life, but I know. You did not come all the way to Napa, just for a conversation that could have took place on the phone. So stop lying!" "We did Zaneeya." "Yeah ok." We stopped and got something to eat. When we made it back to Hayward, I went straight to bed. The next day, Tameka told me that Dan was going to spend the night over the weekend. She wanted to cook for him, but she wasn't that good of a cook as Paris was. Paris said, "I'll cook for you and you can just act like you cooked the food." Tameka said, "I thank God for you sis, because he would have been eating some top ramen." Dan came over on the weekend. Paris was finished cooking. She made some homemade mash potatoes, some string beans, fried chicken and some candy yams and she also made some dinner rolls. Paris brought Jasmine and Dan their food. Then she went to take care of Kelly. Paris loved Kelly. That was like her daughter. When Tameka was at work, Paris would watch her. Kelly face would light up, when she seen her auntie Paris.

After Tameka and Dan ate, they went inside of Tameka's room. I slept in Anthony's bed. Anthony and Aron are Paris kids. The next day, Dan left and Tameka and I had to go to work. When I got off work, I went to Tameka's job and I waited for her to get off. I talked on the phone with David. He really wanted me to come see him. When, we made it to Tameka's house. I told her that David wanted me to go see him, but I was going to take Rebbeca with me. Tameka said, "You should go see him. He is always calling you, morning, day and night! He's a nice guy and you guys are always talking on the phone." I said, "Ok, I'll go see him next week. School starts back in two weeks and I'm going home next week. I'm going to miss you." "You can live with us if you want too. I would just have to talk to Paris about it, but she is not going to say no." "Thanks Tameka, but that's ok. I'm going to continue living with my granny. I'm not moving anymore." "I'm going to miss you too Zaneeya. Kelly is going to miss you too. She got use to you." "I know got use to her as well. That's my baby." When it was time for me to go home, Tameka took me home. I went school shopping with Rebbeca. I called Tammie and Nicky and I asked them could they come pick Rebbeca and me up. I told Tammie, I would give her some gas money for coming to get us. She said, "Ok."

When Nicky and Tammie picked us up, I introduced them to Rebbeca. When we made it to Modesto, Tammie knew she was supposed to take me to my mom house, but she didn't. I told Tammie to take me to my mom's house. Tammie said, "I will take you in the morning. I forgot you wanted to go to your mom house. We are going to Stockton tomorrow tonight." I replied, "Ok." We went to Tammie's house and we spent a night. We made a pallet on the floor. The next morning, Rebbeca and I got dressed then David had called me. He said, "Zaneeya don't forget to come see me today." "I'm not going to forget. I'm coming and I'm bringing my cousin Rebbeca. So hopefully you'll have a cousin there that's single." "I will I have a few she can choose from." "Ok well, I'll see you later." "We always talk for a long time. Why are you trying to get off the phone now?" "I'm helping Tammie do her hair." "Ok, call me when you're done." "Ok bye." I helped Tammie do her hair. Then my mom called me and she told me that she wanted to see me. I said, "You will mom. I'm going to Stockton tonight then I'm coming over your house." "Ok, you better too." When we went to Stockton.Tammie stopped and got some gas and she bought some liquor. Nicky and Tamime asked Rebbeca and I have we ever got drunk before. We said, "No." Nicky and Tammie said, "We do not want y'all to get drunk, but we made a drink for both of you." We drunk are drinks on the way to David's house. When we got to his house, it looked like his whole family was outside partying. David came and he opened the car door for me. I introduced him to Rebbeca. David said hi to Nicky and Tammie. Then he introduced me to his family. David and I went inside of his garage and we sat down and talked.

David said, *"Are you tipsy?"* I replied, *"I think so."* David and I left out of his garage and we went where everybody else was, which was outside. Rebbeca had thrown up and I told her that she does not need to drink nothing else. Rebbeca said, *"I threw up, because I smoked a black a mal."* I said, *"Rebbeca you do not smoke."* *"I know Zaneeya."* David and I flirted. We talked and we all were joking around, but it was cold outside. So, we all went inside of David's house. We all sat down in the livingroom on the couch. Rebbeca sat on the side of David's cousin. His name is Azzy. Rebbeca and Azzy shared a blanket. Rebbeca and I had fun with Nicky and Tammie and we had a good time with everyone else as well. I fell asleep on David it was late. When we all woke up, it was 7:00 AM and I just wanted to sleep. I said bye to David and we hugged.

We went to Tammie's house to get dressed. Then Tammie took me to my mom's house. We stayed over there for a little while then we went back to Tammie's house. David called me and asked me could I come see him? I said, *"Let me see if Tammie will bring me. If so then yeah I'll come, but I'm not going to stay late like last night."* He replied, *"Ok, call me and let me know."* When I got off the phone with David, I asked Tammie could she take me to Stockton to go see David. She told me she would take me. When we made it to Stockton, it was 8:00 PM. Rebbeca came inside of David's house with me. David and I hugged. I asked David, where was his cousin Azzy at, because I knew Rebbeca wanted to see him again. David said, *"Oh, he's at home. Rebbeca did you want to see him?"* *"Yeah I need his number. I forgot to ask him for it last night I was so tired."*

"I'll get his number for you and I'll give it to Zaneeya to give to you." *"Ok, I need that he was cute."* David and I talked and we watched TV. Rebbeca watched TV with us. David asked me did I want a blanket. I told him no, I'm fine. I stayed at David's house for an hour. Then Tammie called and told me she was ready to go. I told David I have to go. He opened the door for me and we hugged. He tried to kiss me, but I pulled away from him. When, I got in the car I smiled at him. He called me on the phone. He said, *"Zaneeya, you didn't even give me a kiss you pulled away."* *"You don't need a kiss."* *"Ok, I got you. Call me when you make it back."* *"I'll think about it."* I giggled. *"You know I really had a good time with you Zaneeya. I'm happy you came to see me. Thank you for spending time with me."* *"You're welcome. I'm happy I came to see you too. I enjoyed myself. I will never drink with you again."* *"You were already drinking before you came to see me."* *"I know, but I'm not going to drink in front of you."* *"That's good you don't have to, but for real, call me when you make it back."* *"Ok, I will."* On our way back to Modesto, we stopped

and got something to eat from Wendy's. Then we went to Tammie's house and we went to sleep. The next day, we went home. Tammie dropped Rebbeca off at home then she dropped me off at my house. When, I went inside the house. My granny said, "Zaneeya did you enjoy your summer?" "Yes I enjoyed it granny. Did you miss me?" "Yeah I missed you. Do you have to work tomorrow?" "Yes I do." "Oh ok, I just wanted to know, because you came home and left again." I put my clothes in the dirty clothes then I called Nathan to see what he was up too.We didn't talk much over the summer. After, I got off the phone with him. I called Jessica to see what she was doing. The next day, I had to go to my 10th grade Orientation. My granny said she could not enroll me in school, because my school had too many stairs for her to climb. I told her not to worry about it. I'll do it myself.

I went to enroll myself in school. I got in line with Rebbeca. We took our id pictures for 10th grade year. I forward my granny's signature on the forms. I had too. After I was finished filling out my forms, I went to turn them in, and they gave me my class schedule. I talked to Jessica, as I was waiting for Rebbeca. After Rebbeca got her schedule, we went to work. We talked about how much fun we had in Stockton. Rebbeca said, "You and David are going to end up together." I replied, "Maybe, I don't know." Jannette called Rebbeca and me to her office. She said, "How are y'all doing?" We replied, "Were doing fine auntie. How are you?"

"I'm good, did y'all enjoy y'all summer?" I said, "Yes I did. I had a nice summer."Rebbeca said, "My summer was nice too." "That's good. I need y'all to clock in early ok. I love y'all." I said, "Auntie I always know, when you want me to clock in early." "You want to get paid don't you?" "Of course, I love clocking in early that's more money for me." "That's right, so go clock in and get to work and I want Rebbeca and you to do the dishes tonight. Everybody has been complaining and saying.That Rebbeca and Zaneeya never do the dishes, and I play favoritism with y'all, because y'all are my nieces. Even though we know that's not true. I'm going to have y'all do the dishes for a week. So when you guys are done serving, just come straight to the kitchen and do the dishes. I'm going to let Vida know, that I want y'all to do the dishes tonight. I have enough servers to bust y'all tables, now let them go talk about that." I said, "Ok auntie that's not a problem and it's a shame how people just sit up and lie on you. You treat everybody equal here. Yes, Rebbeca and I clock in early, but you let all of your employees clock in early as well."Rebbeca said, "That's messed up. When your employees are hungry, and they don't have any money to buy them any food. They will come and ask you can they make something to eat

and you will let them, and I don't get mad." I said, "One day I came to work and I wanted some juice and you told me no! I had to wait until dinner is over, and I did not say you play favoritism, that's crazy." Jannette said, "Your right, but don't worry about that. Let me handle it. I help everybody out and they lied on me, but that's ok. They forgot I'm their boss." Rebbeca and I went to set everything out for dinner. We served the residents their food. After dinner, we went straight to the kitchen as Jannette said.

I racked the dishes, because I was fast at it and Rebbeca sprayed the dishes and she did clean side. Which consist of taking the dishes out of the machine, than placing them where they belonged. I also helped her with spraying the dishes and with clean side. We always worked as a team. If Rebbeca was taking the dishes where they had to go, I would spray them and put them in the machine. Then I would take the dishes out of the machine and place them on a cart to make it easier for her. After, we were finish doing the dishes. We took out the garbage, and we swept and mopped the kitchen floor. We were finish early, so we went to go talk to Jannette. Jannette stayed a work until 8:00 PM that night. After we got off work, we left. We said bye to each other and we went home. David called me when I was on my way home. We talked for a while, but I did not like talking on the phone at night, while I was walking home, because I wanted to be fully aware of my surrounding. So I told David I would call him when I made it home. As I was walking home, I saw the police. Somebody got shot. Everybody was standing outside looking. I knocked on the door. My granny opened it. She said, "Zaneeya, somebody got shot and they kept on shooting too." "All they do is shoot over here." "It's bad over here, but it use to be real bad when I first moved here. It was horrible." "Oh yeah, everybody is dying from left to right. That's all you hear about and see on the news." "How was work?" "It was good, I feel exhausted. I cannot wait to eat and go to sleep." I took a shower then I ate dinner. Then I talked to David on the phone. We stayed up talking until 2:00 AM. My granny woke up. She said, "You're still on the phone girl?" I said, "I just got off granny. You better, go to bed old woman. What are you doing up this late anyways?" I said jokingly "I'm going, you're the one on the phone all late. Who are you talking to anyways?" "I was on the phone with my friend." "Oh ok, what's his name?" "His name is David and don't start asking me a lot of questions. I know how you are." "I'm not. I just wanted to know his name." "Yeah ok, I'm going to sleep. I have to wake up in a couple of hours, so I can get ready for school. I can't believe that I'm a 10th grader now. I'm growing up granny." "I know you better go to sleep girl." "I am granny right now."

Chapter Eleven

My 10th Grade Year

When I woke up, it was 7:00 AM. I had to hurry up and get ready for school. I told my granny that she do not have to walk me to the bus stop anymore. I'm older now and the bus stop is only a block away from home. She said, "Ok, that's fine with me. I can stay in my bed and rest. Have a good day at school. I'll see you when you get off work." "Ok granny. I'll see you tonight bye." I walked to the bus stop and waited for the bus. I had on my new clothes. I cut my banes into china banes. I was ready for school, and I looked good and nobody couldn't tell me otherwise. When I arrived to school, I went straight to my class. At the 15-minute break, I went to the back of the school to go meet Jessica. We ran to each other and we gave each other a hug. Jessica said, "Sis, you cut your hair? It looks nice." I replied, "Thanks sis, I wanted a new look." When the bell ranged to go to class, I saw Nathan in the hallway. I gave him a hug. I said, "Look at you best friend, you got buffer and taller." He replied, "I worked out everyday." "Oh ok, I'll see you later. I'm going to class." "Ok best friend." While I was sitting in class, I kept thinking about David. When it was time for lunch, Jessica, and Desseire and I went to get something to eat. We talked about what we did over the summer. What teachers we had and what we were going to do in school far as in activities. When lunch was over, we went back to school. Then we went to class. On my way to class, I saw my I.E.P teacher. She told me that she needed to talk to me, so she can give me some papers to take home. I asked her could I come get the papers, when everybody else would be in class. I did not want anyone to see me going inside of her office or leaving out. I was a shamed of the fact that I had a learning disability. It was not something I was proud of. She told me she would call my teacher and tell him that she needed to talk to me.

After, I was finish talking to my I.E.P teacher. Jessica said, "Zaneeya who is that?" "Oh, she is one of the helpers in my class and she was asking me did

I get the homework for tomorrow." "Ok, well I'll see you after school. Bye sis."
"Ok, see you later." I had to tell Jessica something, because I did not want her
to know about my learning disability. When I went to my I.E.P teacher office,
Rebbeca was sitting down at the table. I said, "At least I won't be seen leaving
by myself." Rebbeca replied, "That's what I was thinking to myself once I seen
you come in. I just want to leave before the bell ring, so nobody won't see me."
Our I.E.P teacher said, "It want be long. I just need to talk to both of you. First,
I want to say congratulation to both of you for passing on to the 10th grade."
We replied, "Thank you."

"This year will be harder for the both of you. The homework will be harder.
So you will have to try much harder when it comes to finishing up your
classwork. If you are having trouble in class, and your teachers are not helping
you, just come in talk to me, and I will handle it. Both of you have to take
the cahsee, just like everyone else and you have to pass the cahsee in order to
graduate just like everybody else. You have to have a certain score in order to
pass the cahsee." Rebbeca said, "We shouldn't have to take the cahsee just like
everybody else. We have a learning disability." I said, "If we were in special day
classes. We wouldn't have to take the cahsee at all right?" Our I.E.P teacher
replied, "Correct, if you were in special day classes, you would not have to
take the cahsee, but you both have classes like everybody else. So you have to
take the cahsee." I said, "You can put me in a special day class." "I cannot put
you in a special day class. You do not need to be in a special day class. Your
brain is not at the level as someone who needs special day classes. Your brain
is above that and so is yours Rebbeca. You should be happy that you're not in
special day classes." I said, "I was just joking, but I wish we had more help.
Like when we were in middle school. If we did not understand something, are
teacher would help us until we got it right and I really learned a lot from my
middle school teachers." "I know it was a lot better in middle school, far as
the learning goes. It's only going to get harder from here on out. You both still
have to pass the 10th grade, to get to the 11th. You have to pass the 11th grade, to
get to the 12th. It's all a process. You have to take a deep breath and take your
time." "I'm going to pass the 10th grade and that's for sure. I'm not worried
about that, because I'm very determining, and I'm not going to let nothing
stand in my way. I'm going to pass the 10th grade. So I can go to the 11th grade.
I'm going to my juror prom, and I'm going to make it to the 12th grade and I'm
going to try my best to pass the cahsee. I know for a fact that I'm not a good
test taker, but I'm going to work hard to try to pass."

"That's good Zaneeya you are supposed to think like that. You have gotten great grades in middle school and you even gotten rewards in elementary school. You can do it and I will try to help both of you, as much as I can. That's my job." Rebbeca said, "I'm not going to give up either." "Ok, I need both of you to take your parents, this form to sign and bring it back to me tomorrow please." I replied, "Ok, I'm going to ask my teacher can I drop it off at your office, when everybody else is in class." Rebbeca said, "Me too." "That's fine. Both of you can. This meeting is over you can go back to class now." Rebbeca and I looked both ways as we were peeping, our heads out of our I.E.P teacher office. We didn't see anyone in the hallway. We told our I.E.P teacher bye and we hurried up and left. Rebbeca said, "I don't like going to that office." I said, "I don't mind going. I just don't want, none of my friends to see me in there." When I went to class, I sat down in my seat. I looked at my I.E.P forms that my granny was going to sign. When my teacher handed me my classwork I did it. When, I was done with my classwork. I had finished reading my I.E.P forms, and I filled them out and I forward my granny signature on them. When the bell rang to go home, I met up with Rebbeca in the back of the school. I talked to Nathan for a little while. Before he had to go to football, practice and I had to go to work. I saw Jessica on my way to work. When Rebbeca and I made it to work, I was so tired from walking up the hill. I felt like I had ran a marathon and all I wanted was some water. I went to say hi to Jannette and Vida. Jannette told me to clock in early, so I did. She asked me where was Rebbeca. I said, "She is in the breakroom." Jannette said, "Go get her and tell her that I said to go clock in. So we can get everything done. I know it's the first day of school and you both are tired, but y'all still have a job to do." "Ok auntie." I said, "Rebbeca, auntie Jannette told me to tell you to go clock in." "Oh, I am. I need my money. Tell her I'm going to right now." This girl named Amber went to OT High with us. She was a senior. She worked with us and she was nice. Jannette said, "Zaneeya, after you're done putting everything out. I want you to help clean these chairs." Amber, and Rebbeca and I were goofing off. As we were working, because we did not have anything else to do, we were done with everything. Jannette came in the diningroom. She said, "Oh, you guys want to mess around today huh?"Amber said, "Jannette, you know we love you." "If y'all loved me you wouldn't be messing around and talking." Rebbeca said, "Auntie we are finish with are work." I said, "Jannette we have to talk a little. You have always told us, that you do not mind us talking. As long, as were not serving on the floor." Jannette said, "Jannette hell! Since you guys are done, y'all can come clean some busting carts."

"Jannette I love you to death, but I am not cleaning any busting carts." I said while I was joking with her. Amber said, "I love you too Jannette, but I'm not cleaning any either." Jannette said, "Both of you are going to clean them right now! With some soup and water, let's go. Rebbeca, do you have something to say? You can clean some busting carts too." Rebbeca replied, "No auntie, I don't have anything to say. I'm fine with cleaning the chairs." Amber and I were laughing as we were cleaning the busting carts. I said, "Amber watch this, I'm going to tell Jannette that we can't get the corners of the busting carts clean and I know she's going to tell us to use a knife." Amber started laughing. I said, "Jannette." She replied, "What do you want?" "Auntie come here please, it's important." Jannette came inside the kitchen. She said, "What is it?" I said, "We cannot get the corners of the busting carts clean. What do you want us to do?" "That's what you called me in here for?" I smiled while I was giggling. I said, "Yeah." "Don't call me again. Use a knife to clean the corners. You better make sure that they are clean too, because I'm going to come back in check. You and Amber call y'all self's being funny huh? That's ok, I'mma fix y'all. Vida, when Amber and Zaneeya are done cleaning these carts, put them on dishes. Since they like to joke around, their going to be behind today and they have to bust their section too." I said, "That's ok auntie. Amber and I are fast when it comes to doing the dishes and we are going to be done with mopping and sweeping by 7:15 PM watch." "We'll see. Matter of fact, get on the floor and get ready to serve." I went to my section. I knew what my strategy was. When the residents was finish eating, I was going to ask them, was it ok if I take their glasses and cups. That way, I wouldn't have to get a busting cart. I was going to put the dishes on my tray, and take them to the kitchen, and put them in a bucket of water. Then rack them. Jannette did not notice that I was finish busting my tables. When, it was 6:05 PM. I said, "Amber, are you ready to go do the dishes?" "Yeah, but you have to bust your tables first." "I busted my tables already." I sprayed and worked on clean side, Jannette came in the kitchen. She said, "Zaneeya you have to go bust your tables." "I did." "I did not see you take your busting cart out there, come on." "Let me show you auntie." I took Jannette to the section that I was working in. I said, "See, I told you I busted my tables already." Jannette looked me. She said, "You sure did. I know you didn't bring no busting cart out here earlier while you were serving!" "Now Jannette, you know I know better than that, of course not. I'm just a fast worker. Now I have to get back to work." I said as I smiled. "Go ahead and you're going to tell me when you busted your table too." "Ok Jannette."

I went back in the kitchen. Amber was on clean side putting up the dishes. We all worked as a team, mostly when it came to the kitchen. Amber and I were finished with the dishes. Sweeping and mopping by 7:20 PM. Soon as we were finished, we went to the dinningroom and sat down on the side of Jannette. Jannette said, "Why are y'all sitting down?" I said, "We are finish with are job duties. Can I have some juice? I am dying of thirst right now!" "Yeah you can. Then help Rebbeca in the diningroom. Then you can sit down." Amber and I helped Rebbeca put her silverwear out on the tables. Then we sat right back down. When I got off work, I went to the bus stop. David had called me. I told him I was going to call him when I made it home. When, I got home. My granny said, "Zaneeya I know you're tired." "Yes I am granny. My legs are killing me right now. I can't wait to eat. What did you cook for dinner?" "I made some beefstew and some corn bread. You can eat when you want too." "Ok granny thank you." I got in the shower then I ate. Then I called David back. We talked on the phone for a couple of hours then I went to sleep. The next day, Sabreea called me and she asked me did I want to spend the night at her house. I told her I would. After school, I had went to sign up for acting classes. The classes were on Tuesdays and Thursdays, from 3:45 PM until 5:30 PM. I knew the acting teacher already, because one day I sat in her class to see what the class was all about. When she was finished teaching her class, she walked over to me. She said, "Hi, are you thinking about joining my class?" I replied, "Yes I am. I'm thinking about joining your class next year, because I already have two jobs after school and there's no way I would be here on time." "Ok, well my name is Pam." "Nice to meet you Pam, my name is Zaneeya .I'm going to take your class next year." "Ok, I'm looking forward to seeing you." When I walked in the class, it was in the auditorium and their wasn't many students in there. I walked up to Pam. I said, "Hi do you remember me? We talked after you were done teaching one of your classes last year and I told you I was going to take your class this year." "Yes I remember you. Your name is Zaneeya. I didn't forget. I'm happy you're taking my class. We are going to do a worm up. Then I'm going to show you everything you need to know about acting." We all stood in a circle and Pam taught us a few lessons. After we were done, Pam gave us a script that we all had to practice, because we were going to be performing at school in front of everybody. I was nervous, but I knew I liked acting and I liked writing poems. So I was excited to perform in front of my friends. After, class was over. Pam asked me did I want to read a poem out loud in front of my family and friends, because, we also were going to perform after school in three months.

I told Pam yes, I would like that. She said, "The poem can be about whatever you want it to be. When, you are done with your poem show it to me." I said, "Ok thank you. I'm going to start writing my poem this weekend." "Ok, I'll see you next week in class Zaneeya." "Ok, bye Pam. Thanks again." "You're welcome." When I went home, I told my granny that I joined an acting class. She was happy for me. I had to tell Jannette, so she would not put me on the schedule to work on Tuesdays and Thursdays. When the weekend came, I went to Sabreea's house. She was five months pregnant. She was having a girl. I cooked dinner for us. We ate and we stayed up talking. When her boyfriend came over, I went into the livingroom with momma Shay and we listened to music. After he left, Sabreea came out of the room and she sat in the livingroom with us. We stayed up that night. She showed me some of the things that she had bought for my niece. I asked Sabreea was she ready to be a mom. She said, "I wasn't at first, but I am now. I don't have a choice." I said, "I can't believe that you're going to have a baby. I knew you were having sex, but I thought you would have used a condom at least, because you know you can get pregnant." "I did use a condom, it broke." "Yeah right, you damn well that you did not use a condom at all. So stop it, you might be fouling mom, but you are not fooling me. I know better." She smiled. She said, "Yes I did. Shut up, boy your niece is kicking me like crazy. She is always kicking me in my ribs, it hurts so bad to the point where I cry." "Good that's what you get. Welcome to pregnancy, I heard it's not a walk in the park." "I like being pregnant. I get everything I want. Everybody spoils me with gifts and food. I just don't like it when your niece is kicking me. So Zaneeya, are you having sex now?" "No I'm not. I'm still a virgin and I'm proud. I am enjoying working and going to school. No kids for me right now, but I will be spoiling my niece and nephew." "I can see you buying your niece a lot of clothes too. I'm going to bed, good night sis." "Good night sis." I stayed up so I could finish writing my poem then I went to bed. When I woke up the next day, I got dressed and I went home.

As time went on, I kept working and going to school and I was still attending my acting class. My grades were fine and I was making sure that I kept them up. Homecoming was coming up. Jessica, Katelyn, Desiree, Champaign, Lucy and two more other girls and I was participating, in the dances for are class for homecoming. Everyday at lunch, we would practice our dance routine. A couple of days before homecoming, the principal said, "You can talk on your cell phones at lunch, but if the bell rings to go to class. You have to hang up your cell phones and if you don't, they will be taken." Therefore, on the same day that the principal gave that announcement, the bell ranged to go to lunch. I went to get something to eat. Then I went to dance practice. I stayed at practice until the bell ranged to go to class. As I was walking to class, I saw Amber. We were talking for a little while. I pulled my phone out to see what time it was and I put my phone right back in my pocket. Mr. German walked towards me. He said, "I seen that, give me your phone right now. The principal just gave announcement today about talking on your cell phones after the bell ring. So give me your phone." I said, "I was not talkin on my phone. I looked to see what time it was." "You were texting on your phone. Give it to me." "I'm not giving you my phone and I was not texting." Amber said, "She was not using her phone Mr. German. She was looking to see what time it was. You did not see her texting, so stop lying." Dudy walked over to where I was. He said, "German, you're always messing with somebody. Go teach yo class, and mind yo bussiness with your funny looking self." Mr. German said, "If you keep talking young man, I will take you to the principal office too." "You can't make me do nothin." Mr. German told me to walk to the principal office. I said, "For what? I have to go to class. I don't have time for this and you should be teaching your class right now, instead of tryin to get me in trouble by lying on me." "I'm taking you to the principal office or I'm going to call security." "Call security, I don't care." Mr. German told one of the security guards to call Miss. Petter and let her know what was going on. The security guard did. Then the security guard asked me what my name was, but I did not tell him.

I walked to the principal office with the security guard. Miss. Petter came out of her office. The security guard said, "This is the student that refused to give up her cell phone." Miss. Petter said, "Who, which one?" The security guard pointed to me. Miss. Petter said, "Zaneeya. Are you sure this is the student?" He replied, "I'm sure this is her." Miss. Petter said, "Zaneeya come in my office." I went inside of Miss. Petter's office and I sat down. She said, "What's going on? Why were you talking on your phone, after the bell ranged to go to class?" I said, "I was not talking on my phone. Mr. German is lying, and I have two witnesses and they can tell you that I was not talking on my phone. I just looked at the time." "Ok, who are they?" "Amber and Dudy." "Dudy is definitely going to back you up, because that's your cousin, and Amber and you are probably friends. I do believe that you were not talking on your phone, but I still have to take it. Just for five days." "What, are you serious? I like you Miss. Petter, but I am not giving you my phone. I haven't done anything wrong." "Zaneeya you're my girl, trust me. I will give you, your phone back in five days."

"I know you will, that's not the problem at all. I haven't done anything wrong to have my phone taken. So that's why, I'm not going to give it to you." *"Ok, well I don't want to do this, but if you don't give me your phone. I'm going to have to suspend you for the rest of the week, but if you give me your phone, you don't have to worry about getting suspended."* *"I love you Miss. Petter. I really do, but I am not giving you my phone! So go ahead and suspend me. Does that mean I cannot dance for homecoming?"* *"No, you can't dance for homecoming now. I'm going to suspend you for two days. You can come back to school next week."* *"Ok, bye Miss. Petter."* *"Bye Zaneeya, stop by my office when you come back to school."* *"Ok I will."* *I left and I went to the bus stop, so I could go home. On my way home, I stopped at this boutique downtown. I bought me an outfit and I bought Desseire an outfit too, because her birthday was coming up. When I left the boutique, I noticed that I did not have my backpack with me. I left my backpack inside of the store.*

When, I went back to the store. I told the sales associate, that I left my backpack inside of the dressing room. The sales associate gave me my backpack. Then I left. I stopped at Mr. Pizza Man and I bought my granny and me a slice of pizza. Then I went home. When, I made it home. My granny said, "Zaneeya, what are you doing home so early?" I told my granny what happened. I ate my pizza. Then did my homework then I got a call from Lucy. She asked me what happened, so I told her. Jessica called and Desseire called me too. I told them what happened as well. Rebbeca had called me and she asked me. Did I want to spend the night, over Angel's house with her? I told her I would. She told me her and Fred was coming to pick me up. When, Fred and Rebbeca came to pick me up. We went to get something to eat. Then we went to Angel's house. Angel was happy to see me. She said, "Hi Zaneeya. How are you doing?" I gave Angel a hug. I said, "I'm doing good Angel. How are you doing auntie?"

"I'm doing well. I haven't seen you in a long time. Let me ask you something. Why did you leave Rene and Letha's house? Were you tired of Letha's mess?" "I was tired of not seeing my family and being mistreated. I just couldn't take it any more so I left." "Oh ok, I knew you had a reason for leaving. So do you like staying with your granny?" "Yes, I like living with my granny. That's my baby." "Do you guys ever argue?" "We do sometimes, but that's my granny and I love her." I spend the weekend at Angel's house with Rebbeca. We cooked dinner. We talked we watched videos and we just chilled in the house. David and I were still talking. I told David, that Tammie was lying when she told him that I was 18 years old. I told David that I was 16

years old and he still wanted to talk to me. I called Susan to see what she was doing, because I haven't talked to her in a while, but she nerved answered her phone. So I stopped calling her. When the weekend was over, Fred took me home. The next day, I went to school. I seen Lucy and she was telling me how much fun homecoming was. Later on that day, I went to work and I put my phone on the charger so I could charge it. I went to check on my phone, and 15-minutes later and it was not there. I went to tell Jannette that somebody took my phone. Jannette said, "Calm down, don't worry. We are going to find out who took your phone." Jannette called all of her employees to the diningroom.

Jannette said, "Zaneeya phone is missing. Somebody stole it and if I find out who stole her phone, you will be fired. I'm not playing! So who ever got it. Give it up now!" Nobody didn't say nothin. I said, "Somebody has my phone. If I find out who took my phone, I'm taking off. Male or female, I don't care!" Jannette said, "Calm down Zaneeya. Everybody go get your backpacks right now, and before you get them, empty out your pockets." Everybody emptied out their pockets. Then they went to get their backpacks. They knew Jannette wasn't playin about being fired and everybody needed their jobs at this moment. Everybody took their stuff out of their backpacks. Nobody had my phone in their backpacks, but I do believe that somebody had it on them and I was going to raise hell. Before, I left work! I said, "Jannette can we look at the security cameras and run the tapes back?" "Yes, we are going to the front desk and I am going to tell the receptionist to run the cameras back." Jannette and I sat down at the front desk and we looked at the cameras. We did not see anything. I was mad, I just bought that phone and I did not want to spend my money on buying me another one, but I had too. I went home and I told my granny what happened. My granny said, "That's messed up, somebody stole your phone." I said, "I just bought that phone granny. I do not want to buy another one." "I know, but you have too." I called David on my house phone, to let him know, that I was not ignoring his calls and to tell him that my phone had been stolen at work. My granny told me that Dorthy, Mimi and Christy were coming to live with us, because Tony and Dorthy had broken up. I knew Dorthy was moving to the Bay Area, because when I was in Modesto. Tony and her had got into an argument and she said she was moving to the Bay Area. I knew she was going to live Ike or my granny and me. The next day I went to school, I gave Pam my poem. She said she liked it. Pam taught me the ends and outs of acting. She taught me how the lights should be placed on you, while performing. She taught me the difference between stage right and from stage left. She was great at her job and I liked how she taught the class.

She made me want to be an actor even more, even though I wanted to be a lawyer. When I went home, Christy, Mimi and Dorthy was there. My granny had a full house. I slept on one of the couches and Mimi and Christy took turns sleeping on the other couch. Dorthy enrolled Christy and Mimi at OT High, I introduced them to my friends and I told Christy and Mimi if they had a problem with anyone to let me know. I seen Lil Kevin's mom at my school. I called her auntie. She was still family, even though my uncle Kevin and her was not together. She looked at me. She said, "Zaneeya, give me a hug. How are you doing? I did not know you go to school here."

I said, "Hi, auntie I'm doing good. This is my second year at OT." "Do you like this school, is OT a good school?" "I like it here, it's a good school." "Ok, well I'm happy you go here, because I'm enrolling your cousin here. I want you to look after Lil Kevin for me and make sure he stays out of trouble, and if anything happens, call me. I'm going to give you my number." "Ok auntie, but you know your son does not listen to anyone. I would have to put my foot in his butt, because he will not be talkin to me like he's crazy." "When he starts running his mouth, do it." "Lil Kevin is going to have me in so much trouble. I can feel it now. Well, I'll see you later auntie. I'm going to class bye." "Ok, see you later." I saw Rebbeca at school. I told her that Lil Kevin was going to start going to school with us. Rebbeca said, "We are going to be fightin everyday, because of him." I said, "No were not. I'm going to have his back, because he is my little cousin, but I have to talk to him. That's for sure." At lunch, I went to buy me another cell phone. Then I walked backed to school. When school was over, I went to go meet Christy and Mimi in the back of the school. I talked to my friends then I we went home. Christy said, "Zaneeya you have some fine male friends. It's so many fine guys up here I don't know what to do!" "Look at you, you're choosen already." Christy laughed. She said, "You know I am." When we went home, I did my homework at the kitchen table. Then I showered, ate and I talked to David on the phone. The next day, I went to school, I seen Lil Kevin at the 15- minute break. I introduced him to Christy. I told Lil Kevin to stay out of trouble, and do not start any mess with anybody. I also told him to go to class. He said, "I am cousin stop trippin. I just got here." I said, "I'm not trippin. I'm letting you know right now that I am not playin. Where is your backpack and everything?" "I don't need a backpack, I'm good. Can I have some lunch money?" "You don't need any lunch money. I know your mom gave you some money before you came to school." "She only gave me $5 dollars. Come on cousin please?" "Ok, I'm only giving you $5 dollars and that's it. Do not ask me for no more money today." "I'm not, thank you."

Rebbeca walked up to us. She said, "Lil Kevin we are not going to be fighting everybody, because of you. Stay out of trouble and don't start mess with no one." He replied, "I know, I know Zaneeya just got done preaching to me. Y'all better just hope nobody say nothin to me or it's on." I said, "Just stay out of trouble. Just like, I stood in front of that gun for you. I might not be there the next time. Then what?" "Nothing is going to happen to me cousin trust me." "I can't trust you. You do not have all yo marbles. Anyways, you got the message. Now go to class, the break is over. Matter of fact, I'm going to walk with you. My class is right by yours." Lil Kevin and I began to walk to class and it was a lot of students in the hallway. He pushed this girl. He said, "Hurry up and walk damn." I said, "Why did you do that? What if she would have turned around in slapped you?"

"She was walking to slow and if she would have slapped me, I know you would have slapped her." I told him to hurry up and get to class. After school, I went to work. Jannette said, "Zaneeya, the holidays are coming up and you know you have to work every holiday. I need you." "Ok auntie." When I got off work, I went home. Later that on night David called me. Christy was making fun of me while I was on the phone. She said, "You're always Cupcaking." I replied, "I'm not cupcaking. I'm enjoying my conversation so hush." David and I would stay on the phone all night and talk. It was normal for us. Two months had gone by and it was time for me to perform my play at school. I called my dad and I invited him. I invited Jannette and a few other family members. My mom told me that she couldn't come to my play, because she lived in Modesto. Everybody else told me that they were coming to my play. When, it was time for me to go on stage to say my poem. I didn't hear anyone yelling my name and I didn't see any familiar faces. After I was done saying my poem, I went back stage. Pam said, "Zaneeya you did a job great." "Thank you Pam." After the play was over, Pam told us how great of a job we all did. Then I left and I went home. When, I went home. My granny said, "Did your dad go to your performance?" I replied, "No he didn't, but that's ok." I showered then I went to bed. When I would come home from school, I would bring my granny something to eat and I would bring Dorthy something too. When, Dorthy would have money. She would buy Christy, Mimi and my granny something to eat, but she wouldn't buy me anything to eat. Therefore, I told my granny. I was not going to buy Dorthy anything else, because she would never buy me anything, not even a 50-cent soda. Dorthy didn't stay with us for long, she moved back to Modesto. She went to live with my mom. I was still working and going to school. My grades dropped. I had gotten two

F's. I would ask Miss. Petter for my report cards, because it was still going to Letha's house and everytime I would ask Rebbeca to get my report card. She would say somebody opened it or somebody threw it away. So, I just stopped asking her for it. I knew I had to bring my grades up, and I knew how I had to do it. See, I never blamed any of my teachers for giving me a bad grade and I never had any excuses for why my grades dropped.

Rebbeca had wanted me to spend the night at her house. I told her no. She said, "Please Zaneeya." "You have to ask Rene and see what she says." I knew Rene would let me spend the night anytime I wanted to, but I did not know how Letha felt about that. Rebbeca said, "My mom is not trippin and you know that." I said, "You still need to ask her." "Ok, I'm going to ask her." Rebbeca called her mom and asked her could I spend the night. She said, "I told you that she wouldn't mind." When, I went inside of Rebbeca's house. I said, "Hi Auntie Rene." Rene said, "Long time, no see." "I know I know." Letha came out of her room. I said, "Hi Letha." She replied, "Zaneeya, you didn't have to leave my house like that. If you wanted to leave, you should have told me and I would have dropped you off in Modesto." "I don't want to live in Modesto and you know that. You were not going to let me take my clothes with me. I wasn't happy here, and I did not like how you were treating me. So I left." "How was I treating you?" "I am not about to go back in forth with you Letha." "We are not going back in forth, and I'm not letting on one else live here. They would have to go to a foster care. Everybody else that lives here, they run away. Tina, Eva and you, but it will not happen again." Rebbeca I went to the store to get us something to snack on. Then we went in her room. David had called me. We talked and he was telling me, that I was going to fall in love with him. I said, "What if I'm already in love with you?" He replied, "Are you in love with me?" I paused on the phone for a while. David said, "Hello, are you in love with me Zaneeya?" "Yes I am." "I'm in love with you too. I love you SC." "I love you too." SC was my nickname that David called me and I liked it. Rebbeca said, "Aw look at you, how cute." David said, "Tell Rebbeca to be quite, but for really I want you to be my lady. So Zaneeya, will you be my Lady?" "Yes, I will be your lady." "I'm happy we are together." David's brother Cedrick heard us talking. He said, "SC what's up sis?" He yelled threw the phone. I said, "Hi brother." I always called Cedrick brother, because he treated me as if I was his little sister. David and I talked for a little while longer then I went to bed. Rebbeca said, "How do you feel about David? Clearly, you love him, but how long have you been in love with him, you didn't even tell me?"

"I like him. He is so interested in me, even as a friend and we can talk about everything. I like how he cares if I had a bad day. He will try to make me laugh. I'm happy that he's in college and he is doing something with his life. He is not just sitting around and doing nothing. I like how he loves his mom. He is a true mammas boy and he is a good guy and I have to say, that I do love him." Rebbeca said, "Aw you made me cry Zaneeya." "Why are you crying crazy?" "I'm just happy for you. David is really into you and his family likes you and you all get along great." "Thanks Rebbeca." "Are you going to see him for the holidays?" "I wish he wants me too. We talked about this for a while now, but auntie Jannette won't let me take off work. So I don't have a choice, but to work. David will understand." "You know what I think? David has been in love with you for a while." "I think he has too, because he will always say, you're going to fall in love with me watch. I'm going to ask him how long has he been in love with me and see what he says." "I'm happy for y'all Zaneeya." "Thanks Rebbeca." The next day, Rebbeca and I went to work. When I went on my break, I called David. As I was talking to him, Rebbeca was making fun of me. Jannette said, "Who is she talking to niece?" Rebbeca replied, "She is talking to her man, David." I said, "That's right." Jannette said, "I need to ask you something when you get off the phone." "Ok auntie." David and I talked for 15-minutes then I got off the phone, and I went into Jannette's office. I said, "Auntie, what do you want to ask me?" She smiled at me. She said, "Zaneeya are you doing the nasty?" I laughed. I said, "Jannette stop it, no." "Don't tell me no. You don't say no to David when you're giving it up to him. Do you?" "Jannette I am still a virgin! We can call David right now and you can ask him have we ever had sex. You can even ask Rebbeca and she will tell you." "No that's ok, just use a condom. You do not want to have a baby while you're still in high school. You, need to enjoy your life right now, it's harder with a baby." "I am not having a baby at 16 years old or 17 years old or 18 years old. I promise you that." "Good, I'm happy your not, and plus I'm not ready for you to have a baby right now. Not even 3 years from now." "I'm not worried about that auntie." "Good, it's time for me to go home. I'll see you later and Zaneeya. Tell David I said, you are not going to be taking off work for him." "Sometimes I will have to auntie." "Yeah, try it and see what happens." "Jannette you're not going to fire me or suspend me. You love me. I'm one of your best workers. I really work for my money and hands down, I do a damn good job." "You do, but watch your mouth girl, good night." "Good night Jannette."

For the holidays, my granny went to my mom's house and to my uncle Alvin's house. I stayed at Angel's house. Then when my granny came back into town, I went home. I called my mom. I said, "Mom, guess who's pregnant." "Who? I hope your not!" "No, I'm not crazy." "Well who then? I can't think right now," "Sabreea is pregnant." "What? Sabreea is pregnant! How many months is she and why is she having a baby so young? She is only a baby herself, both of y'all are." "She is seven months pregnant and I know were young, but her mom is going to help her. To be honest, I'm happy that my sister is having a baby. I'm not saying that I wanted her to get pregnant, but I'm happy that I'm having a niece. I'm going to spoil her and just love on her." "Well, I'm happy you have a niece, but please do not get pregnant next Cupcake. Just wait to have a baby, you're so young." "Mom, I know I'm young and I don't want a baby right now. My nephew and my niece are going to be my babies. I'm excited about being an auntie. I already know what their nick names are going to be." "Well, tell Sabreea I said congratulation and to take good care of her baby. Tell her to be over protective with her baby too, and tell her to call me." "Ok mom, I love you. I'll talk to you later." "I love you too." David and I made plans to see each other after New Year's. So I asked Jannette, could I work four days straight. So I wouldn't have to work over the weekend. She told me I could. I worked Monday, through Thursday. On Friday, I called Justin Jr., and I asked him did he want to go to Modesto with me. He told me yeah. I went to Angel's house and I got my clothes. I asked Tina could she take me to the Greyhound station, and I told her I will give her $25 dollars for gas. Tina dropped Justin Jr., and I off at the Greyhound station. I bought our tickets then we got on the bus. David wanted me to go straight to Stockton, but I told him. He had to pick me up from my mom's house in Modesto. When I made it to my mom's house, I called David to let him know that I was there. He told me he was on his way to come get me. My mom said, "Do not have sex Cupcake." "Mom, I'm not talking about this." "Well, are you on birth control?" "Mom, I am not answering you." I asked Christy did she want to go with me to Stockton. She said, "Yeah." So I told her to pack her bags. We were only staying out there for one night. I was getting nervous while I was waiting for David. He called and my mom gave him direction to her house. He pulled up in the driveway. My mom opened the door. She said, "Come on in. Which one is David?" David walked over to my mom and gave her a hug. He said, "Hi, how are you doing?" My mom replied, "I am doing well. How are you? We have to have a long talk before you leave with my daughter." "Ok that's fine. This is my cousin Xavier." "How are you doing?" Xavier said, "I'm *doing well. How you are?" "I am going to be much better once I talk to David." David said, "Where is Zaneeya, is she ready?" "Let me go get her for you." My mom came in her room. She said, "Come on Zaneeya. What are you waiting for? You knew he was coming. What are you nervous?" "Mom hush. Yeah I am a little nervous and I'm waiting for Christy."*

Christy said, "I'm ready." I went into the kitchen where David was. He looked at me and he smiled. He got up and gave me a hug. I said hi to Xavier. Xavier was always cracking jokes. He said, "Zaneeya are you nervous?" "I'm a little nervous." "David is nervous too. That's cute." I introduced Christy to David and Xavier. My mom went to her room. When, she came back inside the kitchen. She said, "David let me tell you something. That is my only daughter. She is a virgin and I want her to come back a virgin too. Do you hear me? I have a gun and I am not afraid to use it. Let me show it to you." My mom showed David her gun. She said, "I'm not playin with you. You seem like a nice young man. If you do not want to be with my daughter, you let her down real easy. Do you hear me." He replied, "Yes, I hear you and I will." I asked David was he ready to go. He said, "Yes." So we left. I told my mom bye. She said, "Ok Cupcake. I'mma call you." "Ok mom bye." When we got in the car, David kept staring at me and he was smiling from ear to ear. Xavier said, "Start the car man. Let's go, y'all got all night to look at each other." We all laughed. David picked up my hand and he kissed it. Xavier said, "David, I'm going to need you to focus on the road, before we get into a car accident." I giggled. We stopped and got something to eat. Then we went to David's house. David told Christy she could sleep in his sister room, Xavier left. I put on my pajamas, and David and I went to bed. The next morning, I did not want to wake up. David told me to wake up, but I didn't. So he put some music on and he played it loud. Then he started pulling all the covers off me, so I just gave in. Cedrick came in the room. He said, "What's up SC? Is that all your hair? You came to see yo man! Huh?" "Yeah, this is my hair. I had to come see him" "It's not too many ladies with long hair." After Christy and I got dressed, we waited for David to get dress. Christy said, "So Zaneeya, did you have sex last night? Are you still a virgin?" "I'm not telling you anything. We are going to have a nice day and that's it!" "I know you did, it's all in yo face." I went to David's room to see if he was ready to go. When we left David's house we went to the barbershop where Xavier worked at. We stayed there for a little while then we went to the mall. David and I were holding hands, as we were walking. Christy did not want to walk with us. So she walked in front of us. We stopped at this shoe store, where David's friend worked at, and he introduced me to his friend. Then we left. We took Christy to her Godsister house, so she could pick something up. Then we went to get something to eat. Then we went back to David's house.

When we got to David house, I gave Christy her food. Then David I went to his room, and we talked and laid down for a little while. My mom called me. She said, "Cupcake, make sure you come home tonight." "I'm going to leave in a little while." I was thinking about spending another night. David did not want me to leave. He said, "SC, just spend another night please." I replied, "I wish I can, but I have to go to my mom's house. You can spend the night with me at my mom's house." "I'm not spending the night at your mom house. It's too many people over there." "Oh ok, let's see if I spend the night with you again!" "You will I'm not worried about that. I wish you could spend another night tonight." "I do too, but let's go before it gets late." When we arrived to my mom's house, David came inside. We sat down and talked. My mom said, "David I hope you did what I told you to do." He smiled, but he did not comment. She said, "I don't know why you're not commenting, but you better give me an answer." He replied, "I listened to you. You don't have to worry." David told my mom and my brothers bye. Then I walked him outside. We hugged and kissed, and I told him to call me when he makes it back home. When, I went inside the house. My mom said, "You miss him already. I can tell." I said, "I do, I cannot wait to see him again." "I hope you're not pregnant." "I'm on birth control, and if I was to have sex I would use a condom. Like I told you, I'm not having a baby right now." "Good, I knew you were smart enough to get on birth control and to use condoms. I'm happy you don't want kids right now." I made a pallet in my mom's room on her floor and I went to sleep. 30-minutes later, my phone had ranged so I answered it. David called and told me that he made it home. We stayed on the phone and talked until we fell asleep. The next morning when I woke up, my mom said, "Cupcake I don't want you to leave yet." "I have to mom. I have to go to school and I have to go to work." "Well, you can call into work and tell them that you don't feel good and you can miss a couple of days of school. It's not going to hurt you. You're going to the 11th grade." "I know I am. I just don't want to miss anymore days of school right now and I never call off work." "I know you don't, but I want to spend time with you. Cupcake just call into work and say you don't feel good." "Ok mom, I will this time." I called my job and I talked to Vida. I told Vida that I was not coming into work, because I didn't feel good. Vida said, "Ok, what's wrong, do you have the flu? Their is a lot of people that have the flu right now." "Yes Vida I have the flu, so I probably won't work tomorrow or the next day. Can you tell Jannette I called in? Or I'll call her tomorrow and tell her." "I'll tell her. Go get some rest. You don't never call off work, I know you're sick." "Ok Vida thank you." When I got off the phone, I told my mom what Vida said. My mom was so thrilled, about me staying a couple of more nights. She said, "Cupcake, I'mma make those tostadas that you like." Ramone came in the kitchen. He said, "Zaneeya, I thought you have to go to work?"

"I do have to work, but I just called into work, because mommy wants me to spend a couple of more nights with her." "Well, that's good, because we don't never get to spend time with you. When, you do come out here." "I know, I'm going to start spending sometime with all of you when I come out here." "Ok, I'm going to hold you to your word." "Go ahead, I want you too." David called me. He said, "Did you make it back to the Bay Area yet?" I replied, "No, I'm still at my mom's house." "Why?" "My mom wanted me to spend a couple of nights with her. So I called into work, and I told my supervisor that I was sick." "You can't be missin school, but a couple of days out of school and off work won't hurt you. I want to come see you." "I want to see you too. I'm going to ask my mom can you spend the night. Hold on, I'm going to ask her right now." I went to the kitchen and I asked my mom could David spend the night? My mom said, "Yes he can spend the night, but both of you are going to sleep in my room." "Ok that's fine. David what time are you coming?" He replied, "Did she say yes?" "Yes, I wouldn't be asking what time are you coming if she said no crazy!" "Ok, I'mma leave now." When, I got off the phone with David. My mom said, "Y'all can sleep right here on my floor and make a pallet." I said, "Ok mom." When David came, I was in my mom's room. He leaned over to kiss me and she walked in the room. She said, "Y'all better not kiss." David gave her a hug. Then we took Justin Jr., to Lason's house. Then we went back to my mom's house and we went to sleep. Every night that I spent at my mom's house, David stayed with me. When it was time for me to go home, I caught the Greyhound. David car couldn't make it all the way to the Bay Area. Other wise he would have taken me home. When, I made it back to the Bay Area. I called Ike. So he could pick me up, from the Greyhound station. Ike took me to Angel's house, because I had some clothes over there and I wanted to get them. Then he dropped me off at work, and he took my bags home for me. When, I arrived to work. Jannette said, "Zaneeya are you feeling better?" "Yes I feel much better." Even though, I told Vida I was sick. I really wasn't and I was not going to tell Jannettte that I was not sick. David had called me while I was working to see if I made it home safe. I told him I

was fine, and I will call him later, when I get off work. When I got off work, I went home and I showered. Then I did some homework then I ate dinner. After I was finish eating, I called David so we could talk. We didn't talk long that night, because I told him I was tired.

Sabreea called me and told me she was having a baby shower and she wanted me to spend the night at her house. I went to Sabreea's house a day before her baby shower. Momma Shay said, "Zaneeya, I'mma need you to be the host at your sisters baby shower." "Ok, that's not a problem. Anything you want me to do, I'mma do it." I asked Sabreea was our dad coming to her baby shower. She said, "He was supposed to buy my cake for me, but he is not going to buy it. So Andrea is going to buy it. She said it will be ready by tomorrow." I replied, "Dad could have bought your cake. It's not like, he doesn't have the money. He should really be here for you and support you. What did he say about you being pregnant, when you first told him?"

"I waited to tell him, because I didn't want dad to be mad at me, I really didn't. Mom told me that I have to tell him. So one day he called me and I said dad, I have something to tell you. I'm pregnant! Dad said, "You have to be kidding me." "No I'm really pregnant." He started bursting out laughing I was quite. Dad said, "You know what? That is a damn shame that you're pregnant. You are not going to graduate. You are not going to do anything with your life. You are a teen mom. That's sad, I knew you were going to end up pregnant, and you told me that you are a virgin. I knew you were lying when you said that." Dad hurt my feelings so bad that day, I hung the phone up in his face. I was crying. I could not believe dad said those mean things to me. He said more then that. Dad and Mom got into it. I knew dad was going to be mad, but I didn't think he was going too reacted like that." I replied, "Is he coming to your baby shower?" "He said he is, but we both know dad. I really don't think he's coming." "I don't think he's coming either. I will be shocked and surprised if dad shows up. Do not worry about what dad said. You are going to be a great mom. You need people lifting you up, not putting you down. I am here for you and my Tinky. Do not worry about what other people say. I don't care if he is our dad. If he says negative things to you, just hang up. I would, you do not need any stress right now. You need to enjoy the rest of your pregnancy. You are going to graduate. You're going to be a wonderful mother and you are going to make it in life. Don't let anyone stress you out." "Thanks sis, you always make me feel better. I know you're going to be here for your niece. You're always here for me. You cook for me when you come over. You spoil me too and I love you and I thank you." "I love you too."

The next morning, Sabreea said, "Sis did you bring your brown gauchos?" I said, "Yeah, but I'm not wearing them." "Wear them I'm going to wear my gauchos too, we can dress alike." "Ok, I'll wear them." After we got dressed momma Shay, and Sabreea and I left. We went to the store. Andrea went to pick up Sabreea's cake, it was nice. She had a Winnie the Pooh cake, Sabreea was happy. Momma Shay and I hung up the decorations. As Sabreea's guest was arriving, I told them where to put the gifts. I let them know that I was going to be the host and after we played some games. We were going to eat then open up gifts. Susan called me and I have not spoken to her in a long time. She asked me what I was doing. I told her I was at my sister baby shower. Susan said, "I want to come where is it at?" I told her where it was. Susan said, "I'm going to ask my mom can she drop me off." Susan asked her mom could she drop her off at Sabreea's baby shower. Her mom told her no, because the baby shower was too far, but we were only in San Leandro ca. Susan said, "Zaneeya is there a bus that goes over there?" "There is a bus that stops right in the front of Pizza Hut?" "My mom said you should get on the bus and come meet me." "Girl, I am not gettin on the bus to come meet you. I'm at my sister baby shower and I am not leaven!" "My mom said if you wanted me to come, you will get on the bus." "I am not leaving. If you want to come, you need to get on the bus or have your mom drop you off. She has a car, but that's up to you." "Now my mom said I can't go, because you won't come meet me." "What do I look like leaving my sister baby shower and I am the host? Even if I wasn't the host I would not go meet you!" "Ok, well I'm not going." "Ok, I have to go." When all of Sabreea's guest arrived, we started playing some games. We played the clothespin game. If you cross your legs then somebody can take your clothespin from you. We played the guessing game. Everybody had to guess what the baby name was. We played a word puzzle game, and after playing all the games, we ate and then we opened gifts. Then Sabreea cut her cake. Sabreea had a real good time and so did I.

After the baby shower was over, we said bye to all of Sabreea's guest. Then we put all of her gifts in Andrea's and in Bubba's mom car. After we were finished, we left and we went back to Sabreea's house. I was so exhausted from her baby shower. Sabreea said, "Thank you for helping me sis. You did a real good job." After Sabreea and I were finished talking, I went to bed. When I woke up the next morning, I asked Sabreea did she want me to help her organize Tinky clothes, before I went home. She told me no, she'll do it herself. I got dressed then I told Sabreea and momma Shay bye. I caught the bus home, when I got home. My granny said, "How was Sabreea's baby shower?" I replied, "*It was nice granny. She had fun and she received many gifts.*" "*That's really good. I'm happy you went to help your sister for her baby shower. That was really nice of you. Is she getting big?*" "*Yeah she is due in April. I cannot wait to see my niece.*" "*I know you are going to spoil that baby.*"

"*I sure am granny.*" Later on that night, David called me. We talked, my birthday was coming up and I was going to Modesto for my 17th birthday. My mom asked me did I want a cake for my birthday. I told her I wanted a champagne cake.Tammie and Nicky picked me up. I spend the night at Tammie's house. The next day, I was spouse to be with David. My mom called me and told me happy birthday and all of my friends did too. When Tammie woke up, I told her to take me to my mom's house. She knew I was spending the night at my mom's house and at David's house. Tammie was supposed to take me to Stockton that night to see David. After, Tammie got dressed. She dropped me off at my mom's house, and she went to her mom's house, which was right across the street from my mom's house. When I went inside my mom's house, she gave me a hug. She said, "*Cupcake do you want to go see your nephew?*" "*Yes I do.*" "*Ok, well Ranesha is going to pick us up. She is having a baby shower at her house for her sister.*" Ranesha picked us up. I couldn't wait to see my nephew. His name was Lil Qin. He was named after his dad, but I called him Booda. He was so cute. He had a head full of curly hair. Qin wasn't home. He was in jail. He was 18 years old and he had his first case against him. I knew he wasn't going to be in there long. I held Booda and I took pictures with him the whole time that I was there. David called me and asked what time was Tammie dropping me off.

When, I called Tammie to see what time she was coming. She said, "*I don't know what time I'm going to take you to Stockton, but I'm going to take you no matter what time it. Just call me, when you get to your my mom's house.*" "*Ok, thanks Tammie.*" "*Are you at a party? I know you said you were going with your mom somewhere.*" "*No, I'm at Ranesha's house. My brother Qin girlfriend .I'm visiting my nephew.*" "*Oh, you're over there with Ranesha?*" "*Why you say it like that, do you know her?*" "*Yeah I know her. Were not friends and how long are you going to be over there?*" "*I don't know, you told me to call you when I get to my mom's house. I should be at my mom's house in an hour.*" "*Ok, I don't want to drive my car way out there and it's late.*" "*You just said it don't matter what time it is. You are still going to take me. You know that's why I came out here. So I can see my family and to spend time with David. He leaves for the army this week and we will not see each other for a while.*" "*I know, just call me when you get to your mom's house.*" When

I got off the phone with Tammie, I asked Ranesha could she drop me off at my mom's house. She said, "Yeah."

When, I got to my mom house. I called Tammie, but she did not answer. David called me. He said, "SC, when are you leaving? I have been waiting for you all day. I did not know you were going to take this long. I had plans for us and everything." "I keep calling Tammie, but she's not answering. I'mma go to her mom's house and I'mma call you back." When I went to Tammie's mom house, I knocked on the door. Her mom opened the door for me. Tammie was sitting in the livingroom. I said, "I know you see me calling you." She replied, "Oh, I didn't hear my phone." "What time you are going to take me to Stockton." "Oh, I'm not taking you any more." "Why not?" "It's late and I do not want to drive to Stockton with no car insurance." "Tammie you been driving to Stockton and to the Bay Area with no insurance, but now all of a sudden you can't take me to Stockton after you said you would. You know I want be able to see David for a long time. It's not late, it's only 6:00 PM. Just take me back to the Bay Area tomorrow. I already gave you my gas money for picking me up and dropping me off."

"Ok, I'mma take you home. That's not a problem." I left and went to my mom's house. I was pissed off. I called David. He said, "SC, are you on your way?" "No, Tammie said she's not going to take me, because it's late and she doesn't feel like driving to Stockton with out any insurance." "She could have told you that yesterday or today. I should have just used Cedrick's car and came in got you." "Wait, Cedrick was going to let you use his car to come pick me up, why you didn't come?" "I didn't come, because I thought Tammie was going to bring you out here." "I wish you would have used Cedrick's car." "I know, you would have been out here already and that sounds like a bunch of B.S. Tammie is just mad, because Xavier don't mess with her any more, and now she's sipping on a six pack of haterade. Let me see what Cedrick is doing, so I can come get you. Hopefully, he is staying in the house tonight. If so, I know he will let me use his car. If he is going out he will still let me come get you, but it all depends on how soon he is leaving."

"Ok let me know." "I will, I love you!" "I love you too!" My mom said, "What happen you're not going to Stockton any more?" I told my mom what Tammie said. My mom said, "That's messed up. She knows how important this is to you, and she knew, she didn't have any insurance. When, she went to pick you up from the Bay Area. She is just being mean." "I know one thing mom. I am not messing with Tammie after this. I want her to drop me off at home and that's it." "I don't blame you Cupcake. Come eat some of your cake

that I bought you." "Ok, I'm a little upset, because I'm not going to see David for a while and I'm going to miss him." "I know you are Cupcake." David called me back. He said, "SC, Cedrick is going out tonight with Xavier and their leaving right now. He said if he wasn't leaving right now, he would let me use his car to go pick you up." I said, "Ok." David said, "I'm mad too! I had plans for us. Now I can't see you until I'm done with basic training and that's not until the summer time, five months from now. I don't want you to be sad. I love you SC and I'm only in love with you. I'm not going anywhere and you're not neither. I'm blessed to have you as my woman and to have to stick by my side through everything. I cannot wait to see you! Don't worry about Tammie. She won't have to worry about picking you up ever again. When I come home, we are going to get a rental car, until I go back to where I'm station at."

"Ok, I love you too. I miss you so much, and these months are going to go by fast." "I miss you too and your right, these months are going to go by fast, I can't wait. Cedrick wants to talk to you hold on." Cedrick said, "What's up SC. Happy Birthday. I'm sorry he can't come get you right now, I'm going out. I told him, he could use my car earlier to go get you, but he said Tammie was going to bring you. If I wasn't leaving right now. I would let him go get you, so don't be sad. He is sad over here too, but alright sis. I'll talk to you later here goes David." I replied, "Ok brother. Thank you for offering to let David use your car." "You're welcome SC." David got back on the phone. As we were talking Cedrick and Xavier yelled in the phone, "SC can your man come out with us tonight? David you better ask her, we don't want to get you in trouble, you're going to come back from basic training with no woman." Cedrick and Xavier were always clowning and they were funny. David said, "SC do you mind if I go out with Cedrick and Xavier tonight?" I replied, "This is your last weekend out here and since we are not going to see each other tonight, you should go out and have fun." "Thank you, I love you and I'll call you when I get in." "I love you too."

I ate another piece of cake. Then I went to bed. David had texted me, when he made it to the club. My mom asked me for some money. She said, "Cupcake, I'm going to see Qin tomorrow, but I don't have my id, but I can get an id from the check cashing. Can I have some money?" "Ok mom. I'll give you some money and you better go see my brother too. Don't be lying neither." "I'm not lying Ranesha is going to take me." I knew my mom was still on drugs and she would lie to get money out of anybody, not just me. I did not want my mom to go buy crack, with the money that I was giving her for the id. I told my mom, I would give her the money in the morning. Then I went back to sleep.

David called me, when he got home from the club. We talked for an hour. The next morning I woke up and showered. Then I got dressed, and I gave my mom $20 dollars. My mom said, "Cupcake, Ranesha is here. If you're not here by the time I get back, remember I love you and thank you for the money. You're a great daughter." "You're welcome mom, I love you too. Tell my brother I said hi and when he gets out of jail. He needs to stay out of trouble." I gave my mom a hug before she left. David called me and he told me to call him when I make it home. Tammie called and told me she was going to pick me up in an hour.

While I waited for Tammie, I talked to Patrick, Ramone and Lil Dawane. See I spoiled Lil Dawane. He was my baby and anything he wanted I gave him. I didn't care if it was money, food whatever he wanted from me, he got it. Patrick was telling me how smart mouth Lil Dawane was and my mom would tell me too, but he never acted that way in front of me. 45- minutes went by and my mom came back. I was thinking to myself. I don't know much about jail, but I do know that she would not have been done visiting Qin that quick. I said, "Mom what happen? I thought you were going to get an id to go see Qin?" "I was, but the id cost more than what I originally thought it did." "Oh ok." I walked into the kitchen. Tammie called and told me that she was outside. As I was leaving, I reached inside my pants pocket. So I could give Ramone and Patrick some money, but my money wasn't there. I didn't see any money on the floor. I said, "Did anybody pick up some money on the floor?" They said, "No." My mom was helping me look for my money, but I couldn't find it. I said, "Mom, I know you picked up my money off the floor, and that's messed up! Why would you steal from me after I just gave you $20 dollars today?" "I don't have your money." "Yes you do stop lying. Don't ask me for no more money, because I'm not giving it to you." I told my brothers bye and as I was walking out the door. My mom said, "Cupcake don't forget about your cake." When, Tammie dropped me off at home. I knew that was the last time, I was going to talk to her. My granny asked me did I have fun for my birthday and did I see David. I told her I thank God for letting me see another birthday. Then I told her what happen between Tammie and me. My granny was not too happy about that situation. My granny would always let me know who my real friends were and I love that about her. David called me. We talked about the army and how it was going to be hard on the both of us, because we would not be able to talk to each other morning, day or night.

The next day, I went to work. My friend Evelyn and I made plans to go to San Francisco. So we could go shopping over the weekend. Rebbeca said she wanted to go too. Over the weekend, Rebbeca and I spent the night over

Angel's house. The next day, Evelyn came to over there. So we could meet up. I introduced Evelyn to Angel and Justin. Jr. Then we walked to West MacAuthur Bart station. We got on Bart and went to Evelyn's house. We did not stay long then we went to another Bart station. Then we went to San Francisco, when we got to the city we went shopping first. We went to Old Navy and we went to Forever 21. Which are both clothing stores and we went to a couple of shoe stores. Then we got something to eat. We went to this pizza restaurant called Blondie's. After we were finished eating, Rebbeca and I were going back to Angel's house.

Evelyn said she was going to spend the night at Amber's house. Amber didn't live far from Angel. Evelyn told us she was going to her boyfriend house first, so she can get her clothes. It was late at night and Rebbeca and I did not want Evelyn to be walking around the west side by herself. So we asked her, did she want us to go with her. She said, "Yeah, I was going to ask you guys to walk with me to his house." As we were walking, we were talking about how much fun we had together and how we need to hang out more often. When, we arrived to Evelyn's boyfriend house. We waited for her outside. Her boyfriend was outside and so was his brother. When, Evelyn came back outside. She said, "I got all my clothes, let's go." As we were leaving, she said bye to her boyfriend and he said bye too. Then he said, "Evelyn wait, your not going anywhere! Go inside the house. Rebbeca and Zaneeya y'all can leave, but Evelyn is not going anywhere." Evelyn said, "Zaneeya and Rebbeca don't leave me! I'm coming." Evelyn's boyfriend grabbed her by her arms. He said, "Evelyn, you're not going anywhere! Go inside the house right now." She replied, "Let me go. I'm going to Amber's house, I'm not staying here." "I'mma slap you." "Please don't slap me, please don't! My friends are right here, stop." Her boyfriend slapped her. Rebbeca and I ran over to her boyfriend, because we were going to jump him, but his brother pulled a gun out on us. He said, "Y'all better not touch my brother or I'll shoot both of you in yo head right now." Rebbeca said, "Please don't shoot us. Please don't shoot us." I told Rebbeca to stand behind me, as I got in front of her. The gunman was laughing. I said, "If you shoot me you better kill me, if not you're going to have hell on yo hands." He pointed his gun in my face. He said, "You think you hard huh? You're really not scared huh?"

I said, "No, I'm not scared." The man put his gun down. Evelyn's boyfriend threw her clothes on the roof. I told Evelyn to come on and to forget about those clothes, because she can always go buy her some new ones. She said, "No, I just bought these clothes today and I'm not leaving without them and please don't leave me." I said, "We are not going to leave you, but you need to come *on." Rebbeca said, "Evelyn come on, I will buy you some clothes it is not that serious." I said, "Evelyn come on, his brother just pulled a gun out on us. Let's go and if you don't come I'm leaving and I'll be back. I'm going to get some help." I told Rebbeca I was going to our job and I was going to go get Shanice, which was Evelyn's big sister. I knew she worked that night. I said, "Rebbeca don't worry. I'll be back less then 10-minutes." Rebbeca said, "Zaneeya don't leave me! What if his brother shoots me?" "He is not going to shoot you. If he was he would have shot you earlier. He is not going to do nothing. He's one of those guys, who likes pulling guns out on females to scary them! I'mma call you in 5-minutes, and when I come back, I will be in a car." "Ok Zaneeya, but my phone is dead." "Here, you can use my phone. Matter of fact, let me call Jessica to see if she is home." I called Jessica and I told her what happened. She was upset. She lived right across the street from Evelyn's boyfriend. Jessica wasn't home. I gave Rebbeca my phone and I told her if anything else happens, call the police. As I was leaving, Evelyn boyfriend said, "Zaneeya, don't bring nobody on my block." I didn't say nothing, I just kept runnin. I ran from 38th street, all the way to my job. Which was five, blocks away. My asthma was flaring up, but I just kept on running. When I got to my job, I ranged the doorbell. Shanice was sitting at the front desk. She opened the door for me. She said, "Zaneeya what's wrong?" "Evelyn's boyfriend slapped her, and his brother pulled a gun out on Rebbeca and me, because we were going to jump him." "What? Hell nah. Let me make a phone call real quick." Shanice called her boyfriend. He came in got us less than 5- minutes. Amber was getting off work. She came with us. I used Amber's phone to call Rebbeca. I asked her did Evelyn get her clothes. Rebbeca said, "She is trying to get them right now." I said, "Tell Evelyn to leave those clothes up there. I'm with Shanice and Amber and were on are way." "I'll just stay on the phone with you until you get here."*

When we pulled up to Evelyn's boyfriend house, Rebbeca and Evelyn got in the car. Evelyn was crying. Her boyfriend kept calling her phone. He told Evelyn to tell me. That he is going to go up to my job and he is going to kill me. Shanice took the phone she said, "Don't you ever put your hands on my sister again. I'm calling the police on you and stay the hell away from sister and her friends." Shanice hung up the phone, in Evelyn's boyfriend face. Shanice said, "Evelyn you should have just left, instead of getting your clothes. You don't need to be with him, and you're not, going back to him either." Somebody kept calling my phone. I didn't recognize the number, so I didn't answer it. When I finally answered my phone, it was Evelyn's boyfriend. He said, "I'mma go to your job and I'm going to kill you, watch. I know where you work at and I will be up there when you get off." I replied, "I'll be waiting." I hung up the phone in his face, but he kept calling. I asked Evelyn, how did he get my number. She told me he got it out of her phone. He called Amber's phone, and she cussed him out and she hung up in his face. Shanice and her boyfriend dropped Amber off at home. Evelyn said she was spending the night at Amber's house. Amber told Evelyn, she needs to go home and rest. Shanice dropped Rebbeca and I off at Angel's house. We said bye to Evelyn and to Shanice and we thanked her and her boyfriend for dropping us off. Evelyn told us that she was sorry for what happened. I said, "Don't worry about that go home and get some rest." When we went inside of Angel's house, Justin Jr., asked us what was wrong with us. We said, "Nothing." I didn't want to tell my brother what happened, because I knew he would call my cousins, and David. I knew they wasn't coming to talk! They were coming for blood! I wasn't scared of Evelyn's boyfriend or his brother. I knew they were all talk. Rebbeca and I sat in the livingroom and Evelyn's boyfriend kept calling my phone. I didn't answer, but he kept calling, so I answered my phone. I said, "Stop calling my phone. I don't give a damn about nothing you're talking about." He replied, "I'll see you at work tomorrow watch." Angel came out of her room and she came into the livingroom. She said, "Rebbeca and Zaneeya tell me what's going on." Rebbeca told Angel and Justin. Jr., what happened. They couldn't believe it. Justin. Jr., was mad. He went downstairs to go get our cousins. He told them what happen. Our cousin Eva came in the livingroom. She said, "What did y'all do to make him pull a gun out on y'all?"

We said, "Evelyn's boyfriend slapped her in the face. So we ran over there to jump him and his brother pulled a gun out on us." Eva said, "That don't sound right. Y'all had to say something to make him pull a gun out on y'all! That couldn't be it." Rebbeca said, "That was it." "Zaneeya, did you say something to make him pull a gun out on y'all?" I said, "Are you serious? No I did not, we told you why." "Well, I know that don't add up." Evelyn's boyfriend called my phone again, but I did not answer. Eva said, "Zaneeya who is that?" "Evelyn's boyfriend." "Why is he calling you?" "He keeps calling me, because I went to get Evelyn's sister and he told me not to bring anybody on his block and now he keeps threaten me." Evelyn's boyfriend called my phone back, Eva answered it. She said, "Hello who is this, is this Evelyn's boyfriend?" He replied, "Yeah." "Well, this Zaneeya's cousin. Why are you calling my cousin phone and threating her?" "She should have never brought anybody on my block." "What did she do?" "Ask her, she knows." "Well, don't call her phone ok." He hung up. Eva said, "Zaneeya you did say something to him? He just said you did!" "I don't care what he said, he's lying! I didn't say nothing to him the whole time we was over there." "You had too. So what did you say?" "Stop asking me what I said, because I just told you I didn't say nothin." Rebbeca said, "Zaneeya did not say anything to him." I said, "Angel, I can call Evelyn right now and she will tell you herself. Eva I don't care if you don't believe me." I called Evelyn. I said, "Evelyn your on speakerphone, did I say anything to your boyfriend or his brother to make him pull a gun out on us?" She replied, "No you didn't! He just wanted to do that and he's not going to do nothing." Eva said, "Evelyn this is Zaneeya's cousin. So she didn't say anything to make him pull a gun out on them?" "No she didn't! My boyfriend is mad, because Zaneeya went to go get help. After she left .His brother, was saying how much heart she have, and how brave she is, because she wasn't even scared." I said, "Thanks Evelyn, it's ok .I'll call you later." "Ok Zaneeya." I said, "Angel, I told you her boyfriend is just mad." Angel said, "That's a damn shame. Both of them are some punks. Who pulls a gun out on some females?" Eva said, "Zaneeya, I just thought you said something to make him pull a gun out on y'all." I replied, "Why did it have to be me? It was two of us, but you kept insinuating that it was me, after I told you it wasn't."

"You were right, but I knew it wasn't Rebbeca. You're like me, we have a mouth on us. We have the same birthday, and we are the same sign and you just can't say anything to us and get away with it." "That's true, but I know what to say and when to say it. I was talking mess when he had that gun in my face, because I had a strong feeling, that he was not going to do nothing. Then I remembered having conversations with Evelyn before and she told me, his brother loves pulling guns out on people. I did not know that was his brother at the time. I found that out when he pulled his gun out on us." Eva went downstairs, and I went to put on my pajamas and I waited for David to call me. I really didn't know if I wanted to tell David or not. I knew if I told him, he would get his brother and cousin they was going to come down here and I knew that Evelyn's boyfriend wasn't going to do nothing. Justin Jr., said, "Zaneeya, where does those boys live at? I'mma slide threw." I told Justin Jr., where he stayed. Justin Jr., and my cousin went over there and when they came back, they said nobody was outside. David called me. I talked to him. He asked me did I have fun going shopping. I told him I had fun. He could tell I was hiding something from him. David said, "You're not yourself tonight what's going on?" I replied, "Nothing, why you say that?" Justin Jr., came in the livingroom. He said, "Zaneeya are you talking to David?" "Yeah why?" "Let me talk to him. Did you tell him what happened?" "No, not yet. I'll let

you talk to him after I'm done talking ok." David said, "Tell me what? Let me talk to Justin Jr." I said, "You can talk to him in a minute." Justin Jr., yelled in the phone, "David I have to tell you what happen, since she won't tell you. I'm trying to talk to you, but she won't give up the phone."David said, "SC let me talk to him please, since you won't tell me what happen." "I am going to tell you what happen. Justin Jr., big mouth self is standing right here and he is trying to tell you before I do." "We been on the phone for two hours and you haven't said nothing that's messed up." I told David what happened. He was furious. He said he was on his way down here. I told him to stay at home, because I knew they were not going to do nothin. David said, "Next time something like this happens you better let me know soon as we get on the phone." David told his brother and cousin what happened. They got on the phone. They said, "SC, we on our way out there right now." "No, y'all don't have too come he is not going to do anything." "They are some straight suckas! For a dude to hit a woman and to pull a gun out on a woman, they need to be handled for real! We love you SC and if anything like this happens, again we are coming. We don't care what you say." "Ok, I love y'all too." David got back on the phone. He said, "If that boy goes up to your job call the police, because they can get to you faster than I can. Then call me and I'm not playin. I love you and I don't want anything to happen to you." "Ok, I will. I hear you. I love you too."

"Let me talk to Justin Jr." I gave Justin Jr., the phone. They talked for a while, and I went to sleep. When Justin Jr., woke me up and he gave me back the phone. David said, "SC, did you go to sleep on me?" "You were talking to Justin Jr., you forgot all about me!" "We were just having a little man talk. Wake up, your not going to sleep yet." "I'mma call you in the morning. I'm tired. I love you and I thank you for being concern about me, good night babe." "I love you too, good night SC. I miss you." "I miss you too." The next morning when I woke up, David called me. He said, "I don't think you should go to work today. You should call your boss and tell her what happen and see what she says." I replied, "I'm going to work. I'm not worried about what happened." "Just call your auntie and let her know what happen please and call me back. Thank you." "Ok, I'mma call her right now." As I was calling Jannette, Rebbeca came in the livingroom. She said, "Zaneeya I don't think we should go to work." "You don't want to go to work, because of what happened?" Jannette answered the phone. I said, "Hi auntie." She replied, "I'm happy you called me niece. Can you come in early today? See if you can get Rebbeca to come in early with you." "I have to tell you something." "What is it?" I told Jannette what happen to Rebbeca, and Evelyn and I. Jannette said, "I'm going to take

y'all off the schedule for three days. Call me later on in the week ok." "Ok auntie." When I got off the phone, I told Rebbeca what Jannette said. Then I called David back to tell him as well. Later on that day, my uncle Ike came to pick me up. I asked him to take me home. When I got home, I told my granny what happen. I really didn't want to, because I didn't want her to worry about me. My granny was not too, eased about what happened. She told me I needed to be careful, and I need to stay home more. I told her I would. David called me. We were talking about him leaving for the army. We said we were going to write each other.When, David left for the army I was sad. I kept wondering what he was doing? All kind of thoughts would run threw my head. When I finally received a letter, it was two weeks after he arrived to Oklahoma. That's where he was stationed at for basic training. I was happy to read his letter. He let me know he was doing well, and he told me not worry about him.

He told me he didn't like getting up early, but he would get used to it and he told me he loved me and he couldn't wait to see me. He told me to call his mom. She wanted to talk to me and he wrote her number down, so I could call her. I went to the mailbox after writing him. When, I went back inside the house. My granny said, "What do you want to eat for dinner? I don't feel like cooking." "I don't know. If you don't feel like cooking I want some chinese food." "Ok, order it and get me some rice and see if they have some ribs." "Ok granny." I ordered some Chinese food. I got me some chicken chow main some shrimp fried rice and some beef and broccoli. We lived directly around the corner from the Chinese food restaurant. After I ate my food, I went to bed. Jannette told me after three days, I can come back to work. I called her on the second day and asked her could I come to work. Jannette said, "No!" I said, "But, I'm already here at work." "Come in my office." I went in her office. She said, "I told you to come to work after three days. What are you doing here?" "Auntie I know, but I need some money and I need my check to look like it always has. You know you want me to clock in." "Go ahead and clock in and hurry up too. I'm going to put you on dishes tonight." "Ok auntie thank you." When, I got off work that night. I went to the bus stop and got on the bus to go home. The OG's was looking out for me as I was walking home. My granny came outside on the pouch. The OG's said, "Momma here she come we see her." My granny said, "Ok, thank you. I'm looking." As I walked up the stairs, I said, "Granny, what I tell you about coming outside at night." "You better hush and get in here girl. Dinner is ready you can eat when you want to." "Ok granny thank you." Whatever my granny cooked, I knew it was going to be good. I showered, did my homework and I wrote David a letter. Then I ate dinner and I talked to my granny for a little while. She asked me how was work? I said, "Work was ok today, but my feet hurts from standing on them." My granny said, "When you come home you should soak your feet. Then when you're going to bed, you should elevate them. They might feel a little better." "That's what I'm going to do granny."

The weekend was coming up and I told Sabreea I was going to spend the night over her house for the weekend. Over the weekend, Sabreea and I talked and we listened to music.The next morning, when I woke up, I got dressed. David had called me and this was the first time we have talked since he left and went to the army. I answered my phone. I said, "Hi Babe, I miss you." He replied, "I miss you too SC. I don't have much time on this phone. I called to tell you that I love you so much and I can't wait to see you. You're always on my mind. Have you called my mom yet?" "No not yet, I'm nervous." "Just call her don't be nervous. She can't wait to talk to you and call her mom. I know you're going to call her Miss. Candace, but she's going to tell you to call her mom. How is everything going with you?" "I love you too and everything is going good. I've been working, and going to school and I'm still attending my acting class. Are you ok and how do you like it out there." "I'm fine, but you know I don't like getting up early, but I have to get use to it. I love you so much SC, and I cannot wait to see you. You should get a letter this week and I'm going to call you again this week, so answer your phone. I love you and I miss you. I'll talk to you later."

When we got off the phone, I was a little sad, because I really missed him. Sabreea came in her room. She said, "Aw you miss your man huh?" I said, "Yes I do." "You'll see him soon don't worry. I'm leaving, I'll see you tomorrow if your here." "Where are you going?" "I'm going with Bubba to his family house." "Oh ok, I wish you would of told me you was leaving, I would of stayed home." "I forgot to tell you, but mom is going to be here you can stay with her." Momma Shay said, "I'm leaving, I'm going out with Andrea for a little while. Zaneeya let me see your phone real quick." I gave momma Shay my phone, and when she gave it back to me, it wasn't working. I said, "Mom, why my phone not working?" She replied, "It just went off as I was looking at it." "This is a new phone. I just bought this phone a month ago." "I don't know what happened." "That's strange, now I'mma have to by me another phone."

Sabreea left, she went with Bubba. Momma Shay said, "Zaneeya I'm going to leave." "Ok, I'm going home." "You don't have to go home you can stay here. I'm going to come back later on tonight. You can use my phone and I'll call you from Andrea's phone." "No, that's ok mom. Take your phone with you, but thank you." "No, I'm going to leave my phone with you. If something happens, you can call the police. If anybody comes to that door, don't answer it. This guy I was seeing said he was going to stop by and I don't trust him, but don't worry about that. Just don't answer the door." "Ok." When Shay left, I laid on the couch. It was a lot of walking back in forth in those apartments. I was thinking about what momma Shay said about her friend. I just went to the kitchen, and I got a knife and I put it on the floor beside the couch. I did not feel safe there by myself. I called Sabreea and I talked to her for a little while. Then momma Shay called and told me that she was on her way back home. I saw a red light flashing on mamma Shay's cell phone, so I put it on the charger. I tried to sleep, but I couldn't. I stayed up thinking about David. Momma Shay called me and said she was on her way. When, she came home. She said, "Zaneeya I bought you something to eat." "Ok mom thank you. I put your cell phone on the charger. I also saw a red light flashing on your phone." "Oh ok." She went to grab her phone. She said, "What happen to my phone?" I said, "I don't know, it was working fine before I seen that red light flashing." "I'm going to leave it on the charger. You can sleep in Sabreea's bed." After, I ate my food. I went to sleep, the next morning. Momma Shay said, "Zaneeya my phone isn't coming on. What did you do to my phone?" "I did not do anything to your phone! I only talked to Sabreea once and I talked to you when you called. Maybe, it was messed up before you gave it to me." "No it wasn't and I don't want to hear that. What did you do to my phone?" "I told you I didn't do anything." "Yes you did. You thought I broke your phone, so you broke my phone. You stuck a knife in my phone, that's why it's not working." "I didn't break your phone, and I did not stick a knife in it either. I'm not that type of person. Even if you did break my phone, I still would not have done that! I am a real kindhearted person! I didn't break your phone! I think your phone was already messed up and you're blaming me for it, but I'll buy you another phone."

"Why did you have that knife in the livingroom then?" "I had that knife in the livingroom, because I did not feel safe here and I thought about what you said. You said the guy you were seeing was supposed to come over and you didn't trust him. So I went to the kitchen I grabbed a knife and I put it by the couch." "You broke my phone and I know you did. Sabreea is not here and she's pregnant. I don't know why she got pregnant. She knows better and you broke my phone." "I did not break your phone." "Well come with me to the metro store." "Ok, let's go." We walked to the metro store. When, we got inside the store. Momma Shay was talking to the sales associate. She said, "My daughter stuck a knife in my phone. Now my phone is not working." The sales associate

looked at her phone. Momma Shay said, *"That's what happened huh?"* The woman said, *"Yeah, would you like to buy another phone? I can show you some phones over here if you like."* Momma Shay was yelling in the metro store. She said, *"Zaneeya, why did you do this to me? Why did you break my phone?"* *"I did not break your phone and I told you that!"* The customers were looking at her as we were walking out the store. She was yelling while we were walking down the street. She said, *"Now I don't have any contacts at all! Now I have to wait until Sabreea comes home to use her phone. Why did you do this to me, why? That's how I make my money by doing hair and now I can't make any money."* I replied, *"I did not break your phone! I believe your phone was already messed up when you gave it to me and you just want to blame me for it."* *"You did break my phone and now I have to call your sister from this pay phone."* She called Sabreea. Shay said, *"Sabreea, your sister broke my phone. She stuck a knife in my phone, now it doesn't work and we just came back from metro and they said the same thing."* I said, *"That is not true, I did not break your phone."* Shay said, *"I don't why your sister broke my phone. She probably thinks that I broke her phone."* When she was finished using the pay phone, we walked back to her house. I walked in the front of her, because she kept on yelling and fussing over her phone like a crazy person. When we got back to her house, I got my things and as I started to walk out of the door. Shay said, *"You're not going to say sorry?"* I said, *"No I'm not. I'm not saying sorry for nothing I didn't do."* *"I'm going to tell your dad about this, now he has to buy me a new phone."*

"If you want to lie and tell him or anybody else that I broke your phone. Go ahead, because I didn't and I offered to buy you a brand new phone." *"Well, give me the money so I can get me another phone."* *"I'm not giving you anything after how you just treated me. You were yelling at me as we were walking down the street, acting all crazy, I'm not buying you a new phone."* *"Well, you know what? Stay out of my life until you say sorry and don't come back to my house."* *"That's fine with me, and I will never say sorry for something that I didn't do. You can lie all you want bye."* *"Yeah, get out my house."* *" I'm already out."* I shut the door, and I got on the bus and I went straight home. When I got home, I told my granny what happened. My granny said, *"Shay should be a shame of herself, you have always been kindhearted! I can't even see you breaking her phone. Even if she did break, yours and you offered to buy her another phone! Don't buy her one, let her buy her on phone. Don't worry about that, just stay from over there."* *"Ok, I am granny."* A couple of days went by and I didn't hear from Sabreea. I would call her,

but she wouldn't pick up. So I knew she was not talking to me, because Shay accused me of breaking her phone. I had bought me another cell phone. One night I was getting off work and I received a call, but I did not recognize the number, but I answered my phone anyways. It was Sabreea. She told me that she had her baby. I was so excited. I told her congratulations. We didn't talk long. When I made it home, I told my granny, that Sabreea had her baby. My granny said, "Did she? I know she's a pretty little girl." I replied, "I cannot wait to see her." The next day, my dad came over. He said, "Zaneeya, do you want to go to the hospital with me to see Sabreea and the baby?" "Yeah." My dad asked my granny did she want to come too. My granny said, "Do you think it's ok." My dad replied, "If anybody got something to say, you know I'mma check them." "Ok, let me go put some clothes on." On our way to the hospital, my dad said, "Zaneeya, Shay told me you broke her phone. She said you stuck a knife in it." "Well, that's a lie." I told my dad what happen. My granny said, "Zaneeya didn't do that. She's just not that kind of a person who would do that." My dad said, "That's what I said too. I don't think you did that."

When we went inside the hospital, we went upstairs to labor and delivery. When we went inside of Sabreea's room, nobody was in there, but her and the baby. I said hi to her and I gave her a hug. My granny gave her a hug too. My dad was holding my niece. He was showing Sabreea different ways, of how to burp her. Tinky was little and cute. Sabreea and I wasn't talking much. My dad asked me did want to hold Tinky. I said, "Yeah." When, I was holding her, she was laying there all peaceful. Then my dad asked my granny did she want to hold her too. I gave my granny the baby. She held her for a little while then my dad held her. My dad was telling Sabreea what to do as a parent and what not to do. Shonte came in the room. My dad spoke to her and she spoke back to him. When my granny and I spoke, she didn't say anything. Shonte said, "Why are all these people in the room, and how long are they going to be here?" My dad said, "Calm down Shonte. Their is not a lot of people in here, it's only Zaneeya and her granny. Don't do that." "Well Sabreea, I was going to spend the night. So how long are they going to be up here, because I can go home?" My dad said, "We are going to leave and you can spend the night. We all want to see the baby. Matter of fact, Zaneeya and Miss. Stella were leaving." I said bye to Sabreea and Tinky and we left. As we were going to the car, I told my dad that was crazy and uncalled for. I would have never treated Sabreea's grandma like that. My dad said, "Don't worry about that. Shonte was very rude." My granny said, "I'm telling you, you only have one time to be rude to me and that's it." My dad dropped us off at home. My granny was talking about how pretty my niece was. I had a miss call from Susan. I called her back to see what she wanted. She said she wanted to hang out, I told her we can meet up somewhere over the weekend. When I went to school, I told Jessica that Sabreea had her baby. Jessica said, "Are you excited to be an auntie?" I replied, "Yeah I am. Now I have a niece and a nephew and they are three months a part."

It was getting closer and closer for David to graduate from basic training. We would write each other continually through out the week. I finally got the courage to call David's mother. I was nervous for some reason, when she answered the phone. She said, "Hello." I said, "Hi Miss. Candace. I'm Zaneeya I was calling to see how you was doing." "Hi, how you are doing?" She said all excitedly. "I was waiting for your call. David didn't tell you?" "Yes, he told me. I've been so busy with work and school and I was nervous about calling you." "Don't be nervous and David told me you work and you go to school. He showed me your picture. You are so beautiful and I cannot wait to meet you." "Aw thank you. I can't wait to meet you too. I like how David is a momma's boy and he loves you to death. I like how you made him be a man. He told me when you were moving, you told him. That he come live with you or he can stay in Stockton, but either way. He has to get a job or go to school and he has to do something for himself." "I had to Zaneeya. I raised David and his brother's for a long time by myself. We have lived in the hood and it was not safe. There was drive by shootings, and people selling drugs. I had to make a change and I did. I got married and I love my husband. I told David just like, I told his older brother. I told them I love them, but you have to be a man and take care of yourself! They can always come home, but they have to be a man." "You are such a good mom! When he talks about you his face lights up and it's so cute." "Yeah that's my boy, they all are. He can be hard headed at times, but he is a good man. So he said you're going to his graduation. I'm going out there the day before, so call me when you make it to the airport. David sent me some money for us, he told me to give you whatever you want. So if you don't have enough money for your ticket let me know. He really loves you." "I know I love him too! He is so sweet. I told him I don't need anything. I have my money for my ticket already." "Do you have enough money for a cab? Don't worry about paying for the hotel room?" "Yes I have enough. You can use the money, I'm fine. If I need something while I'm out there, I'll just get some money from him, but I don't need nothing. I'm fine thank you."

"Ok Zaneeya, call me anytime. I'll be calling you to check on you and remember to call me mom. We are family it was nice talking to you." "Ok, it

was nice talking to you as well. Have a wonderful evening and I'll talk to you later." When, we got off the phone. I was thinking to myself, Miss. Candace is so sweet. When, I went to work the next day. I told Jannette the days that I needed off, because I was flying out to go see David. She was making fun of me. She said, "You're flying way out there to go get some huh?" I replied, "No, that's not why I'm going auntie. I'm going to see him graduate. I'm not thinking about that." "Yeah right, you're not going that far for nothing. I know you're going to see him graduate, and you're going to see something else too! Just don't get pregnant and bring me something back too." "Ok, I'm not auntie. I do not want to have any kid's right now. I'm too young and I know that." When I got off work that night, I went home and my little cousin and her mother was over. It was my cousin Wendell's baby. My uncle Alvin son. Wendell's baby was so cute and chucky. She was crawling all over the bed. She wanted my granny and me. She was so adorable. As I was playing with her, David's mom called me. She said she was just calling to check on me. I thought that was sweet. When I got off the phone, I played with my cousin again.Then it was time for them to leave. That night, I looked in my wallet to make sure that my money was there. So I could buy my ticket to go see David and I also looked for my id, but it wasn't there. So I looked in my drawer, and I looked in my backpack, and I looked in my jackets, but there was no id. I started getting mad. I told my granny I couldn't find my id, and I never lose anything. My granny said, "Calm down maybe you over looked it." I replied, "No I didn't granny. I checked everywhere and it's lost. Now I have to find out, how I'm going to get another id, before his graduation and that's in three days." "I hope you find it." "I do too, because David is going to be mad. He already wrote me a letter. He said he feels like nobody is there for him, his mom, his granny or me. I had to reassure him by telling him, that I'm here for him and I have been writing him, and I do love him. At the time, he said that he didn't receive all his letters from me. They didn't give him all of his mail until recently. I cannot miss his graduation, that's not ok." "Yeah, you have to try to make a way to go see him." "I am granny trust me."

The next day I went to school, I asked Miss. Petter if there was anyway I could take another id picture, because I had lost mines and I needed to go to the airport. She said, "No." I said, "Can I get a print out of my id picture?" "Yeah you can, but to fly out, you have to have a real id picture, a hardcover." "Ok thank you. I have to go figure something out." "Where are you going Zaneeya? You need to go to class." "I cannot go to class right now, I'm leaving. I'm going to work. I have to try to get an id." "You cannot leave campus to go to

work early." "I have to bye Miss. Petter. Don't be mad at me I'll see you later."
As I was walking, Miss. Petter was calling my name, but I kept walking. I knew
Miss. Petter wasn't going to be mad at me. She was always understanding, and
nice. She just wanted me to go to school. I went to work and I told Jannette that
I lost my id picture, and I asked her. Did she know how I could get another
one? So I can go see David. Jannette said, "How did you lose your id picture?
It takes a week for an id picture to come. Get a print out from your school."
I replied, "I did, but my principal said I have to have a hardcover id picture
to get on a plane." "Oh yeah, that's right you do. I wanted you to go I wanted
you to bring me something back. What are you going to do?" "I don't know
auntie. I'm so mad at myself. If I knew I didn't have my id picture, I would
have taken a new one. David is going to be mad at me. I'm just going to have
to meet him in Stockton, when he fly's out there." "You have to do what you
have to do. You're not on the schedule for work today. I'll see you later and let
me know if you're going to go out there still." "Ok. I'm going home to search
for it one more time. If I don't find it, I'm going to Modesto the day before he
goes to Stockton." "Ok, you still have those days off." I left my job and I went
to get something to eat. Then I went home. When I got home, I looked for my
id again. I didn't find it, later on that day I called Miss. Candace. She told me
she wasn't going to David's graduation, because she didn't have enough money
to fly out and she had to pay for her son ticket. Plus the hotel room. I told her
to use the money that David gave her. She said, "Even with that it won't be
enough. So I'm going to send Alex, which is David's younger brother with you
and y'all can go see him."

I said, "I looked at some hotel rooms that are only 20-minutes away
from the base and they are reasonable. So I will pay for the hotel room and I
will send you some money, because I can't go. I cannot find my id picture. I
have been looking for it and I do not know where it is. I have a printout, but
I cannot use that to fly and David is going to be mad at me for not coming. If
you don't go he is going to be mad at you too. He already feels alone out there.
I called the Greyhound station, because I was going to get on the bus to go out
there, but I wouldn't get out there in time." "Now I have to go, you have to
have an id to even get on the army base. They will not let you on without it.
I'm going to catch the Greyhound bus. I'll just use the money that David gave
us for the hotel room. I forgot you are not 18 years old. Alex and you are the
same age. You cannot check into any hotel until your 18 years old, but you are
very mature for your age. I want to tell you that I admire you and I'm happy
you're with my son. I wish you were coming, but we will see each other soon.

I'll come out there or you and David can come out here and visit.That will be nice. You are so kind, and so respectful and so nice. You're a sweetheart and I mean that. I'll tell David how much you wanted and tried to come."

"Thank you so much. I cannot wait to meet you. Thanks for being here for David and I and we should go out there to see you. We have to plan everything out." "Yeah, I'm going to call you when I make it out there and when I get with David. You know they made him where glasses." "Yes he told me. He sent me a picture and I was laughing, because the first thing he said was their making me where glasses and I have 20/20 vision." "You know you can't tell him nothing sometimes. I told him you must don't have 20/20 vision if there making you wear glasses. He said after he graduates, he's not going to wear them anymore.I told David he needs to just wear them if he needs them." "That's right, but I'm going to call you to make sure that y'all make it down there safe. Have a good night Miss. Candace." "Call me mom Zaneeya. Good night, I'll talk to you later." "Sorry ok." I was upset. I really wanted to go to David's graduation and there was nothing I can do about it.

The next day, I called the Greyhound station to see when the next bus, was leaving out to go to Modesto. After, that I packed my bags and I told my granny I was going to Modesto, to go see my mom and brothers and David. Jannette called me and she told me that she needed me to come to work. I told her I was going to leave and I was still off work. I never took off work, accept for when I called in, and said I was sick when I wasn't. I never took off work for a week and I have worked ten days straight, without any off days. Jannette said, "Well, come to work today and you can leave tomorrow." I said, "Ok auntie." I told my granny I was going to work and I'll go to Modesto tomorrow. She said, "Ok, I'll see you when you come home." When I went to work Jannette called me in her office. She said, "Zaneeya, I need you to come to work for the rest of the week. I know you asked for those days off months ago, but I'm going to need you to work." "I can't do that. I already worked ten days straight and you know I have requested these days off months ago. I'm going to spend some time with my mom, and I haven't seen David in a long time. You know I couldn't fly out to his graduation. So I'm using the rest of my days to go see my family and him. You have plenty employees that can work, and would want to work. I don't see what the problem is."

"Don't you want to make some more money?" "I don't care about making money this week, that's why I requested these days off months ago. Jannette I cannot work this week." "Well I'm telling you, you can't go.You are not going to be taking off work to go to Modesto to go see your mom either. I need you

to work. You're going to have to figure something out." "I never take off work, and if I want to go to Modesto to go see my mom, I will. There's nothing to figure out. I'm not coming to work, I been had these days off, and that's not right. When everybody else takes off, you don't say nothin to them. I come to work whenever you ask me to. Even on my days off and I'm not coming to work. Sorry, I can't do it." "Is that your final answer?" "Yes it is!" "Ok well, you're suspended for two weeks and I hope it's worth it." "Are you serious right now?" "Yes, I'm telling you to come to work and your telling me no, so your suspended." "I'm telling you no, because I already requested these days off months ago and I am not changing my plans." "You don't have to your suspended." "No. I quit!" As I walked out of Jannette's office, she said, "Call me when you want your job back." I couldn't believe what happened. When, I went home. My granny said, "I thought you had to work?" I told my granny what happen between Jannette and me. I told my granny that I was going to go to the Greyhound station. So I can go to Modesto and I told her I will call her when I get out there.

She said, "Ok, call me soon as you make it." "Ok granny I will." When I made it to the Greyhound station, David called me. He said, "SC, did you make it out here yet? I love you and I cannot wait to see you. Where is my mom? She's not answering her phone and if you wasn't going to answer yours, we were going to have a problem." I replied, "I have some bad news." "What, tell me?" "I couldn't come, because I lost my id and I have been calling you, but you haven't been answering. So I thought you lost your phone, because that's not like you to not answer. I tried to get another id. I really did babe, and I'm so sorry that I'm not there, but I will see you as soon as you make it to Stockton. I love you and I miss you. Don't be mad at me." "I did lose my phone. I don't know where it is. I'm not mad, but I am upset. I miss you too. Did you try to go to the DMV to get another one?" "I was, but my auntie said that it takes a week before my id would even get here. Your mom said I have to have a hard back id to even get on the base." "You do, but dang I wanted to see you. I'm still upset though. Where are you?" "I'm on my way to Modesto right now. I'm going to my mom house. So I can spend some time with her before you get there." "Ok, I'm going to call you tomorrow on my mom's phone, and you know I'm going to call you soon as I make it to Stockton. I don't know if I'm going to get a rental car the same day or the next day, but I'm going to come get you. I love you and I miss you SC." "I love you and I miss you too." When, I arrived to Modesto. I called my granny to let her know that I made it out there. Then I called my mom and she called my brother Qin to come pick *me up. Qin said, "Zaneeya, you never spend anytime with me when you come out here, but you're always spending time with your boyfriend, and when are you going to let me meet that punk?" "Qin he is not a punk and you do not need to meet him. You don't know how to talk to people. You need to work on your people skills first." "I don't need to work on nothing I have good people skills. Look at me. You need to tell him that your big brother Q said he needs to holla at him ASAP."*

"You don't need to talk to him about nothing. You need to stay in your lane." "I'm in my lane. I need to let that punk boyfriend of yours know. If he ever put his hands on my sister then it's a rap and he's going to need way more than his little army friends to help him, because I'mma blow his brains out." "Qin he is not a woman beater. I wouldn't be with him if he was! You don't have to worry about that trust me." "Yeah, I hope so. What are you doing to night? Are you going to see your boyfriend tonight?" "No he's not in town yet. I'm not doing nothing. Why?" "Do you want to watch your nephew tonight?" "Yeah, I was going to ask you could he spend the night with me. Just make sure you have everything that he needs." "I do, and mommy has some stuff at her house for him. That's his second home anyways. I just wanted to ask you to watch him, because mommy said she needs a break, but she will watch him if I ask her too." My mom said, "I call you and tell you to drop him off to me, before you even ask me to keep him. Don't play, he be at my house most of the time." "No he don't mom, he be at home." "Yeah, he be at home when I call you and tell you to come get him, because I need a break. That's my baby." "Well sis, you're going to watch him tonight right?" I replied, "Yeah Qin, I told you I am. Don't ask me that again." "Ok, I'm just making sure." "Take me to get something to eat before you drop me off at mommy's house." "The only thing that's over here is Burger King." "Ok I'll eat that." I bought my mom and me something to eat. Then Qin dropped us off at my mom's house. When we went inside the house, I washed my hands and ate. Then I played with my nephew and I took some pictures of us. I called Miss. Candace to see if she made it to Oklahoma safe. I told her to enjoy herself and to tell David that I love him. She said, "Ok, I'll tell him to call you as soon as I see him tomorrow." I replied, "Ok, I'll talk to you later Miss. Candace." "It's mom and ok." I giggled and said, "Ok mom." When I got off the phone, I played with my nephew some more. Then I fed him then I put him to sleep. I called my nephew Booda. He was a fine baby and he was fat. He was a granny's baby. He loved being under my mom, and she loved her grandson. They was attached to each other.

The next day when I woke up, I showered. Then I got dressed and I played with my nephew. My mom already fed him and gave him, his bath. It looked like she greased him down with a whole gar of the Vaseline. He was shining all over. David called me after his graduation was over. We talked for a long time. I told him to go enjoy his self with his mom and to call me back later. He said, "She don't mind. Plus she talking to Alex and my friend. I was trying to get some alone time with you, but you didn't come see yo man." I said, "Stop it. I tried and you know it. Don't do me like that. I'll see you when you come down here tomorrow." "I'm going to call you on Alex phone. I really wanted to see you, everybody else woman was here accept for mines. I'll see you tomorrow." "I'm going to always here about this. I'll make up for it.

Ok, I love you babe. I'll see you tomorrow. Tell your mom I said hi." "I love you too babe and I will." I stayed in the house that day and I just talked to my brothers and my mom. My nephew was crawling all over the place. My mom said, "Cupcake I know you can't wait to see David and I know he can't wait to see you." "Mom I can't wait to see him. I'm going out there tomorrow. So I'm going to call Qin in the morning, so I can tell him to come, pick up Booda." The next day I got dressed, and I called Miss. Candace. She told me, David already left and he should be in Stockton later on. She told me that she couldn't wait to get home to get in her bed.

I said, "I know you're tired. Did you enjoy yourself?" She replied, "Yes, I did it was nice. It reminded me of when I was in the army." "David told me you were in the army. Did you like it?" "I liked it. I just didn't like it when they talked crazy to me. So I would talk back to them. I didn't listen, and they got tired of me talking back, so they kicked me out of the army. AJ, David's older brother is the same way. I have to tell him to calm down or he's going to end up getting kicked out too." "I think David will be able to handle it." "Yeah, I think he will be fine, but I'm going to talk to you later." "Ok, get some rest bye." Later on that day, David called me and he told me that he made it to Stockton. He said, "SC, it's too late to get a rental car, and Cedrick is doing some work on his car. So I'll pick you up tomorrow or see if you can get someone to bring you out here."

"Ok, I'mma call my cousin and see if she can get someone to bring me out there and I will call you back to let you know." I called Qin and asked him could he take me to Stockton, and I told him I would give him some gas money. He said, "Zaneeya, I'm not taking you to Stockton so you can go see your boyfriend. Why he can't come get you?" "He can't get a rental car, it's too late." "Well, you don't need to go then. I'm not taking you." "Bye." I hung up

the phone. Then I called and asked Mimi did she know anyone that would take me to Stockton. If so I told her, I would give them some gas money. She said, "Yeah, I'm going to call my cousin and see if she can take you." Mimi called me back. She said, "Zaneeya, my cousin is going to take you, but we are going to pick you up in an hour." "Ok Mimi, thank you." "You're welcome, I'll call you when were on our way." I called David and I told him that I was coming and I was going to call him for directions when I got out there. I told him that I needed some gas money so I can give it to Mimi's cousin. When Mimi's cousin came to pick me up, Mimi introduced us to each other and I told her thank you, for taking me to Stockton. When I was in the car, Qin called me. He said, "Sis, you really left? I would have taken you." I said, "Whatever, bye Qin. You did not want to take me or else you would of." "I wasn't at first, but I see that your really were serious about seeing your boyfriend." "Well, now it's too late." "You should have called me back." "I was not going to call you back. To ask you to take me to Stockton after you said you wasn't taking me." "I was just playin sis for real." "No you wasn't and I have to go. I'll talk to you later." "Call me when you come back out here, so we can hang out." "Ok I will." I called David to get the directions. Mimi asked me was I nervous. I said, "No, I have butterflies, but I'm not nervous." When we pulled up to Cedrick's house, it looked like they were having a party. David came to the car, and got my bags. We hugged and kissed and Mimi was laughing. She was making fun of us. David gave me some gas money to give to Mimi's cousin and I told her thank you again. I told Mimi I would see her later. David introduced me to Alex and I said hi to Cedrick and Xavier. They wasn't having a party their neighbor was. While David and I were, hugged up, Xavier and Cedrick were cracking Jokes as usual. Then we left and went to Xavier's house, they was playing dominos. Xavier asked me did I know how to play dominos. I said, "Yeah." He said, "No you don't come play then." "I'll beat you in a game tomorrow." I called my mom and I told her that I made it to Stockton.

I was tired. Xavier told David and me we could sleep in his kid's room. I went to bed. David came in the room after he was finished playing dominos. We stayed up for a little bit, we was talking and cuddling. When I woke up the next morning, I showered then I got dressed. David told me we were going to a jazz festival in San Jose. Xavier came in the room. "SC, did you sleep good last night?" He said with a smile on his face. "Yes I did. Your son bed is very comfortable." "Look at you getting all dolled up for your man." "You know I have too." When we arrived to the jazz festival, we walked around a little. We seen Xavier's mom. David introduced me to his auntie. Xavier's mom had spilled barbecue sauce on his shirt. Xavier said, "Mom, you just spilled BBQ sauce on my new shirt. This is Polo!" She replied, "Oh, you'll be ok wipe it off." We all started laughing, because she did not care. Xavier said, "Dang mom it's like that. You can't even give me a napkin or nothing?" She gave him a kiss. She said, "Bye, I'll see you later have fun." My mom called me. I told her I was at the jazz festival. She wanted to talk to David, so I gave him the phone. Xavier asked me did I want something eat. I told him no, not right now. We walked around and we listened to the jazz music. After, David got off the phone with my mom, Tammie texted my phone. She said, "Hi Zaneeya, I heard you were out here with David. Is Xavier around you? Can you tell him I said hi?" I told Xavier what she said, but he did not care. Tammie texted me again, she said, "I heard Alex is out there David's brother, he use to talk to my cousin." Tammie kept texting, but I didn't reply, because we really didn't have nothing to talk about. After, I stopped responding to Tammie's text messages. I started receiving text messages from this number and it was a girl. She said, "Hi my name is Ginger. David told me to text him on this number." I texted back and said, "Whoever this is stop playin on my phone." The girl kept texting. I knew it had something to do with Tammie. David said, "What wrong babe?" I showed him the text messages. He said, "I do not know her, and I know you don't believe that!" I replied, "No I don't. I know this is Tammie having someone play on my phone." David texted the number back, calling the girl out of her name then I received a text saying, "This is really Olivia. Tammie's cousin, she told me to text your phone, I really just wanted to talk to Alex."

I called Olivia, she answered. I said, "Don't ever play on my phone! Cearly you're not grown, your still a kid and tell Tammie she's hella messy, and she's hella fake. Why, she's trying to start confusion between my man and me it didn't work. She's just mad, because Xavier doesn't want anything to do with her." She replied, "I'm sorry for playin on your phone, I just want to talk to Alex. Can you give him your phone so I can talk to him?" "No I cannot and do not text my phone again." I hung up the phone and I told Alex that Olivia wanted to talk to him. He said he used to talk to her, but he moved away. He asked me do I think he should talk to her. I told him that she is immature, but if you like her and if you want to talk to her then go ahead. I gave Alex her number. I told him, when you are ready to talk to somebody that's mature, let me know and I will hook you up with my cousin Christy. We all had a great time at the festival. We didn't leave until late. When we left, we went to Cedrick's grandpa house. He was a handsome old man. David had showed me a picture of his mom, and stepdad. After we left his grandpa's house, we went to their cousin house. We didn't stay long. Then we went back to Stockton. When we made it back to Xavier's house, David and I went to bed. When we woke up the next day, we went to Cedrick's house and he was having a BBQ. I met Xavier and Cedrick's girlfriends. While the men's was outside bonding us ladies was in the house talking. When the food was finished, we all ate. David and I were talking about me going out there to Hawaii, because that's where he would be stationed at. He wanted me to go out there for my 18th birthday. I told him I would. I had a good time in Stockton. David's auntie had put the rental car in her name. Even though he had license he was not old enough to get a rental car. You had to be older than 20 years old to get a rental car in your name. While I was in Stockton, we went to the mall, we went out to eat and we had a good time. We also went to see David's grandma. His mom's mother, she was sweet. She was the oldest woman that I knew who loved football. She had a notebook with every football team and every coach that was in charge of that team wrote down. She told me that I was beautiful and I told her thank you. After we left David's grandma house, we went to David's auntie house. Then we went back to Cedrick's house. I told David to spend a night with his brothers and I told him to take me to my mom's house. When David took me to my mom's house, she was not home yet. Justin Jr., was there and he was getting ready for work. Cedrick had rode with us. When my mom made it home, I introduced her to Cedrick. My mom said, "David, I know you was excited to see your woman." He replied, "Yes, I couldn't wait to see her." My mom started joking around with Cedrick. They were making fun of David and me. Before David left, we hugged and kissed. Then I went inside the house and I talked to my mom. My mom said, "Cupcake did you have fun?" "I had a great time mom. That's what we both needed. Now he's going to spend some alone time with his brothers and his cousin."

"Well, that's good. He need some alone time with them too before he goes to Hawaii." "I know, I told him, he should spend some time with them. He'll be back tomorrow to pick me up." "Oh ok, at least you guys always enjoy spending time together." "I know, I miss him already and you better not tell him either." "I'm not going to tell him. He's missing you too right now don't think he's not." David called me and told me that he was going to pick me up tomorrow. He said we were going to the movies and out to eat. We talked on the phone for a while. The next day, Qin called me and asked me did I want to go to his house. He said we were going bowling. I told him, I'm going with David, but I'll go bowling with him before I go home. He said, "Come on sis, you always come out here, and spend time with your boyfriend. I'm going to

pick you up, then when he is on his way to come get you. I'll drop you off at mommy's house." I said, *"Ok brother."* David called and told me that he was going to pick me up in a couple of hours. When Qin picked me up, we left. We went to his house and hung out. Ranesha had her family over and Qin had his friends over. Everybody was drinking. I said, *"Qin, I thought you told me we were going bowling?"* He replied, *"We were sis, but we are just going to chill at my house. Have a drink. Do you smoke weed?"* *"I do not want to drink, and no, I don't smoke weed."* *"You gonna smoke today. There's nothing wrong with smoking, it's medicine. It's an herb, and you can drink a wine cooler."* *"I am not smoking any weed and I'm not drinking."* *"Sis, those wine coolers are good. It's nothing wrong with that. I'mma get you high today."* *"No you're not!"* Qin came in brought me a wine cooler. He said, *"Taste it, come on sis taste it, it's good."* I tasted it. I said, *"It is good, ok I'll drink a wine cooler, and that's it."* *"Ok sis, that's what I'm talking about. Now were hanging out."* Patrick was over there, and he tried to take a wine cooler, but Qin was looking right at him. Qin said, *"Patrick put that back I'm not playin with you. You're too young you don't need to be drinking."* Patrick replied, *"Why do Zaneeya gets to have a wine cooler? She's only a year older then me."* I said, *"I am one year and seven months older than you."* Qin said, *"You just turned 16 years old and you don't need to be drinking."* *"I'm going to ask Ranesha and see what she says."* Qin said, *"I don't care if you do ask her. You still can't have one, and Zaneeya will be 18 years old soon, this year is going by fast."* I sat on the couch and dranked my wine cooler, while I waited on David. Qin's best friend Peanut came up to me. He said, *"Sis, Qin wants you."* I said, *"Where is he?"* *"He's outside in the car."* I went outside to see what he wanted. Qin said, *"Sis, so you really like this guy huh?"* I replied, *"Yeah I do."*

"Oh ok, so when are you going to let me meet him?" *"You can meet him when he comes to pick me up just don't have your guns out. There's no need for that really!"* *"Why I can't have my guns out? Those are my friends. I just want to talk to him, and to let him know not to hurt your feelings. Then I'll have to shoot him."* *"You do not have to do all that. You can talk with no guns!"* Peanut said, *"I'm coming to sis we need to talk to him."* I said, *"This is not a family reunion, y'all need to calm down."* I called David to see where he was. He said he was leaving in a little while. I told him to call me when he was on his way. Qin said, *"Zaneeya sit in the car with me so we can talk."* *"I do not trust you."* *"Sis, sit in the car with me, and talk to yo big bruh."* I sat in the car then Peanut got in and so did Ranesha and her best friend Cassondra. Qin said, *"Peanut you ready?"* He said, *"Yeah."* They rolled up all the windows

in the car, and they put the child's lock on the doors so I couldn't get out. Qin said, "Zaneeya, you're going to smoke with me." "I'm not smoking anything and I cannot be around smoke, because I have asthma." "Your asthma will be ok. Mommie use to smoke around us when we were kids all the time. I know you have your pump on you, you don't go nowhere without it." "I sure do, and I am not a shame of it either."

Qin was rolling up a blunt. Ranesha was rolling up a blunt and her friend was rolling up a blunt. They all were smoking in rotation. Qin said, "Zaneeya, this is called hot boxin in the car. You mind as well smoke, because the weed is still gettin into your lungs. It's called second hand smoke." "I know what second hand smoke is, just let me out the car." "No! I'm not letting you out the car until you smoke a whole blunt with me." "Boy is you crazy? I am not smoking a whole blunt with you. Let me out this car!" "You know I'm crazy and I'm not letting you out." Peanut said, "Sis you mind as well smoke with us, that's the only way out." I knew Qin was not playin. We would have been sitting in that car, the whole night, and he would have told everybody not to move and they wouldn't of. I told Qin to give me the blunt. I said, "I don't even know how to smoke." He said, "I'll show you." He showed me how to smoke. When I was smoking, it gave me a feeling that I never felt before, I felt high, and I had the munchies all of a sudden. Before we got out of the car, we smoked nine blunts. When we got out of the car all you seen was smoke from the weed.

I went and sat on Qin's couch and I drunk another wine cooler. Patrick said, "Sis can I have some." I said, "Yeah, just don't let Qin see you." David called and told me that he was on his way, but first he was going to get our tickets for the movies. I told Qin to take me back to my mom's house. Patrick asked me for the rest of my wine cooler, so I gave it to him. Before we went to my mom's house, I told Qin to stop at a store, because I wanted some chips. When, we arrived to my mom's house. Qin said, "Where is he?" My mom said, "Qin who are you looking for?" "Zaneeya's boyfriend?" I said, "He's not here yet. He's on his way." Qin said, "Zaneeya call him back and see where he's at. I'm not about to wait that long." I called David, but he didn't answer. Qin said, "That's ok, I'll meet him next time. I had fun with you sis, eat your chips I'll see you later." "Ok, I had fun with you too." My mom said, "Qin did you get your sister high?" He replied, "Yeah and she had a couple of wine coolers we was chillin." "Why did you do that? She's not use to smokin no damn weed boy. I should kick yo butt." "Mom stop acting crazy. You know you can't hurt me, and she will be alright. She only smoked nine blunts, it's not gonna hurt her. She will sleep it off." "You know she have asthma too, and I can hurt you, try me." "Good night mom, your crazy see you later." My mom said, "Zaneeya, how do you feel, high?" "That's what I feel like. I want to eat these chips and go to bed." I went to sleep on my mom's couch. When I woke up, it was 4:00 AM. I called Alex phone, but there was no answer. So I went back to sleep. When I woke back up, I called his phone again, but there was no answer. It wasn't like David to not answer his brother phone. We would always wake up and talk no matter how late it was. I couldn't believe David lied! He stood me up, and I was upset about it. David called, but I didn't answer, so he texted me and I ignored him. He called again, but I still didn't pick up, so he texted me. He said, "So you're not going to talk to me?" I replied, "What?" "Are you mad at me?" "Yes I am." "Do you want me to come see you?" "I want you to do whatever it is that you want to do!" "I want to come see you."

"You didn't want to come see me last night. You stood me up and lied. So you don't have to come see me today!" "I do want to see you and I didn't lie. Do you want me to come see you?" "Like I said, I want you to do whatever it is that you want to do." "I'm on my way. I'm leaving right now. I'll see you when I get there." My mom said, "Cupcake are you mad, because David didn't come last night?" "Yes I am. He could have said he didn't want to come, and I would have stayed at Qin's house and kicked it with him. Don't tell me that you're on your way and your not. That's not coo and it's not going to fly with me at all, and I'm going to tell him about himself and he knows it." "Qin called me this morning and he asked me did you leave. I told him no, he said momma that punk stood up my sister? I said don't call him a punk Qin that's not nice, and I don't know why she didn't go. He said he stood her up. She could have been over here with me. Tell her to call me when she wakes up." "I'll call Qin later." "Ok, I think David took someone else to the movies last night." "Do not say that mom! I will leave him today, now you're making things worst." Lil Dawane and I walked to the store. I bought him some snacks that he wanted. On our way back to my mom's house, she called me. She said, "Cupcake, David is on his way to pick you up. He came to my house, and I told him you went to the store, but you'll be right back." "Ok, I see him." David said, "SC, get in the car." I replied, "No I'm fine, I am almost to my mom's house. You can meet me in the parking lot." "Get it in the car, it's hot out here. Stop acting like that." Lil Dawane said, "Sister, can I get a ride?" I said, "Yeah you can." I put Lil Dawane in the car then I just sat down too. When we got to my mom's house, Lil Dawane went inside. Justin Jr., came outside, he was talking to David and Nicky was there too. Justin Jr., asked David could he take him to Nicky's house. David said, "Ask your sister it's up to her. If she say yeah, it's good." Justin Jr., said, "What? It's not her car." I said, "There you go runnin yo mouth. All you had to do was ask me, but no y'all can walk to Nicky's house and it's hot outside." "Come on sis, I wasn't saying it like that, but is it ok if David drop us off?" "Yeah he can." We dropped Justin Jr., and Nicky off at her house. Then we went inside for a minute. Then we left and we went back to my mom's house. David and I were talking. Alex was sitting in the car. David said, "SC, you didn't give me a hug or nothing."

I replied, "You better not stand me up again! If you didn't want to come get me. That's all you had to say, but don't stand me up and lie and tell me that you're on your way, when clearly you wasn't!" "I'm sorry baby, and I was going to come get you, but I had Xavier, Cedrick and Alex with me. When, I got to the movies last night. The movie was going to start, and that was the last show and I knew we wouldn't have made it back in time. So I just stayed at the movies with them, then I went back to Xavier's house." "Right, as if I was suppose to believe that. You could have called and said that, but you didn't. So I'm going to ask you, did you take somebody else to the movies last night?" "No I did not! Is that what you think? I went to the movies with my brothers and my cousin." "Ok, whatever. I'm going to ask Alex. I know he's going to lie for you, because that's your brother. Alex tell the truth. Did your brother take someone else to the movies last night?" Alex replied, "No he didn't! I would tell you. Out of all his girlfriends that he had, I like you the most." "Thank you Alex, but if you liked me you would tell me the truth. I know you're not going to tell on your brother." "He really didn't though." "Ok." David said, "Can I have a kiss and a hug? Damn SC you have never been mad at me." "That's, because you haven't done anything to make me mad at you, but you pulled a move like this, and you think I supposed to believe anything. I'm going to leave it alone for now." "Thank you just let it go, because I really didn't do anything. Let's enjoy the rest of our time together." "You were not thinking about spending time with me last night, but that's ok." "I had fun with my brothers. I am enjoying my time with you right now. I was thinking about coming to get you, when I left the movies, but I was tired. Did you go to your brother house?" "Yeah yesterday when, I was waiting for you." "Did you have fun?" "I just chilled with his crazy self. I had couple of wine coolers and I smoked for the first time. Can you believe that?" "You was drinking and smoking?" "Yeah, I did not plan on to, but I got peer pressured." "By who, your brother? I cannot believe you smoked, I wish I was there to see you. How many blunts did you smoke?" "I was high, we smoked nine blunts." "Your brother wasn't playin. He wanted to get you high. I know you were out of it, for real."

When, we went inside my mom's house. She said, "Y'all need to go find that park where y'all met at and reminisce. David, why did you stand my daughter up last night? You know she was waiting for you." He replied, "I didn't mean to. She already gave me the 3rd degree. I'm going to always hear about this. I'm trying to get out the dog house."

"She said she was going to fuss at you, and soon as you dropped her off yesterday. She said I miss him already." "I missed her too. I texted her when I was driving and I told her I missed her and I called her later on that night. I'm going to get me another phone when I get to Hawaii." I said, "Mom, I'm not telling you nothing else. Come on David let's go see if we can find that park." We left and we followed the directions that my mom gave us, but we still couldn't find that park. So we went to a park that I use to play at when I was a little girl. Alex was with us, we all talked. Then David and I walked as we were holding hands. We were talking about marriage. David always told me he wanted to marry me and I told him I wanted to marry him too. We talked about everything. We were very close in our relationship at that moment. We stayed at the park for a long time. Then we went back to my mom's house. We went in her room, and we watched a movie. Alex wanted to go to the car to listen to some music, so he did. David and I were talking and we expressed our love to each other. When we left out of my mom's room, I walked David to the front door. Ramone and David were cracking jokes. My mom said, "David, anytime you want to leave the army, you know you can come here. Let me ask you something. David, do you want to marry my daughter?" He replied, "Yes I do, I tell her that all the time. I don't see myself marrying anyone else and if we were to break up. I know I wouldn't marry anyone else. I know that she's the reason why I do want to get married." "You are a good man and I do like you. If y'all want to get married right now, I would sign off for it." I said, "Mom we are not about to get married right now, slow down woman." "Why not?" "That's something we will plan, and were not ready right now." David said, "I want to have kids too. We talk about all that, but were going to wait until next year. She will be 18 years old then." My mom said, "Ok, that's up to you, but y'all need to get married before y'all have a baby, but that's up to you." David said, "It will happen." "Ok, David you know you're welcome to my house anytime. It was nice seeing you. Are you about to cry?" "I'm fine. It was nice seeing you too. I'mma leave, because I'm getting a little upset." "It's ok to cry. You're sad, because you're going to miss Zaneeya huh?" "Yes, that's my SC. I'll see y'all later." I walked David to the car. I said bye to Alex then David and I was staring into each other eyes, as we were hugging. He began

to cry, and as he cried. His tears was uncontrollable, they rolled down his face like a waterfall!

I wiped his tears from his face. He said, "I love you SC. I don't want to leave you. You got me upset, I never cried over a woman before. I love you so much. I'm going to miss you and I wish we had more time together, and I'm sorry I didn't come last night. Please forgive me. You're going to have to come to Hawaii for your birthday like we planned." I replied, "I do forgive you and I love you too. I cannot wait to go out there. You need to buy you a phone, soon as you get out there." "I am I promise." We hugged, we kissed, and we told each other I love you. Then David started to cry again. I just kept hugging him. I told him not to worry about me and I told him we would see each other soon. I told Alex to start the car so they can leave. David and I hugged again and we did not want to let go, but we had too. As he was pulling out of the driveway, we were blowing kissing to each other and we kept on saying I love you. He stopped the car. I said, "You better go." He said, "Come give me another kiss." I ran to the car, and I gave him another kiss and he watched me as I walked back to the gate. I said, "Leave." He replied, "Go inside, I'm waiting for you to go inside." I just went inside the house. When, I went inside the house. My mom said, "Cupcake is he gone?" "Yeah." "Did he cry outside?" "Yes, he cried." "I knew he did. When he was standing up here, I saw a tear fall from his face. He loves you and y'all should get married and have kids." "We do want to mom, but I just want to wait. I really want to wait to have kids, I miss him." I started crying. Ramone said, "Aww sis, he got you crying now. You never cry." I said, "Shut up Ramone." I started laughing. My mom said, "I know you miss him and you better marry him. If you don't, he's going to get him a girl right there in Hawaii." "I don't want to hear that, and I will marry him, but he has to propose first and were just taking our time. I'm not rushing!" "I know you miss him Cupcake and he's going to cry again. I know he wish he can take you back with him." "I wish I could go with him too." Ramone said, "Enough with all that sweet talk, but David is a coo dude and he treats you right. I like him." "I'm happy you like him Ramone." My mom said, "What about me? I'm the one sitting up here talking to you while you're crying." "You are supposed to. You're my mom."

The next day, I went back home. I called my mom when I made it home. Later on that night, David called and told me, he made it to Hawaii. He said he had more leave time, and he did not even know it. Before he left, he put in a request to leave for a month and they said they denied it, but they didn't. David wanted to come back, but he couldn't. He didn't have enough money *to fly out, and to get another rental car. So, he just stayed out there and it was only for another week. We talked on the phone. He told me he wanted to leave and he did not want to be stationed in Hawaii. He lived on the army base and he had a roommate. David told me he was going to buy him a car, while he was out there. We stayed on the phone late like always. When we got off the phone, I went to sleep. The next morning, David called and told me to wake up. He knew I was still sleeping. He said, "I love you SC. Go back to sleep and call me when you get up." I replied, "I love you too and I will." "I have some good news to tell you when you call back." I went back to sleep. When I woke up, I showered then I ate. Then I called David back. He said, "SC, I found a car that I want, but I have to save for it." I said, "You should save every check that you get and you should only take out money for what you need." "That's what I'm going to do." "I have something to tell you." "Tell me, I hope it's good news like your pregnant." "No, I am not pregnant. So you don't have to worry about that. I quit my job right before you came to Stockton." "Why what happen?" I told David what happen between Jannette and me. He said, "I'm happy you stood up for yourself. You did put your request in, to leave for those days off months ago. That wasn't right, but I don't think you should have quit. I think you should have let your boss suspended you." "I know I was mad at the time. I was not thinking, but I do need my job." "Are you going to call and talk to your auntie about hiring you back?" "She did tell me to call her, when I want my job back. I don't want to call her right now, even though I should, because I do need the money. That's how I take care of myself." "I know, but you cannot let your pride get in the way of getting your job back either. I love you SC, and you know I'mma keep it real. No matter what."*

"I know, and that's what I love about you, and I love you too. I know I will go back to work, but I don't think I should go right now. I'm going to wait for a couple of months. Now, I can do some of the things in school that I wanted to do. That interferes with me going to work. I think I will be fine for a little while. I have some money saved up. I already went school shopping. I'll be fine for a while." "If that's what you want to do. I'll support you a hundred and ten percent you know that. Don't worry about money. I'll send you some money every month, and I'mma still save for my car. I'm going to try to get me a car before you come out here. I love you, don't worry about nothing. Everything will work out." "I love you too. Thank you so much for your help and advice." "That's what I supposed to do. We look out for each other!" When we got off the phone, I could not stop thinking about how I was going to the 11th grade. Time was going by fast. I wanted to continue going to my acting class. I also

wanted to dance for homecoming as well and I wanted to hang out with my friends.

I told my granny, it was time for me to enroll in school again. I told her I couldn't wait to go to Hawaii for my birthday. My granny said, "I want you to bring me something back too. I don't care what it is." I replied, "I know you want something granny. I'm going to bring you something back I just don't know what it is yet." Susan called me. She asked me what I was doing for Thanksgiving. I told her I was going to Modesto to go be with my family. She asked me could she come. I told her I would have to ask my mom. I said, "Why you don't want to spend Thanksgiving with your new sisters?" She replied, "I see them all the time." "Well, I don't know I'll see." Susan would brag all the time about how she has new friends. Susan told me the youngest girl in there gang was 12 years old. I told her that she does not need to be hanging around no 12-year-old girl. Susan changed. She thought she was a tough girl who cussed a lot. She became a bully. Susan told me she tried to fight her mom and she was changing for the worst not the better. I told Susan, all of her friends were going to switch up on her. I told her when they do. I would be there for her, just to listen to her and to see what she have to say and I won't say I told you so.

Chapter Twelve

My 11ᵗʰ Grade Year

*T*he first day of *11ᵗʰ grade, it felt like I was on top of the world. I was proud to be a junior. I was one more grade away from being a senior. Soon as I got to school, I stopped at the attendance office to say hi to Ms. Thomas. She was like a auntie to me. She was always sweet and kind and I love her for that. I also stopped by the main office to say hi to Liz. I called Liz auntie as well. I would go to Liz and talk to her about everything, and she would always be there to listen to me. Liz always gave me great advice and I love her for that as well. I saw all of my friends at school. They were excited as well to be a junior. I knew I had a lot of work cut out for me. Before prom came and I was going to work extra hard to keep my grades up, and I was going to participate and all the activities that I wanted to be in. Nathan and I had 5ᵗʰ period together. Mr.Okieth was our history teacher. He was a great teacher. My best friend and I were happy, we had a class together, because we never had a class together, and we were going to show out. Everybody just chilled and relaxed on the first day of school. When I got home from school, my granny told me, Sabreea called me and she told me to call her back. After I showered and ate, I called David. Even though he was working, we still talked for a little while. Then he told me he was going to call me on his break. David and I would talk every morning. We would talk on my lunch break. When I got home from school and on his breaks and when he got off work. The next day at school, Nathan was telling me who he liked, and he wanted me to hook him up with a few girls and I told him I would. Nathan played football at OT, and he was getting more popular, which we all were. More girls started to like him. This girl I knew wanted to talk to Nathan. She asked me to hook them up, because she knew we were best friends. I told her no! When we were freshmen's, Nathan liked her and she did not like him. I told Nathan who the girl was and he did not want to talk to her. He said, "The only reason why she* *wants to talk to me is, because I'm on the football team. I'm not messing with her." I replied, "That's not the only reason why she wants to talk to you. Your fine, buff and taller and you're on the football team. You don't need to talk to her. There are a lot of girls at school, and I'm going to hook you up with a few."*

I knew 11ᵗʰ grade year was going to be fun. My friend Lucy and I would be together a lot and Jessica and I were too. Lucy was pregnant and she was having a girl. I was happy for her. She had straight A's in school and nothing less. She was a smart girl. The day before Lucy had her baby shower, I spent the night at her house. I stayed up, helping her make her favors and the next day. I cooked all the food for her baby shower and I helped her decorate. We were close. Her baby shower was nice. After the baby shower, I helped her clean up. Then I went home. I called Sabreea to see what she was doing. She asked me to come spend a night at her house. I told her, she has to ask her mom and see if it's ok with her first. The last time I seen Shay, we were not on the best of terms. Sabreea told me she asked her mom. She said she put all of that behind her and we are never going to bring that situation up again. Sabreea told me where she lived and how to get there. I caught the bus to Sabreea's house. When I went inside her house, I said hi to everyone. I couldn't wait to see my niece. I haven't seen her since she was three months old. She was beautiful. She let me hold her and she did not even cry. Sabreea, and Tinky and I took pictures. Sabreea and I talked about school and what was going on in each other lifes, Sabreea had independent studies. She didn't have to go to school everyday. She only went to school to turn in her work. I would go to Sabreea's house on the weekends sometimes, and Jessica would spend the night too. We were the three stooges. Sabreea and I would go swimming late at night. She had a pool in her apartments. I would buy food, everytime I spent the night at her house and I would also buy Tinky things that she needed. When, I bought Sabreea and myself something to eat. I would buy momma Shay something to eat too. I started getting attached to my niece, and she was getting attached to me too. I was looking forward to seeing Tinky. Sabreea would spend the night at my house on weekends too and so would Tinky. She would bring some clothes with her and she would wash them. My granny did not mind. She always told Sabreea, she was her granddaughter too, and my granny treated her like she was. I loved going to school to see my friend Dawight. He was a class clown, and he was so funny. Everytime that I would see him, he always had a joke to tell.

Homecoming was coming up again. Lucy and Champagne was the first dancers who danced for our class for homecoming. We came in first place for homecoming, for the football seasons. We beat the seniors. We all were shocked, but we worked hard. My sis would come to school with me. She liked my best friend and Nathan liked her. He asked me was it ok if he talked to her. I told him he could, and I told him to be honest with her and I told her to be honest with him. You only could have a visitor a couple of times out of the school year. My sis was coming up to my school everyday and she would sit in all of my classes with me. When the security guards would say, she couldn't come today. I would go straight to Miss. Petter's office and I would get a pass for her. I would show it to the security guards and they would be mad. When, girls would flirt with my best friend. My sis would get mad, and when my dude friends would flirt with my sis. My best friend would get mad. They kept their relationship on the low. I would cut my first period class sometimes. It was Spanish. My teacher told me in order to pass with an A+. I had to bake a cake and say the presentation in Spanish. I went home and baked a cake. I stayed up all night studying. When, I brought my cake to school the next day. I stood in front of the whole class and I said my presentation in Spanish. My teach name was Miss. Lopez. She said, "Zaneeya, you gave an excellent presentation and you deserve an A+." I was so happy. I did like Spanish, and I spoke the language very well. Miss. Lopez was an amazing teacher and she was so hands on with her students. She was one of my favorite teachers. Jessica had asked me to save her a piece of cake, and so did Lucy. When the bell ranged, I gave them their cake. After school, I went to my rehearsal for my play that we had to perform at school the next day. I had my own part in the play and I had a part with my class. When, I was performing by myself. I heard Lucy yelling my name from the audience. She said, "Go Zaneeya, I see you." I knew Lucy was going to say something, and I was happy that she did. When the play was over, all of my friends told me that I did a wonderful job. As the school year went on, it was getting closer to my birthday and I couldn't wait to go to Hawaii. Toniya called me. She said, "Zaneeya, what are you doing for your birthday?" "I'm going to Hawaii for my birthday." "Are you buying your ticket?" "No, David is buying my ticket!" "I want to buy your ticket for you and that will be your birthday gift from me." "Ok mom, thank you. I'll tell David when I talk to him." "Ok, let me know what day you're leaving, so I can get your ticket." "Ok, I will." "I love you Zaneeya. I love all my kids." "I love you too mom and we know you love us, thank you." "You're welcome." Toniya had talked to David on the phone before and she told him she wanted to meet him. I told David that Toniya was going to buy my ticket. David said, "Tell Toniya, I will give her half of the money, for your ticket. I really want to buy it myself."

I replied, "Remember, what you told me? Don't let your pride get in the way, just let her buy the ticket." "My pride is not in the way. You're my woman, and I want to buy your ticket, but we can go half." I told Toniya what David said. Toniya said, "That's fine. We can go half on your ticket, but I'm going to pay for your ticket with my card, and I'll take you to the airport the morning that you have to fly out." "Ok, I will give you my half of the money for my ticket, when David sends it to me." "Don't worry about that."

    Susan called me the morning of Thanksgiving. She asked me could she come with me to Modesto. I told her it was too late and she should spend Thanksgiving with her mom. She said, "Please Zaneeya, just ask your mom and see what she says." "No, spend Thanksgiving with your own family." "Zaneeya please, I want us to be close again. Can I come?" "I guess so, let me call my mom." I called my mom and I asked her could Susan spend Thanksgiving with us. She said, "Yeah, but she have to be with you the whole time." I said, "Ok mom." I told Susan she could come. Her mom dropped her off at my house. She said, "Zaneeya take care of my baby." I said, "Your baby is something else." My mom friend Lenny came to pick us up. On our way to Modesto, we caught a flat tire. So he pulled over on the freeway. He replaced that tire with a spear tire. Lenny said, "It's too much weight on the spear tire in the back. Momma can you sit in the back, and Susan can you sit in the front?" My granny sat in the back seat with me and Susan sat in the front seat. Susan had taken off her shoes and she put her feet up in Lenny's window. My granny said, "Susan, put your feet down. You don't put your legs up or feet up and anyones car. That is somebody's husband." Susan put her legs and feet down. When we arrived to Modesto, I introduced my mom and my brothers to Susan. Qin called and asked me, did I want to go over his house? When Qin came to pick me up, I introduced him and Ranesha to Susan. When we got to their house, we played a couple of drinking game and we smoked. We just kicked it. Later on that night, we went back to my mom's house. Susan asked me if she could sleep in my brothers room, I told her no. She was going to sleep in the livingroom with me. The next day, Qin came over to pick us up. Susan said, "Zaneeya, do you think your mom would mind if my boyfriend, come pick me up?" "I don't know. You would have to ask her yourself." "Well, she let you go with your boyfriend when he comes out here." "That's, because I'm her daughter. She would be responsible for you, if anything happens to you, but you would have to ask her yourself and see what she says." Susan asked my mom could her boyfriend come pick her up. My mom said, "Does your mom let your boyfriend pick you up?" Susan replied, "Yes, she does mom." "Well, if it's ok with your mom then yeah, but you have to come back in my house at a decent hour, and I want to meet him." "Ok, thank you mom." Susan's boyfriend came to pick her up. I was eating a piece of sweet potato pie, at the kitchen table. My mom walked outside with Susan. When, she came back inside the house. My mom said, "Cupcake, I told Susan's boyfriend to have her back at a decent hour, and if you don't bring her back. I will be calling the police on you." I said, "Mom your crazy." Qin came and got me. We didn't do nothin at his house, but drink and smoke. When he brought me back to my mom's house, it was late. Susan was already sleep. I put my pajamas on and I went to sleep.

Before, we left the Bay Area. I told Susan we was going to miss a day of school and I was not going back home until Monday, because that is when Lenny could take us back home. Susan's mom called her. She said, "Susan, when are you coming home?" Susan said, "I don't know I'm going to ask Zaneeya. Zaneeya, when are we going home?" I said, "I told you already. You didn't tell your mom?" She put the phone down and said, "No, I did not tell her, because I knew she wouldn't let me come." Then she picked up the phone. She said, "Mom, I'll be home tomorrow." Then she hung up the phone in her moms face. I said, "Susan you need to call your mom back and tell her the truth. You're not coming back out here with me anymore, because you lied to your mom. Now your mom is going to be mad at me, because you didn't tell her the truth. I don't have to lie to my mom about where I'm going and what time I'm coming back. That's not coo." "She'll be fine." We stayed in the house that day. Susan was in my brothers room the whole day. She was all over them. I said, "Susan, do not try to have sex with my little brothers." She replied, "I'm not. I'm just doing Ramone's hair for him, because he asked me to. Huh Ramone?" He said, "No, I did not ask you to. You just came up to me and started twisting my hair, and since I need it done I did not stop you." Later on that night, Qin called and asked me did we want to come over. I said, "Yeah." I told Susan that we were going over Qin's house. She told me she didn't want to go, so I got dressed. My mom said, "Cupcake, why Susan not getting dress? " I said, "She don't want to go. She wants to stay here." My mom called Susan in the kitchen. She said, "Susan, why you don't want to go with Zaneeya?" "I just want to chill at the house with the boy's mom." "You're not going to be in there room. You have to be in my room or in the livingroom. Ain't no body having sex up in here." Susan smiled at my mom. She said, "Mom, I have a boyfriend you met him already." "That don't mean nothin, your going to come in my room with me. Don't you like Justin Jr.?" "Yeah, I think Justin Jr., is fine." "Yeah come in my room, I'm going to keep an eye on you." When Qin came I left, we just hung out at his house. My mom called me. She said, "Cupcake what time are you coming home?" "I'm going to see if Qin will drop me off in a little while." "Ok, I have to keep telling Susan to get out of your brothers room and they had the door closed, but I opened it back up. I said Ramone and Patrick, y'all know better. Keep this door open. They said it wasn't us mom, it was Susan. I told Susan don't shut no doors in my house, unless you're using the bathroom. You need to hurry up in come back. I can't wait for her to go home. She's a fast one. She will do it to all of your brothers. She cannot come back." "Ok mom. I'mma tell Qin to drop me off now."

I said, "Qin can you drop me off at mommy house? Mommy is tired of Susan already." He replied, "She should of came, ain't nobody rushing home for her. Tell mommy to chill out. I want you to spend a night with me. I'm not taking you to mommy's house tonight. I'll take you tomorrow." "Mommy is going to be mad." "I'mma call mommy right now." Qin called my mom and he told her, that he was not bringing me back to her house tonight. When, he got off the phone. He said, "Zaneeya, mommy is mad, but she'll be ok." The next day, Ranesha dropped me off at my mom's house. I asked Susan what was she doing last night and did she have fun with my brothers? Susan said, "Yes I had fun with the boys. We just talked, and I did Ramone's hair while they played the game." I said, "I know you tried to have sex with my brothers." "No I didn't! Why would I? Besides, I like Justin Jr., and your brothers are too young for me." I did not believe her. I was going to ask Ramone what happen, and I knew he would tell me. I went inside of Ramone's room. I said, "Ramone, did Susan try to have sex with you last night?" "Yeah she did! She wanted Patrick and me to have sex with her, but we didn't want to! She begged and begged, but we didn't give in, she's not my type of girl." I let Susan know, that I knew. She tried to have sex with both of my brothers at the same time. She didn't say nothing, because it was true. Justin Jr., called my mom and she told him I was at her house. He told her he wanted to talk to me, so I got on the phone. We talked for a little while then he asked to speak with Susan. I said, "How do you know she's here?" He replied, "Mommy told me." I gave Susan the phone. I just relaxed that day. The next morning, Susan's mom came to get pick us up. When she got to Modesto, it was 7:00 AM. She was mad. Lenny was going to taking us home the same day, but her mom wanted her to come home early in the morning. When Sally came to pick us up, I introduced her to my mom. They spoke, and I said bye to my mom and we left. On our way home, Sally said, "Zaneeya, you got my daughter stuck way out here in Modesto. She was supposed to be home." "I told Susan to tell you that we wasn't coming back home until Monday. She didn't tell you? She lied to you. Don't be mad at me be mad at her." "Susan you lied huh? You're not going anywhere else." Susan said, "I didn't tell you the truth, because I knew you would have said no. Stop being mad mom, you're ok."

When Sally dropped, my granny and I off at home. She said, "Zaneeya, you and Susan won't see each other for a long time." "Ok, thanks for dropping us off take care." When, I went inside the house. I washed my clothes and I put my clothes out for school the next morning. When I went to school, I told Jessica what happened in Modesto. After school, I went home. I talked to David on the phone. He asked me, have I talked to his mom. I told him I called and I talked to her on Thanksgiving. We talked all night, until we fell asleep. As the school year went on, I would go to Merced with Jessica .We would go to her grandma's house. Her grandmother was a sweet old woman. She would call me Pharrell. She could not pronounce my name right. She would call Jessica, Lacole, and auntie Betty said she called Jessica that ever since she was born. When we spend the night at her grandma's house, we slept in her grandma's back room. We would go out to eat, and we would go to Jessica's brother house. Her sister Javonna would come down to visit. We also would go visit her uncle. Champagne, and the rest of my friends, and I wanted to step dance. Like the college, students did as sororities. So, Champagne made up a step routine and we performed at this school in Richmond. We called are self's the OT steppers. We stepped against other step-dancers. We also danced for the basketball homecoming rally. We came in first place again. The seniors told us how great of a job we did. We all went ice-skating that night. The next day, my sis came to school with me. Everybody thought Nathan and I was a couple. It did not bother us at all, because we wasn't. I had a boyfriend and Nathan was dating my sis. As time went on, I called my dad, and I asked him for some lunch money. He came up to my school, and he gave me some money twice. I wanted to surprise Nathan for his birthday. So I told his mom who I called auntie. That I was going to buy, him a cake, and we all were going to sing happy birthday to him after school. My auntie Charnae, which is Nathan's mom, picked me up from school, and she took me to buy Nathan a cake. I put his cake in his teacher classroom. When, school ended. I said, "Nathan, you have to go to Miss.SG class. She's talking to auntie about your grades, and she said you have an F for the semester." Nathan did not believe me at first. He looked at me and said, "Best friend you're not even smiling, your serious." "Yes, I am serious, come on. You better go see what she's talking about."

"Come on best friend, come with me." As we were walking upstairs to Miss. SG classroom, Nathan was talking mess. When he got inside the classroom, everybody said surprise. He was smiling from ear to ear. He said, "Best friend you tricked me, thank you. You know I don't like surprises." He gave me a hug. I said, "You're welcome." I bought his favorite cake. Which was a lemon cake, and I bought some snacks for all of us to eat. As we were singing happy birthday, I grabbed a glove, and I put some whipped cream on Nathan's face. After we cleaned up, we went out to eat. Jessica, and auntie Charnae, and I met up with Nathan and his friends. We went to Chevy, which is a restaurant. I would go to all of Nathan's football games with auntie Charnae. I would ride with her and Jessica and Desseire would ride with us too. When Nathan would get tackled. I would yell and say, "Get off my best friend, let him up." Then Jessica would say, "That 's my best friend, best friend." Nathan was a great football player. He was number-one on the team. My cousin Dudy was on the team too, and he was good as well. Nathan was in the newspaper every week. They talked about, how good he was as a football player. The more time we spent together, the more people thought we were together. Even auntie Charnae thought we were together. So did my granny and my dad, and my mom. I would say, "I don't want him, that's just my best friend." My mom would say, "He's fine. I don't know why you don't want him. Good as he looks. He's lucky I'm not his age, because I would be all over him." "Only you would think like that mom." One day Nathan and I got mad at each other. We stopped, speaking to each other for a couple of days, and Mr.Okieth noticed it. He called us by our last names. He said, "S, M outside now. Step in my office." We walked outside. Mr. Okieth said, "Why y'all not speaking to each other?" Nathan said, "That's her not me." I said, "Stop lying, you been acting funny for three days. I spoke to you and you did not say nothing." "I must didn't hear you Zaneeya." Mr. Okieth said, "You guys better make up right now. You guys are best friends and there is no need to act that way. Y'all don't even know why, y'all are mad at each other." Nathan said, "I'm not mad no more. Are you mad still Cherel?" I replied, "No number 8." That was Nathan's football jersey number. Cherel was nickname that Nathan and Dudy would call me some times. Mr. Okieth said, "Ok, well hug. Y'all been hugging." Mr. Okieth was one of my favorite teachers and he was always helpful. We gave each other a hug then went back inside the classroom. One of the staff members at OT and I use to butt heads. Her name is Rose. I would speak to Rose, and sometimes she wouldn't speak back. I thought Rose didn't like me, but once we sat down *and finally talked to each other. I started to like Rose and she wasn't a mean person at all.*

Toniya called me while I was at school. She told me, she was going to purchase my ticket. When I went home, I felt sick. As if I was getting the flu. David called me and he asked me did Toniya buy my ticket. I said, "She told me, she was purchasing it earlier when I was at school." He replied, "Ok, you sound like you're getting sick." "I am I think I have the flu." "You better get on that plane. I can't wait to see you." "I am. I'm coming sick and all. I love you." "I love you too SC. I'm going to send you the money tomorrow. Ask Toniya what bank, does she have because I can deposit the money into her account. Are your bags packed?" "Ok, I'll ask her tomorrow on my lunch break. Yes my bags are packed. I can't wait to leave." "Ok I love you get some rest SC." "I love you too, good night." The next day at school, Toniya called me while I was in class. She said, "Zaneeya, I'm looking at the prices right now for your ticket. I was tired when I got off work yesterday." "Oh ok mom, David said he could deposit the money into your account, because I'm leaving tomorrow." "Tell him that's ok, you can give it to me when you get back. I'm going to buy your ticket right now. Are you packed already?" "Yes, I am." "Ok, when you get out of school. I'll come get you. So you can spend the night at my house. I'm taking you to the airport in the morning." "Ok mom." I went back to class, than 20- minutes later I got another call from Toniya. She said, "Zaneeya, I'm sorry baby, but your dad doesn't want me to buy your ticket. He said you need to ask him, if you can go. He said he has not met David, and I can't go against your dad." "What is he talking about? I don't have to ask him nothing. I don't live with him. He just wants to be control of things. I can't stand that about him." "If your mom, calls me and tell me it's ok. I'll get the ticket right now." "You don't have to buy my ticket yourself. You can use the money that David has. If I knew this was going to happen, David would have been, bought my ticket. I'm going to call my mom right now and I'm going to tell her to call you." "Ok, I'm sorry. It's your dad not me." My dad was in the background yelling, "That's right, you need to ask me for permission first." I said, "Tell him I will never ask him for permission. It will never happen." I called my mom and I told her to call Toniya. I told my mom what happen. My mom said, "What, he has lost his damn mind. He is always trying to be in control. He don't never want to see his kids happy or having fun. He should be happy, that Toniya wants to buy your ticket. He has not done anything for you. So what, if he gave you lunch money, when you called him. He should have given you more money than that. I am going to call her right now. Then I'll call you back."

When, my mom called me back. She said, "Cupcake, I talked to Toniya and I told her, she can buy your ticket. I told her I met David, and he has spent the night at my house. He is a good young man and I trust y'all. Then your dad got on the phone. He said, "Bella, she needs to ask me. You live all the way in Modesto. I am not going to spend my money that I worked for to buy her a ticket. I haven't even been to Hawaii yet. I do not want to pay for her." "It does not matter where I live. I have custody over my kids, and she does not have to ask you for permission. She does not live with you, and you are not in charge of her. I am her mother, and I said it's ok if she goes out there. Why do you, want to stop your daughter from seeing her boyfriend? She is a good girl. She doesn't ask you for anything. If she does, you should want to help her. You haven't done much, and you know it. You don't never want to see anybody doing good. You want everybody to fail in life. You have always been that way. You are always belittling Qin, and, Justin Jr., and Zaneeya. At least my daughter is in school. She has worked, and she's going back to work soon. She just wants to do take a break." "That's not true Bella. I do not belittle them, that is a damn lie .They just want to do, what they want too do and that's why, they don't like to be around me. I'm not paying for Zaneeya to go to Hawaii, have her boyfriend pay for her." "Your kids don't want to be around you, because you're always mean to them. You have always treated my kids, different from your other kids. You don't know how to be a dad, and her boyfriend was giving Tonyia half of the money for her ticket .He would have paid for the whole ticket, if Toniya didn't offer to pay for it. It's not your money anyways, you don't work. That's, Toniya's money. You don't even pay child support! You should be happy to go half with your daughter's boyfriend to buy her ticket." "Well, I'm not and Toniya money is my money. I don't need to pay child support, they don't live with you. I don't have time for this foolishness." "Whatever Justin Sr., you're the only one that's foolish. Bye and grow up. Cupcake, when I got done telling him off. I knew he was mad at me, but I don't care. That's messed up, and Toniya shouldn't of listened to your dad. Hell, it's her money not his. That house is hers. Those cars are hers. If she leaves him today, he's not going to have nowhere to go. Hopefully Toniya will buy your ticket." I replied, "No she's not. My dad is not going to let her. I'm so mad. Everytime I suppose to see David, something always happens. Thanks mom for helping me. I'm going to call David, and tell him what happened." "Ok Cupcake, call me later."

I called David. I said, "David, Toniya is not going to buy my ticket. My dad said I need to call and ask him, if I can go to Hawaii. He told Toniya not to buy my ticket." He replied, "Both of us were buying your ticket. If she knew, she was going to let your dad, make up the decision for her. I would have been, paid for your ticket. Now, I spent all of my money on this car. The only money I have is the money that I put to the side for us to eat with. I'm hella mad." "I did not think this was going to happen." "I didn't either. I'm going to call you back later. I need to calm down. I love you SC." "I love you too." I left school, and I went home. I told my granny what happened. She said, "Your dad is always doing something. If I had the money, I would give it to you." I replied, "I know granny, I'm going to bed. I don't feel good." David called me later on that night. He said, "I miss you and I love you SC. I really, wanted you to come out here. It's not your fault, I should have just bought your ticket, before I bought this car. Don't worry we will see each other soon." "I do not want to have to wait, for us to see each other until you can get a vacation. That's a long time from now." "I know, but we might have too. This time I'll leave for a month." "Ok, if I work before then, I'll just fly out to see you." "Ok, you sound like you're getting worst. How do you feel?" "I am. I have a fever. I feel like I have the flu. I feel like this everytime I get the flu." "I want you to get plenty of rest. If you want to hang out with your friends, out there for your birthday I'll send you some money. So let me know." "Ok thank you. I love you." "I love you too SC good night. I'll call and check on you later." I went to sleep. The next day, I didn't feel good. I felt horrible. I didn't go to school. I just slept all day. David called, and checked on me to see how I was doing. My mom called me to see how I was doing too. My granny told her I was sleep. My granny knew, not to wake me up, for a phone call. The next day I didn't feel good, but I wanted to go out for my birthday. So, David sent me some money. I had a dinner party. I invited 25 people from school, to come and celebrate my birthday with me. My dinner party was at, PF Chang's. After my dinner party, we went to the movies. After the movies, we went home.

When I got home, I went to sleep. The next day, Lucy called me. She asked me, was I going to prom by myself. I told her, I was taking Sabreea as my date to prom, because David couldn't go. Lucy and I made plans, to go to the mall to shop for prom dresses. Sabreea was happy, that she was going to prom with me, and so was I. She already knew all of my friends. Sabreea, and Lucy, and I went to the Great Mall to go shopping for prom dresses. I had found the dress that I wanted. Sabreea called my dad, and told him that she found a dress that she wanted to wear to prom. My dad told Sabreea, that he would buy her prom dress for her. He told me, he wanted to buy my prom shoes for me. I said, "Dad, don't say you're going to buy them, and your really not." He said, "I'm going to *buy them, I have to buy Sabreea shoes too." After we left the mall, I went back to Sabreea's house. Shonte would always buy wine. I never would drink wine, but one day I came over Sabreea's house, and Shonte told me to try this wine. She bought some Sangria. I tried it and I liked it. I would give my money to Shay, and she would buy wine for us. When we would drink, we would drink inisde the house. The wine was cheap, but we didn't care. As long as it got us tipsy, that's all we wanted. I would buy hard liquor, from my friend's liquor store, because I knew I wasn't going to get carded. Jessica would come over Sabreea's house, and we would drink, and smoke, and listen to music. Jessica, and, Dudy, and I had an English class together. Our teacher name was Mrs. Contantly. She was a nice teacher. I had a mirror that I carried with me in my backpack everyday. I would take my mirror out of my backpack, and I would place it on my desk, in front of me in class. My teachers didn't mind, accept for when I would look in the mirror constantly at myself. Mrs. Contantly would say, "Ok Zaneeya, it's time to put the mirror away, you're not focusing on your work." "Yes I am. I can't help it, because I'm beautiful. Everybody should have a mirror on their desk. Well, I take that back, not everybody." Jessica said, "Yeah, not everybody." Mrs. Contantly would say, "Ok, just make sure your paying attention." "I am, I'm taking notes right now, as we speak." Jessica would say, "Sis, let me see your mirror." I would pass it to her. This boy in my class named Ron had a crush on me. He asked me could he take me out to eat, and can he take me shopping. I would say, "Ron, you know I have a boyfriend. No you cannot." He replied, "Zaneeya, I know, but he's all the way in Hawaii. If he loved you, he wouldn't have left you, and went way out there." "Stop Ron, I'm still not going out with you."*

When I got home, from school, I did my homework. Around 10:00 PM, my granny and I heard gunshots. When, we heard the gunshots. I told my granny, I hope that wasn't one of my friends. My granny said, "That was probably one of your little thug friends, who be hanging out on the corner." I replied, "I hope not. It's too many people that I know, that are getting killed." I went to sleep that night, but I couldn't sleep good. The next day I went to school. I was sitting in Mrs. Contantly class, and Sabreea called me on Jessica's cell phone. Jessica said, "Zaneeya this is Sabreea. She said it's an emergency. Something happened to your cousin." I said, "What? Let me talk to her." Jessica gave me her phone. As I was walking outside to talk to Sabreea, Mrs. Contantly said, "Zaneeya, you cannot talk on the phone, get off the phone." I ignored her, Sabreea said, "Sis, Lil Kevin got shot last night by your house, and he died." I screamed in the phone. I said, "Sabreea thanks for calling me.

I'll call you back." As I was walking, back to class. Tears was all over my face. I gave Jessica back her phone. I gathered up my belongings, and I left. Jessica was yelling, "Sis, what happened? Sis what happened, what's wrong?"

I just kept walking, Desseire seen me. She came up to me and said, "Sis, what's wrong?" She hugged me and I just pushed her off me. Desseire said, "What did I do?" I was just crying, as I shook my head. Jessica ran over to me. She said, "What happened?" I told her little Kevin got shot and he died. Jessica said, "Sis, I'm sorry." Desseire said, "I'm sorry sis. I thought you were mad at me about something." I said, "No, I'm sorry for pushing you Desseire." "It's ok, you should leave. Maybe you should go home for the rest of the day." Jessica said, "I'm going to call my auntie and ask her to come pick us up." She asked her auntie could she come get us. Jessica's auntie picked us up, from school and she took us to Jessica's house. Jessica told her mom what happened. Auntie Betty said, "Zaneeya I'm sorry to hear that. You can spend the night if you want too." I said, "Thank you auntie Betty." When Jessica and I talked about what happened to Lil Kevin. I told her that I heard multiple shots last night, and that was Lil Kevin who got shot. I should have called the police soon as I heard the shots. Jessica said, "It's not your fault sis. You did not know that was your cousin who got shot last night. You cannot blame yourself, for his death. You already stood in front of a gun for him before. You have got into it with people, because of him. You helped out, enough. It was nothing you could do." "I just wish I could have helped him. I should have called the police when I heard those gunshots. No, I didn't know, that was him who got shot, but I heard the shots, and now he's dead. He was young."

"I think you should spend the night at my house tonight. When my dad gets home, we can go get your clothes." When Jessica's, dad got off work, we went to my house. My granny said, "Zaneeya, your cousin Lil Kevin got shot and he died." "I know granny. I'm going to spend the night at Jessica's house tonight, and I'll be back tomorrow. I do not want to be down here in the bottoms. They said he got shot last night right by our house." "So those gunshots we heard last night, that was him who got shot." "Yeah, it was him granny. I cannot believe he's dead. This is too much right now." I gave my granny a hug and kiss and I told her I would see her tomorrow. When we got back to Jessica's house, we just talked and laid down. The next day, auntie Betty woke us up for school. We were late, but I didn't care. I really didn't want to be there. At lunch, Jessica and I were talking to Dudy and Lil Kevin's cousin on his mother side of his family came up to OT. His name is RJ. He came up to me and said, "What's up Zaneeya? The person, who killed Lil Kevin, goes to school here, and I'mma shoot up OT. So just stay out the way." RJ showed Jessica and me his gun. I said, "RJ, you do not know who killed Lil Kevin. You need to leave right now, and go to your own school. Do not come up here with that." Dudy said, "RJ be coo, don't come up here with that." RJ said, "I'mma shoot up OT watch, just stay out the way." RJ kept taking his gun out. I told him to put his gun up, and leave. When he told me he wasn't going anywhere, I told him I was calling uncle Kevin. RJ said, "I'm still not leaving, I'm not scared of him." I called uncle Kevin and told him what RJ said. My uncle Kevin said, "Zaneeya, I'm on my way to come get you right now. Meet me at Burger King." I told Jessica to go to class. She said, "I don't want to be here if he's going to shoot up the school." I replied, "He's not gonna do nothin. He's leaving. Do you want uncle Kevin to take you home? You can call, and ask your mom, can you come with me." "That's ok, I'll stay at school, just call me when you get home sis." Uncle Kevin came to pick me up from Burger King. I asked uncle Kevin how was he doing. He said, "It's hard for me. I called Kimberly to tell her that RJ was up here, and he said he was going to shoot up OT. I told her RJ showed his gun, to you and Jessica. Kimberly said, RJ said that's not true. He said he don't even have a gun, but they believe him." I said, "That is a damn shame they believe him. You can ask Jessica yourself and she will tell you." "I believe you niece." "I'm going to call Jessica, so she can tell you herself." I called Jessica. I said, "Jessica, didn't RJ show us his gun? He kept pulling it out, and he said he was going to, shoot up OT." She replied, "Yeah he did. You told him, to put his gun away and to leave, but he still was saying he was going to shoot up OT."

Uncle Kevin said, "I believe y'all, Jessica he's going to end up in trouble too." I said, "Thanks sis. I'mma call you later. I told you uncle Kevin. If Kimberly do not believe that RJ did that, that's ok." Uncle Kevin and I went to grandma's house and Lil Lamont was over there. My grandma got mad at me, because I did not do what she told me to do. So I told Lil Lamont I was going home. Big Lamont said, "Zaneeya, you can spend the night at my house, with Lil Lamont if you want too." "Ok, thank you Big Lamont." I spent the night at Big Lamont's house with Lil Lamont. Big Lamont said, "Zaneeya, you can stay over here, as long as you want too." "Thanks Big Lamont." Lil Lamont and I watched a movie, then we went to sleep. The next day, we woke up. We got dressed and we went to grandma's house. When we arrived to grandma's house, my dad called. He said, "Zaneeya, do you want to ride with me to the funeral? I want all of my kids to ride together. I talked to Qin, and he said he is going to come out here. He is going to spend the night at my house, and Sabreea is coming to spend a night, and Justin Jr., is too." "Yeah, I'll spend the night." "Ok, I'mma pick you up later on today." "Ok dad, I need to go home, so I can get some more clothes." "I 'll take you home, so you can get some more clothes, when I pick you up." When my dad picked me up, he had brought Sabreea and Tinky with him. They came inside of grandma's house, but we didn't stay long. When, my dad took me to my house, to get my clothes. I told my granny I would see her after the funeral. She said, "Ok." When, we went to my dad's house. Qin and Ranesha were already there. I played with my niece and nephew for a long time that day. Qin and Sabreea was capping on each other kids. Qin said, "Sabreea, I love my niece, but why is she so underweight?" Sabreea replied, "My baby is not underweight. I love my nephew, but why is he so over weight?" "He is not over weight. That's how babies are supposed to look. Mines is healthy." Then they started talking about each other. However, they were only joking, and it was out of love. They had me laughing the whole night. The next day, was Lil Kevin's funeral. I woke up early and showered. Before, Sabreea and Qin got dressed. They asked me could I watch their kids for them. I told them yeah. Booda, was walking already, but he wanted me to hold him. Tinky was making little steps, but she wanted to be held as well. My dad went to get all of us, some breakfast from Burger King. I fed Booda and Tinky their breakfast. When Qin and Sabreea was finished getting dress, they came downstairs and ate. Then they started talking to each other. They forgot I had their kids. I said, "While y'all are sitting up here talking, y'all can come get y'all kids."

Qin said, "Oh sis, you haven't seen your nephew in a long time. I thought you still wanted him." I said, "Don't pull that card." I sat them both down, right beside their parents. Sabreea and Qin both started laughing. When we left for the funeral, everybody met up at my grandma's house. Justin Jr., and Qin rode with my dad. Ranesha, and Sabreea and I rode with Toniya, when we got to the funeral, I saw all of Lil Kevin friends. I knew, most of them, because they went to my school. The funeral was sad. My heart really went out to my uncle Kevin. Lil Kevin was his baby boy, and even though his son did not live with him, he was not a bad father. I remembered what my uncle Kevin told me. He said three things would happen to Lil Kevin. One, he would go to jail. Two, he would sell drugs. Three, he would die at a young age, because the life that he lived was a fast life, and it was too much for him. Lil Kevin did all three things. My uncle Kevin knew what he was talking about.

The look on my uncle Kevin's face, the day of the funeral. Was a look of a man, who was heart broken. He was a father, who tried to fight for his son.

When all odds were against him, he still remained strong. A man who did not get the respect as a father, to know, that his beloved son was dead. Until the next day after he died. Uncle Kevin was Lil Kevin's, only living parent left on Earth. My heart went out to my uncle Kevin. After the funeral, everybody ate. Then we all went to grandma's house. When it got late, Toniya, Sabreea, and Ranesha, and I were ready to leave. So we went back to Antioch. We stayed up talking. When my dad and my brothers made it back home, it was late. We stayed up, for a little while. Then we all went to bed. The next morning, was Lil Kevin's burial. They were barring him in Manteca CA. Toniya had left early that morning, and Qin and Ranesha went home. Sabreea and Justin Jr., and I road with our dad to the burial, my dad was running behind schedule. So he told us, to make sure that we had our seat belts on, because he was speeding. My dad is a great driver, and he should have been a racecar driver.

We made it to the burial. As they were putting the dirt, on his coffin, we all stood around and talked. My dad told my cousin Lil Dana, to drive his car back to grandma's house for him. My dad rode with Toniya back to the Bay Area, and Justin Jr., Sabreea, and Tinky and I rode with Lil Dana. When we got to grandma's house, we went inside, but my dad wasn't there yet. Lil Dana had my dad keys to his car. He put my dad's keys on grandma's livingroom table. Justin Jr., said, "Lil Dana, let me see my dad car keys." He replied, "I'm not giving you, your dad keys. If he comes back, and you're not here with his car, he is going to be mad, and you know it." "I'm going to be back, way before he gets here. I'm only, going to the store, right around the corner." "You can walk to the store." I went outside. Then Justin Jr., came outside. He said, "Sis, you think I should take dad's car?" I replied, "No, if he comes back and his car is not here, he is going to be mad and you know it. Then you guys are going to get into it, it's not worth it." "You took his car before, and he wasn't mad at you?" "I did take his car before, and I hit somebody else's car, but I didn't tell him about it. Nothing was wrong, with dad's car. The other person's car was, messed up. Qin told dad that I drove his car. He told on me. That's how dad knew, but I told dad I would pay for the other persons car to get fix, but he didn't want me too. Don't take his car, just walk to the store. I'll walk with you." "No, I'm going to take it." Justin Jr., went inside the house and got my dad's car keys. I said, "You're, really going to take his car?" He replied, "Yeah I'll be right back, I don't feel like walking." Sabreea said, "Dad is going to be mad, when he gets back and his car is not here. I feel sorry for Justin Jr." My dad and Toniya pulled up in front of my grandma's house. My dad said, "Where is my car, where is my car?" I did not say anything. My dad went inside the house. He said, "Lil Dana where is my car?" "Your son has it. I told him not to take it, but he didn't want to listen to me, and he took it anyways." "You gave him the keys to my car? Are you kidding me?" "No, I didn't give him the keys to your car. I came inside the house and sat your keys on the table." "Justin Jr., must have lost his Damn mind. Zaneeya so Justin Jr., left with my car huh? Where did he go?" I replied, "He'll be back. He only went to the store." "He could have walked to the store, that's what he have feet for."

When Justin Jr., came back, he pulled up on the side of Toniya. My dad said, "What makes you think, you can take my car, and disrespect me? I didn't give you permission to take my car. So why did you take it?" He replied, "Dad I just went to the store, and I came right back. You don't trust me?" "You should have never left with my car. It's not about trust. You don't have license, and don't never disrespect me again, by taking what belongs to me. This is a $75,000 dollar car. That you cannot afford. If the police pull you over, my car will be taken, don't take my car again, and give me my keys." "Alright dad, I'm sorry for taking your car, and you don't have any license either, but ok." "I don't have any license, but I still have a car to drive, Sabreea and Zaneeya let's go." We said bye to Lil Dana and we left. My dad was supposed to take us to Sabreea's school. So, she could get this paper sign, stating that it will be ok, for her to go to my prom. My dad said, "I can't take y'all to Sabreea's school, today to get that paper sign. It's too late." Sabreea said, "Dad, it's still early, and we need this paper sign, because prom is this week." "Well, I can't do it today. Maybe I'll take y'all tomorrow, and I don't know if I can buy you a dress. You might not go to prom with your sister." "Dad you said you were going to get my dress, and now you can't get it." "Look, I can't get it right now, and that's that." I said, "That's messed up. You knew how important this was to us, and Shay was going to buy her dress, but you said you were going to do it." My dad, yelled and said, "Listen Zaneeya. It's other things in life, besides this damn prom that is only going to last for a couple of hours. I don't have to do anything. You and Qin are the most disrespectful, out spoken kids that I have, and I can't stand that about y'all! Keep your mouth shut." "I don't have to keep my mouth shut, and I already know you don't really care about, Qin or me. You just put up with us, but that's ok. I won't ask you for nothing." "Good don't, that's makes the both of us happy. We can agree on that." "We sure can." When, my dad dropped us off at Shay's house. I got my bags out of his car. He told Sabreea and Justin Jr., bye. I walked up the stairs. He said, "You're, not going to say bye? Well that's ok, bye Zaneeya." "Bye dad." "I'm sorry for saying what I said. I have a lot going on right now, that's all. I don't *have money like I use to, but I'll come get y'all in two days, and take you to get the rest of the things, that y'all need I promise."*

"Ok dad." Sabreea told momma Shay what happened. Shay said, "Y'all dad is always saying something mean to y'all. When is he going to change?" I said, "He's not mom, but I'm not worried about that, I just want Sabreea to come to prom with me." "I know that's right. Y'all dad better come through, or else I'm going to let him have it for real. Y'all do not ask him for much, he can do this." Sabreea said, "Zaneeya I really want to go to prom with you. We already bought our tickets all I need is my dress." "I know, I think Dad is going to come up with the money. He knows that I really want you to go to prom with me, and we still have to get our shoes. I think he'll come through this time, I hope so." The morning of prom, our dad picked us up. He called and said, "I'm outside, y'all have 5-minutes to get dress." Momma Shay was going to do our hair. Sabreea and I were going to wear our hair alike for prom.

When, we went downstairs. My dad said, "Sabreea, Sindy is going to let you wear one of Baybay's old prom dresses to prom." When we got to Sindy's house, Baybay let Sabreea choose what dress she wanted to wear. Sabreea picked this Turquoise dress that Baybay had. It was the same dress, that I had, but my dress was fuchsia red. Baybay told Sabreea she could have that dress, because she was not going to prom again. She even gave Sabreea the bracelet to go with the dress. Sabreea told Baybay thank you and we left. My dad took us to Sindy's job. Sindy gave Sabreea and me $100 dollars each for prom. We told her thank you, and we left. My dad told Sindy that he would give her the money back, that she gave us. After we left Sindy's job, my dad took us to a shoe store. So we could buy us, some shoes. We bought our shoes with the money that Sindy gave us. Then he took us to buy a few accessories, to go with our dress. When we went back to the car, my dad was eating some pizza. He had enough pizza to share with Sabreea and me but he didn't give us none. Sabreea said, "That pizza sure smells good." My dad said, "It tastes good too." He dropped us off, at Sabreea's house. He told us he was going to come back, so he could see us in our prom dresses. We both said, "Dad, are you really going to come back?" "Of course I am. We are going to take pictures and everything." "Ok dad." We went upstairs and showered. Then momma Shay did our hair for us. Then we put on our dresses. Lucy called and told me, she was on her way. When Lucy picked us up, Jessica was with her. We all took pictures, and we took pictures with Tinky too. Then we left.

We went to Lucy house, because she had to get dress. Jessica's parents had picked her up. After Lucy got dress, we took pictures. Then we went to prom. When we arrived to prom, everybody was so overly excited to be there. Nobody wasn't dancing on the dance floor. So, I told Sabreea, and Jessica, and Lucy to let's go dance. Soon as we started dancing, everybody else got up and joined us. When, I seen Rebbeca, we gave each other a hug. I told her to sit with us. We took pictures, and we had a great time. My sis was there too, and she was dancing with Nathan. She broke him off on the dance floor, he couldn't handle her. We danced the whole night, and we took pictures. When prom was over, the only restaurant that was open was Denny's. We all went to Denny's. I gave Lucy some gas money, for letting us ride with her to prom, and Sabreea gave her some money too. We stayed at Denny's for a while. We ate, we talked and we joked around. We had a real good time. I told Lucy to drop me off at my house. Then Lucy took Sabreea home. When, I got home. Justin Jr., said, "Zaneeya, you went to prom with that dress on?" "Yeah boy." "I'm telling David. Does, he know your wearing that?" "Tell him, yeah he knows. There is nothing wrong with my dress." My granny said, "Zaneeya did you have fun?" "I had a wonderful time. We danced the whole night, it was nice." "I'm happy you had a good time with your sister, and your friends." David called me. He said, "SC, how was prom?" I replied, "I had a great time." "Did you, dance with any boys?" "No. I did not. I danced with my sister, and my friends." "Ok, I'm happy you had fun. I wish I were there with you, but go ahead, get some sleep. I know you're probably tired." "Ok, I'll call you in the morning and I wish you were there with me too." "I miss you, and I love you, SC good night." When I got off the phone, with David I went to bed. The next morning, Sabreea called me, and she asked me when was I coming back over to her house? I told her in a couple of days. When I went to school, everybody was talking about prom, and how much fun we had. Everybody got along. Even the people, that didn't like each other. My sis and Sabreea had came to school with me, and we went to the office, because I wanted to see my counselor. This girl named Nae wasn't speaking to me anymore, because Ron liked me, and she liked him. My counselor was busy. So we went back to my class.

When, I went to class. I was talking to Dudy, and Nathan, and Nae came in my classroom. She said, "What was said in the office?" I said, "What are you talking about, and who are you talking to?" "I'm talking to you. What was said in the office? I heard you said something." I walked up to her. I said, "If I had something to say, I would say it. You know I don't have a problem speaking up. Don't ever walk in my class, acting like you big and bad, because your not. We can catch fades all day. You ain't checking me about nothin!" "Like I said, I came to see what was said in the office." Nae walked out of my classroom. Sabreea said, "What was said in the office? You didn't even say nothin to her. What is she talking about?" I replied, "I don't know, but that just made me hella mad." Dudy said, "Don't worry about that cousin just stay in class. You already checked her, she don't want it." "I'm bout to go see what's up." Sabreea said, "I'm coming with you." Sabreea and I went inside the hallway. I seen my friend Jackie, which is Nae best friend, and Trudy was with them. I said, "Nae, you want to come to my classroom like you bad, I'm right here! What's up?" She replied, "I don't want to fight you. Trudy told me you said something about me in the office, and that's why I went to your classroom." "Trudy you know damn well, I haven't said anything about Nae. You told me hi and I said hi back, and that was it. If you're looking to start a fight, I can start with you. If anybody else want it they can get it too. Line up let's go." Trudy said, "Ain't nobody trying to fight you." "Well stop going around lying on me then, straight up. You hella fake, don't say nothin to me when you see me." Jackie looked at Sabreea. She said, "What is this, a stare down, what's up Sabreea?" Jackie dropped her stuff. Sabreea started crying. She said, "What are you talking about?" I said, "Jackie that's my sister straight up, it's not gonna happen. Ain't nobody, gonna touch her. We can catch fades all day." Jackie said, "Zaneeya you know I don't have a problem with you, but your sister is lookin at me like she wants to fight." "I don't care how she looks at you. Ain't nobody gonna touch my sister! Sabreea stop crying for real. Go back to my classroom. I'll be in there in a minute." Jackie, Nae and Trudy left. I called Jessica to see where she was. She told me she was leaving her house. I told her what happened, between Nae and me. I told her, to meet me in the hallway, on the side of the school. Nae, Jackie, and Trudy came back by my classroom, but they didn't say nothin. Sabreea came looking for me.

I opened the door for Jessica. She said, "Sis what's going on." Jackie said, "Zaneeya, you know you and I are friends." I said, "That's my sister, don't nobody come before her period! No friend, and I'm not gonna let nobody touch my sister. I would fight all of y'all before that even happen." "Nae is mad, because somebody told her you're jealous of her, because Ron took her to prom, and you wanted to go with him." "I'm not jealous of nobody, and I'm in a relationship. My man couldn't come, because he's too old, so I went to prom with my sister. I don't care who he took to prom, that's not my man. He likes me and he been chasing me, the whole school year. You can ask Jessica and my sister and they will tell you. If I wanted to go to prom with Ron, I could have. It's not hard. I don't believe nobody told you that. Nae, you're just coming up with a reason to not like me, and that's ok. Don't come to my classroom like *that again." Nae said, "Well I did." "I know you did, and you got checked to huh? Now go run and tell that!" "Ain't nobody worried." Jackie said, "Sabreea, I'm sorry for coming at you like that. I don't know what came over me. I like you I don't have a problem with you." Sabreea replied, "I was crying, because of what you said. You and I have always got alone, but ok." "Yeah, I'm sorry about that, give me a hug." Sabreea and Jackie hugged. Then we all left. Jessica said, "Nae is mad, because she probably found out, that Ron likes you. I don't know why, she came to your classroom, like she was gonna fight you. She knew she wasn't, that was just stupid." I said, "Sabreea, next time I get into it with someone, don't never bust out crying like that again. Sis I love you, and I'm not gonna let nothing happen to you. I always have your back, and you know it, but don't do that again." She replied, "I was so shocked, about what Jackie said. I just started crying." The school year had ended, and we were looking forward to the summer. Sabreea birthday was coming up. David had sent me some money. I told him, I wanted to take Sabreea to dinner, for her birthday. Jessica and I had spent the night at Sabreea's house. We took her to Apple Bee's, for her birthday. After we left Apple Bee's, Shonte called us. She told us to get on Bart, and her boyfriend and her, was going to pick us up, from the Bart station. We were going bowling. When Shonte and her boyfriend picked us up, she had a big bottle of Vanilla Bacardi. We drunk some, then we went bowling. We had a great time. We were tipsy while we were bowling. After we left the bowling alley, Shonte took us to Sabreea's house. When, we got inside the house. Shay said, "Shonte, why did you get them drunk?" Momma Shay was wetting us with water guns.*

Shonte said, "Mom, their not drunk. They are a little buzzed, they will be fine. Don't worry they just need to sleep it off." David called me, I talked to him for a little while. Then I went to bed. The next morning, we woke up, and my sis called me. She told me, she was going to my best friend house. She told her mom, that she had a job interview. I told her to have fun, and to let me know all the details when she gets back. I got in the shower. Then Jessica got dressed, her parents picked her up, later on that day. We had a good time together. Over the summer, I went to my uncle Alvin's house. He lived in Gridley. I would go out there, and spend time with my cousins. My cousin, Savanna and I were very close. We would go to the movies, and we would hang out, at the mall. My cousin Ben, and Savanna and I would play pool together. Mike is their baby brother. My uncle Alvin, made sure all of his kids stayed active, far as in activities. My uncle wife name is Gloria. She is very humble and sweet. My uncle Alvin took us to the State Fair, in Sacramento. That was my first time going to the State Fair. We ate some good food, and we got on most of the rides. The State Fair was huge. My uncle Avin was always nice to me and I could talk to him about anything. When I went back home, I called Jannette, and I asked her could I have my job back. She told me yes. I was happy to start back working. I needed the money. Even though, I would call my cousin Meech and he would, bring me bus passes, and he would give me money as well. I still wanted to work, and make my own money. My granny would fuss at me, because I would not take the lunch money that she would give me. She would fuss at me, and say, "I don't know why you won't take this money, and you need to eat lunch." I would say, "Granny I'm fine, don't worry about me." Even though, I was getting help from Meech. It was nothing like making your own money, and I got use to that. When I went back to work, I was happy to be back. I told David that I asked Jannette, for my job back. He was happy that I put my pride to the side. For the first time, everything was going well for me.

Over the summer, Susan called me. She said that she wanted, to talk to Jessica and me. She told me it was very important, and she wanted to meet up. I told her I would meet her at Denny's, in Emeryville. When we met up with Susan, we all sat down and ordered our food. I asked Susan what did she want to talk about. Jessica said, "The last time I talked to you. You had a new group of friends. You didn't want to be bothered, with us." Susan said, "The girls, who I was hanging with, they tried to jump me. They turned on me. One of the girls who I was the closest to, set me up." I said, "Well, what happen, how did all this take place? I know your friends didn't try to jump you?" Susan replied, "We all were on Bart, and one of our friends wasn't there. One of my friends asked me, how did I feel about the girl who wasn't there. I told them, that I think she's fake, and I was talking about her and they were too. However, one of my friends had her phone out, the whole time I was talking. She had me on speakerphone. My friend heard the whole conversation, of what I said. They all turned on me." Jessica said, "What did she say after she heard you?" Susan replied, "She called me out of my name. She told me she was going to beat me up, and they all were talking mess on the Bart to me. So I got off Bart, and I got on another train, and I went home. Then I called you, Zaneeya." I said, "So, how do you feel about your friends now? You chose those friends. You said you knew them every since you were a little girl, which I knew you was lying. One of your friends got disrespectful and I had to check her, and you got on the phone trying to take up, for the girl. Now you're calling me, because they want to jump you. These are your sisters, your best friends!" Susan replied,

"Zaneeya, I understand where you're coming from, but I didn't see this coming. You were right, they did turn on me, and they were not my true friends. I never should have been friends with them. I want us to be close again. You know I love you, and I'm sorry. You can tell me I told you so." "I don't need to tell you that. You don't switch up on your friends, who are loyal to you. Who has been there for you! You been acting funny. Ever since you started hanging around those girls, it's alright though." "So are you mad at me?" "I don't have a reason to be mad at you. I see who you are and that's that." Jessica said, "That's crazy they did that to you, but they were not your real friends. You had to learn the hard way." Susan said, "I did, and I will not be hanging around them. When I told my mom what happen, she said oh no, call Zaneeya." I said, "You haven't been calling me, so you don't have to start." After Susan was finished talking, we left and I went home.

The next day, I went to work, and as I was working Susan's mom called me. She said, "Zaneeya this is auntie Sally. I need you to hook your sister up with a job." "Who Susan?" "Yeah who else." "I can get Susan a job, but I don't know if I want to do that, because Susan is lazy. She don't even like to wake up for school, early in the morning. She has to be here on time, and my boss does not play. If Susan doesn't come to work, on the day that she is supposed to, she will get fired. It's a lot of work, and it's going to be hard for her. She is always late to everything." "I'll get her to work on time everyday, if you can get her hired. She needs to work, and have some responsibilities. So can you get her a job? I know you can." "I'mma talk to my boss, and I'll call you back later." "Ok, thank you." "You're welcome." When I went to work, I went inside of Jannette's office. I said, "Auntie, I need a favor." She replied, "What is it?" "I have a friend that needs a job real bad, so I wanted to ask you can you hire her." "Has she ever worked before, and why does she want a job here? You know I don't take no mess." "I know, and no she has not worked before but she is a good kid." "Who takes care of her?" "She lives with her mom." "Ok, I'll hire her, and tell her I don't play. If she doesn't come to work when she is supposed to. She will be fired, and I don't want no mess from her." "Ok Jannette, thank you." "You're welcome. Tell her to be ready to work, and come to work tomorrow at 4:00 PM." When I went home after work, I called Susan and I told her what Jannette said. I told Susan what she had to wear, and I told her to make sure that she gets to work on time. She said, "Thank you so much sis. I can't wait to work." I replied, "My name is Zaneeya, not sis and you're welcome. I'll see you tomorrow at work." I told my granny I hooked Susan up with a job. She told me that was nice of me. The next day I went to work. My *auntie said, "Zaneeya, I hope Susan shows up on time, if she's late that's it." "She'll be on time Jannette, don't worry." When 4 o'clock came, Susan was there on time. Jannette had her fill out her paper work and she had me train her. Kathy and I still wasn't gettin along. Susan asked me who was Kathy, she knew I didn't like her, because I told her. When, I showed Susan who Kathy was. Kathy rolled her eyes at Susan. I told Susan not to worry about that. After work, I went home. I couldn't wait to go to bed.*

Everyday Susan came to work. She would be late, and she wasn't just 5-minutes late. She would be 30- minutes late. Jannette said, "Zaneeya, you need to talk to your friend, because if she shows up to work late one more time. She don't have to worry about working here." I had a talk with Susan. I told her if she was going to be late, one more time, Jannette was going to fire her. Susan said, "You really think your auntie will fire me? I'm your friend." I replied, "Yeah, that's doesn't mean anything. Business is business, and Jannette will fire her family. You think she really won't fire you? You don't know my auntie like you think you do. I would fire you too. You're always late. I'm the one who asked her to give you a job." "Ok Zaneeya. I'll be on time for now on." "You should want to come to work on time. I have my job. I know what it consist of, and if you worked somewhere else, and you were 30- minutes late for work. They would have, been fired you. Jannette haven't fired you, because I told her we were friends, but that's out the window now. You need to appreciate that you have a job. It's a lot of people out there, that are looking for a job and they don't have one."

"Ok Zaneeya, I get what you're saying. I'll be on time. It's not like I live around the corner. Before I come to work, I'm usually somewhere else. That's why I'm always late." "That doesn't matter. You can go anywhere you want to before work. When you have a job, you need to make sure you arrive to work on time with your uniform on. I live further then you do. If you don't want to be here, you need to let Jannette know. She can hire someone who needs this job, and who will appreciate it. I did you a favor. You're not doing me a favor, by being here." "You right, I'm not doing you a favor. If I'm late, I'm late. I can't make it to work on time everyday, but I will call in. My mom wanted me to work, I didn't want too." "Ok, I'm done talking to you about this." I knew Susan had to learn on her on, and I knew she didn't care, and I did not care if Jannette fired her. I knew she was going to get fired soon. At work, Rebbeca and I would eat lunch together. We would take are breaks together, and she would spend the night with me at Sabreea's house sometimes. Rebbeca and I would go to work around the same time. We would go to work early, so we

could hang out. We would sit in the breakroom at work, and eat are food, until Jannette asked us to clock in.

One day, Rebbeca and I were sitting in the breakroom at work, and she said, "Zaneeya, you know if Susan be late one more time, auntie is going to fire her. That was nice of you to get her a job. You didn't have to do that. You know Kathy and Susan are friends now. I walked in the breakroom yesterday, and they was laughing and talking. That's messed up, because Susan know you and Kathy don't like each other. She is supposed to be your friend, she's hella fake." I replied, "I'm not worry about that. I didn't know they was friends, but that's fine. If she wants to hang out with Kathy, she can. I mean, I wouldn't of did that to her. I don't trust her and she's not loyal." Susan and Kathy walked in the breakroom. They were talking and laughing. Susan didn't say anything to me and I didn't say anything to her. Rebbeca and I kept talking. When it was time for us to start work, we clocked in. I did not want to be bothered with Susan. She already stopped hanging around me, when she became friends with those girls, who traded on her. When Jannette seen Susan, she said, "Susan, I'm happy your here on time, because if you wasn't on time today. I was going to fire you." Susan said, "I will be here on time for now on Jannette. Please don't fire me." "If you don't come on time, you will not have a job here." When it was time to go home, Susan said, "Zaneeya are you mad at me?" "No, I'm not. I just don't want nothing to do with you." "Why, because I talk to Kathy now?" "I don't care who you talk too. Your not loyal, and don't call me when things don't work out between you and your friends." "I talk to Kathy, because she speaks to me, and I been trying to find out information about her." "I don't believe you, I have to go." Rebbeca said, "Come on Zaneeya." Rebbeca and I walked to the bus stop together. She spent the night at my house. We stayed up talking. My granny had cooked some greens. Rebbeca loved my granny greens and she could not wait to get her hands on some. Rebbeca said, "Zaneeya, Susan stopped hanging out with me too, remember we use to be close." I said, "Susan and I were close, but y'all were even closer. I always told both of you to continue being friends. I did not come between that! You and Susan would still kick it and hang out and you would still go spend the night at her house. At the time you was in a relationship with her cousin, Willy remember." "Yeah I remember, but she just switched up, for no reason, and we are not use to people like that."

"I see Susan for who she really is, and I don't want any part of that. I had Susan's back. When she told Jessica and me that her friend Carly, slept with Spencer and she said she was coming up to OT High to fight her. I stopped

talking to Carly and so did Jessica. We really had her back. I will never be friends with her again. I'm a great friend and I don't need anybody like that in my circle." "We are not close and I'm not going to be friends with her neither. What if Jessica did something like that to you, what if she betrayed you?" "I don't think Jessica would do something like that to me. If Jessica don't like someone. Then I'm not going to be friends with that person, and if I don't like someone, she's not going to be friends with that person. We are best friends, and we have loyalty for each other." "I don't think she would do that either. I just wanted to ask you, what you would do." "Oh, I'm tired. I'm going to sleep good night." "I'm tired too, good night Zneeya." When we woke up the next day, Rebbeca and our co-worker Danny and I went to get my tongue pierced. I got my tongue pierced at this place called the smoke shop. After I got my tongue pierced, my tongue was bleeding. Rebbeca said, "Why is her tongue bleeding? It doesn't suppose to be bleeding?" The guy said, "Sometimes it does that, the bleeding will stop." He gave me instruction on how to keep my tongue ring clean. I bought me another tongue ring, because after a week. I would be able to change my tongue ring. Danny had to go to work, so Rebbeca and I went to Emeryville to have lunch. I could only eat food that was soft. Like fries and mash potatoes, and soup. Rebbeca had order a lot of food and all I ate was some soup. I said, "Rebbeca, why did you order all this food and you know, I can't eat any of it?" "I still ate after I got my tongue pierced. Take a bite of my sandwich and see if it hurts." "My tongue hurts right now. I'm not taking a bite of your sandwich, I barely could speak." When I went home, I told my granny I got my tongue pierced. She said, "There's no way, I would have did that. I know that hurts." I told her it did.

Later on, that night I woke up, and my tongue was bleeding. I had blood on top of my tongue ring. I cleaned my tongue with the salt water that the guy had gave me. As I gargled with the salt water, my tongue was bleeding more and more. Then it started to burn. So I went back to bed. As I laid down, my tongue was hurting even more. When I woke up, I got dressed for work. When, I arrived to work. Rebbeca said, "Zaneeya does your tongue feel better?" "My tongue hurts, and it has been bleeding all night. My tongue should not be bleeding at all." "Let me see your tongue." I showed Rebbeca my tongue. She said, "Oh no, your tongue is still bleeding." I said, "I need to go to the hospital. I'm going to show Jannette." Rebbeca came with me to Jannette's office. Jannette said, "Zaneeya, I heard you got your tongue pierced. Let me see it." I showed Jannette my tongue. She said, "Your tongue ring is purple." I said, "That's blood, it has been bleeding all night." "You need to go to the hospital. That's a blood clog on the top of your tongue ring. Go to the hospital. Don't worry about work right now. Go get that taken care of. Do you have some body that will take you to the hospital?" Rebbeca said, "I'm going to call Letha. She have a car, she can take you." I said, "You need to ask her first." Rebbeca called Letha and she asked her could she take me to the hospital. Letha said, "Yeah."Jannette said, "I'll see you later niece, let me know what happen. Call me tomorrow ok." "Ok auntie, thank you." Rebbeca said, "Zaneeya, I'll call you later and check on you." "Ok, thanks for calling Letha." I walked to Rebbeca's house. When I got there, Letha was sitting on the porch. She said, "Let me see your tongue." I showed it to her. She said, "Yeah that's a blood clog, I know that hurts. We have to pick your granny up. Then I'm going to drop y'all off at the hospital." "Ok, thank you Letha." Alisha rode with us, my pain was excruciating. I have never experienced anything like that before. When we got to my house, Alisha went to knock on the door, and she told my granny what happened. My granny hurried up and got dressed, and came to the car. Letha dropped us off at the hospital. My granny said, "Letha, thank you for dropping us off." We went inside of Children's hospital Emergency room. My pain was getting worst and worst. I started screaming. My granny said, "Zaneeya you can't scream in here." I yelled, "It hurts." As I was waiting for the doctor, I was screaming, and crying, and the blood clog from tongue ring was getting enormous. I didn't see a doctor for two hours. When I seen the doctor, they told me to open my mouth. When, the doctor looked at my tongue. He said, "I never had a patient with a blood clog on a tongue ring. I never dealt with anything like this before."He went to get another doctor.

When the other doctor came in the room, he asked me to open my mouth. He said, "It's going to hurt, so if you need to hold on to my arm and squeeze it, you can. We have to get this tongue ring out your mouth." The doctors used these tools to try to get the tongue ring out of my mouth, but it didn't work. I was losing more blood. They said, "We are going to try something else." When they asked me to open up my mouth, again I shook my head no. The doctors said, "You have to open your mouth, so we can get your tongue ring out." I shook my head no. My granny said, "Zaneeya, you have to open your mouth. So they can remove your tongue ring." I said, "It hurts no!" The doctors said, "Just open your mouth one more time please." I opened my mouth, and they still couldn't get it out. The doctors said, "We have to take her to OR." I said, "My tongue ring twist. Can you guys try to twist it?" They said, "Oh, it twists? Let's try to take the tongue ring out by twisting it." They went inside my mouth, and they tried to twist the ball of the tongue ring off, but it was so much blood around the ball it made it slippery. When they removed my tongue ring, they placed it in a container. I told the doctor's I wanted to keep my tongue ring. The doctors said, "Whoever pierced your tongue, they pierced your artery in your tongue, and that's why you have a blood clog." The doctor gave me some antibiotics. They told me to eat some soup, and my tongue will close and heal buy it self. I told both of the doctors thank you, for your patience, and for taking my tongue ring out of my mouth. My granny told the doctors thank you too. My granny called my uncle Ike to come pick us up from the hospital. As we were leaving out the emergency room, it was a girl coming in the emergency room, and she had a blood clog on her tongue too. When Ike picked us up, he took us to Walgreens. So I could put my prescription in the pharmacy. Then I bought me some soup. After my prescription was ready, we left. He dropped my granny and I off at home. I told my granny thank you, for coming with me to the hospital. She said, "You're welcome. I know one thing you better not go back and get your tongue pierced." I replied, "I'm going to go get it pierced next week granny. It's going to be done right this time." "I'm not going back to the hospital with you, don't call me." I laughed. I said, "Granny, I'm not getting my tongue pierced again. My tongue hurts to bad, and that scared me." The next day Rebbeca called and checked on me. I called Jannette and told her what the doctor said. I stayed home and rested. I took my medicine and I ate my soup. David would call and check on me.

After my tongue healed, I went back to work. Susan was supposed to be at work, and it was time for us to serve dinner and she still wasn't there. Jannette called my name. She said, "Zaneeya come here for a minute." I went to see what Jannette wanted. Jannette said, "It's 5:10 PM and Susan still isn't here, that's it. I'm going to fire her. I'm done she can go be late somewhere else." I replied, "I don't blame you Jannette. You gave her chance, after chance and when you have a job, you have to be on time. You're the boss, do what you have to do." "I am. It's a lot of people who needs a job, and would like to have her job. When she gets here tell her to come to my office, thank you niece." "You're welcome auntie." I went back on the floor to serve. When Susan came to work, she started serving and I told her to go to Jannette's office. Susan said, "I'm going to her office, after I'm done serving my residents their food." I said, "You need to go now." Susan didn't listen to me. Vida said, "Susan put your tray down and go to Jannette's office right now." Susan went to Jannette's office. Then she came back in the diningroom with her belongings and she left. I got a call from Sally. I went to the breakroom so I could answer my phone, even though I was not supposed to leave the floor. Sally said, "Zaneeya, your auntie fired Susan, because she was late. Can you talk to your auntie for me or can I talk to her?" "It's nothing I can do. I'm not helping Susan anymore, and Susan has been late every since I got her this job. She doesn't want to work. I told her time after time to be on time, and if she keeps being late, Jannette is going to fire her. She didn't care, she got her on self-fired. She can't blame anyone, but herself." "Susan was late, because of me and she do want to work. She don't be late everyday. I just want to talk to Jannette. Can you tell her I want to talk to her?" "I'll go tell her you want to talk to her, but she's not going to talk to you, hold on." I went in the kitchen. I said, "Jannette, Susan's mom is on the phone, and she wants to talk to you." Jannette said, "I am not hiring Susan back. That is not going to happen. I am working right now and I'm not taking any calls, and you need to get on the floor. So tell her I cannot talk right now." I told Sally what Jannette said. Then I went back to my section. After work, I went home. Rebbeca called me we made plans to go school shopping.

The next day, I went to Sabreea's house and David had called me. He said, "I really love you SC and I really want to marry you. I'm going to propose to you soon, and I want to get you pregnant, when I come home to visit." I said, "I do want to get married, and we always talked about that, but I'm not ready to have a baby right now." "I want to get you pregnant, when I come home. Then you can move out here with me. The army will give us our own place to live. I'm ready right now." "I'm not ready to have a baby right now, I think we should wait." "Ok, I'm bout to get off the phone, I'll call you later." "So you're getting off the phone, because you're mad that I don't want to have a baby right now?" "Yes I am. I don't see why it's a problem. We have been together for 3 years and I'm ready to have a baby right now." "I know we have been together for 3 years, but I just want us to wait, let's wait. What wrong with that?" "OK, whatever I'll talk to you later." "Ok." When, I got off the phone with David. I called my mom and I told her what David and I talked about. My mom said, "David wants to get you pregnant, so he'll know that you're not going anywhere. He does want you to have his baby, but you don't need to have a baby right now. Tell him if he wants you to have his baby, he needs to marry you. You know I like David. He is a good guy, but like you said, y'all can wait. You have your head on right." I replied, "Ok, thanks mom. I'll call you later, I just wanted your opinion on what David and I was talking about. You know I never talk to you about my relationship. I love you and I'll call you later bye mom." "I know Cupcake, I love you too bye." When, I got off the phone with my mom. I kept thinking about how David was mad at me, because I did not want to have a baby right now. I did not want him to be mad at me, and I had a feeling, this was going to start a problem in our relationship. I wasn't ready to have a baby, and I knew no matter what, I was not going to get pregnant at 18 years old. Toniya, had called me and asked me to come to her house, so I can go grocery shopping for her. I told her I would have to call into work. She said, "I just got out of the hospital, I had surgery on my neck. I need some food, and I'm not able to go to the store myself." I said, "Ok mom, I'll come and you do not have to pay me." "Ok baby, thank you." Jessica and I went to Antioch. We went grocery shopping for Toniya and I cleaned up her house for her. I said, "Mom, if you need me to come out here to go grocery shopping for you, and to clean up your house for you I will." She said, "Thank you, so much. I'll give Jessica some gas money for coming." "You don't have to pay us." "Zaneeya, before you leave, can you put my credit card in my pillow case for me, because your dad will rob me blind?" I laughed. See, my dad and Toniya was not together any more.

Chapter Thirteen

My 12th grade year

*T*oniya and I still had a stepmother and daughter relationship. She told me, even though her and my dad was not together. She would always be there for me, and my siblings. Jessica and I would go to her house and spend nights. When her sister came down to visit Jessica and I went to Antioch. Toniya gave all of us some money and we went shopping. We went to the movies and we went out to eat. When Toniya moved, Jessica and I helped her move, and after she moved, I never seen her again. I would call Toniya, but she wouldn't answer. She wasn't there for me, and it did hurt my feelings. I thought she would always be around. I thought we would always have a relationship, but we didn't. Toniya went on with her life, as if we never had a stepmother and daughter relationship. I told myself. If I ever had a child, and my child's father and I was not together, and I got into another relationship with a different man. I would tell that person. Do not say, you're going to be in my child's life, and have a relationship with them. If you're really not, because at the end of the day. The only one is hurting is that child. Even though I was 18 years old, I did not think Toniya would just leave like she did. I told my dad that I was not going to get close to none of his girlfriends and I did not want to meet them. I was finally a senior in high school. I was working more hours at work, and I knew, I wanted to work full time and I wanted graduate. I did not pass my cahsee. I had to take two cahsee classes. One was for math, and one was for English. The cahsee classes were only for the people who needed to graduate. I had my cahsee math class with Nathan and Dudy. We had a teacher who taught us well, and he was very helpful. Senior year was different. It was more pressure. I knew I wasn't going to pass my cahsee. It was just too hard for me, with my learning disability. I didn't understand it, my teacher knew that I needed help and he would help me, but he had twenty-five other students who he had to help as well. I liked my English teacher Mr.

Nicholas. He was very nice, and he was always calm and I had his class my 9ᵗʰ grade year as well. He taught 9ᵗʰ graders and 12ᵗʰ graders.

I talked to my I.E.P teacher and I told her even though, I'm in a cahsee class. It's still difficult for me to focus, because in one of my classes. Some of the students didn't get along, and the teacher would spend most of the time yelling at the students and trying to get them to calm down. I still wanted to try my hardest to graduate, even if I had to leave OT High, and go to another school, to succeed and to do better. I had a wonderful counselor at school. Her name was Ms. Johnson. I would go to Ms. Johnson's office sometimes when I needed to talk to her about my classes, and she would help me. I would go to school then work. After work, I would go home and that was my routine. I would spend some nights at Sabreea's house. Jessica, Sabreea, and Lucy and I would go to the movies and out to eat and we would go shopping. My sis would still come up to my school, and sit in my classes with me. My best friend and her, wasn't on the best of terms anymore, but they still liked each other. Over the summer, my sis and my best friend fail in love with each other, and even though she had a dude and he was seeing other girls. They still were attached to each other, until one day he couldn't take it anymore. He stopped calling my sis and she didn't know why. So I had called and asked him. I said, "Best friend how are doing?" He replied, "What's up best friend. I'm good." "Have you talked to my sis?" "No, she be calling me sometimes, but I just don't answer. I be wanting to answer though." "Oh, why don't you want to talk to my sis anymore? I thought y'all were in love and I thought you had strong feelings for her. Why is there a change all of a sudden?" "I do love her, and I do have feelings for her, but I'm not down with that any more. She has a dude. I'm not comfortable with her seeing me and seeing him too. So I'm just coo." "You knew that she had a dude, just like she knows that you have other females. You have a right to feel that way. I understand it." "I told her if she leaves her dude. I'll be with her, and I would stop talking to all these females. She's not ready for that. She is not about to have her cake and ice cream and eat it too. Not with me anymore." "Do you really want her to be your woman?" "Yeah, I do if she would leave her dude, but she's not. So I can't talk to her like I use to." "I get it and you are a good man Nathan, and I don't want to see neither one of you hurt. She does want to be with you, but she's not ready to leave her dude right now, but she's hurting too. Her feelings are hurt. She really loves you, but I do understand your point of view as well. I think y'all will still hook up and mess around." "We probably will, we can be friends. That can be my sis now." "Real funny best friend ha-ha, no. That is not your sis. That's my sis, and I'mma kick yo butt about hurting my sis feelings too." "She hurt my feelings too. I didn't mean to hurt her feelings at all trust me. I still want her. I will always talk to her, and to be honest, I really like her big booty self. I'm not going to continue to be in love with her. Hell nah, we can still mess around for sure. I'll still hit that. I can see that happening." "Ok thanks for the clarity, but you should tell her. She deserves to know." "You can tell her for me and if she calls me, I will tell her too." "Ok, I'll talk to you later best friend bye." When, I told my sis what Nathan said. She was crying. She was upset, but they talked and they were still seeing each other. If another guy would talk to my sis, while she was at my school, Nathan would get jealous. If another girl was talking to him, she would get jealous, and she would roll her eyes at him. Nathan would say, "Why are you rolling your eyes at me sis?" She replied, "Oh, now I'm sis? Ok bruh."

As a teenager, I became very hot headed. I never took any mess from anyone. I always stood up for myself. I had a lot of anger inside of me and when I use to get mad I would want to shoot the person who made me mad. I knew that was nothing, but the devil, but at the time I couldn't shake it. My attitude was like my brother Qin's, and I also looked up to him as well. Everytime I went to work, there was a lot of eye rolling. Their was a lot of girls that didn't like me for no reason, and they didn't even know me. I would always have my hair done in different styles, and I would always dress cute. One day I was at work, and some of my co-workers stood around me, while I was putting on my mascara. They were talking amongst each other. They said, "What are you going to wear, Maybelline or CoverGirl?" They just looked at me and laughed. I said, "You guys are so envy of me, and it's so sad. It's nothing like the next woman, haten on the next. I forgot none of you are a woman yet! You still have a lot of growing to do, poor babies. Continue to hate on me! As I wear my nice dresses and as I give you a catwalk, as if I was on the runway in my high heels." I laughed. They were talking mess, but I did not care. Jannette heard us arguing and she told all of us to come here. Jannette said, "I'm going to have a meeting with all of you right now, and y'all are going to get everything out on the table. Why you guys don't like Zaneeya? What did she do to you? Danny you use to like Zaneeya. Now you have your friends here, and you started acting funny." Danny said, "I just don't like her anymore, because she thinks she's better than me." Danny's friends said, "I don't like her, because she thinks she's better than us and she is always looking at herself in the mirror. Telling herself how good she looks. She don't never speak to us." Jannette said, "Zaneeya, why you don't like them?" I replied, "I don't think I'm better then anyone. If I want to look in the mirror at myself, I am! What's wrong with that? I know that I am beautiful, and I like to look good. I will never go out of my way, to speak to you guys. All of you are jealous of me, because I look good and I have a lot of pride about myself, and you all know it. Danny don't like me, because her ex-boyfriend Dre, has a crush on me. That's the real reason. When I come to work he flirts with me, and he's always complimenting me. By telling me how good I look and Danny, you don't like that. Y'all don't like me, because Danny don't like me and that's fine. Just woman up, and tell Jannette the reason why, and stop lying damn." Danny said, *"He does flirt with you, and I don't like it. I did like you at first, we was coo." "When, Dre flirts with me. I never flirt back with him. I'm in a relationship. I do not want him! You should have came up to me, and said something, but you didn't. You started talking mess with your friends like a kid. We are not friends, and we are not coo, period."*

"That's fine with me and I don't care what he does." "Oh, you care honey!" Jannette said, *"Y'all have to get along, and that's, that. I'm not going for this and Danny you can't be mad, because Dre flirts with Zaneeya. You take that up with him. You guys are not even together, and you are just starting mess, and I'm not going to have it. So what if Zaneeya, looks in the mirror at herself. If she looks in the mirror all day long, what does that have to do with y'all? Nothing, if y'all look in the mirror all day long. What does that have to do with Zaneeya? Nothing, she is supposed to know that she looks good. Just like y'all are supposed to know, that you look good. Do y'all think y'all look good?"* They replied, *"Yes, we do Jannette." "Well, I don't want to hear, nothing else about this again. Stop with the jealousy, because all of you are going to be jobless. Zaneeya, do you come to work and stand on the side of them, and make fun of them with Rebbeca?"* I replied, *"No, I do not behave like that, only kids do!" "I want all of you to stop doing that too. Danny, I don't have time for no childish behavior. We all are grown adults here, and if you won't stop. You will not have a job and I mean it."* Danny said, *"Jannette I just don't like looking at her. Sometimes, I just want to slap her."* Jannette said, *"Well, that's not going to happen, so you can forget about that."* I said, *"I don't like looking at you either. However, I don't have a choice. I wish, I really wish, you would slap me. You wouldn't make it out of here alive! Trust that, and you know it. Jannette, I wish you would just line all of them up, and I will fight all of them one on one."* Danny said, *"I'm not worried about you Zaneeya." "Right, but you was just saying, you wanted to slap me. I'm just letting you know, the invitation is always out there if you ever want to catch fades, remember that."* Jannette said, *"Ok that's enough. I'm not, going to have that here. Everybody said what they wanted to say, and if there is any more mess, y'all don't have*

to worry about nothing. You will be looking for another job, so get back to work." I went in the kitchen. Jannette said, "Danny, I'm going to have you do the dishes tonight, stay in here. You don't have to serve tonight." She replied, "Why, do I have to do the dishes? Why Zaneeya can't do them?" "Zaneeya, is always doing the dishes, and she don't have a problem doing them, when I tell her too. If you have a problem doing the dishes, you can leave." Danny got mad and she started talking back to Jannette. Jannette said, "You better, stop talkin back to me Danny. Have some respect because you're not doing me a favor by being here honey, know that!"

Danny kept talking back to Jannette. I said, "Talk to my auntie like that again, and I'mma reach over there and touch you. Won't nobody be able to get me off of you, say another word." Jannette said, "Zaneeya, I can handle myself, thank you. Go to the diningroom." I went inside the diningroom. After I was finished serving, I went to the kitchen. I was mad, because Danny was disrespecting Jannette, and my auntie did not deserve that. I wanted to make Danny mad, so she could hit me. That would give me a reason to beat her up. Jannette already told me. If I hit her first, or if I fought by the job, I was going to get fired, and I needed my job, but I wasn't going to let Danny get away with talking to Jannette like she was crazy. I went to the kitchen. I said, "Danny, you need to hurry up with my dishes." Then, I walked back to the diningroom. 15-minutes later, I walked back to the kitchen. I said, "Danny, you need to hurry up with my dishes, and move faster. I'm going to come in here, every 5-minutes until you're done." She did not say nothing, so I went back into the diningroom. When, I went back in the kitchen. I said, "Danny, are my dishes done?" She replied, "You need to stop talking to me, because I'm going to take my time doing yo dishes." "You're not stupid, you are not going to do that, so hurry up and come on little girl." "I am not a little girl. What's up? I'm tired of you." Danny started taking off her gloves I said, "If you feelin froggy leap." There were five busting carts in the middle of us, and I started kicking some of the busting carts out of the way. I swung on Danny. Thomas ran between us. He said, "Zaneeya, no don't hit her." I was tired of her talking back to Jannette, and that wasn't her first time talking crazy to her. I kicked a few busting carts at Danny, and threw a few things as well. I was upset. Thomas was yelling Dre, and Vida and Jannette's name, but only Dre heard him. Dre, ran over to me and he picked me up, and he took me towards the back of the kitchen. I was yelling at Danny I said, "The next time you talk crazy to Jannette want nobody be here to help you." She replied, "We get off work at 8 o'clock, see me than." "I'll be waiting, don't leave." Thomas said, "Donate go get Jannette." Donate came back and said, "Thomas,

Jannette lefted." Thomas said, "Zaneeya, get out the kitchen and I'll get your dishes for you." Dre said, "Zaneeya, I'll get your dishes for you, let me walk you to the diningroom. When you get mad, there is no stopping you. You don't need to fight. You look too good to fight." "Shut up Dre. Can you just go get my dishes for me, thank you?" Dre went to the kitchen to get my dishes for me. When it was time to get off work, Danny clocked out and I was right behind her. When I went outside, Thomas was right by us. I said, "Danny, it's 8 o'clock what's up?" She kept on walking, and she did not say anything. One thing about me, I never fought anybody that did not want to fight me, no matter how much mess they talked. To me, that was a bully and that was something that I was not.

As it was getting closer for David to come home, the less we would talk. When I called him, he wouldn't answer. His behavior towards me had changed. I saw on the news, that there was going to be a tsunami in Hawaii. Qin had came to my house, he told me he needed a cell phone. He asked me could he have my phone. I said, "No, this is the only phone that I have. You need to go buy you a phone, you have money." Qin said he did not want to buy him a new phone. He didn't stay long. I wanted to call David, so I could tell him about the tsunami warning in Hawaii. I noticed that my phone was gone. I said, "Granny, have you seen my phone?" My granny said, "No." Qin, stoled my phone, I couldn't believe it. I called my phone, but it was turned off. I called Ranesha phone, but she didn't answer. So I called Cassandra phone, because I knew, she was going to answer. I said, "Cassandra, does Qin have my phone?" She replied, "Yeah he does. I told him to put it back." "Put me on speakerphone. Qin, bring me my phone and my phone charger right now. You are supposed to be this big time drug dealer. Buy your own damn phone."

Qin laughed in the phone. He said, "Sis, I need a new phone, so I took yours. I knew, if I would have asked you could I have your phone again, you would have said no. So I just took it. I'll bring it back later, I'm not coming back right now. I have a lot of things to do, while I'm out here. I love you. Thanks, for letting me use your phone." "I'm not playin with you. Bring me back my phone. You are a theft." Qin hung up the phone. Qin brought my phone back to me. I said, "That is a damn shame, you come to people house stealing." "I didn't steal your phone, I took it. You're lucky I came back, because I didn't want too. So be happy. I should have just driven to Modesto and you would of been mad." "We are not kids no more." "What does that suppose to mean? I will still beat you up." "Try it and see what happens." "Yeah ok Zaneeya, I have to go. Don't have your phone around me next time, because I'm not coming back." "I'mma always keep my phone by me when I see you."

The next day I went to work. When I came home from work, Rebbeca had called me, and she said Dre wanted my number. I told her not to give it to him. She said, "Zaneeya, what if you just talk to him on the phone and I threeway for y'all? Since, you don't want him to have your number." "No, that's not coo." David was calling me, while I was on the phone with Rebbeca. I said, "Rebbeca, I'm going to call you back, that's David." "Ok Zaneeya." I answered the phone. I said, "I haven't talked to you in a couple of days, we need to talk." He replied, "I know, I been busy. What have you been doing, and what took you so long to answer the phone?" "I was talking to Rebbeca. You know me. I just work and go to school. I'm happy it's getting closer for you to come home." "Yeah." "Why do you sound so down? Like, you're not happy." "I'm stressed out right now, that's all. I miss you a lot." "I miss you too. Are you going to your room, because I can hear you walking up the stairs?" "Yeah I am." I heard a girl's voice. I said, "David who is that?" "Do you want to talk to her? Since you're asking who she is?" It was a different side of David, that I never seen before. I said, "Put her on the phone." She said, "Hello." I said, "Who are you?" "I'm David's girlfriend, and I have been sleeping in his bed every night. I'm pregnant and we are going to have a family together." "Oh really, so you're his girlfriend? So, you be quite everytime we talk on the phone. Now you want to speak up. So you're the type of chick, who doesn't mind, if a man have two or three girlfriends! Just as long, as he sleeps with you too!" "I think he likes sleeping with me." "Put David back on the phone." "No." "Put David back on the phone. What are you scared of?" "I'm not scared. You don't need to talk to him, you can talk to me." "You are a simple NCLBAB. See, the one thing I cannot stand. Is for another female to sleep with a man, knowing he has a woman. I don't have any respect for a female like you at all. I'm not mad at you. I'm in a relationship with David. My problem is with him, put me on speakerphone." "You are on speaker." I said, "David, you are weak and you are a liar. You do not deserve a wonderful woman like me. You are going to rep, what you soul and I hope you do. Just like you cheated on me and got a NCLBAB pregnant. She is going to cheat on you, and her baby is not going to be yours watch!" David did not say anything. The girl said, "We are having a family and this is his baby.

I am not a scandals female. I have been cheated on, and my ex had a baby on me too. I know how you feel right now. I am pregnant and it's too late. His family knows that I'm pregnant and everything." "If that happend to you, why would you, continue having a relationship with someone, knowing that they have a woman? I don't have no respect for a female like you period. If he cheated on me, he's going to cheat on you too, believe that." "I don't think he'll cheat on me." "David you are a coward for real. I did not know you were this soft!" I told David off. I said, "David, you can have her, and she can have you. I don't want you! Do not ever contact me in life again." I hung up the phone, but David kept calling me, back to back nonstop. I did not answer the phone, I called Jessica and I told her to come over. When Jessica came over, we sat in her van and we talked. I told her what happened. David kept calling me, so I answered the phone and I put him on speakerphone. I said, "Stop calling me." David said, "I have never heard you talk like that before, and you're going to call me out of my name." "It's a first time for everything, even you know that. Hell yeah, I called you out of your name. You're lucky it was just that. Stop calling me. I don't, want nothing, to do with you." I hug up the phone, but David kept calling. Jessica said, "He's calling you, but his girlfriend is right there and she is allowing him to call you. She is stupid. She must be a simple female." "She is too simple, she is a basic female." My heart was just not there anymore and I was hurt. I had my first heartbeak, and it did not feel good. When David called back, I answered the phone. I said, "Why are you still calling me? Your girl is right there, talk to her." He replied, "Who are you with?" "Look you're not runnin nothin over here. No questions will be answered at all. You are a liar, and your heart is going to be broke. When you find out that her baby is not yours, and don't call me. I'mma laugh at you. When the test results say, you are not the father. Jokes on me right now, but your going to be the joker in the end!" "I'm not worried about that, you didn't want to have my baby. I told you, I wanted us to have a baby when I come home, but you don't want to." "So that gives you a right to cheat on me? I'm happy I'm not having your baby. She's not having your baby either. So you're going to really be depressed, you made your bed now lay in it." "I tried to have a baby with you, but you don't want too. Are you sure you don't want us to be together?" "Yes I'm sure! You can have her and she can have you. I don't want you!" David's girlfriend gabbed, the phone. She said, "You keep saying that this is not his baby, like you know it's not. I am with David now, and we have a family. The ring he got you, I'm getting." "I told you, that you are a NCLBAB. See, I am the type of woman that would not accept a ring that a man has for the next woman. He would have to get me another ring. That's bigger and better, but you're so simple you'll take anything. You're a basic female."

"Whatever that's, why I have your man." "He's not my man anymore! He's yours. Since you want to brag, I'll tell you what. I'll do you a favor, when he comes home. I am going to see him, and he is going to call me when he

comes out here. Don't think he's not. We have been together for over 3 years. He's going to call me, and when he does, I'm going to answer and I'm going to keep him company for two weeks. When I'm done with him. I'll send him home to you, and I promise you I am believe that." "Yeah right, you couldn't have David back if you wanted too." "That's your man, but he just asked me if I want to be done with our relationship. Girl wake up. You're a joke, bye joker. I'll see you when you come out here." When I hug up the phone, David called me back. He said, "SC, so you're really done with our relationship?" "What do you mean? You cheated on me. You got a NCLBAB pregnant, and I'm supposed to stay with you, and be faithful to you, and stay loyal to you. Hell no bye! Call me when you get out here." I hung up the phone. David called back, but I didn't answer. I cried to Jessica. She was there for me as a best friend, through my break up with David. After Jessica left, I went back inside the house. I did not sleep well. I cried myself to sleep. When I went to school the next day, I cried and Jessica was there for me. She would say, "Sis, it's going to get better, you deserve to have someone better then that." When I got out of school, I went home. I called David's mom and I told her David, and I was no longer together.

Miss. Candace said, "Zaneeya, I adore you, and I always will. I'm not happy with the decision that David has made. Even though he is my son, he is wrong for cheating on you, and getting another girl pregnant. No woman deserves that. I'm sorry that you're hurting right now. My heart goes out to you. You are a beautiful woman and you deserve a better man. I don't care if he is my son. David is wrong, and he does not know anything about that girl. I wish y'all could stay together. I am a woman, and I know you're hurting, and I know you're in pain. I am sorry this had to happen to you. I am very, disappointed in David and I told him that. You are the right woman for him. Some men have to learn the hard way. You can call me anytime you want too, you have my number." "Thank you so much Miss. Candace. That's why I like you, you always keep it real. I knew you would feel for me, as a woman. Thank you again." "You're welcome. Everyday, it will get easier for you, and I am still your mom ok!" "Ok, thank you." I hung up the phone then I called Xavier. I said, "David and I are not together anymore. I wish you could have told me he cheated."

"I'm sorry SC, but I couldn't tell you. He needed to tell you that, but he shouldn't have cheated on you. I'm sorry you have to go through that. We are still family. You can call me anytime, and Cedrick wants to talk to you, hold on." Cedrick said, "SC, I'm sorry you have to go through that. Like Xavier said we are still family, you can call me anytime. If you want to party, if you

want to talk or whatever, were here for you." "Ok, thanks brother." "You're welcome sis. Y'all need to get back together." "No, that's not gonna happen. I do not want him." When I got off the phone, I told my granny that David and I was not together anymore, and I told her the reason why. My granny said, "I know you're hurt, but it's plenty of men out there, that's going to like you and love you. You're going to look back at this and laugh. Trust me, you don't see it now, but you will soon." I did not care about that, I did not want to feel, what I was feeling. David had called me later on that night. I answered my phone. I said, "What do you want?" He replied, "I'm just calling to check on you and to see how you're doing." "You have the nerve to call me and check on me, as if I want to talk to you, after what you just did." "I know what I did was wrong. She was supposed to have, an abortion. I told her too, and she was fine with that. She just flipped the script and said she was keeping the baby. I do not want to have a baby with her. You just through away our relationship, like it wasn't nothing." "I didn't throw away our relationship. You did, when you cheated and got a NCLBAB pregnant. You thought I was going to stay with you!" "I still have feelings for you SC." "You don't have feelings for me. I can't believe you got mad and cheated on me, just because I don't want to have a baby right now." "I'm ready for us to have a baby. I did not want to have a baby with her!" "If you didn't want to have a baby with her you should have used protection, but you didn't care." "I did care and I do now. That's why I'm calling you. I hope you feel better. My mom told me, she talked to you." "I talked to her, Xavier, and Cedrick." "Oh really, what did they say?" "None of your business, I have to go." "Where are you going?" "I'm not answering that question." "Is your boyfriend calling you?" "You're such a coward. You just want to know, if I'm talking to someone else.I don't have to answer you, but the truth is, I'm not. I never cheated on you, but you are going to know how it feels to get cheated on, because that baby isn't yours. Just like my heart is broken, yours is going to be too." "I don't think she'll do that. Can I call you and check on you tomorrow please?" "No you cannot."

David would call in check on me to see how I was doing. One night, I went out to eat with Jessica, Desseire and Trina. When, I got back home. My granny said, "Zaneeya, David called you." I knew he was out here and he wanted to see me, so I called David. He said, "SC, how are you doing?" "I am doing well, you must be out here." "I am and I want to come see you. So can I come see you?" "Yeah you can." I told David how to get to my house. He made it to my house less than 2 hours. He was smiling as he was looking at me. He gave me a hug and I pushed him off me. We sat down and we talked. He said, "SC,

I know I messed up big time, you will never take me back." I replied, "Your right about that, you're lucky you're here. I told your so called baby momma I would keep my promise and I am a woman of my word." My granny was getting ready for church. David said hi to her. My granny said, "David, you came back huh?" "Yes I did, I wanted to see Zaneeya." "I'm going to leave you too love birds alone and I'll see y'all later." I told my granny bye as she was leaving. I asked David, why he's not rubbing his baby momma belly right now. He said, "That is not my girlfriend anymore." I said, "I know you guys did not break up, not the one you love." "I'm not in love with her. It was lust. She did cheat on me. She had a dude when I met her, and she knew that I had woman, but she didn't care." "No, you did not care, but you are going back to her." "Do you still love me?" "No I don't!" I was not going to tell David, that I was still in love with him. I was trying to get over my feelings for him, but I was still in love with him. We just hung out that day. We watched movies and chilled. David had spent a couple of nights with me. He took me out to breakfast and we went to the movies. Then we went to Barnes & Noble. When, he dropped me off at home. He told me he was going to come back and pick me up when I got off work Friday. He said he was going to spend the rest of his vacation with me. On Friday, David came to my house, and his so called baby momma called my phone, but I didn't answer. So she called my granny's phone. My granny answered her phone. She said, "Zaneeya, tell that girl not to call my phone."

I went into my granny's room and she handed me her cell phone. I got on the phone. I said, "Your hella disrespectful, do not call my granny's cell phone." She said, "I'm sorry for calling your granny's cell phone, but you didn't answer your phone. I'm not calling to be disrespectful. I just want to know if David is with you." "Yes he is. I told you I was going to keep my promise that I made to you, and I did." "Well, if he is over there with you he must don't want me. I'm so mad at David with his lying self." "Don't worry, when I'm done with him, I'll send him right back to you! He'll be home soon." I hung up the phone. Jessica called me. She said, "Sis, I never seen David before, and I cannot believe your crazy self kept your word. Can I come over? I just want to see what he looks like." I replied, "He's sleeping Jessica." "Ok, I want stay long." "Ok, come on." When Jessica came over David was sleep and she was laughing. She said, "You are so crazy. I'm not even mad at you. That girl deserves it, all that mess she was talkin." Jessica smiled and gave me a high five. I said, "Ok, I'll call you tomorrow." The next day Sabreea called me and asked me what I was doing. I told her I was with David. She said, "Well come over my house, I have not seen him in a long time." We left and went to Sabreea's house. I introduced,

David to momma Shay, they talked for a little while. Sabreea was leaving. I said, "I did not know you were leaving." She replied, "I'll be back later on. I see you came back to see my sister huh David?" "Yeah I did. It was nice seeing you again." David and I went to get something to eat. We just stayed in the house that day watching TV. When Sabreea came back, it was late. We spent the night at Sabreea's house. The next morning, Sabreea left. She had to go to work. David and I left, we went to my house. David told me, he never meant to hurt me and he wish, he could take it back. David had to go back to Hawaii, his vacation was over. We stayed at my house until it was time for him to leave. We hugged and we said bye to each other, then he left. I was happy, that I had some closure, after he left I felt better.

I wasn't doing good in school. I did not pass my cahsee, but I wanted to graduate on time. I went to see Miss. Petter, so I could talk to her about my grades. I told her, I wanted to go to a school that was independent study so I could graduate on time. She told me about this school called Trump and it was independent studies. She told me that was a great way to bring up my grades and I would be able to take the cahsee over. I had to write Trump a letter. Stating why they should let me go to their school. They accepted my letter. I asked Shay, could I use her address, so I could go to Trump. She said, "Yeah." I asked Shay could she come with me to Trump, because they were not going to let me enroll myself into school. Even though I was 18 years old, and I have been putting myself in school all this time. I had to go to school twice a week. My class started at 8:00 AM and I did not get out of school until 10:00 AM. I worked Monday through Friday. I started work at 11:30 AM and I did not get off work until 8:00 PM. My teacher was amazing her name was Mrs. Colman. She was very understanding and helpful. She would help me with my work. I was getting better grades and things were starting to change for me. When it was time for me to take my cahsee again, I did, but I didn't pass the math part. I knew that I could go to summer school and I would be able to take the cahsee over, and I was happy about that. I asked Jannette to hire Lucy for me, and she did. Lucy and I would go to the bar on Tuesdays. We would go to the 21 and up clubs on Wednesdays and Thursdays. On Fridays, Sabreea, Jessica, and Lucy and I would go have ladiesnights at Apple bee's and other restaurants. On Saturdays, all of us would go to the strip club. Jessica had gave me a ticket to go to her graduation, I rode with her and her parents to the graduation. When the graduation was over, we went to Desseire's house. Then we went to a party. I would get rental cars and have hotel parties. Jessica and I would ask uncle Henry to get our rental cars for us and he would. We would give him our money for the rental car. I hooked Xavier and Jessica up together and they started seeing each other. Jessica and I would go to Modesto. Then we would go to Stockton and party with Xavier and Cedrick. Sometime I would take Christy with me. We would spend the night at Xavier's house. Then we would get up the next morning and go to my mom's house, and sleep for a couple of hours. Then we would go back to Stockton. Xavier and Jessica liked each other a lot. We would go to Stockton, a lot and Xavier would come to the Bay Area to see Jessica. One night Lucy had called me, when we were in Stockton. She told me, that she had got into an argument with one of the girls at our job.

The next day Lucy went to work, and our boss Ryan fired her. The receptionist told Ryan, that Lucy tried to jump her and she pulled a gun out on her. Everything, that the receptionist said was a lie. Lucy was mad, that she got fired for no reason and so was I. Jessica wanted to work at my job. So, I asked Jannette once again, could she hire another friend of mines and she did. I did not mind getting Jessica a job, because that was my best friend and we looked out for each other. Jessica started working with me. Jannette would let her clock into work early and she would give Jessica the same hours that I had. When I went back to school to take my cahsee, my teacher told me that they did not have a cahsee for me. I was devastated. I knew if I had taken my cahsee. I would have passed it and I would have gotten my diploma. I just wanted my diploma. I was upset about that for a long time. As I got older, I knew that Letha didn't want me to work in high school, so I can focus and finish school. I didn't know how hard it was going to be, but I did find out. As time went on, I kept working and David and I would talk everyday. He would call me while I was at work, and I would sneak off to go talk to him. He would call me at least four times a day. Jessica and I would still get rental cars to go to Modesto... One day, I had rented a Dodge charger. I called Sabreea and asked her did she want to go to Modesto, with me. She said, "Yeah." I also called Rebbeca, and I asked her did she want to go to Modesto, as well. On our way to Modesto, Jessica would drive out there, because she had license and I did not, but I would drive while we were in Modesto. When we made it to Modesto, we went to my mom's house first. Then we went to Qin's house, but we were not speaking, because we had a fight a couple of months before I went out there. When, we arrived to Qin's house. He said, "Zaneeya, you cannot come in my house." "I'm not, but I'm going to stand right here on your porch." "Don't stand on my porch either, you're not my sister, Sabreea is my sister." "Make me get off your porch, and I do not care about Sabreea being your sister, we are not kids anymore. That does not bother me." "I'm just playin sis, you can come in. Did you miss me?" "No I did not." I gave my nephew a hug and kiss. Qin said, "Where y'all goin all dressed up?" I said, "We are going to Stockton." "You and Big Bird are always going to Stockton. What do y'all do out there?" Big Bird was Jessica's nickname that Qin gave her. I said, "We be hanging out with my brother and my cousin." "Those people are not your brothers or cousins. That is your ex-boyfriend family. Which one is Big Bird seeing?" "None of your bussiness Qin dang and they are my family."

Qin said, "I'm going to ask Big Bird, since you won't tell me. Big Bird, which one of those dudes are you having sex with." She replied, "None of your business Qin, you're not my man." "I know I'm not, but I'm just asking a question and don't get smart neither, because I will kick you out just like I kick everybody else out." I said, "Shut up Qin." Jessica said, "I know, that's why were leaving." I made us a few drinks before we left. I made us some caramel apple tines. Dorthy was there, so I made her a drink too. Qin said, "What time are y'all leaving tomorrow? When are y'all coming back out here?" Jessica said, "That's up to Zaneeya." I said, "I don't know, we probably won't leave until later on, after the sun goes down. Why what's up? No you cannot use our rental car." "No, it's not that, I'm going to BBQ tomorrow for us, if you guys stay out here. Just come to my house when y'all get dress." Qin started laughing. I said, "Ok, I'll see you tomorrow." He replied, "Ok and I do need to use y'all rental car tomorrow too." "Bye Qin." Rebbeca didn't know, Azzy was going to be at Xavier's house. So I told her while we were in the car, and she was happy. She said, "I haven't seen him in a long time, I wonder what he looks like." When, we got to Xavier's house. Cedrick and Xavier were cracking jokes as usual, and we all were drinking and talking mess and we all had a good time. Rebbeca was a kid in the candy store while she was around Azzy. I put Rebbeca on blasts about her wanting to see Azzy. She was denying it, but Jessica and Sabreea backed me up. We all were dinking and talking mess. I was tired, so I told everyone that I was going to bed. Xavier said, "SC, you know where everything is help yourself." I went in the back room so I could lay down, Sabreea came with me. Jessica went to bed with Xavier and Rebbeca went to bed with Azzy. Sabreea and I heard Jessica having sex. Sabreea said, "Did you hear that?" I smiled and said, "Yeah, go Jessica." Sabreea said, "Xavier is puttin it down on Big Bird, get it girl. I wonder if Rebbeca is having sex right now." "Yes she is and I am not walking out there until later, I do not want to see that." "I have to go to the bathroom." When, Sabreea came back from the bathroom. She said, "Rebbeca is having sex, I heard her moaning." I replied, "I'm going to sleep, I heard enough tonight." "I'm right behind you." The next morning, Xavier's daughter woke up. I haven't seen her since she was a little girl. She walked over to me. She said, "What's your name?" I said, "Zaneeya, what's your name? I remember you when you were a little girl" She told me her name, then she showed me her Barbie dolls and I played with her.

When, Jessica and Xavier came out the room. I said, "Y'all was up all night, we heard a lot of smacking last night." They both started smiling Jessica was blushing. Xavier said, "I had to put her to sleep, I had to teach her a few things." Jessica was still blushing. Sabreea said, "Jessica was you keeping up with him?" "You know I was." Xavier said, "Yeah right." We all got up and headed to the livingroom then Cedrick came over. Cedrick lived next door to Xavier. Cedrick said, "Rebbeca are you happy you seen Azzy, did you have fun last night?" She replied, "Yeah I had fun. I enjoyed myself." Sabreea said, "Good, all that moaning you was doing you should of had fun." We said bye to Xavier, and Azzy and Cedrick. When we arrived in Modesto, we went to my mom's house. We got dressed then we went to Qin's house. I went to pick Lisa up and I took my mom a few places that she wanted to go. Then, I took my brothers a few places that they wanted to go. Christy called me and she asked me could I pick her up, so I did. I asked Justin Jr., to come with me and Rebbeca came with us too. After I picked up Christy, we went back to Qin's house. I made some drinks for us, we ate and we partied. I let Qin use my rental car. When he got back, Justin Jr., wanted to use the car to go to the store so I let him. We took pictures, we ate and we talked mess to each other. When we left Modesto, it was 8 o'clock. Earlier that day, Rebbeca had called into work. She said she was sick. Rebbeca's ex-boyfriend CJ called Jessica, and he asked her was Rebbeca with us. Jessica said, "Yeah, she's right here." Jessica gave Rebbeca the phone, Rebbeca was mad. Rebbeca said, "Now I have to go to the emergency room and act like I'm sick." When we made it to the Bay Area, we dropped Sabreea off at home. Then I drove Rebbeca to the hospital. Then I went home. Then Jessica went home. Jessica picked me up the next morning to take me to work. We had a good time in Modesto. Jessica always talked about how much she liked Xavier. When we got off work that night, we went to meet uncle Henry at the airport, so we could return the rental car. Justin Jr., had called me. He asked me, could I buy him a ticket from the Greyhound station. So he could go back to Modesto, because his girlfriend and him got into. Jessica picked me up and she took me to the Greyhound station, so I could buy his ticket. I called Justin Jr., when I got back home. Justin Jr., was cussing out his girlfriend, while I was on the phone with him. I told him to stop calling her out of her name, but he didn't listen. The next day this guy called my phone.

He said, "Is this Justin Jr., sister?" I replied, "Yes this is. Who is this?" "I'm Justin's Jr., friend. Somebody came to my house today and they were looking for him, and they said they are going to kill him, when they see him. So maybe you should come and get him."

"Thank you for the information." When I got off the phone, I called Qin and I told him what Justin's Jr., friend said. Qin told me he was going to Reno to pick up, Justin Jr. I told Qin, I bought Justin Jr., a ticket to go to Modesto. I paid, $77 dollars for that ticket, I thought Justin Jr., left Reno. David I became friends. I did forgive him for cheating on me and for getting a NCLBAB pregnant. We would talk about life, and relationships, and if he was having a bad day, he would call me. All of a sudden, I stopped getting calls from David. One day Jessica and I went to Stockton. Xavier and Cedrick said, "SC, have you talked to David lately?" I replied, "No." They said, "Well, his girlfriend had her baby." "Oh, that's why I haven't heard from him." Cedrick said, "Well, they had a DNA test and he found out that the baby isn't his!" Xavier said, "He's devastated." I said, "I told him that he is going to rep what he soul. I knew that baby was not going to be his. Plus, she is a NCH. You guys told me that!" Cedrick said, "She is, and y'all should have just stayed together and she was a NCH when he met her. You can't turn no, NCH into a house wife anyways." Jessica said, "Damn, he went through all of that and the baby ain't even his." Later on, that day, Jessica and I went back to the Bay Area. I was still working, and I did want to go back to school, but I did not want to fail my cahsee test again. I knew I had to face it one day. Jessica and I wanted to live together, so we looked at a few apartments. We would fill out applications, but we did not make three times the rent. That's why we did not move together. Jessica and I would hang out everyday and we would spend nights at Sabreea's house. We would go shopping, and out to eat. Nathan and I would talk on the phone. I missed seeing him. He went to college in Santa Barbra. When, Nathan and I would talk on the phone. His girlfriend would get mad and she would fuss at him. She thought Nathan was cheating on her with me. I told Nathan, I wanted to talk to his girlfriend, so I could tell her that we are nothing but best friends and that's it. Nathan said, "That's ok best friend. I told her, that we are only best friends and we are close. I told her, if I wanted to be with my best friend I could have been a long time ago." I replied, "Maybe she'll get over it. You know what I'm going to tell her? He might be gettin it in with Miss. S, but it's not this one. Tell her, she shouldn't be so insecure, that's not cute." "Right, I'm coming home for break and I want to see sis, so call her for me." "Ok I will."

Chapter Fourteen

Learning My Strength

J couldn't believe it was a new year. It was finally 2009. Christy, and Jessica and I went to Modesto, we went to my mom's house. I always would stop at my mom's house first, and then I would stop at Qin's house. When I got to my mom's house, she was happy to see us. She said, "I like your rental car Cupcake, y'all look cute." I said, "Thanks mom." I had rented a Chrysler 300, the big body. I was just paying for the rental cars myself. Jessica told me she did not have enough money to go half with me on the rental cars. I told her not to worry about it, because that was my sister and I knew if she had the money, she would have given it to me. My mom said, "Where are y'all going tonight for New Years." I replied, "I don't know, I'm going to see what Qin is doing." "Oh, do you have some wine?" "No, but I will take you to the store to go buy you some." "Ok, thank you Cupcake." I would let my mom use my rental cars, but I wouldn't let her leave by herself, because one day I did, and she used all of my gas out of my rental car. She was gone for two hours. After, I took my mom to the store Jessica, and Christy and I went to Qin's house, but he was not there. I knew I would find him at this Am Pm gas station.

So, we went to the Am Pm gas station and Qin was there with his friends. I walked up to his car. He was surprised to see me. He said, "Zaneeya, when did you come out here?" "Like an hour ago. Where are you going? Let's go out tonight." "I'm going to the casino right now, come with me. Is that your rental car? Let me drive it." "No, you are not driving my car." "You let Big Bird drive, I'm going to tell her you said I can drive." "Go ahead and tell her, she is not going to fall for that, because she know I would tell her myself." Qin said, "What's up Big Bird? Get out the car and get in the back. Zaneeya said I can drive." Jessica said, "No she didn't, because she would have told me herself, so stop lying." "I can't fool you huh?" I said, "See, I told you we know each other to well." Qin replied, "Yeah ok, y'all just follow me, but I need to drive your car tomorrow sis." I said, "I'll think about it." On our way to the casino, the police pulled us over. The officer told us he was pulling us over, because we did not have any back license plates. The police officer was niece he did not give us a ticket. After the police officer left, Qin came up to the car to see if we were ok. Then we went to the casino. It was a two-hour drive, we went to Black Oak Casino, and we had fun. Peanut was there, and Ranesha, and her brother, and cousin and their girlfriends. When Qin was gambling, I asked him for some money, because I knew he would give it to me, so I would leave him alone. I played black jack. We had a few drinks. We stayed at the casino for five hours. When we went back to Modesto, we went to Qin's house we ate and went to sleep. When Jessica and I woke up, we went to my mom's house and we went out to eat. We stayed in the house for a little while. We were talking to my mom and my brothers. Later on that night, we went back to Qin's house. Ranesha and her two friends and Christy, and Jessica and I went to the club. Ranesha friend could not find her id. So we left and we went to the bar. We danced and we had a few drinks. Then we went to Stockton, to Xavier's house. I told Ranesha I would see her later. When we arrived to Xavier's house, we all went to the club. Cedrick said, "Zaneeya, if anyone bothers you, let me know and I'll handle it." "Ok brother." I ordered me a drink. I had a Hennessy and coke. As Christy and I were dancing, Xavier and Jessica were, hugged up. Xavier and Jessica was a cute couple. Jessica was happy and you could see it all over her face.

After we left the club, we went back to Xavier's house, and we went to sleep. The next morning, we went to my mom's house. We stayed in Modesto for a couple of hours, and then we went home. A few weeks went by since I left Modesto, one day I came home from work, and my granny said, "Zaneeya, Qin called and he said, that your mom is in jail in New Mexico." I replied, "Qin is lying, no she's not. How did she get out there?" "Yes she is. She was supposed to be going to LA, with a guy friend of her's. He was supposed to be taking her shopping, they were on Amtrack and the police stopped them. Your mom did not have any drugs on her, but her friend did, but the police arrested her too and they took her to jail." I thought about my little brothers. They were use to seeing my mom at home, especially my baby brother. I had made reservation, for my 20th birthday to go to Hawaii for a week. Jessica and Sabreea were coming with me. I was buying my plane ticket and Sabreea's ticket. I told my granny, I wasn't going to Hawaii anymore. I told her, that I am going to use the money that I had saved for my birthday, to rent a car.

So I could go to Modesto, so I can meet with my mom's landlord. To see what she owes on her rent and pg&e, so I could pay it. I told my granny, that I'm going to take my brothers grocery shopping and I'm going to buy them, all their personal items that they need. My granny said, "That's really nice of you and I'm happy you're going to help your mom. Some kids wouldn't even help their parents, if a situation like this took place. I'm happy that you're helping and I'm going to help too." I replied, "I have to help granny, those are my little brothers, and as long as I'm working. I'm going to make sure that my mom has her house, when she gets back and her bills are going to be paid." The next day I went to work. I thought I was going to be ok, but as I was serving the residents their food. I started thinking about my mom and I began to cry. I walked out the diningroom and I went into the breakroom. Vida came in the breakroom. She said, "Zaneeya, what's wrong? This is the first time that I've seen you cry, as long as I have been knowing you." I told Vida what happen. She said, "It's going to be ok Zaneeya, things are going to get better. You need to go home and take care of your business." Vida went to get our boss Steven. We had new owners. Ryan and his dad had sold the Claremont House. It was now, called The Monarch Place and Jannette was no longer working there. They fired her, when she was in the hospital having surgery.

When Steven came in the breakroom, I did not go into many details, but I did tell him that my mom was in jail. I was not in the best mood at work. So I did not want to be bothered by no one. Steven understood, and he told me to take a few days off work. When I got home from work, I called Jessica and I told her what happened. She couldn't believe it. Later on that night, uncle Henry had rented a car for me, so I could go to Modesto. When Jessica and I arrived to Modesto, we went to my mom's house. My brothers and I cleaned up my mom's house. We did a spring-cleaning. That consisted of cleaning the walls, bathroom, scrubbing any and everything that needed to be scrubbed. My brothers and I stayed up cracking jokes. The next day, was my nephew's birthday party. I dropped Ramone off at basketball practice. When I picked him up from practice, we went back to my mom's house, because I had to meet up with her Landlord. My mom's landlord came over. I told him what happened. I also told him that I was going to pay all of my mom's bills and I was going to pay him, the same amount of money that she was paying him. He told me that was fine. He was a nice man. His name is Mr. Prescott. After, I was finished talking to Mr. Prescott., we went to Lil Qin's party. I was happy to see my nephew. Jessica and I got on a couple of rides at Lil Qin's party. When the party was over, we left. I took the boys shopping. I bought them a lot of things. I also bought my mom, her personal items, so when she comes home, she could shower and be comfortable. After we went shopping, I droped my brothers off at my mom's house, and I told them I was going to Stockton. Christy went with us to Stockton. Jessica, Xavier, and Christy and Cedrick and I went out to the club. I was dancing so hard that my glasses fell off my face. I didn't know where they were. I asked Christy to look for my glasses for me, and she did. After we left the club, we went back to Xavier's house. We went to sleep. Then the next morning we woke up and left. When we arrived to Modesto, we went to my mom's house. We showered, and then we went out to eat.

After we were finished eating, we went to Qin's house. He was barbecuing. He was giving Lil Qin another birthday party. When Jessica and I went inside of Qin's house, it was two guys sitting on his couch. I said, "Jessica I wonder where my brother is." One of the guys said, "Who is your brother?" I said, "Qin." "Oh, he is in the backyard." When, I went to the backyard. Qin said, "Zaneeya where are your glasses?" I told him they had broken and I told him how it happened. He said, "I don't care about all that." I said, "Why do you always have to show out in front of your friends?" When I went back in the house, Jessica and I sat down on the couch and we watched the football game. One of Qin's friends was sitting on the side of me. He stepped on my boots. He said, "My bad for stepping on your boots." I wiped my boots off. I replied, "You mean I am sorry, for stepping on your boots." I got up and went to Qin's room. He was laying in his bed on his stomach, so I laid on his back. He said, "Get off me Zaneeya, and move." "You bother me when you want too. I can lay on your back, you don't never want anyone bothering you. Qin that's crazy, how mommy is way in New Mexico in jail." "Oh well, she did that to herself. She'll be alright." "Mommy shouldn't have left, but she did not know he had $85, 0000 dollars worth of dope on him." "She probably did know, oh well." Qin started laughing. I said, "That's not funny." He replied, "It is funny. I don't care she did it to herself." Qin's friend walked in the room. He looked at me. He said, "Can I take you out to eat? What is your name?" I replied, "I don't think that's a good idea and I don't tell people what my name, is and your probably just a baby." "I'm not a baby. I can take you anywhere you want to go. Do you like Red Lobsters?" Qin said, "Zaneeya he is the same age as you. He ain't no baby." I said, "What is your name and are you in a relationship?" He replied, "My name is Allen and no I'm not in a relationship. Are you?" "I'm not seeing anyone right now." Allen said, "Qin is it ok if I take your sister out on a date? Is it ok if we talk?" "You guys are both grown, you can do whatever you want *too. I'm not trippin."* Qin left out the room. Allen asked me for my number. I gave him Jessica's number and I told him, he could call me on her phone. He said, "I don't want her number. I want your number. You are so beautiful. I did not know that Qin had a sister." I said, "You can call me on her phone for now and maybe, I will give you my number. I'm going in the livingroom." "When are you leaving?" "I'm leaving after they sing happy birthday to my nephew. Why?" "I just wanted to know, because I want to take you out to eat tomorrow, but I'm going to call you tonight."

"Oh, ok." I went inside the livingroom and I sat on the side of Jessica. When, Allen came in the livingroom, he sat on the side of me and he was asking me questions. Jessica said, "Zaneeya, do you know him?" I replied, "I just met him today." "Girl, he is flirting with you, you should give him your number." "I gave him your number and I told him to call me on your phone. I'll probably give him my number, depending on how the conversation goes." "I feel you on that one." Patrick walked by. He said, "Allen, your sitting to close to my sister and don't try to talk to her." Allen said, "Patrick I'm not worried about you." Then Allen and I kept on talking, but Lil Dawane came and sat right between us. He said, "Allen don't talk to my sister straight up, because you're going to have to deal with me." Allen replied, "Lil Dawane, I'm not worried about you either. You need to go sit down some where and read a book." I said, "Allen, you cannot be mean to my lil brother. That's, my baby. You have to get along with him." He replied, "I get along with Lil Dawane. That's my little potna."Lil Dawane said, "We are not friends." "Oh, now were not friends, because your sister is going to be my woman." "My sister is not going to be your woman. You're not even her type of guy."

"We will see and that's ok, she's my type of woman." I went to the kitchen. I said, "Qin make me a plate before I leave and make Jessica one too." Allen came in the kitchen. Qin said, "Allen, make my sister a plate." Allen said, "Zaneeya what do you want on your plate?" I told Allen what I wanted on my plate. After we ate, I said bye to everybody then we left. I went to drop the boys off at home. Patrick and Lil Dawane started arguing. Patrick hit Lil Dawane in his chest. I said, "Patrick you need to keep your hands to yourself, you should be nice to your little brother. Don't beat him up." Patrick replied, "Sis, he has a smart mouth. Everytime he says something smart, I am going to hit him. Sis, you don't live with him, so you don't know the things he say. When mommy is home I can't really hit him, but mommy is gone now. So, I'm going to beat the mess out of him everytime he says something smart." "That's not right Patrick. He is not your child, or your punching bag, and you should not want to put your hands on your brother." Lil Dawane yelled, "That's why I don't like Patrick. He is nothing, but a bully. All he wants to do is beat me up and I'm his little brother, who is much younger then him." I said, "It's ok Lil Dawane. I'mma take you back to Qin's house. Maybe, you can live with him until mommy comes home." I told Patrick and Ramone bye, and I gave them a hug. Then I took Lil Dawane to Qin's house. I told Qin what happen between Patrick and Lil Dawane. Qin said, "Lil Dawane can live with me sis."

I replied, "Ok brother." I gave Lil Dawane a hug and I gave him some more money, then Jessica and I left. On our way back home, Jessica was asking me did I enjoy my conversation that I had with Allen. I told her it was ok. When we got back to the Bay Area, we sat in the front of my house and we talked like always. Allen called me on Jessica's phone. I said, "Hello." He said, "Hi, can I speak to Qin's sister? This is Allen." "This is she." "I was hoping you didn't give me a fake number. Did you make it home yet?" "Yes I did. I'm having a conversation right now with my best friend." "Oh ok. Can I call you on your phone in like an hour? Hopefully, you will be in the house. Then you can talk to me." "You can do that." I gave Allen my number. After Jessica and I were finish talking, I went in the house. I put on my pajamas and I talked to my granny before Allen called.

When Allen called, we talked. He asked me did I have any kids. I told him that I have five kids. He said, "No you don't, because they would have been with you, when you went to Modesto." I started giggling. I replied, "Your right, I don't have any kids. Do you?" "Yes, I have kids." "Did you say kids with an s at the end?" "I have kids. I didn't want to have kids, I wanted my ex's to get an abortion. They said they were, but they didn't." "I'm going to tell you something right now. That is not going to make me like you. Never talk about your kids or your baby mothers to anyone. That's not coo! How many kids do you have?" "I have three kids and I'm not trying to not have you like me. I was just telling you the truth." "Damn, three kids at 19 years old. I'm shocked and I hope you take care of your kids. It doesn't matter if you didn't want them, they are here now. So, the best thing that you can do, is to man up and take care of them. You need to love them and you should be there for them no matter what." "I take care of them. I see them everyday and I do love them, but I am shocked everyday. I did not think I would be 19 years old, with three kids! Do you like kids?" "Yes I like kids. I also like it when their parents, take care of them. I love how my brother loves his son. Qin is a great father and he really would do anything for his son." "That's true, Qin is a good dad. So when are you coming back to Modesto?" "I don't know soon. Why?" "I *just want to make sure when you come back in town, you'll let me see you. So I can take you out. You are really beautiful and I mean that." "Thank you. I'll let you know when I'm going back to Modesto." Allen and I talked on the phone for over two hours. I told him I have to go to sleep, because I have to get up and go to work tomorrow. He said, "Ok, well I'll call you tomorrow. Have a good night and thanks for giving me a chance to become your man." "Who said that you are going to be my man?" "Hopefully you will give me a chance, everything will be good."*

"We will see good night. I'll talk to you later." "Good night Zaneeya." The next morning Jessica picked me up. We went to Burger King to get some breakfast. Then we sat and ate in the car. While Jessica and I were talking, Allen called me. He said, "Good morning, Zaneeya. I hope it's not too early for you." "Real funny, no it's not. You're a late bird." "I was a little tired. Are you at work yet?" "Yes I am." "Ok well, when is your lunch break? Can I call you on your break?" "You can, that will be fine. I take my lunch at 2 o'clock." "Ok I'll call you on your lunch break, have a good day." "Thank you I will, enjoy your day as well." Jessica said, "Look at you all smiling and blushing." "I am not blushing, stop it." "Yes you are, but that's ok. You need to get in another relationship. It's been a while and it's time for a change." "It has been a while, but I'm fine with that. We will see how this goes." I said bye to Jessica, and I told her I would see her at work later. When I went to work, Vida asked me was I ok. I told her yeah, and I'm taking everything one day at a time.

Vida was like an auntie to me, and when Jannette left, we became closer. I would eat lunch with Vida and I would go to her for advice. When Vida would get on my nerves, I still respected her, and I still would listen to her and I still looked at her like an auntie. When it was time for me to take my lunch break, Allen called me. I was sitting at the table with Vida, and my co-worker Vicky. I answered my phone and I walked outside. Allen said, "You probably thought I wasn't going to call you huh?" I giggled. I said, "I knew you were going to call me." "You're right about that. How are you doing? Hopefully I made your day better by calling you." "My day is going well, thanks for asking." Allen and I talked until my lunch break was over. When Jessica and I were finished working, we sat down and Allen had called me again. He said, "I'm just thinking about you. I know it's time for you to get off work. So I'll call you in a couple of hours, that way I can give you a chance to settle in." "So I'm on your mind huh? That's always good to know. I'll be waiting for your call." I hung up the phone. When Jessica and I got off work, we took the rental car back to the airport. Then she dropped me off at home. When I got in the house, I showered, ate and I laid down.

When Allen called me, we talked for a few hours before getting off the phone. Allen and I would talk on the phone, before I went to work. He would call me on my lunch break and we would talk when I got home from work. I liked him, the more I thought I was getting to know him. Allen told me he loved me two weeks after I met him. I didn't tell him I loved him, because I didn't! After a while, I grew feelings for him, but I didn't know if I loved him or if it was lust, but soon I was going to find out. I made plans with Allen for my birthday. He said he had a surprise for me when I go to Modesto. Allen and I made it official to be in a relationship with each other a couple of days before my birthday. I asked uncle Henry could he rent me a car for two weeks, I gave him my money for my rental car as usual. On my birthday, Jessica and I went to the bar with are supervisor Thomas. He was like an uncle to me. We had a good time. The next day Jessica and I went to Modesto. Allen was calling me while I was in the car. He said, "Zaneeya are you really on your way? Please don't stand me up." "I'm coming I'm only 30-minutes away. I should stand you up." "Don't do that, I'll see you when you get here I love you." "I love you too." When we made it to Modesto, we went to Qin's house to pick up Allen. Jessica said, "Zaneeya are you nervous sis?" "A little bit." I had on a dress and my high heels shoes. I liked wearing dresses and I would always wear heels. As we were walking in Qin's house, Qin was leaving. He gave me a hug and he told me happy birthday. He said, "I'll be back sis. Can I use your rental car real quick please? I'm only going to bust this move and I'll be back. I promise I'm not lying." I said, "Ok Qin, but come right back, because I have to leave." "Ok sis, I'll be back." Jessica and I went inside of Qin's house. Allen was sitting at the kitchen table. I walked over to him. He stood up and gave me a hug and kiss. I introduced Jessica to him, even though she saw him when I did. We waited for Qin to come back. When Qin came back to the house, it was an hour later. I said, "Qin you're not using my car again." He replied, "Sis my bad. I didn't mean to take that long." "Whatever, come on Jessica let's go. Qin I'll see you later." "Come over tomorrow sis. Allen I'm going to take you home in a couple of minutes." Allen said, "That's ok I have a ride." "Is my sister taking you home? Zaneeya are you taking Allen home?" "Yes I am." I was staying in Modesto for two weeks and Jessica was staying with me. The plan was, Jessica was going to stay at my mom's house, but she was only going to be there at night. In the morning, after Allen and I got dress. We would pick her up. Jessica drove to my mom house, I told her I would see her in the morning.

Christy was living at my mom's house, and so was Dorthy and my brothers. So, Jessica wasn't alone at night and she knew them, and she was comfortable with them and she was only there at night.

Allen and I went to check in our hotel room. The next morning, Qin called my phone. I didn't answer, so he called Allen's phone, and he did not answer. So he called Allen's phone again, then he answered. It was too early in the morning, to be dealing with Qin and his drama. Allen said, "What's up Qin." Qin said, "Allen are you with my sister? I been callin yo phone, and her phone, since 6 o'clock this morning and neither one of y'all answered. I went to your house early this morning, and your momma answered the door. She still had sleep in her eyes and everything. I said, hi mom is Allen here? She said no he didn't come home last night, so I said he must be with my sister. Where is she at?" Allen said, "She's right here. Why are you hunting us down like a mad man?" "Let me talk to her." When, I got on the phone. I said, "Hi brother." Qin said, "Don't hi brother me, where are you? I've been looking all over for you, I went to mommy's house, and Jessica was sleep. I woke her up, I said Big Bird where is Zaneeya? She said I don't know Qin. I told her you do know, you're her best friend. You be with her all the time, don't tell me you don't know. She kept saying I don't know Qin. So I kept kicking her, and taking her blankets off of her. I was messing with her, but she still didn't tell me. So I went to Allen's house and y'all wasn't over there. I'm calling you, and you're not answering. He's not answering. Where are y'all?" "Leave Jessica alone, I'm grown. You're out there looking for me like I'm your child. You should have been sleep at 6 o'clock this morning. We got a hotel room, that's where I'm going to be staying at while I'm out here." "Allen stayed with you in your hotel room?" "Yeah, we got a hotel room together." "Let me talk to him." I gave the phone to Allen. Qin said, "Allen did you stay the night with my sister?" He replied, "Yes I did that's my woman." "My sister is not your woman. Stop playin with me come to my house we have to get this money." "She is my woman. I'm going to get dress then we will be on are way." After we got dressed, we went to Qin's house. I felt like I did something bad and I was going to the principal office and I was going to be, expelled from school. When we went inside of Qin's house I said hi to him, but he just looked at me, and shook his head. He said, "Zaneeya, don't have me go around looking for you again. I can't believe you're with Allen sis! Allen did you tell my sister how you be lying, and how many females you have." Allen said, "Qin, stop lying don't start saying that. I don't need yo sister mad at me. You said it was ok if I took her out and if we talked. So what's the problem?"

Qin said, "It's ok. I'm not trippin go ahead you guys are grown." I said, "Ok then, why are you looking at me as if I disappointed you. You don't want me talking to your friend?" "I'm fine, do whatever you want too. Allen we still have to get this money, we are too far in." Allen replied, "We are don't worry." After, Allen and I left Qin's house we went to pick Jessica up. Jessica said, "Zaneeya did you have fun last night?" I replied, "Yes I did. How did you sleep?" "I slept well, until Qin came and woke me up, by kicking me and asking me where you were. Your brother is so crazy." Jessica, and Allen and I went out to breakfast. Then we went to Qin's house. The whole time that Jessica and I were in Modesto, Allen and I would pick her up in the morning. Then go out to eat, then go to Qin's house. We would hang out, ride around and we would drink and smoke. Jessica didn't have to pay for nothing. I paid for her. One day Jessica, and Allen and I went to Chili's restaurant to eat lunch. Jessica did not have any money, so I told Allen to pay for her. Allen was cracking jokes about Jessica. He said, "Jessica, I don't know how you're going to pay for your meal, you better go do some dishes or you're going to jail. I'm only paying for my woman." Jessica said, "Please, I'm not worried about you. That's my sis, and she is not going to let that happen." I replied, "That's right. Allen is going to pay for your food, he is just messing with you." When we left Chili's. Jessica said, "Allen, are you ready for your woman to leave you for a couple of nights?" Allen replied, "Zaneeya is not going anywhere! What are you talking about?" "Yes she is. She is going with me to Merced to spend the night at my grandma house." "No she's not. You are going to spend the night at your grandma's house. We are going to drop you off and you can call us when you want us to pick you up." "You're going to be lonely at night when she's not there with you." "I'm not worried Jessica, because she's not going." We went to Qin's house. Allen went inside the house. Jessica and I stayed in the car, we were talking. I said, "Jessica, I'm not going to Merced with you. I don't have that many days left out here and you should go spend some time with your family. Your grandma would love that." Jessica replied, "Zaneeya, I already told my grandma you were coming, so you have to come." "Well, you shouldn't have done that. You don't know if I wanted to go or not. I will drop you off and you can call me when you want me to pick you up." "Ok whatever." I knew Jessica was mad at me, but I did not care. One night with her family without me, was not going to hurt her, and I knew she would get over it. I spent a night with Jessica at my mom's house. The next day, we took Jessica to her grandma's house. Allen and I went back to our hotel room. We *watched a movie and we cuddled. The next day we picked Jessica up. Then we went to her brother house.*

When we got back to Modesto, we went to Qin's house. When it got late, we dropped Jessica off at my mom's house. The next day, we picked Jessica up and we went out to eat. Then we went back to our hotel room. Jessica hung out with us in our hotel room. Then we went to the mall. Allen took me shopping. Then we dropped, Jessica off at my mom's house. I called Sabreea and I told her I was going to pick her up Friday, but she has to stay in Modesto, until we go back to the Bay Area. I told Jessica that Allen is going to surprise me for my birthday. I told Jessica that I was going to be gone all day and I was not coming back until night, and I told her, she could go to Qin's house. Allen told Qin where he was taking me. Qin said, "Zaneeya, tell Big Bird she can come to my house and hang out with us, she's family. She always be over here when y'all come out here." I told Jessica what Qin said. Jessica said, "I don't want to go to your brother house and sit there." I replied, "Well, you knew that Allen was going to take me somewhere and surprise me before we came to Modesto. So, if you don't want to go to Qin's house you can stay in my hotel room until I get back." "No I don't want to stay there either, don't go sis. He don't have to surprise you, let's just do something all together. I know I knew, I just don't want to be by myself today." "Jessica we be together everyday. Except for when you spent the night at your grandma's house and yes, Allen does have to surprise me. I am not changing my plans. It's not going to happen. So we will pick you up and take you to get something to eat before we leave. When I get back, I will pick you up and take you to get something to eat and we will drink and kick it for a little while." "Ok and you don't be with me everyday, because you don't be with me at night." "Are you serious? I be with you everyday, and at night I be with Allen. I suppose to. If you were in a relationship and we was together everyday. Except for at night, because you have to be with your man, I would not be mad at you. You are supposed to do that. That's normal! I do not have a two-room suite. I have a one-room suite. So it's not like you can spend the night with us." "Ok, Zaneeya." The next morning when Allen and I woke up, we went to Qin's house. We did not stay long. Then we went to my mom's house to pick up Jessica, so we could take her to get something to eat.

When, Allen and I were on the freeway. I said, "Where are you taking me, tell me?" He replied, "It's a surprise. I'm not telling you." He did not tell me either, we was in the car for over two hours. When we made it to our destination, there were a lot of hills and it was a beautiful place. Allen said, "We are in Monterey." I said, "Aww, thank you. You're so sweet." Allen took me out to eat. We went to a restaurant that was on the beach. I could see the ocean from inside the restaurant. After we were finish eating, I called Jessica to check on her. Then we went to the Candy Factory. Then we walked to the beach and we stayed there for a while. When we made it back to Modesto, we picked up Jessica. We took her to get something to eat then we went to Qin's house. Later on that night, we dropped her off. I called Sabreea and I told her what time we were going to pick her up. Sabreea said, "Sis, Jessica called me and she said that you haven't been with her, most of the time that you guys have been out there. She barely sees you. She only saw you a couple of times, and you leave her to go be with Allen. She said she is happy that I'm coming. So she can have somebody to talk too, because she doesn't have anybody to talk too and you're never around." I replied, "First off, I see Jessica every damn day! I hate to be lied on, and I have spent a night with her, but I am supposed to be spending my nights with my man. Allen and I pick Jessica up everyday and we both have been paying for her meals. I do not have to make Allen pay for her food. I do it, because she is my best friend and as long as I'm eating, she is too. The only time that I am not with Jessica is when I go to bed, and that's at night! We pick her up every morning. When I'm eating, she's eating. When I'm smoking, she's smoking too. If I'm drinking, she's drinking! You can ask Allen and he will tell you." "I believe you sis. I think Jessica is so use to it being just you, and her, she don't know how to handle it." "Jessica is pissing me off. I'm going to see you in a little while." When I got off the phone with Sabreea, I told Allen what she told me. Allen said, "I can't believe Big Bird lied like that. That's messed up. You be with her everyday and she's going to call your sister and lie to her, that's not coo at all." I said, "I know right." We went to pick up Jessica then we dropped Allen off at Qin's house. We went to the Bay Area to pick up Sabreea and to get our feet and nails done. I took Booda with me. After we picked up Sabreea, we went to the nail shop. Then we went to my house, so my granny could see Booda.

When we went back to Modesto, we picked Allen up and we dropped Booda off at home. I asked Sabreea and Jessica did they want to spend the night at Qin's house. They told me no. They wanted to go to my mom's house. So we dropped them off and I told them I would see them tomorrow. The next day, I called Sabreea and asked her did they want to go to Qin's house and did they want me to take them to get something to eat. Sabreea said, "No, sis that's ok. We are going to walk and get something to eat everything is close by mom's house. Enjoy the rest of your time with your man. I'll call you later when we are ready to leave." I replied, "Ok." Allen and I just went out to eat. Then *we went back to our hotel room and laid down. Later on that day, around 4 o'clock, Jessica called me. She said, "Hey sis. Can you come get us? I want to go to the mall so I can buy me a new belt." I replied, "Yeah, I'll be there in an hour, Allen is taking a nap. I would drive, but I cannot see at night."*

"Ok that's fine. I'll see you when you get here." I woke Allen up at 5 o'clock. Sabreea called me. She said, "Are you still going to take us to the mall?" I replied, "Yeah, I'm on my way right now. I'll call you when I'm outside." When we got to my mom's house, I called Sabreea and I told her to come outside. When we got to the mall, I didn't want to go inside, I wanted to stay in the car. Sabreea said, "Zaneeya are you coming?" I replied, "No, I'm going to stay in the car." They did not stay in the mall long. When they got back in the car, we went to Qin's house. Ranesha, and Sabreea and Jessica said they wanted to go out. Sabreea told me that she didn't have a babysitter for Tinky. So I told her I would watch her and I will bring her back in the morning. Sabreea said, "Zaneeya, you're not going out with us?" I replied, "No, I'm not! I want to spend my last two nights that I have left, cuddled up in my hotel room with Allen." "Ok, I'm getting Tinky clothes right now." Allen and I left. We went to get Tinky something to eat then we went to our hotel room. I gave Tinky her food, and then I put her to bed. Sabreea called me twice. We talked and after we got off the phone, she called me right back, but I did not answer. The next morning, Sabreea called me. I told her that I was on my way to drop Tinky off. I bought Tinky something to eat then I took her to Qin's house. Sabreea and Jessica both had an attitude, but I did not care. Allen and I left. We went to pick up his dad and we took him to his house.

Later on that day, I met Allen's oldest son. His name is Lil Allen. He was so cute. I fell in love with him. Allen and I went to Qin's house. Lil Allen and I stayed in the car. Jessica and Sabreea came outside to see Lil Allen. They said, "He is so handsome, he looks just like his dad." When we left Qin's house, we went back to our hotel room. Later on that day, Lil Allen's mom came to pick him up. Sabreea and Jessica wanted to go bowling and they wanted me to go too. I told them I mite go. Jessica called me. She said, "Are you going bowling with us?" I replied, "No, I don't feel like going bowling." The next day I went to Qin's house. Sabreea and Jessica had an attitude. Sabreea wasn't speaking and I wasn't either. Later on that day, we went home. When we made it to the Bay Area, we dropped Sabreea off at home. She did not speak to me while we were in the car, but she was talking to Jessica and I didn't speak to her either. Jessica said, "I'm so happy, to be back home. I'm not going out there for a while, no more rental cars for me." I said, "That's fine. I'm not taking nobody with me when I go back out there. I hate to be lied on. Being in Modesto is no different from us being out here. I was with you, until it was time for me to go to bed. I did not leave you except for one day. When Allen surprised me and took me out." "I'm not getting any more rental cars that's all." "You didn't pay for this rental car. I did, and if you want to tell your dad to stop getting rental cars for me, that's really messed up, but go ahead. One monkey don't stop no show! I will still get rental cars with or with out you." Jessica and I went to the airport to take my rental car back then I went home. My granny asked me did I have fun. I told my granny what happen between Jessica and me. My granny said, "Just start going to Modesto by yourself. That was nice of you to even pay for Jessica when she didn't have any money. Then she's going to turn around and lie on you. That's not nice at all." Allen called me later on that night. I would go to Modesto on the weekends and Allen would come to my house. I would give my uncle Ike my money to get my rental cars for me. My granny and I went to Modesto for Mother's Day. Allen and I took my granny out to eat for Mother's Day and Lil Allen went with us. My granny thought Lil Allen was so cute and my granny liked Allen a lot.

One day, I was going to Modesto and Jessica called and asked me. Could I drop her off at her grandma's house in Merced, I told her yeah. Allen and I took Jessica to Merced. I didn't charge her any gas money, but everytime I was in her car I gave her gas money. If we were going shopping, or out to eat or where ever we were going, I always gave her gas money. Allen and I had fun over the weekend. We hung out with Qin. He was barbecuing at this park, my brothers, and cousins and some of Ranesha's family members was there. The next day, we picked up Jessica from Merced. Then we went to the Bay Area. I missed my mom. She would write me letters from prison. She told me thank you for paying her bills for her. Once a month, I would go grocery shopping for my brothers and Allen would go with me. It was Lil Dawane's birthday. I told him I would take him wherever he wanted to go and he could bring one of his friends with him. He told me he wanted to go to Boomers and he wanted to go to Apple Bee's. Allen and I took Lil Dawane and his friend Dan to Boomers. Lil Dawane wanted to get on the go-carts, but he was too short to get on the go-carts. So he got mad and he wanted to leave. Dan asked me could he get on the go-carts I told him yeah. Lil Dawane said, "Zaneeya, I'm ready to go." I said, "We are not leaving just, because you cannot get on the go-carts. You knew you were too short, go play some games." "I don't want to play nothing else." "Well, you have to wait until Dan is done." After, Dan got off the go-carts we left. Then we went to Apple Bee's. After we ate, we dropped *them off at Qin's house. Then we went back to our hotel room. I always ate a lot, but my weight was going up and down and it always would. Allen noticed that I was eating way more then I usually would. I didn't think nothing of it. Allen said, "Zaneeya, you're pregnant. Your breast is getting bigger. Let me see your stomach." He lifted up my shirt as he smiled. Allen said, "You have that pregnant line on your stomach, your pregnant." I replied, "I am not pregnant. Stop saying that." "Yes you are. I hope we have a boy. I want another boy." "I don't think I'm pregnant. If so I want a girl." When I went home, I made me a doctor's appointment, so I could find out if I was pregnant. My doctor name is Patchase. She has been my doctor every since I was born. When Patchase told me that my test came back positive, I did not believe her. She said, "Congratulation Zaneeya. I have been your doctor every since you were a baby. Now I am going to be your baby's doctor. I am so happy for you."*

I said, "Thank you Patchase. I just can't believe that I'm pregnant." I was so excited and happy. Patchase told me she had to go to a meeting, but she wanted me to get something to eat. Then she wanted me to come back in an hour. So I could talk to Tanesha who was a counselor. Tanesha was like a big sister to me. She would call and check on me and I would go to her office to see how she was doing, and we would talk about everything. Her life and what she was going through and we would talk about my life. She would even call my house phone, if I didn't answer my cell phone. When Tanesha would call my house, phone her and my granny would talk for a little while. One day Tanesha called me. My granny said, "Thank you Tanesha, for being a good friend to my granddaughter." Tanesha replied, "I love Zaneeya, that's my little sister. You're welcome." After Patchase told me I was, pregnant I went to have lunch with Jessica. I went to this sandwich restaurant. I bought me a sandwich, some chips, and some lasagna and I bought Jessica a sandwich too. I told Jessica she had to hurry up and meet me, because I had to go back to my doctor's office. She told me she was on her way. I started eating my food. I called Allen and I told him, that he was right I am pregnant. He just kept stating, "We are going to have a boy." An hour went by and Jessica still was not there. So I called her and I told her that I had to leave. She said, "Zaneeya I'm on my way." "I have to leave." I went back to my doctor's office and I talked to Tanesha. When I left my doctor's office, I went home. My granny was cooking some fish. I asked her could I have some. My granny said, "You don't like fish, but of course you can have some." I ate some fish and some potato salad then I went to bed. Lil Dawane graduation was coming up and Allen was supposed to come get me. I bought Lil Dawane his graduation clothes, but I couldn't take them to him, because Allen didn't come get me. So I had Jessica take me to the mall, so I could return his clothes. Then she took me to the Greyhound station so I could go to Modesto. When I got to Modesto, I called Ramone. Ramone and his girlfriend Leeza picked me up from the Greyhound station. Then we went to Qin's house. Qin was talking mess to me, because I was not at Lil Dawane's graduation. I already felt bad for missing his graduation. Ranesha bought Lil Dawane a shirt for his graduation and I gave her, her money back. Allen called me to see where I was. I told him I was in Modesto. I was mad at him. I didn't know what was going on, but I knew I did not like the way how he was acting towards me. I went to take Lil Dawane to get his ears pierced. Then Leeza took me to my hotel room. Allen came and he brought me some food. He told me he was going to come back, but he didn't. The next morning, Allen called me and he brought me something to eat. Later on that night, he came and he brought me some dinner. He was supposed to come back and spend the night. He told me, he was going out with his friends. A few hours later, he called me and told me that he was on his way, but he never showed up.

The next morning, I called Ranesha and I asked her to pick me up. My mom told me to buy some food for Ranesha, because Lil Dawane lived there. Ranesha and I went grocery shopping. She said, "Zaneeya, are you pregnant?" I replied, "What made you ask me that?' "I think you're pregnant. You don't want to drink and we always drink when you come out here." "Yes, I'm pregnant." Ranesha smiled. She said, "I knew it. Are you excited?" "Yes I am. I cannot wait until I have my baby. I want a girl." "You're going to have a boy, and Qin is going to have a fit, but oh well, you're grown. He can't do anything about it." "I am not worried about Qin." "I know where Allen is. He lives with his baby momma. Qin and I went over there one morning and he answered the door in his underwear. He showed us around her house and everything." "Take me over there, but first I have to go change my clothes." I changed my clothes, because I was wearing some high heels and a dress. Ranesha said, "We are going to have to tell Qin that I'm taking you to get something to eat." As we were leaving, Qin said, "Where are y'all going?" Ranesha said, "I'm taking Zaneeya to get something to eat." Ranesha took me to Allen's baby momma house. She showed me which door was hers. Then she went back to her car and waited for me. I walked up to the door and I knock on it. No one answered the door, so I knocked harder. Somebody was going to answer the door for me. Allen answered the door. He came outside smiling. I said, "So this is where you be at? This is where you live at big timer?" He replied, "I don't live here, this is my baby momma house. How did you get over here?" "Don't worry about all that. You said you were coming back to the room last night and you didn't. I don't have time for your lies. You can play games with yo baby momma." "I came over here this morning. I didn't have a ride to go back to the room, that's why I didn't go." "Stop lying. You didn't have a ride to come to the room, but you had a ride to come over here. I want you to see your kids. That's fine, but I know that's not why you came over here." *Allen's baby mother came outside. She said, "What's going? What's the problem?" I said, "Allen, do you want to tell her or do you want me to tell her?" Allen, replied, "Tell her. I told you I'm not with my baby momma." I said, "Are you and Allen together?" She said, "That's just my baby daddy." "Ok, are y'all intimate with each other?" "That's just my baby daddy." "Since both of you don't want to confess to nothing. I'll be right back, stay right here." I walked to the car, and I told Ranesha to open her trunk. She said, "No, come on Zaneeya. I'mma have to beat his baby momma up, because I'm not going to let you fight her. You're pregnant." I replied, "No you're not, open your trunk."*

Allen ran towards me. He said, "I'm not even cheating on you." I said, "Whatever, you didn't come back to the hotel room for two nights. If you're not sleeping with me, you're sleeping with somebody. I'm done with you. I'm going to drop your stuff off at your momma house. I'm going to let her know that she have another grand baby on the way." Allen nodded his head up and down. He said, "Ok." I got in the car and Ranesha and I left. Qin called Ranesha's phone. He said, "Ranesha, why did you take Zaneeya over there? That was hella messy of you." Ranesha said, "Zaneeya already knew where she lived." "Stop lying Ranesha, hurry up and come home." When, we got to Qin's house. He said, "Zaneeya, you knew he was staying at his baby momma's house." "No I did not! I am not going to be in a relationship with him while he lives with his baby momma. I have been to those apartments before, because he said his uncle stays there." "He does have an uncle that lives there. Ranesha, I don't care that was messy of you. You shouldn't have did that. Allen called me and his baby momma is fussing with him in the back ground." Ranesha said, "Oh well Qin. I did, so what, she is grown." Qin said, "Zaneeya did you brake up with him?" I replied, "Yeah I did. He didn't come back to the hotel room and he has been acting funny. When I come to Modesto, we are always together. If he didn't want to come back to the hotel room that's fine, but I'm not going to stay with him." "Well, eat some crab with me. At least you're not pregnant by him." "Yes I am pregnant." "If you're pregnant, you have to leave right now. You're not going be pregnant in here?" "Shut up Qin. This is not your house. This is Ranesha house, and I'm not going anywhere now!" Ranesha said, "She

*is a grown woman and she doesn't have to leave just, because she's pregnant."
Qin said, "Why did you let him get you pregnant? I'm throwing your stuff
out of my house, right now." Qin took my bags and he acted as if he was going
to throw them outside. I went to door and I grabbed my bags. I went to put
my bags in Lil Qin's room. Then I laid down in my nephews bed. Qin came
in the room and he laid down on the side of me. He said, "Sis, are you really
pregnant?" I replied, "Yes I am." Qin rubbed my stomach. He said, "This is
my baby. Did Allen hurt your feelings?" "A little bit. I'm not gonna lie, but I'll
be ok. Move your hands off of my stomach." "Don't worry sis, that's my baby
and your going to be a great mom anyways. You have been working since you
were 15 years old. You're going to take care of my baby." "This is my baby, not
yours and thank you." "You're going to have a boy too. My first nephew, you
should name him after me." "I am not naming my son after you. His name is
going to be Zarelle." "Ok I like that, that's close enough." "I want a girl, but
I'll be happy if I have a boy. Just as long, as my baby is healthy."*

*"He is going to be healthy sis don't worry. You can take care of your own
baby, but you are going to have a boy and he is going to have a big head just like
Allen watch." I was happy that Qin came and talked to me. I felt like he loved
me and he was going to be there for me, if I needed him too. At that moment,
I needed to hear those words. Ranesha took me shopping for Lil Dawane. I
bought him seven pair of shorts. Eight shirts to go with his shorts, and I bought
him all kinds of stuff. My granny bought my mom some things for her house.
When I went back home, I told my granny that I was pregnant. She said, "I
knew you were, because you were eating fish. I was just waiting for you to
tell me. You're going to have a boy and your baby is going to look just like his
dad." I replied, "Granny, I'm going to have a girl." "No you're not, your going
to have a boy." "I'll be happy if I have a boy or girl, just as long as my baby is
healthy." I went to see Tanesha at the hospital. I needed to talk to her. I told
her that I was stressed out. She told me that she was going to tell Patchase to
take me off work. Until after I deliver my baby. Tanesha did not want me to
have a miscarriage. After Patchase was finished seeing her patients, she came
upstairs and Tanesha told her what we talked about. Patchase said, "I'm
going to take you off work and put you on disability, until after you have your
baby." I told her thank you. I was really stressed out and I did not want to
have a miscarriage either. Tanesha and I would talk everyday. She would call
me and I would call her. It was time for me to go to the main hospital, where
I was going to have my baby at. So I could find out if I was having a boy or a
girl. When I went to the hospital, they gave me an ultrasound, and the nurse*

showed me my baby. She said, "You are having a boy." I did not believe her. I said, "Can you show me his private part? I just can't believe that I'm having a boy." She printed a picture of his private, and she gave me a lot of pictures. The nurse said, "Zaneeya, I'm going to need you to come upstairs to the third floor, to labor and delivery." "Why, what's wrong with my baby?" "Nothing is wrong with your baby, he is fine. We just need you to go to the third floor and the doctor will explain everything to you." When I went upstairs, they already had a room for me, and they gave me a hospital robe and they told me to get undress. I said, "I'm not putting on anything, until somebody tells me what's going on with my baby." The nurse said, "Your baby is fine, the doctor will be in to talk to you. Please just get into your robe and I promise you that the doctor will come in to explain what's going on." I started crying uncontrollably. The nurse was rubbing my back. She said, "Everything is going to be ok. I need you to stop crying, because when you cry that puts stress on the baby and we do not want that."

After, I put on my robe. The nurse said, "When you have to use the bathroom, please paige me. We do not want you to get up by yourself." The doctor came in my room. He said, "Hi Zaneeya, I wanted to tell you that you have a healthy baby boy. The reason why you have to stay in the hospital is, because your cervix is a few inches short. Your cervix is not the length that it needs to be while your four months pregnant. So, you have to have surgery tomorrow morning at 8:00 AM. We have to keep the baby inside of you. If your baby comes early the baby might not make it. So we are going to keep you in the hospital until December. You cannot go to the bathroom by yourself. If you need anything, you need to paige the nurse." I was crying. I did not understand why me. I said, "I am not staying in the hospital until December. I'm going home. My cervix is going to grow the right length that it needs to be and I am going to be fine." The doctor said, "I'm sorry to tell you that your cervix isn't going to grow. That's why you have to have surgery in the morning." I started praying and asking God to let my cervix grow, so I would not have to have surgery the next morning. I asked God to heal me and to protect my baby. After, I was finish praying. I called my granny and I told her what the doctor said. My granny said, "Oh Lord, I can't believe that. Don't stress Zaneeya." "I'm trying not to. I'm going to call you back later." When, I got off the phone with my granny. I called my dad and I told him that I was in the hospital. He said, "I'll see you in 5-minutes." When my dad came inside my room, he gave me a hug, and he said he wanted to talk to my doctor. My dad was talking loud. He was asking my nurse what was going on. My nurse told my dad that she did not have to give him any information, and needed him to calm down. My dad told my nurse, he wanted to talk to the person that was in charge of the hospital. My nurse told my dad ok. This woman came in my room. She asked me how I was doing. I told her I was doing fine. She said, "I'm the chief of this hospital and I'm going to make sure that you are taking care of. You are in good hands." My dad said, "I wanted to speak to you. I want to know everything that's going to take place and why. We need everything to be clean in Zaneeya's room. That is very important." I said, "Dad, I already told you what's going on." My dad replied, "I know, I just want her to tell me." The chief said, "I don't have to explain anything to you, and I'm going to need you to lower your voice. My patient cannot be stressed out and you are too loud." "You do have to tell me what's going on. That's my daughter, I lost a daughter already." My dad told the chief how Angelique died. The chief said, "I'm sorry for your lost, but this does not have anything to do with the death of your daughter. These are two different situations, and if you don't lower your voice I will make you leave."

My dad started raising his voice. He said, "You can't make me go nowhere. That's my daughter, and you cannot with hold information from her parents and I don't care about you being the chief. I know a lot about hospitals more then what you know." "Let me tell you something. This is my hospital and you will lower your voice and if you want. I will call the police and you will leave. My patient is an adult and I do not have to give you any information about my patient at all. That's her business, and we have that right." I said, "Dad, you know why I'm in the hospital and you do not need to know any more of my business. You do not need to talk to my doctor about anything." My dad replied, "Zaneeya, I just want to make sure everything is ok." "I told you what's going on with me. That's all you need to know and I'm not about to go back and forth with you while I'm in the hospital." The chief said, "Zaneeya, if your dad is going to stress you out, I have to tell him to leave." My dad said, "That's my daughter talk to me." The chief replied, "I'm talking to her, that's my patient and if you keep talking you will leave. Zaneeya, I'm going to leave. If I come back down here and your dad is still talking loud and keeping up mess he will have to leave." "Ok, thank you so much for your support." My dad just wanted to be in control and to be nosy. The chief was a strong woman she did not back down to my dad. He tried to belittle her, but it didn't work. She stood her ground, and she let him know who was boss and I was happy she did. My dad's friend was there her name is Jennifer. She brought him to the hospital. She told my dad to calm down. My dad told her to mind her business. I said,

"Dad that's not right and you have to lower your voice." My dad told me, he wanted to spend the night with me at the hospital. I told him, he could. I knew I was not going to get any sleep with my dad being there. Later on that night, my dad was so loud while he was talking on the phone. I could not sleep. I just kept praying to God. The next morning my doctor came in my room. He said, "Zaneeya, let's get ready for surgery." On my way to surgery, the doctor said, "Wait let me examine you first." He examined my cervix with this camera that he put inside of me. He said, "That's strange, your cervix grew. You don't need to have surgery, but first I'm going to examine you by placing two figures inside of you." My doctor took me back to my room. My dad said, "That was too quick. What happen?" I replied, "My cervix grew and I don't have to have surgery. God answered my prayers." My doctor said, "I'm going to need your dad to step outside while I examine you. Zaneeya it's going to hurt and you are going to feel pressure, but I have to examine you." While the doctor was examining me, I screamed it hurted real bad. The doctor said, "You don't have to have surgery. I see that your prayers worked." The doctor said that I have to stay in the hospital for another night. Then I would be able to go home.

After my doctor left out of the room, my dad came back inside the room. He said, "Girl, are you crazy? I cannot believe you were yelling like that. I could hear you all the way down the hall. So what's going on?" I replied, "I do not have to have surgery any more thank God. I have to stay in the hospital tonight. Then I can leave tomorrow." "Ok, well I'm happy you don't have to stay in the hospital until December anymore. I'm going home so you can get some rest. I'll call you later on." "Ok, thanks for spending the night with me dad. I love you." "I love you too. Everything is going to be ok." When my dad left, my doctor came back inside the room. He said, "Zaneeya, you have to come to the hospital every week to get your cervix checked. I want to make sure that your cervix does not shrink back, and you have to get an ultrasound every week as well. So the nurse will give you an ultrasound and they will check your cervix on the same day." My doctor told me that I couldn't travel long distanced, because I was having contractions early in my pregnancy. I told my doctor thank you for being so helpful. Later on that day, Lucy came to see me, but she didn't stay long. The next day, I was released from the hospital. Before I left the hospital, I told my nurse Ms. Judy thank you, for being here for me. My granny and Ike came to pick me up. We went to Modesto, because my mom just got home from prison and my granny was going to stay a few nights with her. Ike did not know his way to Modesto or his way back home. Even though, he has been there several times. On our way to Modesto, I was a *little uncomfortable in the car. I kept praying. When we arrived to Modesto, we went to Qin's house. When I seen my mom, I gave her a hug. I was happy to see her, she had gained a lot of weight and she looked good. I have not seen my mom with weight on her, since I was a little girl. We stayed in Modesto for a little while. Then we went back to the Bay Area. My granny called me later on that night to check on me. I told her I wasn't feeling good and my contractions was getting stronger. My doctor taught me how to time my contractions. I knew, I wasn't going into labor early, but I needed help. My granny told me to call Sabreea to ask her can she over to spend the night with me, so she can help me out. I called Sabreea. I said, "Sis, can you come spend the night with me tonight or tomorrow? My contractions are getting stronger and I need help." She replied, "I don't know. I think I have to help Bubba's grandma clean up her house, but maybe after I'm done helping her I will." I was upset, because I was there for my sister when she was pregnant and I cooked for her, and I was there for my niece. I said, "Ok, call and let me know if you're not going to come."*

Later on the next day, Sabreea did not call and she did not come over. My granny would call and check on me. My granny stayed in Modesto for a couple of days. When it was time for Ike to pick her up, Ike wanted me to ride with him, because he didn't know his way. We picked my granny up, from my mom's house. When we made it home, I talked to my granny about everything that I wanted to buy my son. The next day I had a doctor's appointment. While I was on the bus on my way to my doctor's appointment, I started having contraction back to back. The bus driver asked me was I ok, I told him yes. He asked me did I want him to call 911. I told him no, I'll be fine, but thank you. When I got off the bus, I started walking to the hospital and I fell down, and I couldn't get up. My contractions were coming stronger, and I was yelling for help, but no one helped me. People kept on driving and walking by. I called 911. I wasn't far from the hospital. This man had his earplugs in his ears, but he seen me yelling. He came and sat by me, until the fire, truck came and the ambulance came. I told the man thank you for helping me. The paramedics, was timing my contractions and they were 2-minutes apart. When I got to the hospital, I called my granny and told her what happen. Then I called Jennifer. She told me she was coming to see me. When Jennifer came to the hospital, my doctor was giving me instructions on what not to do anymore. Far as my pregnancy goes, my doctor told me that I was bedridden. I only could go to the bathroom and back to bed. He said I only could sit up for 5- minutes threw out my day. I only could go to my doctor's appointments and I had to go straight home after that. He told me I would have contractions everyday until I give birth to my baby and they will become even stronger. My doctor said, "You know you have a high-risk pregnancy and you have to be careful at all times." I told my doctor that was going to be hard for me, because I was use to doing everything. I said, "I have to have my baby shower. I'm throwing it myself and I'm going to have to stand up and decorate and I have to go shopping for my baby." My Doctor replied, "You cannot have a baby shower. You will not be able to sit or stand for more then 15-minutes without having contractions and you do not need to go shopping. You should send someone to go get the things that you need. Your contractions are only going to get worst. So please listen to me, you are bedridden. You need to have someone cook for you and to help you out at home." "Ok, I understand." I knew, no matter what my doctor said, I was still going to get my baby everything that he needed and I had to go shopping. Jennifer said, "Zaneeya, I will take you to your doctor's appointments every week." "Ok, thank you Jennifer." I stayed in the hospital for seven hours. Then I was discharged to go home. When Jennifer, and I was in the car. I said, "Jennifer, after my doctor appointments can you take me shopping? So I can get my baby some more things that I need for him?" "Yes, I'll take you. I was going to tell you we should go shopping after your doctor appointments, but I'm only giving you 30-minutes to shop, because I do not want you to go into labor early."

"I don't think, I'll go into labor early, but I know I'mma be in a lot of pain while walking and shopping. I have to do this. I never shopped in 30-minutes before, but I will be the first pregnant woman, who gets everything that she needs in 30-minutes." When Jennifer dropped me off at home, I told my granny what my doctor said. My granny said, "Zaneeya, you don't want your baby to come early! So you have to make sure that you listen to your doctors." I replied, "I am granny, you better listen to your doctors too." "Listen, I'm not the one pregnant and I'm not bedridden. You better go lay down while you're talking mess." "I'm going to lay down right now." Even though, I had a high-risk pregnancy. I was still blessed to have a healthy baby and to be living! I was happy while I was pregnant, even through my pain. Jennifer would pick me up and we would go shopping. Then we would go out to eat. Everytime I would go out to eat, my contractions would get stronger and my pain was unbearable. So we would have to leave the first 15- minutes after arriving. Jessica and I stopped speaking after I was two and an half months pregnant. She never called me to see how I was doing. She knew I was in the hospital, because I told Lucy to call her and tell her. Thanksgiving was coming up and I wanted to go to Modesto for Thanksgiving to be with my mom and my brothers. So *my granny and I went to Modesto for Thanksgiving. While I was at my mom's house, I notice her behavior would change at moments. She was acting like, she was back on drugs, and I wanted to catch my mom using drugs so I could see for myself. One night, my mom went inside of Patrick's room, and as I was going to opened the door, I heard a lighter flick. So I hurried up, and opened the door. My mom was using a crack pipe and she hurried up, and put it down. She said, "Zaneeya knock next time damn." She had an attitude. I sat down on the side of my mom on the bed, and I looked at her. I said, "Mom, you're not on drugs still huh? I know you wouldn't risk your freedom to go back to jail, knowing that you're going to get 5 years if you violate your probation." My mom replied, "No, I'm not on drugs. I'm clean don't worry Cupcake, I'm fine." I wanted my mom to confess that she was back on drugs, but she did not, and even though I caught her using drugs. She still was in denial. My granny and my mom cooked for Thanksgiving. Leeza came down to visit and she spent a night with us. Jay came to my mom's house and he spent the night. I was in my mom's bed laying down. Jay asked my mom a question. He said, "Bella, why do we have to sleep in Patrick's room? Why you didn't make Zaneeya sleep in here?" My mom replied, "Why did you say that out loud, so Zaneeya could hear you? Do you want to sleep in my room?" "Hell yeah. Make her come sleep in this cold room." I went in the livingroom and I told my granny what Jay had said. My mom would call my brothers out of their names and they were use to it, but I wasn't and I wasn't going to get used to it either.*

The next morning, I woke up and my mom was getting dress. She said, "Good morning Cupcake." I replied, "Good morning mom." "What's wrong with you?" "I heard what Jay said last night." "Oh, he was just playing." "No he was not playing around, and do not start taking up for him." My mom got mad. She said, "He was playin. If he wanted you out of my bed, I would have put you out." "So, you're telling me. If your man wanted me to get out of your bed, you would have put me out?" "Yes I would of." "What mother would put their daughter, who have a high-risk pregnancy, and who have chronic asthma. Out of her bed, and make her go sleep in a freezing cold room where there is no window in? No other woman but you, it's sad how you still would put a man before your kids." "There's nothing sad about that, and if he wanted you out of my bed, I would have put you out now!" "That's ok. I will never treat my son how you treat your kids." "I don't care you stupid B." My mom called me out of my name for the first time and I wasn't going for it. I said, "You're stupid. Your with a man who beats you, and who don't even like your kids! Since you called me out of my name, you can stay away from me, and my baby! I wish I didn't have parents like you or my dad!" My granny said, *"Bella, you don't talk to your daughter like that. You do not cuss at your kids and call them out of there names. I did not cuss at you or your siblings and you should not cuss at your kids. Calling your kids B's isn't nice at all."* My mom replied, *"Oh well, that's how I talk to my kids."* I said, *"That's the first and the last time you will ever call me out of my name! I don't want nothin to do with you. Do not call me at all. Are relationship is over."* I got dressed. I was so mad. Leeza came in the room. She said, *"Sis, are you ok?"* I was talking loud so my mom could hear me. I said, *"I'm fine, but the next time she goes to jail. I'm not helping out with nothing. She better take care of her own business, and I'm not paying none of her bills for her either."* *"Sis, don't say that, that's your mom."* *"I don't care who she is. She's not acting like a mom."* My granny called me and told me to come here. She said, *"Zaneeya, do you want something eat from Taco Bell?"* *"Yes, I want five tacos with everything on it, accept for no tomatoes."* *"Ok, I'm going to send Patrick to Taco Bell."* When Patrick came back from Taco Bell, he gave me my food and I told him thank you. When I looked at my food, the only thing that was in my taco shell was meat and sour cream. I went inside of Patrick's room. I said, *"Granny, did you tell Patrick what I wanted on my taco? I only have meat and sour cream on my tacos."* *"Yeah, I told him what you wanted. You can have one of my tacos."* *"No, it's ok granny eat your food, thank you."*

I said, *"Patrick, what happen to my tacos? They must have forgotten and messed up my order."* He replied, *"I don't know, straight up and I don't care now?"* *"Why are you talking to me like that? I just asked you a question."* *"Like I said, I don't care."* *"I do not know why, all of a sudden you think you can talk to me as if you're crazy, but lose the attitude and act like yourself."* *"I am acting like myself and if you keep talkin, I'll hit you."* I smiled and said, *"Boy, just because I'm pregnant, don't let it foul you! If you think for a second, that I will let you or anybody else put their hands on me while I'm pregnant or not pregnant you are stupid! You better think again. I will pick up that hot iron and knock you in yo head with it trust me."* Patrick called me out of my name. He said, *"Get out of my room for I put you out."* *"Oh, you think just because your mom called me out of my name you can too. Put me out your room since you say you can do it. Go ahead I want to see you try. I will lay you out on that floor."* My granny said, *"Zaneeya, just get of out his room, do it for granny."* *"Ok granny."* Patrick was still talking mess. As I was walking out of his room, I turned around and he tried to hit me with his room door. So I put my foot between the door. If I didn't he would have hit me with the

door on my back. I said, "Oh, you tried to hit me while I'm pregnant huh?"
He backed up and said, "I sure did. I don't care about you being pregnant."
My mom came in the room yelling. She said, "Zaneeya just leave." I had my
tacos in my hand. I took my tacos, and I opened them up a little and I threw
them right in Patrick's face and I giggled. Patrick came towards me as if he
was going to hit me. So I picked up the iron. I said, "Come on, so I can crack
you in yo head." My mom said, "No, Patrick it's ok. You don't have to worry
about her. She will not be here for a long time, just get out of his room." I said,
"You don't never have to see me again and you shouldn't have raised your
kids to be woman beaters." I called a cab. When the cab came, Ramone put
my bags in the car, I told Ramone bye then I gave him a hug. He said, "Don't
worry about them sis." I said, "I'm not brother. I'll call you when I have my
baby." "Make sure you do. I want to see my nephew." I was sitting in the cab.
I was waiting for my granny to get in. When my granny got in the cab, my
mom came outside and told my granny and me bye, but I did not say anything
to her. I couldn't even look at my mom. When we made it back home, I told
my granny I don't want anything to do with my mom or dad. I was tired of
going through the same thing. No matter how much I tried to get along with
my parents, it would never last.

My dad and I got into one day. Jennifer was taking me to the hospital and
she was dropping him off somewhere that he needed to be. I asked Jennifer,
when we leave my doctor's appointment could she take me to Burger King,
because I wanted a burger. She said, "Yes, you know we always get something
to eat after your doctor's appointments." My dad said, "Well, don't take her
to Burger King she does not need to eat that poison." Jennifer said, "She can
eat Burger King." "That's my daughter, just stay out of it and don't take her
there." I said, "Dad, I am a grown woman that's having a baby. You don't
tell me what I can eat, and what I cannot eat. If my doctors tells me that I
can't eat fast food then I won't eat it. Until then, I'm going to eat whatever it
is that I am craving at the moment and today I'm going to eat Burger King!"
My dad replied, "You need to eat home cooked meals." "I do eat home cooked
meals, five days a week and after my doctor's appointment. I'm going to eat
me some fast food. It's nothing wrong with me eating fast food once a week."
"It is something wrong with that. Your doctors doesn't know everything. Go
ahead and give your baby that poison. You're already a bad mother." "I'm not
giving my baby poison, and I'm not a bad mother. If I want to eat fast food, I
will. I don't need your approval to do so. Sorry you're not in control of me, and
how are you going to say I'm giving my baby poison when you eat fast food."

"I don't eat fast food anymore and I already had a daughter that died and the doctors doesn't know everything. So you can put that poison in your body if you want too." "The doctors do not know everything. You're right, but no one knows everything. However, I am going to listen to my doctors, and they did not say that I couldn't eat fast food. Angelique's death does not have anything to do with this. These are two different situations." "It's not that different. If your baby dies, because you're feeding it poison then you won't be saying it's so different." "My baby is not going to die because I'm eating a cheeseburger. And stop bringing up Angelique's death and trying to compare it to every situation, because it's not the same." My dad started going off. He said, "Keep believing that, and oh yeah, I don't like your pregnancy pictures. You look like a hooker pregnant, and I told Jennifer to keep them, I don't want them." "I don't care if you don't like my pictures and let's not talk about looks, because you need to work on your appearance yourself. There is nothing wrong with my pictures. You're opinion does not matter to me." My dad turned around in the car and put his finger in my face. I said, "You better take your finger out of my face. If you think about slapping me, I will call the police and hit you up side your head with your crutches." My dad took his finger out of my face. He said, "That's what you said when you lived with Toniya and me. You said you were going to call the police on both of us.

Jennifer pull over here. So I can get out the car. I don't want to be nowhere near this girl." "Good, I'm happy you don't, the feeling is mutual. You need to stop lying to every woman that you meet! I have never told you I would call the police on you or Toniya, so stop lying. I know it's a hard thing for you to do." My dad grabbed his crutches and his briefcase as he was getting out of the car. He said, "Your mothers is a liar, and she is on drugs and you have a messed up attitude just like her." "Don't worry, you're on drugs too and you're a liar! I rather have my mom's attitude then have yours any day, now! That's why you don't have nothing. All you do is depend on every woman that you meet, and that's going to run out." My dad was still talking mess as Jennifer was pulling off. When, Jennifer and I were in the car. She said, "I never seen that side of your dad before." I replied, "We do not get along. Out of all his children, Qin and I do not get along with our dad and we never have." "I never heard a dad speak like that to his daughter before. My husband would have never said those things to my daughter." "I would have never said those things to my dad. If he didn't say the things he said." "I would have spoken like that to if I was you. You stood up for yourself and I don't blame you." After my doctor's appointment Jennifer and I went to my grandma's house.

Jennifer started telling Vanessa what happen between my dad and me. My uncle Dana was there. Vanessa said, "Jennifer, you know Zaneeya and her dad does not get along.You shouldn't have had both of them in the car together." "I didn't know they didn't get along. That's the first time I ever heard about this." "You did know." I said, "No, Jennifer did not know that my dad and I didn't get along." My uncle Dana was always kind, and he never would put me down and he always had an understanding for everything that went on. My uncle Dana said, "Zaneeya, don't let your dad or anyone else stress you out. You already have a high-risk pregnancy. Your Dad is wrong for saying those things to you. No matter what you said and I'm going to tell him about his self too." Jennifer took me home. I told my granny what happen between my dad and me. I told my granny that I was going to stay away from my dad for the rest of my pregnancy. Which is not hard for me to do, because my dad and I never had a father daughter relationship. When we seen each other, we would speak and laugh some times, but if we was around each other for more than 45-minutes or a day or two. We would get into an argument and it has always been that way, ever since I was younger. There has been multiple times where my dad has introduced Sabreea as his daughter to someone, right in the front of me, but he didn't introduced me as his daughter. My dad has done more hurtful things than that. My dad still play favoritism between Sabreea and I, but won't allow him to hurt my feelings any more, because I don't feed into it!

I had ordered my cake for my baby shower, when I was four months pregnant. My doctor told me I couldn't have a baby shower, but I already put down my deposited on the location. For where my baby shower was going to be. I had bought everything for my son. I bought clothes, shoes, blankets, a car seat a stroller, and diapers. He had more clothes than my granny and me put together. I would get paid every two weeks and I would save my money and I would go shopping every week for my son. I knew I was going to be a wonderful mother and I wasn't going to ask anybody for help. Some of my family members on my dad side would call me. They would say, "Zaneeya what's your income and how much money do you make?" I would say, "I don't tell no one what my income is and how much money I make. What good is that going to do you by knowing?" They would get mad, but I did not care. The less people knew the better. When people couldn't find out your business. They would just lie and say what your income was, and how much money you were getting. When they didn't know and it wasn't true. I looked up to my cousin Christa! She is a great mother! Christa is a phenomenal woman! Christa had took me to lunch once when I was pregnant. She bought me my first pregnancy

book. It's called "What To Expect When Your Expecting." One day, Christa
had called me. She said, "Zaneeya when is your baby shower?" I replied, "I'm
not having one, because I won't be able to decorate and sit up in interacted
while I'm pregnant. My doctor told me I could not have a baby shower, because
I have a high-risk pregnancy. He said my contractions will only get worst, as
I get further along in my pregnancy and he was right. "Zaneeya, you have to
have a baby shower. Your baby is going to need things. Have you bought a lot
of stuff already?" "Yes, I bought him some clothes, and diapers. He has a lot
of things already. I don't need a stroller or a car set. I wanted to have a baby
shower, but I can't and I don't really care about having one anymore." "You
have to have a baby shower, and you do not need to throw it yourself. Let
every one buy you a gift. I'm going to give you a baby shower." "I don't know
Christa." "Look, I am going to throw you a baby shower. Rather you come or
not. I just need a list of the people that you want to come to your baby shower."

"Ok Christa, for my baby shower I have 76 guests." "You don't need 76
guest and we are not going to have any mans there. What type of food do you
want and what type of cake do you want?" "I already ordered my cake, and I
wanted Mexican food. Some chicken and beef enchilada's. I can order my food
myself and I can buy all of my decorations Christa, I have money." "I don't
need your money Miss. Independent. Let someone help you for a change. It's
ok to let people give you things and for you to accept them, just relax." "I just
don't want you to spend a lot of money on my baby shower, and I do not want
anyone else in the family spending money on my baby shower." "I'm going to
throw your baby shower. I'm not going to let anyone else buy nothing ok. I love
you, don't worry let me throw you a nice baby shower. Do you want to keep
your baby shower on the same day that it was originally going to be?" "Yes,
that's fine. I love you too and I am going to try to relax, but I like to be so hands
on with everything." "I know you do, but don't worry. I got this. I just want you
to go get your cake and come to your baby shower, and when you start having
contractions, you can lay down on Montrella's couch. She does not mind.
That's where your baby shower is going to be at." "Ok Christa, thank you so
much. Let me know if you need me to buy anything like, decoration or food."
"Zaneeya I don't need your money, but thank you, I love you and I'll talk to
you later." "Ok, I love you too." I told my granny that Christa was throwing
me a baby shower and she wouldn't take no for an answer. My granny said,
"That's nice of her, she is a kindhearted person." I said, "She sure is granny."
When, I moved from Letha's house. Christa took me to get my birth certificate
and my social security card and she has took me school shopping, before as

well. I wanted my friend Tanesha to come to my baby shower, but she wasn't answering her phone. Jennifer told me that Patchase wanted me to sign some papers and she needed to see me. When we went to see Patchase, I was nervous for some reason. I did not believe that she needed me to sign some papers, because she would have called me herself or Tanesha would have called me. When, Patchase came into the lobby. She said, "Jennifer, you haven't told her yet right?" Jennifer replied, "No, you said you were going to tell her." I said, "Tell me what? What's going on?" Patchase said, "Well Zaneeya, I wanted to tell you that Tanesha died and she has been dead for over three weeks now." I started crying. I said, "Why didn't you tell me? I have been calling her for over three weeks."

Patchase said, "I didn't tell you, because you have a high -risk pregnancy and I do not want you to stress out and Tanesha, wouldn't have either." "I could have gone to her funeral that was my friend." "I know you're going to miss her. I told Jennifer, you and Tanesha were extremely close. I just did not want you to stress out, I'm sorry." Patchase gave me a hug, and she was a great doctor and I truly loved her. She said, "Don't worry about that. I'll see you after you deliver your baby." When I got in the car, I just cried. Jennifer rubbed my back. We got something to eat then I went home. I told my granny that Tanesha died. My granny said, "I know your hurt, but don't stress yourself out." I replied, "I'm not granny. I just wish I could have seen her in the hospital before she died or I could have gone to her funeral." "I know, but maybe it's a good thing that you didn't go. You probably could not have handled seeing her like that. Tanesha probably did not want to tell you, that she was in the hospital, because she don't want you to stress."

"Yeah your right granny, but I am going to miss her. At least she does not have to suffer any more. I'm happy about that." I started thinking about the times that I would go visit Tanesha. We would have lunch in her office. We would talk about our life, and we would laugh and we would call each other on the phone. We would lift each other up, when we were down. She was a great friend and I will always miss her. One day Sabreea called me. She said, "Sis, I would of threw your baby shower for you, but I know how hands on you are and plus I don't have any money." I said, "You could have gotten the money from me and you could have still thrown my baby shower for me. I just would have been paying for it, but it doesn't matter. I'm not mad it's ok. Christa is throwing me a baby shower." "I know, but I am going to help out at your baby shower. I wish I had the money, because I would have really thrown you an amazing baby shower. You helped me out at my baby shower and I thank you.

I don't want you to be mad at me." "I am not mad at you, I'm fine." "Ok, I love you and I'll see you at your baby shower." "Ok, I love you too."

My baby shower was December 12ᵗʰ 2009. The day of my baby shower, I wore this purple sweater dress and my black tights and my black boots. Jennifer picked my granny and me up. Then we went to pick up my cake. Then we headed to my baby shower. The people who came to my baby shower were. Sabreea, Jessica, and auntie Charnae. Krystal, and Christa. Jannette, and April. Montrella and Vida, and two of Christa friends. Evon, and Davena. Monica, and Lucy. Desseire, and Trina, and Jonnie, and Lamonica. When, I arrived to my baby shower. Christa said, "Zaneeya do you like your decorations? Do you like your baby shower?" I replied, "Yes, I like them you did a wonderful job. Thank you so much, and thank you too Montrella for opening up your home to me, and for letting me have my baby shower at your house."

Christa and Montrella said, "You're welcome. No problem, just have fun today and if you have any contractions just lay down." "Ok thank you." I always enjoy seeing my auntie Monica. She has always been the life of the party and she didn't back down to anyone and I liked that about her. My auntie Evon was always sweet and kind. When everybody arrived to my baby shower, we talked. We ate and we played games. My granny had a good time at my baby shower. She liked the food and everybody said it was good. Christa made sure that everybody left with a gift. We took pictures and I opened up my gifts. My cake was ginormous. The name of my cake was called, "Baby in a Blanket." It was enough cake to feed a hundred people. My granny was sitting down on the couch, and Evon and Jannette came up to my granny and they started asking her questions. They said, "So, how do you feel about Zaneeya being pregnant. Are you still going to let her live with you? What about her baby daddy where do he live?" My granny said, "I'm happy my granddaughter is having a baby. I have five kids and no I'm not kicking her out! She can live with me as long as she wants too, and her baby father lives in Modesto. Zaneeya is going to be just fine." My aunties were just being nosy. They couldn't wait to ask my granny those questions. I walked in the livingroom. I said, "What's going on?" My granny said, "Are you almost ready to go?" "Yes, Jennifer and Sabreea are putting my gifts in the car. Then we are going to leave. Did you have fun granny?" "I really enjoyed myself your baby shower was nice."

My granny and I said bye to everyone and I thanked Christa again for giving me a baby shower. Jennifer took my granny and I home. She helped me *carry my gifts inside the house. I gave her a hug and I told her thank you for helping me. I told my granny I would put all of my gifts up tomorrow, because I was going to bed. The next day, I opened up my gifts and I put them away. Jannette bought my baby a lot of pajamas which a kid could never have too much of. Jennette bought my son a beautiful Carter Piggy Bank. It was baby blue and brown. After I put all of my baby gifts away, I had a talk with my granny about my mom and dad. My dad would always say hurtful things and he would always belittle me, and he loves to be in control of people. My mom just really hurt it my feelings and I did not look at her the same. She should have never called me out of my name. My granny said, "Both of your parents are wrong, but just don't turn your back on them. You can't turn your back on your parents. If something else big happens then I understand, but right now, just don't turn your back on them. Give them another chance." I replied, "Ok granny, I will give them another chance and see how this goes." "That's what I'm talking about Zaneeya, you can do it."*

My mom called, so I answered the phone. I said, "Hello." My mom said, "Cupcake!" "Hold on, here granny come get the phone." My mom said, "Cupcake talk to me." I could hear in her voice that she felt sorry, for what she did. I said, "What?" She replied, "I'm sorry for calling you out of your name. I shouldn't have did that. I'm sorry, but you made me mad." "I don't care how mad I made you. You shouldn't have called me out of my name. I didn't call you out of your name and I was mad at you, but I accept your apology. I forgive you. I'm sorry for saying what I said too." "Now I'm happy. You wouldn't talk to me at all. I had to ask granny how you were doing. I'm happy we are back talking now." "Yeah I am too, but if you ever call me out of my name again. I'm not gonna have nothing to do with you at all." "I'm not going to call you out of your name again. I call your brothers out of their names. All the time and they don't say nothing and they don't even get mad, but you got mad. I said oh yeah, I can't call her that. She don't like it." "No I don't like it. Just like, you wouldn't like it if I called you out of your name and my brothers, don't like it either. You probably have been calling them that for so long, their just use to it now, but that doesn't mean their feelings, isn't hurt."

"Yeah your right, I'm going to stop calling them out of their names too. I wanted to ask you, do you want to come live with me after your baby is born." "No, we don't even get along, and we would be arguing everyday, and I don't want to raise my son in an environment like that. Plus I wouldn't have my own room if I moved with you. I want to live by myself with my son, and I can't afford it right now, but everything will take place when it's time." "You

will have your own room. You can have my room, and we are not going to argue. I can help you with your baby. You're going to need your sleep, and you can pay the pg&e bill and we will go half on the rest of the bills." "That's why you want me to live with you. So I can help you pay your bills." "No, that's not why. You haven't lived with me since you was younger and I thought that it would be nice if we had a better relationship. You're having a baby and I want to be close to my grandson." "I don't know mom. I have to think about that. We have not lived together in a long time and I have to make sure that my son is safe at all times." "He is going to be safe, just think about it." "Ok, I will." When I got off the phone with my mom, Jessica called me. She said, "Hi Zaneey, how are you doing?" I replied, "Hi, I'm fine. How are you doing?" "I'm fine, I just called to see how you were doing, and I wanted to talk to you. I don't know why we haven't spoken." "I don't know, but we should all go to lunch and catch up. So we can talk and have a good time." "Ok, that's fine with me." "Ok, I'll call Sabreea and Lucy later on and tell them." When all of us would get together, we would always have a good time. Christa came over my house and she brought me some bottle for my baby. She didn't stay long, because she had to go. Jessica and Sabreea came to pick me up, so we could go to lunch. When I got in the car, I gave Jessica and Sabreea a hug. When we pulled up to the resturaunt, Jessica and I began to talk. Jessica said, "I don't know why we haven't been speaking to each other. My dad would ask me. Jessica have you spoke to Zaneeya and I would say no, I have not spoken to her. He would tell me to call you, but I thought you were mad at me. I would cry all the time, because I missed you. We would always be together, and we would talk everyday. I miss talking to you. You're my best friend." I said, "I miss talking to you too. I was mad, because you didn't call me and I tried to call you, but you wouldn't answer. So I stopped calling. You wasn't there for me through out my pregnancy and I didn't know why. I cried too, this is the first time that we have never spoken to each other and we are best friends."

Jessica started crying. She said, "You're my best friend, we are sisters and I don't never want us to not speak again. I'm sorry for not being there for you, through out your pregnancy and for not helping out with your baby shower. I wish I could take it back. I think about that everyday." I replied, "You know I treat you just like I treat Sabreea. We are sisters and I forgive you. I'm sorry for hurting your feelings. Stop crying. Next time we need to just express how we feel towards each other, instead of waiting and not speaking." I started wiping Jessica tears from her face. We hugged then we went inside the resturaunt to eat. When, we went inside the restaurant. Lucy and Sabreea said, "Did y'all make up?" We said, "Yes we did." Sabreea said, "Well, don't let this happen again." We laughed, and ordered our food. We ate and we cracked jokes. After we ate, we went home. Everyday I was getting more and more excited to have my baby. I could not wait to give birth to my son. Jessica birthday was coming up and she called me. She said, "Hey sis, my birthday is coming up and I know you can't come, because you're pregnant." I said, "Yeah, I'm staying in the house. Have fun enjoy your birthday. I'll talk to you later."

Qin came to my house with his new friend. He would always mess with me while I was pregnant. He would grab my butt and say, "Damn sis you got butt, you never had a butt like this before. I know you're happy." I said, "Qin stop grabbing my butt. Everytime I see you, you're grabbing my butt. You have plenty of girls, go grab their butts and leave mines alone thank you." He would laugh and grab it again. I would fuss, but he did not care. Until I told him, I was going to pick something up and hit him with it. Then he would stop. My granny and I would eat and watch TV together. I would go out to eat with Jennifer, and Jessica and Lucy. Jennifer and I went to Chili's restaurant on the 5th of February. I went to the Olive Garden with Jessica and Lucy on the 6th of February. As I was eating, my contractions were getting stronger and I knew I was going into labor soon. Jessica said, "Sis are you ok? Maybe you should go to the hospital." I said, "No, my contractions are strong, but they are too far apart. It's not time for me to go to the hospital yet, but I can't wait to have my baby." When I went home, my contractions were getting stronger and stronger, but I just dealt with the pain, because I was used to it. I just laid down on my side, that's all I could do. I was praying that my baby turned back around, because when I went to my last doctor's appointment. My doctor told me that my baby was breech. I was in pain all night, but I kept dealing with it. I told my granny that my contractions were getting stronger and they were less than 5- minutes apart. She said, "You should call 911." I replied, "I'm fine granny."

Chapter Fifteen

My Biggest Blessing That God Has Given Me My Baby Zarelle

J woke up and I went to the bathroom. As I wiped myself, there was blood on the tissue. I jumped up and down. I was happy! I knew it was time for me to have my baby. After, I was finish using the bathroom. I went to tell my granny that it's time for me to have my baby. She said, "Call 911." I replied, "Granny, I am not going anywhere until after I'm done eating my breakfast." "You're so greedy. Your baby is going to be greedy just like you. After you eat, you have to go to the hospital." "I am granny." Zarelle diaper bag was already packed. I was getting my outfit out that I was going to wear to the hospital. My granny came in the room and she brought me my plate. She made me some grits, egg, bacon, and some toast and she brought me a big glass of juice. I said, "Thank you granny. I cannot wait to eat." "Hurry up, so you can go to the hospital." As I was eating my food, my granny kept on pacing back and forth while she was on the phone with my mom. She came in the room. She said, "Zaneeya, are you almost done eating?" "Granny calm down. I'm almost finished." When I was finish eating, I took my plate to the kitchen. My granny said, "Did you call 911?" "No not yet granny, I'm fine. I have to take a shower first. Then I will call." "You don't need to shower. You can go like that, keep your pajamas on." "Granny I am not going anywhere in my pajamas and you know that. I'm going to get in the shower and I'll see you when I get out."

When I was in the shower, my granny kept coming to the door. She said, "Zaneeya are you almost finish, what's taking you so long?" I replied, "Granny, go sit down. I'm fine. I'll be out in a minute." "Just hurry up girl." After I got out of the shower, I got dressed. My granny said, "What are you doing now?" "I'm putting on my eye shadow." "Girl you don't need that on."

After I was finished putting on my eye shadow, I did my hair. Then I got my bags and placed them in the livingroom then I called 911. When the fire truck came, my granny was pacing back and forth. When the paramedics came she was breathing fast, and she was still pacing back and forth. The paramedics told my granny, "We need you to calm down. She's having a baby and she is having contractions that are very close together and she's calmer then you." My granny said, "I haven't given birth to a baby by self, since I gave birth to my son Alvin." I said, "Granny, I'll call you when I get to the hospital." "Ok, make sure you call me. I'll see you later on today." "Ok granny." As I was on my way to the hospital, the paramedics said, "You are doing quite well, for your contractions to be so close together. You're a champ." I said, "Thank you." When we arrived to the hospital, they took me to labor and delivery. I had my own room just like, I always did. The nurse came in the room, and she told me I could not eat anything, because my contractions were so close together. The nurse said my baby was going to come in a couple of hours. I said, "My baby is not going to come until later on tonight." The nurse replied, "Well, you can't eat anything. I do not want the food to get stuck in your baby's throat." "Well, can I have some water or some juice?" "I'll bring you some water and juice." "Ok, thank you." Jennifer called me. She said, "Hi Zaneeya, I'm on my way to the hospital right now. I'll see you in a little while." When I got off the phone with Jennifer, I started looking for my phone charger, but I couldn't find it. When Jennifer came to the hospital, she was smiling. She gave me a hug. She said, "Zaneeya, how do you feel? Your contractions are very close together and you're all dolled up like you're ready for a photo shoot." I laughed and said, "My contractions are strong, but I think I'm taking my pain so well, because I've been having contractions most of my pregnancy. I do not want the epidural, but if my pain gets worst then I'm going to get it." "You're doing good Zaneeya. I'm going to pick up your granny and Sabrrea. Call me if you need me."

When Jennifer left, I asked my nurse could I have something to eat. She said, "No, because you're going to have your baby soon." I said, "If I do not have my baby in the next hour or so. I'mma eat something, rather you like it or not, I'm hungry." "Ok, just wait a little longer. Then I'll see what I can give you to eat." When, Jennifer came back to the hospital with my granny and Sabreea. I asked her could she go get me something to eat. My granny said, "Zaneeya, you haven't eaten since early?" I replied, "No, I haven't eaten since I left the house and you know I'm hungry. I like to eat every hour, and I want something from Jack in the Box. I want four egg rolls, potato wedges, two tacos and some fires." Sabreea said, "Girl you're greedy." My granny said, "I'm tellin you, your baby is going to be greedy too." Jennifer said, "Ok, I'mma get you something to eat when I drop your granny off at home." Sabreea said, "Zaneeya how do you feel?" I replied, "Hungry, I'm ready to eat like yesterday. Do you have some snacks in your purse?" Sabreea laughed and said, "No I don't have any snacks in my purse crazy." Jennifer took my granny home and Sabreea went with her.

I waited for them to come back. My nurse came in my room. I said, "I'm going to eat when my sister comes back. I haven't eaten since earlier." My nurse replied, "Ok, when your sister and your auntie gets back, with your food. I'm going to give you 15-minutes to eat, because you do not suppose to have any food in your system before giving birth to your child." "Ok, thank you. That's all I need." "The doctor is going to come in and check you again, to see if your baby is still breech." "Ok." As the doctor was examining me, she said, "He is still breech. I need you to lay on your side, but a little bit on your stomach. This will not hurt you or the baby. This will make him move and he will turn around in the right position." I was not comfortable at all, while I was laying down. I just wanted Zarelle to hurry up and turn around. When Sabreea and Jennifer came back, I couldn't wait to eat. Sabreea said, "Why do they have you in that position?" I said, "So my baby will turn around, he's breech. He has been whooping my butt my whole pregnancy. I started having contractions while I was four months pregnant. This is his second time turning around. Zarelle and I is going to have a nice talk, when he comes into this world." Sabreea said, "You better leave my nephew alone. He's having fun in there swimming all around."

Jennifer said, "Zaneeya, you took everything so well during your pregnancy. Even though you got into it with your dad and your mom, you still was happy your whole pregnancy. I can't wait to see my man, when he comes out. I'm going to leave, I'll be back in the morning when Zarelle is born. So, Sabreea call me soon as Zarelle gets here. I love you both." Sabreea said, "Ok Jennifer I will." I said, "I'll see you tomorrow, love you too." When Jennifer left, Sabreea and I just talked. I wanted her to record me while I was in labor. My pain was getting worst and on a scale from 1 to 10, my pain was a 7. My nurse came in the room. She said, "Zaneeya we are going to induce your labor." My nurse gave me some medicine to make my contractions come faster. After she gave me my medicine, I told her I was going to take a hot bath, because I was in enough pain. I knew my contractions were only going to get stronger. My nurse said, "When you get out of the tub just paige me, because *the doctor is going to bust your water bag, because your water bag have not been broken." "Ok." Sabreea recorded everything. She ran my bath water for me. She was recording me while I was in the tub. We were cracking jokes, and we were taking turns singing parts of different songs, like we always would. As I was in the bathtub, Allen called me. He said, "Zaneeya, how are you feeling?" "I'm in pain." "I just called to check on you, and to see how you was doing. Is it almost time for you to have my son?" "I don't know when my baby is coming, but he should be here soon." My pain started getting worst. Allen said, "Ok, I'll call you back and check on you in a little while." I stayed in the tub for an hour. When I got out the bathtub, I had to use the toilet. As I was peeing, I couldn't control myself. I knew I was done, but I just kept on peeing. Sabreea said, "Sis, are you done, do you need help?" "No, I can't stop peeing." "Let me know when you're done and I will help you get back in bed." When I was finished using the bathroom, I went to get in the bed. Sabreea said, "You're so hard headed. I thought I told you to let me know when you're done, so I can help you." I said, "Help me by paging the nurse. So we can get this show on the road." Sabreea went to get the nurse. When, the doctor came in the room to bust my water bag. She said, "Your water bag has already been bust. Let me check your bed to see if it's wet." The doctor checked my bed. She said, "Your water bag didn't bust in the bed. Maybe your water bag broke in the tub. Did you feel something warm coming down your legs? Like you were peeing on yourself?" I replied, "When I was peeing I knew I was finish, but I couldn't control myself. So, my water bag must have broken while I was on the toilet.*

When my doctor left out of my room, everybody started calling me. Qin called me. Ramone called me and my mom and momma Shay called me. My friends and a few other family members called me too. My pain was getting worst. I told Sabreea I might need the epidural. She said, "If you need some medicine it's ok. You have been in pain long enough. If you want me to paige the nurse I will." I said, "Ok, I'm going to wait a little longer to see how worst my pain gets." Sabreea went to get my nurse, when my nurse came in the room. She said, "Zaneeya do you want the epidural right now? If you wait another hour we won't be able to give it to you." "Ok, I want it right now." "The doctor will be in, to give it to you. Do you want me to bring you some ice?" "Some ice to eat?" "Yes. If you don't want it now, I'll give it to you later. You are going to need it." "Ok, not right now. I just want my medicine." The doctor came in the room to give me my medicine. He said, "Do not move, it's going to hurt just a little." I moved on an accident. The doctor said, "This time do not move. I'm going to do it again." Sabreea said, "I can't look, I can't look." *After the doctor was finished giving me my epidural, I told him thank you. My pain was stronger then ever. I said, "Sabreea when is this medicine going to start working?" She rubbed my hair. She said, "It should work real soon baby. Do you want some ice?" "No, I only like ice when I am drinking something, like some juice." "Well, I'm going to sleep. If you need me just wake me up." "Ok sis, thank you." Sabreea and I went to sleep for a little bit. When I woke up, I woke Sabreea up. I said, "Sabreea, I want some ice." "Ok, let me paige the nurse." My nurse came in the room, and she brought me some ice. Sabreea started feeding me the ice. My body started shaking. My nurse came and rubbed my arms. She said, "Zaneeya, it's going to be ok." I was so cold for some reason. After, my body stopped shaking, I asked the nurse for some more medicine. Sabreea told me she was going back to sleep. She said, "Let me know if you need me sis." I replied, "Go ahead and get some rest. You helped me out enough." "Ok, thank you."*

I kept waking Sabreea up, because I wanted some ice. I said, "Sis wake up, I need some more ice." She got up and paige the nurse. The nurse brought me some more ice. She said, "Get ready to have your baby in the next hour or so." Sabreea was feeding me some ice. Sabreea said, "Here, I'm going to give you a spoon so you can feed yourself. Now I'm going to sleep sis. So I can get a little rest. I love you, but man I'm tired and if you need anything you know what to do." "Ok sis. I' m going to let you sleep this time, I promise." Sabreea just looked at me, and smiled. She said, "Yeah ok." I waited until Sabreea was sleep. I looked at her and I yelled, "Sissy, sissy wake up, wake up." She did not move. I said, "I know you hear me. Wake up I need some more ice." She kept laying down. I was messing with Sabreea on purpose. I drove her crazy that night. My nurse came in the room. She said, "Zaneeya, I'm happy you're woke. It's almost time for me to get off work. I wanted to tell you, that you are one of the best patients that I ever had and I thank you." "You're welcome. Thank you for putting up with me, and don't leave. I'm going to have my baby soon, I can feel it." "Ok, I get off work in 10- minutes just paige me, and let me know if you feel like it's time for you to push." "Ok I will." The nurse went out the room and 5-minutes later the nurse came back inside my room and I told her that I was ready to push. She said, "I'm going to get the doctor." When, my doctor came in the room, my nurse woke Sabreea up. Sabreea said, "Sis, are you ready to push?" "Yes I am." Sabreea started recording me. I was holding my legs. My nurse was rubbing my hair. My doctor said, "We are all going to count when you are ready. Then you're going to push." I replied, "Ok I'm ready 1, 2, and 3." I pushed and I got tired. My doctor said, "Come on, you can do it." Sabreea said, "You can do it sis. Come on your strong." I said, "Ok, I'm ready 1, 2, and 3." I pushed. The doctor said, "I can see his hair." I got my right hand and I touched the top of my baby's head. Then I pushed again. His head was out. Then I pushed for the fourth time and his whole body came out. My son was born February 8, 2010. Sabreea said, "Look at him, he looks just like Allen." My doctor said, "Good job Zaneeya." My nurse said, "Well, I am proud of you, see you did it." She gave me a hug. Then she went home. My doctor said, "Do you want us to wash him off or do you want to hold your baby first?" I said, "I want to hold him." I laid my Daddy Love across my chest and I started crying tears of joy. I knew I was going to be a great mother. I was going to protect my son and give him the love that I never had from my parents. I was going to be there for my baby. Daddy Love is Zarelle's nick, name that I called him. I kissed him on his checks and lips and he started crying. Then he boo-booed all over me, so I told the nurse to come get him.

Sabreea called everybody and told them that I had my baby. I moved to another room. I was happy I had my own room still. Jennifer came up to the hospital, she held Zarelle. Then my granny, my mom and Lil Dawane, and my mom's friend came to see me. Sabreea and Jennifer left. I told my sister thank you for being here for me, while I was in labor. She said, "You're welcome sis, no problem. I can't wait to get some sleep." I said, "Get some rest. You deserve it and kiss my niece for me." "Ok, I'll call you later to check on you." I told my mom and everybody to wash their hands before they held Zarelle. My granny said, "He is finally here." My granny and everyone else stayed for a couple of hours then they left. Lucy called me and she told me congratulations and so did Desseire and Jessica. The first night, that I stayed in the hospital. I told the nurse that I did not want my son to sleep in the nursery. I told the nurse he was going to sleep in the room with me. My nurse said, "You are going to be tired, you should let us help you." I replied, "I'm going to be fine. Even if I am tired, I'll be ok." I laid Zarelle on my chest and we went to sleep. He didn't want to eat much, he just wanted to sleep. The nurse told me it was normal. I breast fed Zarelle while I was in the hospital. The next day Christa came to see me. She held Zarelle as we were talking. She said, "Zaneeya, I can't believe you're a mother now. I remember when you were a little girl. Now you have your own baby." "I know, I cannot wait to just love on him and to teach him everything. I can't wait until we have mother son days." Christa didn't stay long. After she left Jessica called me. She said, "Zaneeya, my mom and dad is already at the hospital and they want to see you and the Baby. Is it ok if they come see you?" "Yeah they can come." I gave Jessica my room number.

When Henry and Betty came to see me, they looked at Zarelle and said, "He is a fine baby. Congratulations Zaneeya, well we are going to leave. We just wanted to stop by and say hi." I replied, "Thanks for stopping by. I'll see y'all later." I went to sleep after they left. The next day, Jessica called me and told me she was coming to see me. When she got to the hospital, she called me. She said, "Zaneeya, is it ok if my boyfriend, come inside your room? If not, he can wait in the lobby." "He can come in." When Jessica came in the room, she introduced me to her boyfriend. She didn't stay long, I was tired anyways. I slept good that night and so did Zarelle. The next day I left the hospital, Ike came to pick me up and he took me home. My granny was smiling while she was looking at Zarelle. She said, "Look at him. He is such a fine baby, he looks just like Allen." I said, "Granny, do not wake him up. He is a light sleeper just like me, and if you wake him up. You are going to put him back to sleep." She would ease back.

The first night that I came home from the hospital, I was hungry and there wasn't any food to eat. So I called my mom and told her that I was hungry. I said, "Mom, I'm hungry and if I knew granny wasn't going to cook. I would have had Ike take me to get something to eat. I know, I could call my uncle Kevin and he would come, but I hate asking people for stuff." My mom replied, "Granny should have cooked you something. She knows when a woman comes home from the hospital after having a baby.They need to eat a hot meal or you'll be weak and you need all your strength. I'm going to call your uncle Kevin right now." "No, don't do that, I'll be ok. I did not know it was nothing to eat." "I'm going to call your uncle Kevin anyways. I'll call you back." My uncle Kevin called me. He said, "Zaneeya, what do you want to eat?" "I just want some soup uncle Kevin and some juice and I'll give you your money back, when you get here and I'll give you some gas money too." "Ok niece, I'll be there in 30-minutes." When uncle Kevin made it to the store he called and asked me what kind of soup did I want. When, uncle Kevin brought me my soup. He said, "Look at my baby, damn he's light skinned! Is his dad light?" I said, "Yeah, he is light skinned just like his dad." I gave uncle Kevin some gas money, and I gave him, his money back, and I told him thank you. He said, "Call me anytime niece." My mom called me. She said, "Your uncle Kevin said he is going to call you." I replied, "He just left mom, thank you." "You're welcome. You have to eat. You just had a baby. You need your energy. That's why you need to live with me. I can cook for you and help you with you're baby." "I do not need help with my baby mom and I like to be hands on at all times." "You're not going to be able to sleep, and you're going to need me to watch him while you're in the shower." "Mom, I have it all planned out. I'm going to take Daddy Love everywhere I go, and maybe I should live with you, but I'm only going to stay with you until I get my own place. You don't owe any money on your bills or nothing right?" "No, I don't owe any back pay on my bills." "Ok mom, don't be lying. I don't want to move out there and you're getting evicted, and I'm going to have to move right back out here and I can just stay where I'm at right now." "Girl, that is not going to happen just come. I'm going to take everything out of my room, and I'm going to start putting everything in Patrick's room." "Ok, I'mma call you back. I'mma move down there this week." "Ok, I can't wait until you and my grandson come." When I got off the phone with my mom, I told my granny that I was moving to Modesto. She said, "That will be nice you can always come back home."

Chapter Sixteen

My Move Was Not The Right Move

*E*va took me to Modesto. Justin Jr., and Brain, and Mercy helped me move. We put all of my belongings in my mom's room. I told them thank you for helping me move and I told Eva thank you for taking me to Modesto. When everybody left, Qin and his friend, Mickey came over. Qin told me to call him soon as I made it to Modesto. Qin couldn't wait to see Zarelle. Qin kept saying, "look at my nephew, I can't wait until he gets older so I can take him everywhere with me. He is going to have his first girlfriend at 8 years old, and she is going to be 5 years older than him." I said, "Boy please, my son will not be with you, and he is not going to have his first girlfriend at 8 years old and she will not be 5 years older than him." He laughed and said, "I like getting you mad. Get some clothes, so you can spend the night with me for a couple of days." "No, I'mma stay with mommy and watch some movies." "Come on sis, just come spend a few nights with me, so I could see my nephew and spend some time with him." My mom said, "Yeah, go ahead Cupcake, because I don't have no cable here. That way you can watch your TV shows and hang out with your brother." I replied, "Ok, I have to get my son some clothes and I have to pack me a bag too." Qin said, "Hurry up. You don't need a lot of clothes and I'm sure you have at least ten outfits in his diaper bag." "I do, but I need to get some more clothes and I don't need you to telling me how to pack my bags and what to bring, thank you." After I was done, packing my bags we left. Mickey had a daughter and she was so cute.

Qin and Ranesha had broke up, when I was pregnant. At the time, he wanted his family to work, but he was hurt. I told my brother I know how he feels, because I got hurt before and it's not a good feeling at all, especially when you love that person. I said, "Qin, you are fine and you are a good man, and you can have any woman that you want." I was happy to see him smiling and dating again. When we got to Mickey's house, we talked and they told me I *could eat whatever I wanted. The next day, we all went to the mall. I bought Lil Qin some shoes, and I bought Zarelle some stuff and I bought my mom a pair of shoes too. After we left the mall, we went to get something to eat. I stayed a few more nights at Qin's house. Allen would come see Zarelle and he would call and check on him. Allen's mom came to see Zarelle and she picked us up over the weekend so we could go to her house. So Zarelle brothers could see him and his great granny, who is his Allen's granny on his father side. I had a good time seeing my son siblings. Zarelle's great grandmother bought him a big case of diapers and some clothes. I told her thank you. I told Qin I wanted to buy me a car. He told me he would help me look for a car, but he didn't. He acted as if he was too busy, but he was really running around with everybody else. He would go see Ranesha and take her out to breakfast while Mickey was at work. Peanut would come over and he would tell me everything that was going on with Qin, and whatever else they did. Qin and I began to have a closer brother and sister relationship, so I thought. I would fill out job applications and look for apartments while I was at Mickey's house. My mom called me. She said, "Cupcake what are you doing?" I replied, "Nothing, just feeding my Daddy Love." "Oh, I have to move." "Why you say that?" "I just have to move. I'm going to get me a one bedroom." "Are you serious? You're going to get you a one bedroom? You knew you had to move when you told me to move out here, and I just moved out here with my baby." "I have kids too, and I have to think about them." "If I knew you were going to do this, I would have never given you that money. You used me and you probably did not give that money to your landlord!" "Whatever Zaneeya, I did give that money to Mr. Prescott." "I'm done talking to you." I hung up the phone and I called my granny. As I was crying, I told my granny what my mom said. My granny said, "You can always come home. You don't have to stay out there. I know you want your own place, but you just can't afford it right now." "I know granny. I am going to call Mr. Prescott and see if she gave him that money." "Ok, call me back."*

I called my mom's landlord. I said, "Hi Mr. Prescott this is Zaneeya your tenant Bella's daughter." He said, "Oh, hi Zaneeya. How are you doing?" "I'm doing fine. I was calling you to ask you did my mom give you her rent money and her pg&e money for this month?" "Zaneeya, I have only received rent from your mother three times since she has been home and she have not paid her pg&e at all. I told Bella she has to pay her rent and her pg&e. If she doesn't I am going to evicted her, and I know she needs a place to stay. You have helped your mother out when she went to jail and everything was fine, but since she came home. She has not paid her pg&e and she owes me rent." "How much money does she owe you? I can give you $250 dollars, and I can talk to my brother and see what he can do and I'll call you back." "Ok, your mom owes me way more money then that but just call me back. Zaneeya, I just wanted to tell you. That you are a good daughter and your mom should be happy to have you as her daughter." "Thank you Mr. Prescott." When I got off the phone, I called my granny and I told her what Mr. Prescott said. I said, "Granny, my mom used me. She knew she was getting evicted before I came down here." I told my granny I was going to call her back.

I called my mom. I said, "That's messed up. You told me to move out here, and you knew you were getting evicted and I gave you all that money. I paid your cell phone bill for two months and Lil Dawane's." My mom said, "I'm not getting evicted, so stop saying that." "Yes you are. Stop, lying I just talked to your landlord. So, what did you do with the money that I gave you? I know you didn't give it to him, and I could have kept that money for my child. You will never use me again, and I promise you that." "I gave him the money, he's lying and all I need is $350 dollars and I'm done paying him. So can you give me the money and I will give it to him?" "I'm not giving you nothin. If I give up any money, I will give it to him myself, and I don't feel like talking to you right now. You're not even thinking about my brothers. It's no reason why you should be getting evicted." "I don't have an eviction and we can get a place together. Now, we can get a one bedroom." "I'm not moving with you. You get enough money for my brothers to get a two bedroom. I would have paid half of the rent, but I'm not gonna do that, I have to go."

When Qin and Mickey came home, Qin asked me what's wrong. I told him what happen. He didn't believe that my mom had an eviction. He said, "If, mommy have an eviction. I'm going to call and tell her about herself, because like you said sis. She's not thinking about our brothers and she told you to move way out here, that's not right." Qin called my mom. He said, "Mom, why do you have an eviction? Momma that's stupid. You should have paid your bills." My mom said, "Qin, if you and Zaneeya give me the money that I owe, I won't have to move." Qin said he will give her $100 dollars and I told Qin I would give her $250. I said, "Qin, mommy owes way more money then that. I talked to her landlord." Qin said, "We will see." The next day, Qin and I went to meet Mr. Prescott at my mom's house and we gave him are money. Mr. Prescott said, "I told your mom. She owes me way more money then this and I already gave her, an eviction. She told me she would give me the rest of the money next month, which is not far from now. If Bella pays me

I will not evicted her. I like Bella, but she have to pay her bills, and thank you Zaneeya." "You're welcome, hopefully my mom will pay you, but I can't stress about that." I went back to the car and I waited for Qin. When he got in the car, we left. Qin said, "Sis, if mommy gets evicted, what are you going to do?" "I am going to stay in a hotel until I find me a place, I have enough money too." "You don't need to stay in a hotel." "I can move back to the Bay Area, but I want to live on my own." When, we got back to Mickey's house. She said, "Zaneeya, you can stay here until you find a place. You're not a problem at all or your baby. You always clean up after yourself and we get along. Y'all can stay here, and I got use to Zarelle and I'm going to miss him if you leave." "I don't know about that. I don't want you to get mad at Qin. Then trun around and kick me out. I'm not use to that and I should have just stayed in the Bay Area." Qin said, "You're going to stay here just like she said sis." "Ok, well Mickey I'm going to give you some rent money every month, and I'm going to buy some groceries starting tomorrow." "You don't have to give me anything. My rent is already paid for six months, and if you want to buy some food that's fine. We can go to the store tomorrow." "Ok, thank you." The next day Mickey and I went grocery shopping. Ramone came over. He said, "Sis, can I have some of your snacks and food, because I don't have any food at the house?" I gave Ramone some juice, and some food. He said, "Thank you sis. I appreciate it." "You're welcome brother." I stayed at Mickey's house for two weeks total. I bought me a car and I was filling out job applications. I went to look at an apartment it was nice. I just didn't have an income to move in, I was waiting for my unemployment to come.

One evening, Mickey took me to my mom's house, so I could get my son swing. I wanted to put him in it while I was doing her hair. She said, "Zaneeya you can put the swing in my hall closet." One morning I woke up, and it was early. I heard Qin fussing and Mickey said, "Qin, can you take that swing to the garage? I don't want it in my closet." Qin said, "I don't know why you went to get this swing for her anyways. Don't let her bring no more stuff here." I went out of the room and I said, "Qin, give me my baby's swing." Qin said, "It's in the garage. I just put it out there." "I know you did." I took my baby swing and I put it in my car. Qin was yelling out the window. He said, "Why are you putting the swing in your car? If it gets stolen don't say nothing to me." "Why would I say something to you? What are you going to do about it? I'm putting my swing in my car, because you and Mickey were complaining about me having it in her closet, after she told me I could put it there." "That's ok. The first is coming up real soon." "What does that supposed to mean?" "You

*will see." I would let Ramone and Necco use my car to go out, because Necco
had license. I would say, "Ramone, you can use my car, but just bring my car
back to me before I get up in the morning." I would pick Ramone up and take
him places where he needed to go some times. After Qin and I got into it, we
were not speaking. One day I went in the kitchen to make my baby a bottle and
Qin said, "Zaneeya, you have to move on the first. You have been here for two
weeks. Mickey said you're not a problem, but she just wants to get her house
together for next month, because her daughter will be turning 3 years old. If
it was my house, I would let you live here." I said, "Ok." I called Stephanie,
because we became friends, and we would hang out. I asked her for Becky's
number. I wanted Becky to take me to look at this apartment. I asked Ramone
could we get a place together. He said, "Yeah." When I called Becky, she came
to pick me up. I told her what happen. She said, "Zaneeya you don't have to
stay there, you can come live with me. I will not kick you out, and they should
have kept their word and let you stay there longer than two weeks. We can
get your stuff today and you can move in. I have a two bedroom. You do not
have to worry about nothing. We will get along good." I told Becky thank you.
We went back to Mickey's house, but Qin and Mickey was not there. I got my
stuff and I left. When we made it to Becky's house, we took my stuff upstairs.
Later on that night, Qin called me. He said, "Zaneeya, where are you?" I
said, "Don't worry about it. I'm going to come over tomorrow, so I can give
Mickey her key back. Thanks for letting me and my son stay with you and
your girlfriend." "You didn't have to leave until the first, but just bring her
key back." "I am, don't worry and why would I wait until the first to move?*

*Mickey is the one who said I could, live there until I find me a place and
you did not, want me there either. I was good to you as well Qin. I would give
you money, and you would charge me for doing little things for me. Like going
to get me something to eat, when I didn't have my car. It's good, I won't ask
you for nothing neither and don't ask me to brow any money, because I'm not
going to give it to you. If you go back to jail, you better make sure whatever
girl that you're with have your bail money, to bail you out. You better make
sure that the bank is open, because there won't be any IOU's this time and I'm
not bailing you out." Qin would treat Ranesha's family better then he would
treat his own. He would take her family member's places and he wouldn't
charge them. He would even treat them out to lunch and they would come
over Mickey's house. Qin would let his friends, and whatever girl, that they
were sleeping with at the time come over and spend a night. Mickey texted my
phone, she said, "Zaneeya you didn't have to leave." I replied, "You told Qin*

that you didn't want me there. After, you told me I could stay with you until
I get my own place. That's your house, you could of came to me and told me
that yourself, but that's ok. I'm going to bring you, your key back tomorrow
and thank you for letting me and my son stay with you for two weeks." "You
could have waited to move until the first." "Why would I wait until the first to
move and I can move now?" The next day, Becky and I went to Mickey's house,
so I could give her, her key back. Mickey came outside. She said, "Zaneeya, I
didn't want you to leave like that. I came home, and I went inside of Lee Lee's
room, but I didn't see you. I looked in her closet and I didn't see your stuff. I
said Qin, your sister moved. She left, with the baby and he said no she didn't
she'll be back. I told him to come here. That's when he looked and said she
did leave." "I was not going to wait until the first to move, that's your house
you should of came to me and told me how you felt." Qin came outside to see
Zarelle. He tried to take him out of his car seat. I said, "Put my baby back,
don't take him out of his car seat. I'm leaving." Qin said, "I can see my nephew.
I'm not worried about you." "You don't have to be worried, just don't take
him out of his seat. Come on Becky let's go." Becky and Stephanie introduced
me to their friends stevie and Sofia and Stephanie sister Millie. I got along
with all of the girls. I was close to Stephaine and Rin. They would come over,
and I would cook and we would kick it at Stephaine's house sometimes. I told
Becky and Stephanie we should have ladiesnights, but we should take turns
cooking at each other houses. We would cook at Stephanie house. We would
cook at stevei's house and we would cook at Becky's house. We all would go
out sometimes. I stayed with Becky for two weeks. I wanted to move, because
Becky was a prostitute and her tricks would come in and out of the house. I
couldn't live like that with my newborn baby, and I just wanted to go back
home to my granny's house, so I did. Jessica and I still kept in contact. We
would talk to each other all the time. She didn't want me to move to Modesto.
I called Jessica and I told her I was moving back to the Bay Area. Jessica said,
"For real, are you playing with me?" I said, "No, I'm serious." "When are you
coming?" "I want to leave in two days, tomorrow I'm going to take pictures
with my son and I'm going to take Lil Dawane to buy some shoes and I'm going
out to lunch with Marrie."

"Oh, ok I'll come get you if you want me too." "Ok, that will be nice
and you know I will give you some gas money, and I will pay you as well."
"Ok, don't worry. I'm going to call you before I leave, so you can give me the
directions. I can't wait. Now we can start doing everything together again."
"I know I miss that. You still owe me a gift for my birthday too, I have not

forgotten." "*I know I am going to get you something. I have not forgotten.*"
"*Remember, before I moved I took you shopping, and I took you out to lunch
and I got your feet done for you as a birthday gift.*" "*What do you want for
your birthday?*" "*I want a dress. That's all I want.*" "*Ok well, when you come
out here we are going to go shopping.*" "*Ok, thanks sis. I'll talk to you later.*" *I
told Stephanie and Becky I was moving. Stephanie said, "You're really going to
leave and you're going to take my baby away from me. I'm going to miss y'all?*"
*Rin said, "Zaneeya, it's not going to be the same. Nobody is going to cook and
I'm going to miss you and the baby.*" *I said, "I'mma miss y'all too. I'll be back
to visit.*" *Becky said, "I'm going to miss you and Zarelle. Every morning I come
in your room and look at him. You can always stay here when you come down
to visit.*" *The next morning, Marrie picked me up, and we went to the mall.
Zarelle and I took pictures. We went shopping, and we went out to eat. Then
we dropped Lil Dawane off at home. I bought my mom some Roses and I gave
her some money for an early birthday gift. Jessica picked me up the next day.
Before we left Modesto, we stopped at my mom's house. So she could see Zarelle
before I left. When we got to the Bay Area, Jessica took me to my granny house.
We made plans to hang out over the weekend. I gave Jessica some money and I
told her thank you for coming to get me. My granny was laughing as she looked
at Zarelle. I said, "Granny, why are you laughing?" My granny replied, "Look
at him. Bella said he was a fat baby, he is fat and fine. You can tell your feeding
him baby. He's not missing any meals, look at him." My granny kept laughing.
I said, "Granny, don't be laughing at my baby. He gained a lot of weight." My
granny said, "Girl, I'm tellin you." I was happy to be back at home with my
granny. I knew I made the right decision. Every morning I would wake up at
7:00 AM. I would put Zarelle's clothes out, and I would give him a bath and I
would have his bottle ready. I would change his clothes five times a day. He had
a head full of curly hair. I kept him clean, and I made sure he ate. I nevered
ran out of pampers or food for him. I would take my baby everywhere that I
would go, and I did not mind. When I did move back to the Bay Area, I got
back in contact with my friend Jasmine. Jasmine and I started hanging out.
We would go to Santa Cruz and we would go shopping. We always had a great
time together. I started working at Wal-Mart, and I received my guard card,
so I could work as a security officer. While, I was working at Wal-Mart my
friend Robin and I became close. We would eat lunch together and we would
help each other out at work. I worked as a security guard in San Francisco CA.
My granny would babysit my son for me while I was working. I would take
Zarelle out to eat and we would have mother and son days on my off days.*

I love spending time with my son. Even though he is young, that does not stop me from having fun with him and I enjoy every minute of it. A friend a mines called me to inform me that Rebecca was speaking badly about my child and me. So I told my granny what was said. See, the person that Rebbeca talked about me to, worked at my old job and I having been knowing that person for a long time. I could not believe what Rebbeca said about my child. So I stopped liking her. I know longer wanted anything to do with her. Jessica betrayed me by being close with Rebecca. Jessica knew I did not like her, because of what she said about my son and me. I thought Jessica and I were going to be close again. I would call Jessica, so we could hang out. She would say, "Oh, I'm doing something with Rebecca." Jessica would say that everytime I would call her. Jessica stopped hanging out with me and she started hanging out with Rebecca. Everything that we would do together, she started doing it with Rebecca. Jessica had a friend who betrayed her, and she did not like it. Jessica would cry to me about how she felt at that time. When her friend had betrayed her, and I did not understand why would she betray me. Knowing, that I didn't like Rebecca. Rebecca knew what she was doing. She wanted to come between our friendship and Jessica acted as if she didn't see it at the time. Rebecca only went out with us a couple of times and she never came back out with us. I was hurt more, because Jessica knew I didn't like her and she was a family member of mines. Rebecca did not want Jessica and me to be friends. Jessica fell right into a trap. When Jessica and I talked, we made up and I told her how I felt. Jessica said, "When you moved to Modesto, I didn't have no one in the Bay Area to talk too. So I started talking to Rebbeca and we would smoke together." I said, "You already knew what happen between us and I told you everything and you could have called Sabreea and Lucy, those are your friends too. Don't betray me by being friends with a family member of mines that I don't even like! I would never do that to you. I have always had your back, out of y'all your friends. All you had to do was call me and I was there for you. Through your break-up's, when you got jumped and your friends where there, and they didn't help you. You called me." "That's true. I did and you have always had my back." "Rebecca needs a friend, that's why she wants to hang out with you. She haven't been close to you in all these years, and to be honest, she's just using you. Rebecca talks about you and she talks about Desseire. She don't like her. She puts up with Desseire, because she is your best friend. Rebbeca told me, "The only thing that I don't like about Jessica is that she cannot think for herself!"

Jessica said, "Wow, I'm going to have to talk to her about that. I don't like that at all. That means, I do whatever somebody else says and that's not true." "Ask Sabreea." Sabreea told Jessica, "Rebbeca did come between y'all friendship and she did say that." Jessica and I would make up and I tried reaching out to her, even after she wasn't loyal to me. Jessica never reached, out to see how I was doing. She nevered called and checked on her Godson, not one time. She would say, "I want to be there for you and I'm going too." It was a lie and it never happened on her end. So I stopped calling her and I know longer was upset about it. The more friends she got. The more she didn't need me. I would call and check on my Godson every week. I would call and talk to Jessica's mom. To see how my Godson was doing. When I wanted to see my Godson, Jessica wouldn't let me. I still bought him gifts for his birthday, Christmas and when it wasn't a holiday I have bought him things. I truly loved him. I did miss him a lot and I would tell my granny I wish I could see him.

When, I did get a chance to see my Godson, we both were overly excited to see each other. He was hugging me and crawling to me. He wanted me to hold him the whole time that we were together. Before he left, I hugged him and he did not want to let go of me. I only saw him once, after that visit. As time went on, I stayed to myself and I stared getting my career together. I started going to school at the City College of San Francisco. I went to school for Adminstration of Justice and CSI. I had gotten real sick due to an illness that I have, and I had to stop going to school. The illness started taking over my body. When I would go to school, I would call my granny to let her know that I made it. I told my teachers about my illness, and they were very understanding. My teachers told me if I needed to email them my homework that would be fine, and if I could not come to class, I could call them and let them know. I was thankful to have such kindhearted teacher's who were, understanding. My family and friends knew about my illness. The people that I was the closest to the most left, and they acted like I never existed! Having my illness taught me, that you can be there for someone, but that does not mean that they are going to be there for you. Just, because someone tells you they love you. That does not mean their telling you the truth. When someone loves you, they will show it with their actions! Not just by words. I know, who I can trust with everything, and I know who I cannot trust. I am no longer putting my dreams on hold. I want to spend every second with my son. I told myself, that I am still going to go to school for CSI, because that is something that I want to do, no matter how successful I become. I finally have all of the answers to my past, which I have been waiting for.

Chapter Seventeen

How I Over Came My Past and It's No Longer Welcomed Into My Future

I *finally did the homework on my life. So I have a clear understanding of my life and everything makes sense. See, I over came my past, by Worshiping God and seeking his guidance. I worship God, because he is worthy to me. I have to thank God for my blessing, and for allowing me to live and for allowing me to worship him. I thank God for my son Zarelle. I wouldn't know what I would do without him. He is the reason why I strive harder and harder everyday. My son is who keeps me motivate at all times. He gives me strength just by looking at him. I know longer care about the small things in life. I know longer care about the friends and family who are not there for me. I know longer care whose friends with whom! With all the backstabbing and the betrayal that happened to me in relationships with others. I am no longer blaming them. I am a grown woman who takes responsibility for my actions. I allowed people to treat me that way, but never again will I allow it. I am the only one who gets to say what goes on in my life, and I am taking a stand. I do not blame my parents for all of my issues. See, I was a product of what I was exposed to growing up, but I am no longer that product. I have let go, and I have moved on and I forgave myself for the things that I have done wrong in life. I have called certain people and said I am sorry for hurting you please forgive me. In order to progress in life you have to change your whole surroundings. I no longer buy love from my family or friends. I have learned by having a past like mines. I can either repeat my past or I can make a difference by changing and accepting my past for what is it. I am not a shame of the fact that I have a learning disability. It's nothing to be a shame of. Their, are so many kids that have learning disabilities. They are bright, and they grow up to be young ladies and men and they become very successful. They are doctors. Lawyers, authors, singers and they have many other successful jobs. I am not that little girl anymore who was crying out for help. I am not that teenager, who was turning into a young woman, but was hot headed. I know that violence is not the answer to anything, but I do believe when someone is harming you fiscally. You should protect yourself with all means necessary. I am a mother, and that is how I conduct myself, and I know what I want out of life and I know who I am! I am Zaneeya. S. Who worships God! I am humble, and thankful no matter how successful I become in life. I am kindhearted and I have compassion and love for everyone, the way that God say I should. I know that God loves me. I know that I am worthy to God. Do not let your past interfere with your future. Judge Mathis and Tyler Perry are two people who inspired me and they made me look at life differently. Remember, you can be anything that you want to be in life, but you have to have faith and believe. Everyone has a purpose in life. You have to find your purpose, I found mines, my dream is no longer a dream, it's a reality. I no longer hold grudges against people. I am at peace with my past and I only have God to thank for it. Remember, your struggle can be ten times worst than mines, but you can over come your past too. So do not allow your past to become apart of your future. Find your purpose, and fulfill it and remember to keep God first at all times.*

Printed in the United States
By Bookmasters